Patience

20th Century Samurai

Richard Kim 1917–2001

Patience

Special Collector's Edition # SC #3 **of 1000**

ISBN #0-920129-26-9

628 N. Doheny Dr., Hollywood, CA 90069 USA
www.risingsunproductions.net
1-310-248-3633

ACKNOWLEDGEMENTS

This book has taken close to a year to create and without the help of the following people it would have never been possible: Brian Conaughton, Chuck Siani, Pat McCarthy, Louis Jemison, Frank Gaviola, Brian Ricci, Greg Mellor, Mr. Leong, David Grover, Ken Shockey, Leroy Rodriguez, Jim Larkin, Nobu Kazi, Dr. Alex Bennett, Jean Chalamon, Charles Goodan, Emil Farkas, Isaac Florentine, and Mr. Naito.

The graphics production of this book, including design and concept, was spearheaded by Tosha Lord. Scanning, typing and graphic assistance came from Annette Hellingrath, Colin Arnold and Angel Lemus.

Table of Contents

 People who touch their nose while they are talking to people are usually lying.

Dedication

How could this book be dedicated to anyone other than Sensei?

May all his students and students' students continue his teachings for centuries to come.

Introduction

Rarely does a man come into our lives and leave footprints on our mind that last for ever.

Richard Kim was such a man.

For the thousands of students who have been touched by this great martial arts master already and for the thousands who will come to understand only his legacy, we, his students, have created this book called "The 20th Century Samurai".

It is our hope that we will do him justice, if even only in a small way. We know that it will not come close to being in the dojo studying the martial arts with him in a way only he could teach; which the rest of us can only try to imitate in some small way.

We, the senior students of Sensei Kim, want to personally thank everyone who has so kindly and graciously contributed to the making of this book, whether in a small or large way. We know that it could not have come to fruition without your help.

At the risk of forgetting someone, we will mention no one person in particular.

As Sensei Kim would often say when he was given something, we will also say, "Until the English language comes up with a better phrase than 'thank you very much' we will simply say to each and every one of you who contributed, 'Thank you very much.'"

Foreword

When I began this challenge of compiling this book on Sensei Kim, I knew that there would be much dispute from two diverse camps: those who loved the man and those who hated him. But I also knew that they all respected the man.

I found there to be many misleading statements that Sensei Kim told over the years. I want to emphasize the word misleading, not lies. For an example, he often talked about his education, saying to me that he had equivalent knowledge to a Ph.D. in Political Science, and Oriental Philosophy. That did not mean he said he had them, just that he had equivalent education to these. Many people took it as he had these in Ph.D.s.

The purpose of this book is not to justify any of his actions or to question any of them. It is to only share with you those things that I know are fact from my lengthy, sometimes difficult, research on the man.

I also realize that this book will not make either of the camps happy because it does not meet either of their agendas. It is not meant to meet anyone's agenda except the truth, as best I can source it out. Many of my findings are subject to criticism, as I do not have any hard proof one way or another on some of the information I offer you.

Many have said, 'go here and you will find that out,' or 'here and you will find this out'. I have done my best in all areas and in many cases people would simply not give me any information at all.

In summary, I can only say every fact in this book is the truth as to the best of my knowledge – both the good and the bad.

The one thing I do believe we can all agree on is that our lives are in many ways better and fuller because we met and trained with Richard Kim.

History of Dai Nippon Bu Toku Kai

The Dai Nippon Bu Toku Kai was a section of the Japanese Ministry of Education since 1895. The masters of that time joined together to create the Dai Nippon Bu Toku Kai, with the virtues of respect, compassion, gratitude, integrity, and honor as it's core. They established standards and awarded all ranks, up to the end of World War II when it was disbanded by the occupation forces leader, General Douglas MacArthur.

General Douglas MacArthur

Practising at the Dai Nippon Bu Toku Kai

The actual Bu Toku Den building was built in 1899.

On September 18, 1911, the Budo Semmo Gakko (Busen), or Martial Art Specialty School, was created, which increased the proficiency of it's masters for generations to come. In some ways, the Busen was regarded as Japan's West Point Academy.

1977 outside the Bu Toku Den

Kyudo experts demonstrating at the Bu Toku Den.

Ohno Kumao, head of the reformation of the DNBK (early 1950s).
Courtesy Pat McCarthy www.society.webcentral.com.au/

The Mecca of Japan's fighting traditions, the Bu Toku Den was where budo juhapin (the 18 martial ways) were vigorously cultivated and highly revered. With both a two- and four-year program and a host of brilliant instructors, the Busen disciplined its flock in kendo and judo, while teaching military strategy, history, philosophy, and associated academic studies.

The 50th Emperor of Japan, Kanmu Zou

In 1954, the Dai Nippon Bu Toku Kai was reactivated under the auspices of a member of the Japanese Diet named Ma Chino and the legendary Ohno Kumao, a prominent Hokkiryu swordsman. Higashi Fushimi, a member of the Showa emperor's immediate family, served as patron.

DNBK group shot, including two sword legends: Sugino, and Ohno.
Courtesy Pat McCarthy www.society.webcentral.com.au/

The Bu Toku Kai is a martial art, organization which traces its origin to the Emperor Kanmu the 50th emperor of Japan, 781-806 A.D. He opened up the Imperial grounds the Bu Toku Den in March, 797 A.D. Eriryaku Jugonen or the 15th year of the Emperor Kanmu.

In Emperor Kanmu's time, the Bu Toku Den was tied in with the begin-

Archery on horseback was a traditional part of the opening ceremonies of the DNBK.
Courtesy Hal Sharp.

The Grand Hall of the DNBK – photo taken during the 1977 Japan Tour.

ning of the Heian Shrine. This was the beginning of true samurai spirit and training. They say that May 5th of 818 A.D. the imperial order of Emperor Saga, the Yabusame ceremony (Samurai Archery on Horseback) was conducted in honor of the warriors' tradition to promote aristocratic authority of the imperial majesty in the Bu Toku Den (Hall of Martial Virtues) located near Heian Shrine (circa 781A.D.) in Kyoto, Japan. Since then, Bu Toku Den became the center of all Martial Arts training throughout the history of Japan.

Samurai in old-style dress.

The Samurai warriors, as ruling nobles by virtue of their professional and lifelong commitment, dedicated their lives to developing such superior martial skills and the cult of military excellence. The manifold Heiho (Martial Strategy) systems were developed during the proliferation of warfare, Sengoku Jidai (Period of Nations at War) from 15th century to early 17th century Japan. In the decisive battle of Sekigahara in 1600 A.D., the Tokugawa military clans destroyed the Toyotomi allied

Samurai in old style dress, prior to 1868 Meiji Restoration.

Baron Orura and the Prince of Japan were the prime movers in the reorganization of the DNBK in 1895.
Courtesy Pat McCarthy www.society.webcentral.com.au/

troops. The powerful Shogunate military feudal government called Bakufu was established in Edo, present day Tokyo.

Under the ruling Bakufu regime, Japanese warrior class by and large faithfully maintained the traditional order of martial disciplines for critical readiness for the next two hundred years. We knew the Bushi (warrior class, often called Samurai) was not only the champion of societal elite for their military skills but also they epitomized the exemplary moral leadership by living under the code of Bushido ethics they relentlessly adhered to.

When the Dai Nippon Bu Toku Kai opened as a section of the Ministry of Education in 1895, the prime movers were Prince Fushimi and Baron Orura. This was the first official Martial Arts institution of Japan sanctioned by the authority of the national government. The Prince Kuniyoshi Kunino Miya, General of the Imperial Army had served as the first Supreme Chair of the Dai Nippon Bu Toku Kai. Consequently, DNBK became the prestigious headquarters empowered by the nation's leading experts, and established as the center for training, research, licensing, and publication of Martial Arts.

The Busen is where much of the non-technical teaching took place - where the real art of Bushido was taught. The Busen.
Courtesy Pat McCarthy www.society.webcentral.com.au/

Established in conjunction

Heinan Shrine next door to the DNBK headquarters.

with the Heinan Shrine, Emperor Kanmu was revered as a deity in the shrine. The modern Bu Toku Den was opened in Kyoto, Japan in 1899. Only kendo and judo were practiced at first. Therefore, both of these arts developed one international standard for ranks that prevails today. The Bujutsu Semmon Gakko later on, it was changed to the Budo Semmon Gakko, popularly known as the Busen was established within a framework of Dai Nippon Bu Toku Kai to administer national accreditation, certification and professional training of all Martial Arts disciplines throughout Japan. By 1930, National Government Record on Martial Arts Profile showed more than two and half million Black Belt holders, and more then two hundred fifteen thousand high-ranking experts registered in the eight major martial disciplines.

The kendo section was headed by Naito Takahara, a swordsman of the Hokushi Itto Ryu, and the judo section was headed by one of Kano sensei's top students of the Kodokan, Isogai Hajime.

Then, in December 1941, the Bu

Isogai Hajime, as a young man, was very formidable as an opponent on the Tatami.

Courtesy Pat McCarthy www.society.webcentral.com.au/

Ohno Kumao and the heads of the Dai Nippon Bu Toku Kai.

Above and at right, demonstration by a sword master in the Bu Toku Den boys day 1977.

Toku Kai formed a committee to report on the progress of the different budo groups. Konishi Yasuhiro (1893-1983, Shindo Jinenryu) and Ueshima Sannosuke (1895-1986, Kushinryu) were petitioned to report on the progress of karatedo. However, in the following year, because of World War II, the Bu Toku Kai was reorganized under the auspices of five ministries: Welfare, Education, War, Navy, and National Affairs.

When the Dai Nippon Bu Toku Kai was established in 1895, the Sosai, or president was a member of the royal family Komatsu-Rio-Miya, Akihito Shinno Denka- the kaicho or chairman, was Watanabe. The Governor of Kyoto, and the Fuku-Kaicho or vice chairman, was Minobu, the Bishop of the Heian Shrine and another vice-chair man,

The offices of the DNBK in Kyoto, Japan.

 A friend is someone who uses you and allows you to use him.

The DNBK grounds looks like a castle out of a samurai movie.
Courtesy Pat McCarthy www.society.webcentral.com.au/

was Toriumi, also the head of the Kyoto Chamber of Commerce.

The first Bu Toku Matsuri (martial art festival) was held on October 25, 1896, in a makeshift tent and temporary hall, Kata and shiai were held in kendo and judo.

A few years after the opening of the permanent Bu Toku Den, the samurai titles Hanshi ("Model Expert" or "Teacher by Example", and Kyoshi, originally known as Tasshi ("Teaching Expert") were bestowed upon deserving recipients. The first recipients of the title of Hanshi were given in kendo, and the titles conferred on Watanabe Noboru, Ishiyama Magoroku, Takao Tesso, Eno Kanshiro, Sakabe Daisaku, Dobashi and Murasaki. On April 1, 1906, the title of Kyoshi was conferred.

The practice is continued up to the present time. A training apprentice title Renshi was also designated later.

Jigoro Kano outside the Bu Toku Den in the 1920s.

Jigoro Kano and a group of Ju Jitsu masters outside the DNBK in Kyoto, Japan. *Courtesy Pat McCarthy www.society.webcentral.com.au/*

Naito Takaharu was the kendo and a master swordsman in 1899 for the DNBK. Courtesy Pat McCarthy www.society.webcentral.com.au/

Some of the more recognizable experts of karatedo to receive the Bu Toku Kai titles have been: Mabuni Kenwa (Shitoryu), Miyagi Chojun (Gojuryu), Funakoshi Gichin (Shotokan), Chosen Chibana (Shoren Ryu), Funakoshi Giko (Shotokan), Konishi Yasuhiro (Shindo Jinenryu), Ohtsuka Hironori (Wadoryu), Yamaguchi Gogen (Gojukai), Nagamine Shoshin (Matsubayashi Shorinryu), Shinzato Jinan (Gojuryu), Higa Seiko (Gojuryu), Yagi Meitoku (Gojuryu), Ueshima Sannosuke (Kushinryu), Tomoyori Ryusei (Kenyuryu), Kinjo Hiroshi (Koryu), Richard Kim (Shorinjiryu), and Sakagami Ryusho (Itosukai Shitoryu).

Swordmaster posing outside the BuTokuDen, 1977.

The aim and purpose of the Dai Nippon Bu Toku Kai was / is to promote and cultivate Budo in a true samurai spirit, to produce teachers to go out and propagate the real Japanese Martial Arts. The dan system was introduced by Kano Sensei, the founder of the Kodokan, and basically involved six steps known as kyu, three white belt steps and three brown belt steps, followed by the dans or grades, of which the shodan was the first grade. This was the first black belt degree or step.

There were and are until today ten steps in the black belt ranks.

The Bu Toku Kai Insignia

Zen Archer at BuTokuDen, 1977.

A variety of DNBK publications.
Courtesy Pat McCarthy www.society.webcentral.com.au/

In January 1946, the Education Ministry was put in charge of the Budo, which was to serve only as physical education within the school system. Later that year, ex-Bu Toku Kai officials successfully made a strong effort to have the association reinstated.

However, the judgement was short-lived as senior allied officials once again terminated it.

With the Bu Toku Kai dormant for the next seven years during the American occupation, various groups used its old honbu, the Bu Toku Den. From 1945 to 1950, it was Allied Forces "GHQ"; following that, the Legal Affairs and Finance Ministries used it, then the Kyoto Police Department used it for their official training hall, and finally, it was the site of the Tokyo

Municipal Koto (13-stringed zither) Association until it was declared a national treasure in 1970. The old dilapidated Bu Toku Den was restored to its original splendor in 1987, although the surrounding buildings were torn down to make room for a new budo dojo.

This stone was placed here when the DNBK was started in 1895. Courtesy Pat McCarthy www.society.webcentral.com.au/

In 1998, the unprecedented First World Bu Toku Sai was held in Old Dominion University by the present International Division leader Hanshi Tesshin Hamada twelve nations participated in the event. The honored guests included Fuku Sosai, Jiko Higashi Fushimi, and a cousin to Emperor Akihito led the Honbu delegations comprised of twenty-two top elite members of DNBK.

The official participants demonstrated the respective disciplines of Kendo, Jiujutsu, Naginata, Jojutsu, Iaido, Sojutsu, Aikido, Karatedo, and various Kobudojutsu.

Although no longer exclusively in charge of budo in Japan, the Dai Nippon Bu Toku Kai still maintains that it is only through understanding the common principles upon which the Martial arts rest, embracing its moral precepts, and pursuing its spiritual magnitude, that one can ever truly master the self, the inner-most message of budo.

The Dai Nippon Bu Toku Kai symbol takes its shape from the eight point chrysanthemum, a flower first introduced to Japan in 650 AD from China. The nectar extracted from this flower was at that time made into a wine that was thought to have ensured longevity. The flower became associated with the Emperor, and ultimately became the national flower of Japan, which is still remembered every year on September 9.

The insignia has gold characters on a royal purple background. The color gold represents the idea of richness: the Bu Toku Kai believes that the generations of learning transmitted through budo are an invaluable asset to its supporters. The royal purple, the official color of the Emperor, represents the virtuous ideology that governs the behavior of its supporters. The eight points of the flower represent the conceivable gates of attack and defense, a principle that unites all combative disciplines.

The Chinese characters "butoku" represent the martial virtues of the feudal samurai: respect, compassion, gratitude, loyalty, honor, and integrity. The rays emanating from its center represent the various koryu (feudal combative disciplines) that served as the platform upon which budo was established. The bow and two arrows represent Japan's very first line of defense during its feudal beginnings.

Note: We want to thank both Mr. Ken Shocky and Dr. H. Tesshin Hamada, Chair, International Division Dai Nippon Bu Toku Kai and USA Honbu for allowing us to use information and facts from their web site in the creation of this chapter. The official Dai Nippon Bu Toku Kai web site is http://personal.picusnet.com/butoku/. Plus, a very special thank you to Patrick McCarthy for so much information, not just in this section but also on Sensei Kim, and the loan of many photos.

The Life and Times of Richard Kim

Richard Kim, 1917-2001. Sensei always had a great smile for the camera. Courtesy Brian Ricci

Author's Note:

Much of Sensei Kim's background information has been disputed by his foes who say some of it is made up, while his supporters swear it all to be true. Some of the information compiled in this book cannot be proven to be either true or false. Much of it has been proven to be factual and true. If anything, Sensei Kim understated many of his accomplishments, but it has nevertheless all become part of the legend and mystique that surrounds Richard Kim and will, more than likely, continue to be added to as years go by.

I have found much of the information from both camps to be out and out exaggerations. For example, the comments that Sensei Kim had 3 PhDs. He may have had 3 PhDs but were they accredited or non accredited? Since we are unable to see the actual certificates or contact the actual universities (as some of them, like St John's University in Shanghai is no longer in operation) we cannot prove them to be one way or the other...

Were those scrolls in Black Belt Magazine nothing more than old Chinese menus rolled up? Was he in Shanghai during WWII? He was there

for the duration of WWII, 100%; and the scrolls are 100% legitimate.

I can only say that I have interviewed countless people in person, on the phone, and on the internet. I have compiled and read, in depth, over 50 personal handwritten letters by Sensei Kim, traveled considerably and read every book and article I could get my hands on, had many documents translated from Japanese to English, and I believe what I have written to be the truth.

At the end of the day we must satisfy ourselves – I have exhausted every possible avenue trying to unearth as much as I possibly can about Sensei Richard Kim, in an attempt to understand him as much as possible. After nearly a year of research and digging, I am satisfied and this is the best I can do.

~~~~~

Richard Sun Sung Kim was born on November 17, 1917, in Papaaloa Hawaii. (His mother was part Korean and part Japanese – her name was Tok Nam Park – and his father was pure Korean – his name was Mong Young Kim). His social insurance application in 1937 says that he was of Korean ancestry but, he in fact, was part Japanese and part Korean.

Known to many by his nickname, 'Biggie' (he had a brother who was smaller and therefore named 'Smallie'), he was raised by his mother in a Pearl City, Hawaii neighborhood. His childhood friends included Betty Nakamura, So Young and Junichi Buto (who became instrumental in his life later on as you will soon see). When he was six years old, his mother enrolled him in a Judo class under the direction of Kaneko Sensei.

In 1927, the young Kim watched a Karate demonstration at the Nuuanu YMCA by Yabu Kentsu. Yabu Kentsu was visiting Hawaii on his way back to Okinawa. The young Kim was so impressed by the demonstration that he joined a karate class being given by Sadao Arakaki. (It has been documented that Sensei Kim also trained with Ankichi Arakaki but Ankichi Arakaki never visited Hawaii.) Sadao Arakaki was Yabu Kentsu's disciple in Hawaii. Many of Sensei Kim's katas were prefixed 'Yabu' like 'Yabu Chinto.' (Sensei Kim told me this information personally and is why he called them Yabu Chinto etc.)

In 1930, Richard Kim finished his schooling at one of Hawaii's oldest
~~~~~

Nuuanu, December 26, 1927. Back row: Koto Shiroma, Shingi Higa, Saburo Teruya, Kamezo Uyehara, Sadao Arakaki, Ryosonkin Nakama, and Taro Azama. Front row: Kyusei Kiyabu, Kitatsu "Kanshun" Kawamae, Kentsu Yabu, Kitaro Kawakami, and Sadao Asato. - *Hawaii Karate Museum collection.*

McKinley High School, Honolulu, where Sensei Kim went to school during the early 1930s.

high schools, McKinley High, which was established in 1865 in Honolulu, Hawaii. The school was primarily made up of Oriental students, with 84 per cent of the students being Asian. These were the roots that allowed Richard Kim to become one of America's leading Karate pioneers, particularly in the area of research and journalism.

He then went on to study at the University of Hawaii (he did not graduate from this University), as well as Tung Wen College (where he studied languages and the art of investigation), and St. John's University both in Shanghai, China, during WWII. No documentation can be found as to what degree or how long he studied at either institution.

He did claim a PhD from St John's University though. *(He told me this, personally, when I asked him how long he studied at St. John's University. He said, "Well, let me put it this way – it was amazing what you could get*

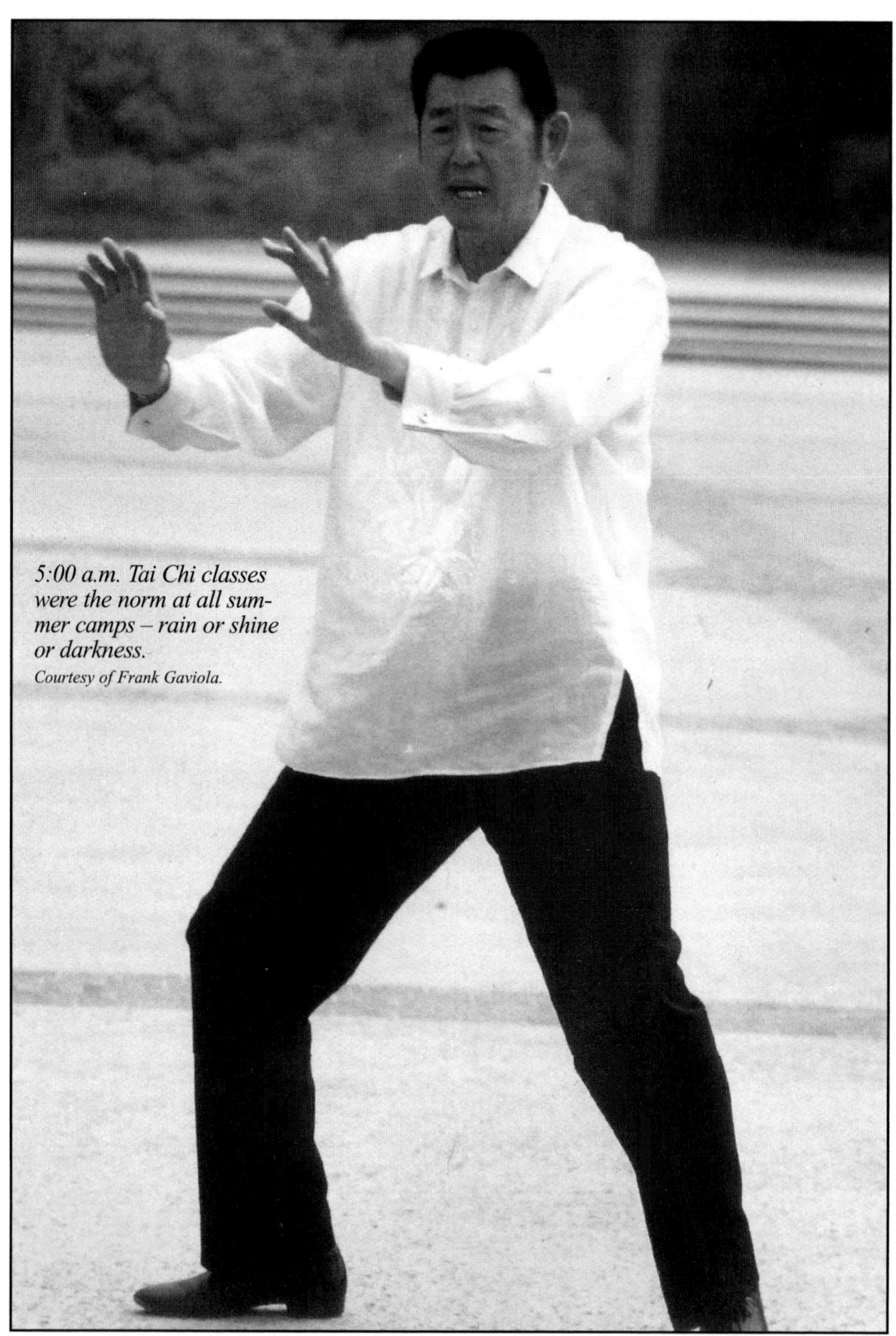

5:00 a.m. Tai Chi classes were the norm at all summer camps – rain or shine or darkness.

Courtesy of Frank Gaviola.

 To obtain happiness you must eliminate the three Ds: Death, Disease, and Desire.

from people when you had a gun at your side and were part of the Kempei Tei during WWII in Shanghai." That said volumes to me and I never forgot it. ~D.W.)

Tung Wen College was where Sensei went to school in Shanghai – it was a spy school for the Kempei Tei. Here, he perfected his language skills and his ability to interrogate individuals and who knows what else.

One of Sensei Kim's earliest teacher's, Higashionna, performing tamashiwara technique.
Courtesy of Charles Goodin.

Mizuho Mutsu (also known as Zuiho Mutsu and Mizuho Takada) and Kamesuke Higashionna (also known as Hiroshi Higaonna), upon their arrival in Honolulu, Hawaii, 1933.
– Hawaii Karate Museum collection

In 1933, Richard Kim met and trained with Mutsu Mizuho (Mizuho Takada was a student of Gichin Funakoshi's), who was visiting Hawaii from Tokyo with Kamesuke Higashionna. Sensei Kim trained in Honolulu with Tachibana Sensei, as well, in 1933.

The young Richard Kim spent a great deal of time at Sato's Boxing Gym

Thomas Shigeru Miyashiro, Taro Azama, Kamesuke Higashionna (also known as Hiroshi Higaonna), and Seishin Uehara. Kalihi, Hawaii 1933. – Hawaii Karate Museum collection.

on Maunakea Street where, like many young Hawaiians, he acquired his boxing skills. While training and boxing with some of the top world contenders of the era, including Midgett Wolgast (World Flyweight Champion 1930), with whom he was a sparring partner.

Richard Kim had 42 fights in the ring and managed to attain a record of 42-0. These were the classic smokers of the 1930s.

In one fight, Sensei Kim nearly lost the vision in his left eye by being thumbed with rosin spread on his opponent's glove.

In 1935, he joined the merchant marines and was soon Orient-bound to further his study of the Martial Arts.

Midget Wolgast was the champion of the world at one time and Sensei Kim was his sparring partner in Hawaii.

He eventually found his way to Japan where he studied under some of the great karate masters of the time, including the legendary Yabu Kentsu, whom he remembered having seen as a young boy in Hawaii.

It soon became apparent that being in the merchant marines allowed him to travel throughout the Orient and gather knowledge on the subject that would become his lifelong pursuit and passion – the Martial Arts.

Eventually, Sensei Kim's career as a merchant marine working for the American

Presidents Line, led him to be trapped behind enemy lines in Shanghai on December 8, 1941, during World War II at the age of 23. (Keep in mind that December 7, 1941 is the date the Japanese attacked Pearl Harbor).

According to the Sailor's Union of The Pacific many ships were captured by the Japanese and the crews were interned in Asia until after the war. One of these ships was the S.S. President Harrison on which Richard Sun Sung Kim O.S. (Ordinary Seaman) was at the time.

The S.S. Harrison was on its way to Shanghai to evacuate the US Fourth Marines, when it was intercepted by a Japanese Zero that fired its machine guns across the bow of the ship ordering it to stop. This is when the captain, Orel Pierson, chose to head for the Shaweishan Islands and ram the freighter into a stone cliff, rendering it useless to the Japanese military since it had been outfitted for carrying troops already. Eventually it was fixed and used by the Japanese military to carry troops.

Sensei Kim was in Shanghai for the entire length of WWII. According to the author of Captives of Shanghai, no one was released early except for two people – a stewardess and a man who eventually had both legs amputated. So there is no doubt he was there for the war.

The S.S. President Harrison – the boat Sensei Kim was on when he was trapped behind enemy lines.

Because of his partial Japanese mother and his Korean father, he was not looked at as an ordinary American. According to Sensei Kim himself, he became a translator (remember Sensei Kim spoke Russian, Korean, Mandarin, Japanese and English fluently) and eventually acted as a double for an unnamed high-ranking Japanese Officer who he often referred to just as the Colonel.

NOTE: The Japanese military did not have a rank of Colonel – the equivalent rank was Major General.

According to my notes and after talking to some of his students from the early years, it was also during this time period that he met many high ranking Japanese officers, including Major General Kenji Doihara

(Lawrence of Asia) who was eventually hung for War Crimes on December 23, 1948.

According to Hiroshi Kinjo, one of Sensei Kim's associates during the 1950s, Sensei Kim told him that he was in Shanghai during World War II where he studied Chuan Fa, or Chinese Martial Arts. Hiroshi Kinjo also mentioned that Mr. Kim was not very forthcoming about his past, or where he came from, and he rarely discussed his years in the war.

Major General Kenji Doihara, one of Japan's most ruthless militants before and during WWII.

While in China, Richard Kim studied Tai Chi Chuan under the tutelage of Chen Chin Yuan, and Pa Kua under the guiding hand of Chao Hsu Lie a Taoist monk.

Later, Wang Xiang Zhay taught him Yi Chuan. Much of his training in the internal arts was done in Jessefield

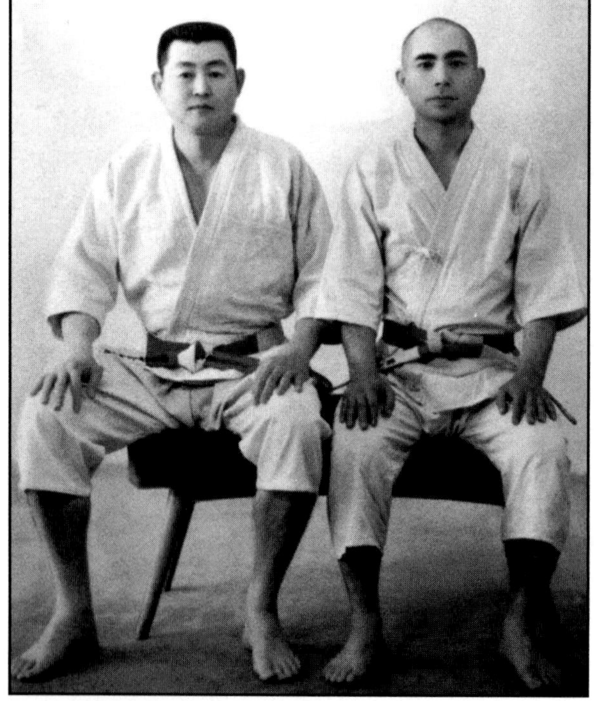

Richard Kim with Hiroshi Kinjo.
Courtesy Pat McCarthy www.society.webcentral.com.au/

Wang Xiang Zhay taught Sensei Kim in Shanghai, China, during WWII. He was one of the great internal masters of all time.

Jessefield Park, Shanghai, where Sensei Kim learned a great deal of Paqua, Tai Chi and Yi Chuan during WWII.

Park, which is now called Zhongshan Park. All the English names were changed to Chinese after the Revolution by Mao Tse Tung. Wang was a famous Chinese master of the internal system.

Kim first met Yoshida Kotaro in the City of Sendai (northern Japan) during the late 1930s, and then again in 1941 in Shanghai, when Kotaro was working as a spy for the Japanese (as he had done in Manchuria and in the Russo-Japanese War, as well).

According to other books we have read, Shanghai was full of spies for all sides during the war, because of the multi-national citizens there at the time. Russians were working for the Chinese and Chinese were working for the Japanese and Germans were working for the Russians – it is quite logical that Sensei Kim, a Korean, was working for the Japanese.

Sensei Kim told many of us that one day at the end of the war, while at the home of one of the Japanese officers in Shanghai (who had used his services as a translator and double), when there was a knock on the door. It was an American officer, 1st Lieutenant Junichi Buto, looking for war criminals. Fortunately for Sensei Kim, Junichi Buto was the same childhood friend from Hawaii that he had protected as a kid. Junichi Buto was also credited for getting Sensei Kim out of Shanghai and back to Hawaii as a repatriate. Knowing Sensei Kim well, Junichi Buto was not surprised to find him in this tricky situation – and he asked no questions. According to three sources, Sensei Kim's Japanese name was Masaki and this is probably who Junichi Buto was looking for in the first place. (It was not usual for Koreans to take Japanese names, due to the prejudice in Japan towards the Koreans. For example, Mas Oyama is a Japanese name, but he was 100% Korean.) The Japanese government made it easy for them to change their names to Japanese, as part of the government policy to incorporate Koreans into the Japanese empire.

On September 27, 1945, he was put on board a hospital ship called "The Refuge", formerly known as the US President Madison, for a short trip that landed him in Naha, Okinawa. It was here that he, along with 454 other repatriots, service men, women and children, was put on to the U.S.S.

The U.S.S. Sanctuary, the ship which brought Sensei Kim back to Hawaii after the WWII.

Sanctuary. Destination – San Francisco. The U.S.S. Sanctuary had successfully avoided a typhoon while at sea, when the call came in from the commander of the 5th Fleet for the U.S.S. Sanctuary to report to Naha, Okinawa, for what was called 'magic carpet duty' – a term used by the Navy to describe that this oceanliner was being used to assist in an air lift evacuation to save the POWs (women and children, servicemen, etc.).

On October 18, 1941, Sensei Kim got off the U.S.S. Sanctuary in Hawaii and was reunited with his family.

After only three months back and a short visit in Hawaii with his family and a check up, Sensei Kim went back to Japan, as his research in the Martial Arts was not complete.

Later, he continued to shuttle back and forth between Hawaii and Japan. While in Hawaii, he visited, trained and taught in many Karate dojos.

During this time, Sensei Kim worked for the President's Shipping Line (in the Deck department). In August 1949, it is documented in a US Coast Guard trial, that merchant marines Manual Medeiros and Richard Sun Sung Kim were involved in a knife fight onboard the S.S. Wilson in which they were attacked by a gang wielding knives. During this fight, Kim and Medeiros were cut. They defended themselves using fireman axes when backed into a corner. No one was killed, but it certainly shows that Sensei Kim had to put his Martial Arts into action. He often showed those cuts on his arm as he told this story to many of his students. The fight had started when a drunken sailor had bashed Medeiros over the head with a whiskey bottle.

Around 1948-49, Sensei Kim moved back to Japan from Hawaii on a permanent basis, and studied with many Martial Arts masters. In 1949, he trained under Kenichi Sawai, who was a student of Wang Xiang Zhay's in Shanghai. Sawai never taught indoors and, in fact, held classes at the base

 The original mind deals with intuitive processes (it's warm, paradoxical, compassionate, creative, and loves).

Kenichi Sawai was a student of Wang Xiang Zhay and he also taught Sensei Kim when Sensei lived in Japan.

Wang Xiang Zhay demonstrating a Yi Chuan posture.

of the Meiji Shrine in Tokyo where all of Japan's war heroes are buried. Sawai's book, called "Taikei Ken", is one of those super rare books on the Martial Arts that depicts his style, the way he learned it directly from Wang Xiang Zhay. Sawai had over 100 fights and he never lost one. He used only 8 techniques that he learned from Master Wang.

Later on, Sensei Kim was employed by the Sailor's Union of The Pacific as their Yokohama Branch Agent, he worked closely with Harry Lundburg. The photo below shows him and Lundburg in Guam resolving Union matters.

Sensei Kim lost his maritime papers due to a court martial in 1949. Then Harry Lundburg appointed Sensei Kim as the Yokohama agent, which he maintained until he left Japan in 1959. It wasn't until 1959 that he made San Francisco, California, his permanent base.

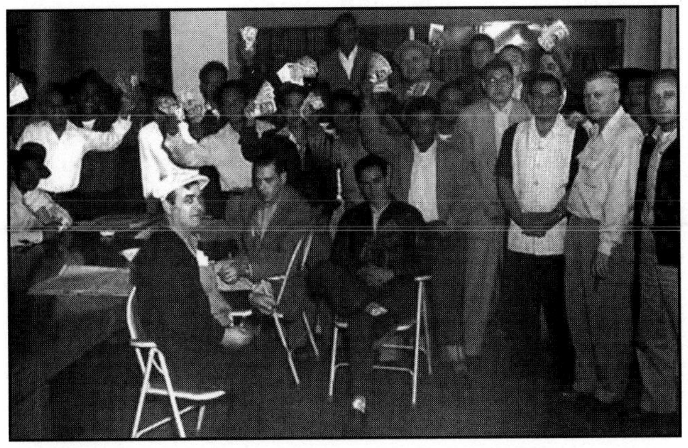

Biggie Kim with Harry Lundburg (seated forefront in the white hat). Courtesy of Louis Jemison.

Sensei Kim was married four times. His first wife was of Russian origin and was killed during an air raid in Shanghai. He met his second wife in Honolulu. She was of Korean decent. They had a son together.

Later in Yokohama he met his third wife, with whom he had a baby girl. His third wife was educated in America, and was of Okinawan/Japanese origin. He met karate master Hiroshi Kinjo through his wife's family, since Hiroshi Kinjo came from the same town in Okinawa as did Sensei Kim's father-in-law. (Sensei Kim often called Hiroshi Kinjo a walking Encyclopedia.) Kinjo was a famous Martial Artist who was associated with Mr. Ohno Kumao, the head of the reformation of the Dai Nippon Bu Toku Kai. Sensei Kim was first introduced (as was the Japanese custom) to Ohno Sensei by Toyomo Mitsuro (the head of the Black Dragon Society) in 1927. Ohno Sensei (as he was referred to by Sensei Kim) was one of the Japan's most famous kendo masters. He had over 100 matches and was never beaten. Sensei Kim was recommended by Hiroshi Kinjo to Ohno Sensei for his 7th, 8th and 9th degree black belts.

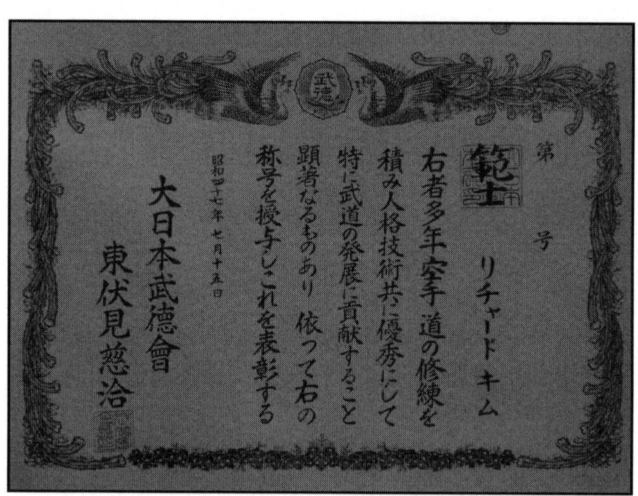

第　号
範士
リチャード キム
右者多年空手道の修練を
積み人格技術共に優秀にして
特に武道の発展に貢献すること
顕著なるものあり 依って右の
称号を授与しこれを表彰する
昭和四十七年七月十五日
大日本武徳會
東伏見慈洽

One of Sensei Kim's certificates signed by Ohno Kumao.
Courtesy Pat McCarthy http://www.society.webcentral.com.au/

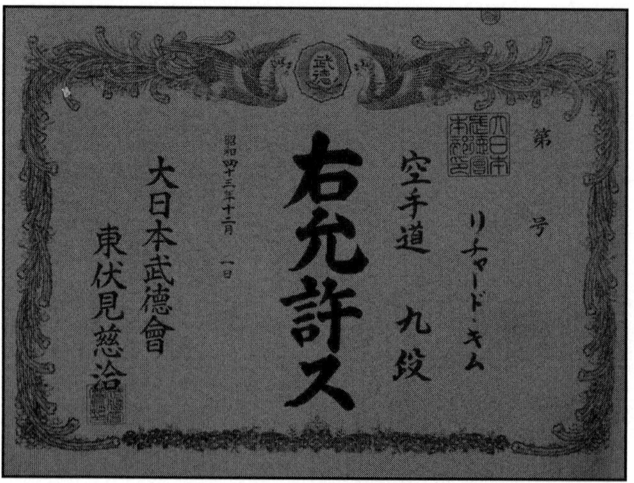

第　号
リチャード・キム
空手道　九段
右允許ス
昭和四十三年十二月 一日
大日本武徳會
東伏見慈洽

Another of Sensei Kim's certificates signed by Ohno Kumao.
Courtesy Pat McCarthy http://www.society.webcentral.com.au/

It should also be noted at this point in time the Dai Nippon

Bu Toku Kai (DNBK), and Martial Arts in general, were in a disarray throughout Japan. Nobody was allowed to practice since General Douglas MacArthur had outlawed all Martial Arts.

MacArthur was convinced that the Dai Nippon Bu Toku Kai was one of the reasons WWII had started. The thinking being that since many high-ranking officers were members of the DNBK they must have had a big part in the start of the war. It should be noted that the DNBK was a strong supporter of the Emperor and its members believed strongly in the ways of Budo and the Samurai. This was indicated in its name, DAI = All, NIPPON = Japan, BU = Military, TOKU = Virtue, KAI = Organization

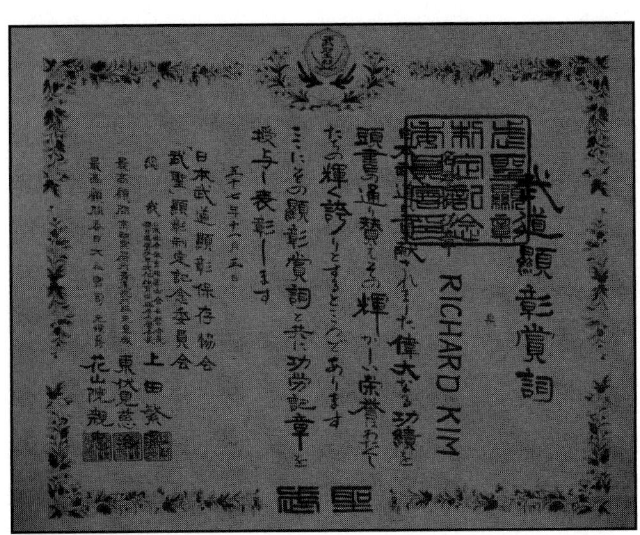

Another of Sensei Kim's certificates signed by Ohno Kumao.
Courtesy Pat McCarthy *http://www.society.webcentral.com.au/*

There were some exhibitions of the Martial Arts during this time, but they were not official by any means whatsoever. The Dai Nippon Bu Toku Kai was not officially reformed until 1954 when it was reactivated under the auspices of a member of the Japanese Diet named MaChino and the legendary Ohno Kumao

With the end of war, as is common, came the mass burning of many of the records kept during the war. This included the records of the DNBK. Hence, there is much confusion as to who was in and who wasn't in the DNBK prior to the end of WWII. This is partly why many believe that the Dai Nippon Bu Toku Kai of post WWII had its roots in the Black Dragon Society, an elite group of spies who were dedicated to restoring the ideals of bushido, casting out the foreigners and restoring Imperial Reign.

Sensei Kim and his third wife owned and ran a bar called The Pilot House in Yokohama's 'China town'. It was known to be a bar frequented

Inside the infamous Pilot House: Mas Oyama, Sensei Kim, Muka, and Higa Yuchoku.
Courtesy Pat McCarthy http://www.society.webcentral.com.au/

by US sailors visiting Yokohama. The Pilot House also became well known to martial artists living in Tokyo and Yokohama.

They gathered there, and considered it as a place they could meet freely and talk about what they loved. It was here that Sensei Kim met many legends, including Yoshida Kotaro again, who he had first met in Sendai and then again in Shanghai in 1941. Eventually, Yoshida Kotaro moved in with Sensei Kim and his family for seven years, from 1949 until approximately 1956. During this period he also trained in Shotokan karate with Minatoya who rented a second floor room from Sensei Kim at The Pilot House. Yoshida left when Sensei Kim took up his merchant marine job and had to ship out again.

Nobuyoshi Tamura, a student of O'Sensei Ueshiba, became very good friends with Sensei when he was training with Ueshiba Sensei in the 1940s.

Yoshida was an "odd duck" as Sensei would say, but one of the things that Yoshida Sensei insisted on was the training with many of Japan's top masters, which included Moreihei Ueshiba (founder of Aikido) in his dojo in Wakumatsu Cho. Sensei Kim became very friendly with Ueshiba's top students, including Nobuyoshi Tamura, who moved to France in 1964. Tamura was one of Ueshiba's favorite ukes and is seen in many of the films on Ueshiba. He trained 6 days a week with Ueshiba Sensei for one year from 6-9 each morning.

It was Yoshida Kotaro who trained Sensei Kim to become proficient in Japanese weaponry, including the sword, spear, tanto and bo. He also

Mrs. May Kim, Sensei Kim's fourth wife.
Courtesy of Ken Shockey.

taught him the art of Aiki. In 1952, Yoshida Sensei gave Sensei Kim his 'Menkyo Kaiden' (a certificate of full proficiency given by a master to a chosen student best suited to carry on the style). He also gave him the scrolls of the style depicting the history of Daito Ryu, as well as all the techniques. Today these scrolls are in the possession of Sensei Kim's fourth wife Mrs. May Kim, who resides in Sacramento, California.

When Sensei Kim first met May he was fascinated by her singing abilities and eventually fell deeply in love with her. He would often say that 'nothing is too good for my wife'. May Kim is a staunch supporter and protector of Sensei Kim's name, his reputation and legacy. She continues to run the "Way Of Man Kind", an organization that strives for the betterment of all.

Gogen Yamaguchi sanchin no kamae.
Courtesy of Hal Sharp.

Sou Nei-chu was Yamaguchi's right-hand man.

Perhaps Peter Urban was exaggerating when he said in his book, "The Karate Sensei" that Sensei Kim had over 100 marriage proposals, but it is the absolute truth that he was admired and loved by many.

"His intellect often upset the intellectual pygmies," is another quote from Sensei Urban's book.

During this period he also studied with Gogen "The Cat" Yamaguchi and both he and Mas Oyama were brown belts in 1948-49. Both Sensei Kim and Oyama received their shodan from Yamaguchi Gogen in 1950. This was just before Oyama moved into the mountains to train for 18 months at the suggestion of Sou Nei-Chu. Sou Nei-Chu was one of Yamaguchi's senior and best students.

Sensei Oyama and Sensei Kim became very good friends during the next short period of time, and continued training together. In Mas Oyama's 1958 book, the revised edition of 'What Is Karate' (written in 1956), Sensei Kim is thanked by Oyama for helping create the book. He is also seen in the book with Mas Oyama acting as Oyama's uke in many photos.

During this time frame, Peter Urban also began his training with Mas Oyama. As it happens, it was Sensei Kim who introduced Oyama and Urban. Urban is also seen extensively throughout Oyama's book. Sensei Kim and Oyama were actually each other's benefactors, meaning that if one of them were killed the other would inherit the other's worldly possessions.

According to Hiroshi Kinjo, he and Richard Kim were also very close friends and Kinjo taught Sensei Kim many kata including Chinto, Kusanku-dai/sho Kanku Dai and many others. Kinjo and Toyama Kanken also taught him the Okinawan weapons forms. Kinjo was a noted Okinawan Karate/Kobudo master and was appointed the official representative for the Dai Nippon Bu Toku Kai for Karate. The post was then turned over to Gogen Yamaguchi in the mid-1970s. It was Hiroshi Kinjo who recommended his training partners both Sensei Oyama and Sensei Kim for 7th dan.

Kinjo eventually recommended Sensei Kim to the Dai Nippon Bu Toku Kai for both his 8th and 9th dan, as well. Sensei Kim attained his 9th dan early in 1968, also from the Dai Nippon Bu Toku Kai. This is the highest rank that is issued to anyone alive. Only at a person's passing are they promoted to 10th dan. This was done for Sensei Kim when he died in 2001, by the International Traditional Karate-Do Federation's Chief Instructor, Master Hidetaka Nishiyama at Sensei Kim's memorial in Sacramento. He was also promoted to 10th dan on May 14, 1999, by Hawaii Karate Kodanshakai.

Sensei Kim never used his 9th dan rank until the early 1990s. We have no idea why. One explanation might be that he felt it was given to him prematurely by Higashi Fushime (the Prince of Japan) whose official seal is

Toyama Kanken, one of Sensei Kim's kobudo teachers.

William Chow was one of the Godfathers of Hawaiian Martial Arts when Sensei Kim was a young boy.

on the certificate. Some say that these certificates were forgeries, but when they were shown to an expert in Japanese Martial arts history at the Kyoto University, he said they did not appear to be forgeries and not having numbers on them meant very little.

After the war, Sensei Kim continued to shuttle back and forth between Japan and the United States as a merchant marine. During this period, he often returned to Hawaii, teaching and training at many Karate dojos there, including the Te Ken Jutsu Kai dojo of Masaichi Oshiro (originally a Kenpo Karate student of William H. Chow and later a Goju-Ryu student of Gogen Yamaguchi's).

Master Hidetaka Nishiyama, a dear friend of Sensei Kim's since 1961.

In 1957, Sensei Kim visited San Francisco while continuing his work as a representative for the Sailor's Union representing the other merchant marines. He also traveled extensively back and forth to the Orient while he worked on the ships as a 3rd Stewart in charge of the crew which took care of the passengers. He went back to Japan in 1957 and tried to attain permanent status. Due to his questionable background in Japan he was denied permanent status and in 1959 he returned to the USA permanently.

It was also in 1957 that he met Clarence Lee and began teaching karate in Clarence Lee's mother's garage on Taraval Street in San Francisco. His first group of students in the United States included Clarence Lee, Richard

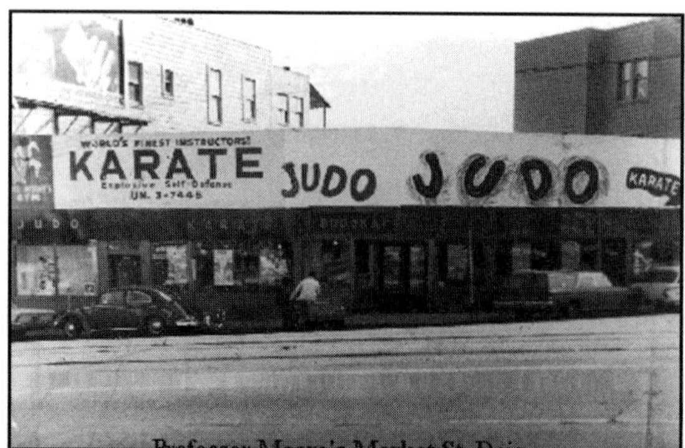

Duke Moore's dojo on Market Street in San Francisco, 1958.

Sensei Kim presenting Urbano Tejo with a Ju Jitsu Dan Ranking Certificate
Courtesy Lenore and Frank Gaviola

Lee and Herbert Lee, all of whom became very proficient under Sensei Kim's tutelage. During this time, he met Duke Moore, who was one of the American Martial Arts pioneers and also taught at his school on Market Street.

It was at this club that Sensei Kim also taught Judo. In 1961, Tony Troche began his training and then in 1962 Urbano Tejo joined with his daughter Lenore and her brothers. The Market Street Dojo was one of those special dojos in the USA that really started the Martial Arts rolling. Others, who either taught or trained at this dojo, were names like Wally Jay, Willy Cahill, Harold Getz, Jerry Streeter, LeRoy Rodriguez, Johnny Pereira and many others.

When I interviewed LeRoy Rodriguez, who was one Sensei's earliest students, he could not emphasize enough the severity of the training at this dojo. He said that at one point Chuck Siani was training very hard for a big Judo competition and they trained for three-hours-a-day, non-stop. He,

Wally Jay, and others, trained at the Market Street Dojo of Duke Moore's in the early 1960s.

Troche, Chuck and Robert Leong and a few others would work out together. According to Siani and Rodriguez, Sensei Kim's groundwork and matwork were exceptional. When he lived in Shanghai he was a student at the Shanghai Busen, and Judo's Michigami was one of the true judo legends that taught in Shanghai.

Sensei Kim eventually moved his headquarters to the Chinese YMCA in Chinatown around 1964 at 855 Sacramento Street. Clarence Lee had established the Chinese YMCA Karate program and turned it over to Sensei Kim.

Sensei Kim was the unofficial international representative of the Dai Nippon Bu Toku Kai, establishing branches in the United States, Canada, Germany and France.

In 1959, when Sensei Kim moved from Japan to the United States, he lived in the Haight/Ashbury section of San Francisco during the hippy revolution of the '60s and '70s.

He established the Zen Bei Bu Toku Kai, which was later called the Bu Toku Kai, which unfortunately lead to much confusion and many misunderstandings. Many understood that this was the official Dai Nippon Bu Toku Kai, which it was not. All the certificates handed out during this time said Zen Bei Bu Toku Kai, not Dai Nippon Bu Toku Kai. According to Sensei Kim, he was asked to do this by the Head of the DNBK at the time,

Don Warrener outside the famous Chinese YMCA dojo, 2005.

Ohno Kumao. It should be pointed out that after WWII, Martial Arts was not allowed to be practiced in Japan.

Judo was considered a sport rather then a Martial Art. It wasn't until September 8, 1951, that the official peace treaty was signed allowing the Martial Arts to once again be practiced in Japan. At which time, each Martial Art established its own federation.

Considering the state of things in Japan after WWII, the Martial Arts was not at the top of the list of peoples' priorities. It was more important to survive, make a living and get Japan back on its feet. There are few records available of the Dai Nippon Bu Toku Kai, as it was considered an ultra-right-wing nationalist group. In fact, it was not removed from the United States enemy list until 1973, by President Richard Nixon, at Sensei Kim's request. I recall Sensei Kim often saying this is one of the few things Nixon did that was good. I personally believe that Sensei Kim considered this one his biggest accomplishments.

During a team trip to Japan in 1977, for Hidetaka Nishiyama's International Amateur Traditional Karate Federation, Sensei Kim arranged for the team to be taken on a special tour of the old Dai Nippon Bu Toku Kai headquarters in Kyoto, established in 1895.

Also during this trip, Sensei Kim met with Ohno Sensei and was given three dan ranks for foreigners: Don Warrener, Brian Ricci, and Tony Molinar. Although these certificates are not numbered, they are

1977 Japan Tour, waiting to depart San Francisco International airport. Courtesy Ken Shockey

Sensei Kim and Don Warrener in San Francisco's China Town, 1975, at a banquet for the first time the Canadians brought a huge contingent to train with Sensei at the YMCA.

Sensei and Brian Ricci.
Courtesy Brian Ricci

signed by Ohno Kumao and have his official seal on them.

Sensei Kim continued to develop the Zen Bei Bu Toku Kai outside of Japan over the next 15 years. It was also established in Canada, France, Germany, England, and Finland.

In the early 1990s, he resigned from the Dai Nippon Bu Toku Kai, as the old guard had changed and a new Dai Nippon Bu Toku Kai was emerging. It was heading in a different direction and Sensei Kim chose not to be a part of their plans.

Sensei Kim often told us that he had the equivalent knowledge to three PhD.s in Political Science, Oriental Philosophy, and the Martial Arts. He did receive a degree from Rockwell College at Eurotechnical University, and Universal Life Church. He also received Ph.D.s from St. John's University for Political Science, and Tung

The Grand Hall of the DNBK photo taken during the 1977 Japan Tour.

Wen College, which he acquired during WWII. Rockwell and Universal Life Church are both unaccredited universities. Prior to WWII, the Tung Wen College and St. John's University were very prestigious. These degrees can not be substantiated as both were closed at the end of the war.

It may seem strange to some that he devoted his life to teaching the

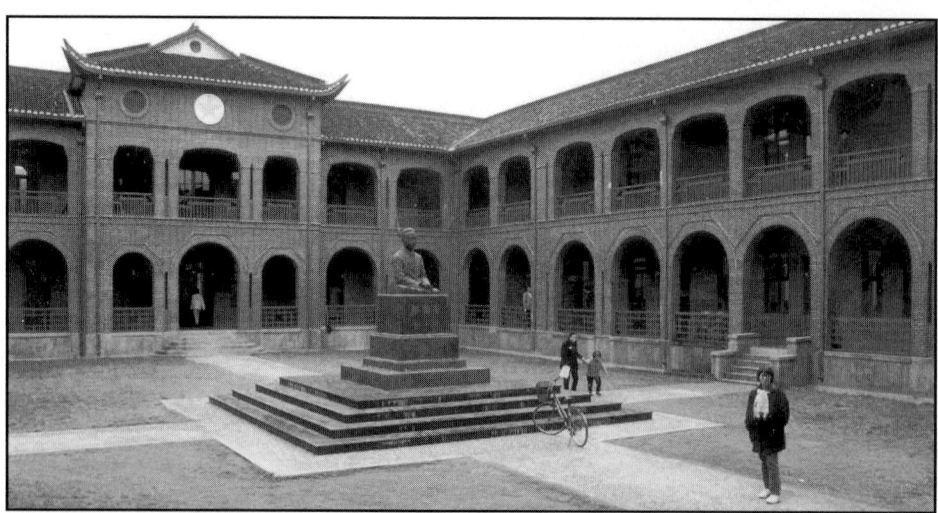

St. John's University in Shanghai, where Sensei Kim went to school during WWII. The hard part about being a P.O.W. during WWII was finding something to do with your time – Sensei went to school and trained in Martial Arts.

Martial Arts, but his love of them was apparent. This became obvious to anyone watching him lead a group of students either in California, Massachusetts, Canada, or in Europe.

One story told by Chuck Siani is quite humorous, and only if you knew Sensei Kim could you imagine it to be true. Chuck asked Sensei Kim if he would like to go with him to his calculus class. Sensei said he would most definitely like to go. Within ten minutes of sitting in on the class, Sensei Kim was standing at the front of the class, and teaching, with the professor sitting, listening and learning.

Richard Kim was a distinguished author several times over. He wrote

Sensei receiving his Ph.D. from the Eurotechnical University. In attendance, Mrs. Kim, Robert Leong, Ken Shockey. Courtesy Ken Shockey

classic books like: 'The Weaponless Warriors', 1974; 'The Classical Man', 1982; The Okinawan Kobudo Weapons Series, including the weapons of 'Matsu Higa', 1983, 'Chatan Yara', 1985, and 'Hama Higa', 1987

Sensei Kim was also featured on numerous magazine front covers, countless articles were written about him and by him, and published in various noteworthy publications throughout the Martial Arts world, including Dojo and BUDO magazines. He was a regular columnist for 'Black Belt Magazine' and 'Karate Illustrated' during the early 1970s. His column, 'The Classical Man', featured short stories about Japanese martial artists. They depicted a particular philosophy, or a lesson in psychology, and were

Some of the classic books written by Sensei Kim over the years.

one of the magazines' most popular columns.

He was given many top honors over the years. Some of the most noteworthy are as follows:

- Earned the rank of 4th Dan in Judo during WWII
- 1967: 'Sensei of the Year' by Black Belt Magazine
- 1967: Mentioned in the 'Who's Who of Martial Arts'
- 1968: He became a Director of the U.S. Team for I.A.K.F. World Championships and held this position for many years to come.
- 1970s: Resident Instructor at Hidetaka Nishiyama's San Diego Summer Camp (until his passing)
- 1970s-1990s: Was the official weapons teacher to the JKA, according to Keinosuke Enoeda
- 1973: Voted into the 'Black Belt Magazine Hall of Fame' as 'Man Of The Year'
- 1977: Chief Instructor at the Guelph, Ontario, Canada, Summer Camp (until his passing)
- 1983: Chief Instructor at the Victoria, BC Summer Camp (until his passing)
- 1999: May 14, Hawaii Karate Kodanshakai presented Certificate Number 65 to Sensei Kim for a 10th Dan. This prestigious organization also awarded high ranks to other outstanding martial artists, like Bobby Lowe, Kenneth Funakoshi and James Miyaji.
- 2001: Was promoted posthumously to Judan (10th Dan) by Sensei Hidetaka Nishiyama (one of the most famous and respected karate masters alive) his long-time karate associate and dear friend since 1961.

San Diego official camp instructors, including Senseis Shirai Mabuni, Kim and Nishiyama, plus many more. Courtesy Rod Sanford

武德

CERTIFICATE

This is to certify that

Don Warrener has attended a summer camp taught by Dai Nippon Butoku Kai International Representative O, Sensei R. Kim.

on the 30th

day of Aug 19 87

International Rep.

Master Richard Kim, 9th Degree Blackbelt
Dai Nippon Butoku Kai

Guelph Summer Camp participation certificate, August 30, 1987.

It is clear that Sensei Kim embodied the spirit of the Martial Arts, and mastered being 'the artist of life.'

BUTOKU–KAI of CANADA

Certificate

Mr Don Warrener

participated June 28th *to* July 3rd 1987

in the Canadian Butoku-Kai Summer Camp

organized at University Of Guelph

and satisfied all requirements thereof.

Director: Richard Kim, Hanshi

July 3rd1987 Guelph Summer Camp Bu Toku kai Certificate

Sensei Kim's Life at a Glance

1917 - Born in Papaaloa, Hawaii

1924 - Began Judo instruction

1927 - First saw Karate and began instruction under Yabu Kentsu.

1930 - Graduated from McKinley High School.

1932 - He studied at University of Hawaii for three years, but did not graduate.

1933 - Studied Karate under Sadao Arakai, Tachibanna, Higashionna, Mizuho in Hawaii.

1930s - Trained in boxing in Hawaii.

1935 - Joined the merchant marines.

1937 - Met Yoshida Kotaro for the first time in Sendai, Japan.

1941 - December 7th. Japanese attacked Pearl Harbor.

1941 - December 8th. Trapped behind enemy lines while working on S.S. Harrison.

1941 - Again met Yoshida Kotaro in Shang Hai.

1941-1945 - Was in Shang Hai, working for the Japanese Kempei Tei as a translator and double for a Major General of the Japanese Kempei Tei. Studied Chinese Internal systems in China with Chen Chin Wan, Hsu Chao Lie and Wang Xiang Zhay. He went to both St. John's and Tung Wen College in Shang Hai.

1945 - He was repatriated by his childhood friend, LT. Junichi Buto and arrives in San Francisco.

1945-1948 - worked on the boats as a merchant marine.

1948 - moved to Yokohama, Japan.

1949 - met and trained with many of the great Japanese masters of the time – names like Sawai, Oyama, Kotaro, Ueshiba, Minatoya, Kinjo, Yamaguchi, Kanken and Ohno Kumao.

1949-1959 - He worked for the Sailor's Union Of The Pacific as an agent for them, traveling and enforcing Union rules.

1957 - Met the Lee brothers in San Francisco. Taught in the Lee's mother's garage until 1964.

1959 - Moved permanently to San Francisco, California. Taught at Duke Moore's dojo on Market Street.

1964 - took over the Chinese YMCA Karate program.

1967 - Voted Sensei of the Year by Black belt Magazine.

1968 - Became director of the IAKF US Team.

1970 - Became a resident instructor at the San Diego summer camp hosted by Sensei Nishiyama.

1971-1974 - wrote regular monthly column in Karate Illustrated magazine called The Classical Man.

1973 - Voted as the Man Of The Year by Black Belt Magazine.

1974 - Produced The Weaponless Warrior published by O'Hara Magazine.

1974 - Came to Canada for the first time.

1977 - Became Chief Instructor of the Guelph, Ontario, Canada, summer camp.

1982 - Released The Classical Man.

1983 - Released Kobudo #1. First Western Canadian Summer Camp.

1985 - Released Kobudo #2.

1987 - Released Kobudo #3.

 The greatest life force (ki) is given out through the fingers.

1999 - Promoted to 10th Dan by The Hawaii Karate Kodanshakai.

2001 - Passed away. Was posthumously promoted to 10th Dan by the ITKF and Hidetaka Nishiyama.

Senior Students of Richard Kim

Sensei Richard Kim taught literally thousands of students over his career. In one seminar alone he taught well over 550 students at one time.

Following is a list of his students who were the most prominent over the years, from his first American student, Peter Urban, to his students in Canada, France, Australia and the famous Chinese YMCA dojo in San Francisco.

We have listed them by the year that they attained their black belt from him rather then the highest rank or alphabetical order.

We realize that there were many more students and we do apologize for the poor quality of some of the photos but these are the best we could get.

Peter Urban, 1934-2004

Peter Urban

Peter Urban made Shodan around 1955.

"I was the only one fortunate enough to train under Japan's big three: Oyama, Yamaguchi and my Sensei, Richard Kim" ....1982.

In 1953, a young sailor was introduced to karate, in Yokohama, Japan. His name was Peter Urban. He was boxing with a guy named Schmidt at the Black Friar's Gym in Yokohama and Sensei Kim saw them sparring. He saw that Peter Urban was being given a lesson but would not quit, so he stopped the fight and told him, "Hey kid, you should do Karate or Judo, not boxing, you're not built for it." That was the beginning.

After training for one year with Richard Kim, Peter Urban traveled to Tokyo and was introduced first to Mas Oyama, and later to Gogen "The Cat" Yamaguchi, by Sensei Kim, where he was accepted as a student by them both. In 1957, Peter Urban opened a small dojo in Tokyo, and competed in the All-Japan College Championships that same year. In 1959, Urban moved back to America with a 5th dan by Gogen Yamaguchi – the highest rank a foreigner was given at that time – and opened his first American Dojo, in Union City, N.J. The following year, he opened another school on 17th Street in Manhattan and then came the infamous China Town Dojo, located at 232 Canal Street in 1965-1966, making Japanese karate open to the public.

Peter Urban is one of the men responsible for establishing structured tournaments in America, one of the first of those being the North American Karate Championships in 1962 (where he fought Isshin Ryu Karate Master Don Nagle in an exhibition match where, as Sensei Urban would say, this was the first time two masters put it on the line. This tournament was held at Madison Square Garden. In his early 20s, Urban self published his first book, "The Karate Dojo". In 1967, The Karate Dojo was published by Charles Tuttle but much of the original book was left out and, as Sensei Urban said, it was left on the cutting room floor. Only a few copies remain of the original book.

A student of Sensei Kim's in the late 1960s, Urban eventually decided to start his own organization with the blessing of Sensei Kim, called USA Goju. He then proclaimed himself a 10th Dan.

Chief Grand Patriarch of all American Goju Systems, Peter Urban is credited with training some of the greatest North American martial artists in this generation. Names like Merriman, Dalgleish, Ingraham, Banks, Ruiz, Gote, Hooker, Van Clief, and Maldanato.

Upon Sensei Kim's passing, one single lily was laid at the alter for Sensei Urban and a simple message that simply said, "Thank you Sensei your student, Peter".

One of his greatest treasures came in 1999, when Sensei Kim sent him a note saying, *"Dear Peter, I saw you on your web site. Remarkable achievement. I am proud of you. You are the best martial artist among the "Gaijin", The Best. Sincerely, Sensei Kim. P.S. regards to all your students."*

Sensei Kim often said that Peter Urban was the only man he ever met that had no fear whatsoever.

James Miyaji

James Miyaji

Born in June 17, 1928, James Miyaji made Shodan in the late 1950s.

"I trained with Sensei for nearly 40 years."

Jimmy Miyaji was born in downtown Honolulu in 1928. A skinny and asthmatic child, he began his Martial Arts training in Judo around 1949. He studied with several sensei, including Richard Takamoto (son-in-law of Henry Seishiro Okazaki) at the Aiea Recreation Center, Yasuyuki Sakabe (on Maui), and Yukiso Yamamoto at the old Nuuanu YMCA.

Around 1955, Miyaji saw an advertisement for a new dojo opened by Masaichi Oshiro. This was the Te-Ken Jutsu Kai dojo at the McCully Community Center. Oshiro had been a student of William Chow at the Nuuanu YMCA. Chow, in turn, was a student of Masayoshi James Mitose, who popularized Kenpo Karate (or Kempo Jiu-Jitsu) in Hawaii. In 1959, Oshiro Sensei visited Japan for one year, where he studied Goju-Ryu under Gogen Yamaguchi, and Okinawa, where he studied under Yagi Meitoku.

In the late 1950s, Sensei Oshiro began converting his school to the Goju karate system. Senseis Bingo and Miyagi decided to start their own school and separated from Sensei Oshiro.

Miyaji then began to train with Richard Kim, whom he had met around 1957. Sensei Miyagi then separated from Sensei Bingo and started his own school under the Bu Toku Kai system which was headed by Professor Richard Kim of San Francisco, California. Kim was a merchant seaman, and visited Hawaii often on his way to and from the Orient. Miyaji trained with Kim for about the next 40 years and became one of his strongest supporters.

In 1961, Miyaji (along with Tommy Morita and Winfred Ho) co-sponsored the visit of Tsuyoshi Chitose, founder of Chito-Ryu and a student of several prominent instructors, including Seisho Aragaki, Kanryo Higashionna, Chomo Hanashiro, and Chotoku Kyan. In the 1960s, he trained with Hirokawa Kanazawa (for a few months), and in the 1970s he trained with Kenneth Murakami (for 3 or 4 years).

Because of the wide range of his experience, Miyaji practices and teaches over 50 Karate and Kobudo kata. Once, when he was visiting a neighboring island, he discussed Karate with some first generation Okinawans. They immediately recognized the Naihanchi Shodan kata when he performed it for them.

Miyaji was a founding member of the Hawaii Karate Congress and the Hawaii Karate Kodanshakai. He is one of only a few people in Hawaii to be a member of the Dai Nippon Bu Toku Kai. On November 13, 2004, he was inducted as a member of the Martial Art Hall of Fame of the International Division of the Dai Nippon Bu Toku Kai.

Miyaji has always kept the fees for his Karate and Kobudo classes at the Kenshukan dojo in Waipahu very low. He has taught innumerable children and adults, some of whom have gone on to teach their own classes.

James Miyaji's top students include, Rudy Castro (Shihan Dai), Dennis Sato, Ralph Sakauye, Nito Batalon, Eddie Santos, Shawna Carino, Darcie Mikami, Garin Miyaji (his grandson), and Clayton Gushiken.

Raymond Duke Moore, 1915-2003

Duke Moore

Earned Shodan in the 1940s.

"Yes, I knew Biggie really well. He was something else."

One of the true American pioneers, "Duke" Moore was a student of Sensei Kim's right when he came back to the USA in 1959. In fact, Sensei Kim taught at Duke Moore's dojo at 1819 Market Street where he also taught Duke privately Shorinji Ryu Karate, Daito Ryu Aiki Jitsu and Judo.

In 1965, Moore Sensei received the rank of 7th Dan (Shichidan, Prof.) in Aiki-Jujutsu from Master Richard Kim, representative of the Dai Nippon Bu Toku Kai of Kyoto, Japan.

We all owe Duke Moore a great deal of gratitude for he was the conduit to Sensei Kim getting started in the USA. Duke also was responsible for getting Mas Oyama started in the USA and it was he and Sensei Kim that invited Sensei Nishiyama to San Francisco in 1961 for a Shotokan Karate Tournament. This was the beginning of a friendship that would last for over 40 years between Sensei Kim and Sensei Nishiyama.

It was Duke Moore and Sensei Kim that started the Northern California Karate Federation.

Richard Lee

Richard Lee

Made Shodan in the early 1960s, around 1962.

"A master of masters – a traditional and modern day samurai – Sensei Kim's short stories of Budo are like a dictionary of Martial Arts, a guide to each reader for a deeper understanding."

Lee began his training in the late 1950s under Richard Kim in the now historic garage dojo run by Lee and his brothers Clarence and Herbert – where Sensei Kim would come and teach. The garage was owned by the Lee's mother.

He became a karate champion in the early- to mid-1960s, fighting some of the best the west coast traditional karate tournaments could muster up. His expertise in kumite and, in particular sweeps and takedowns, was well known. He fought one of the west coast's very best: Tonny Tulleners – a student of Master Tak Kubota's at the Long Beach Internationals in 1965 – and he put a foot sweep on him that was second-to-none, leaving Tulleners scratching his head trying to figure out how he did it.

He moved to Paris, France, in 1974 where he started his dojo and became the representative for Sensei Kim's Bu Toku Kai in Europe.

Not only did he teach Tai Chi and Shorinji Ryu karate, he also taught kobudo and became an acclaimed author with his book, "Karate Competition Sweeping Techniques", published both in English and in French. Until this day there has not been a book written that comes close to the quality of this little treasure.

In 1975, Richard Lee, along with his student Andre Loucka, formed one of the best karate magazines ever published: "Karate Bushido", which is still in print and is considered by most to be one of the top two magazines in the world today on karate.

Master Lee still lives in Paris and, although he is not a high profile teacher now, still teaches his karate in the way of Bushido.

He trained many top martial artists in Europe – names like Andre Loucka, Rick Marsh, Rick Attix, Jean Pierre Loucka, Jean Chalamon, and Jean Luc Bricard, to mention but a few.

Anthony "Tony" Troche

Tony Troche

Born 1929, Tony Troche made Shodan in the 1950s.

"One of the skills I learned from Sensei Kim was the extensive grappling applications present in Karate kata."

Tony Troche began his study of the Martial Arts in 1939 at the Fort Street and School Street dojo of Tetsuo Higami. Higami was a Ju Jutsu and Judo expert, as well as a professional wrestler. His ring name was "The Rubberman". Troche went on to study Judo in Japan under Watanabe Sensei and Daigo Sensei.

In 1949, Troche lived in San Francisco, where he continued his study of Judo and also Aiki Ju Jutsu under Raymond "Duke" Moore. Troche also studied under Mits Kimura, Richard Kim (Daito-Ryu Aiki Ju Jutsu and Shorinji Ryu), and Frank Matsuyama (Aiki Jujutsu) from 1957 to 1966.

In the 1950s, Troche began the study of Karate under Yuko Takahashi, the San Francisco representative of the Shudokan under Kanken Toyama (1888-1966, student of Anko Itosu). Troche also trained under and was tested in Japan by Toyama.

In San Francisco he trained under Sensei Kim for 14 years and formed a relationship that lasted for many years. Troche later moved back to Hawaii where he was a member of the Hawaii Karate Congress, as well as the Hawaii Karate Kodanshakai. He trained with many sensei in Hawaii and has taught at numerous seminars.

Troche's Martial Arts training spans over six decades and several arts and styles. He currently teaches a free children's Karate class in Waianae, Hawaii.

These are Mr. Troche's senior students: Makana Troche, Norman Kato, Kishin, Gopani, Sandra Lopes, Jose' Guzman.

Johnny Pereira, 1941-1993

Johnny Pereira

Pereira made Shodan in 1964.

"The purpose of training karate is to become a good teacher."

In every dojo there are the ones who start the quality of students. In Sensei Kim's dojo on Market Street, that he ran with Professor Duke Moore, that person was Johnny Pereira. He was known for his attention to detail and his quality of kata.

He left his training with Sensei Kim in the mid- to late-1960s as Martial Arts politics were not for him. He believed firmly that karate was Okinawan not Japanese. One of his protégés was Nobu Kaji.

His students still remember him and their description of him says it all, "He was a good guy".

Leroy Rodriguez

LeRoy Rodriguez

Rodriguez made Shodan in 1964.

"The most important lesson I received from Sensei Kim was the power of a creative imagination."

Leroy Rodriguez began his Martial Arts training in 1963 with Duke Moore. He began his training with Sensei Kim around 1965. He continued training off and on until 1976, when he left and began his own group.

"One of the things I remember about the training with Sensei Kim was those Monday to Friday 1-4 p.m. classes at Duke Moore's where we practiced judo under his close supervision. There was Richard Lee, Chuck Siani, Robert Leong and Frank Yuen (China). They were the best and talk about hard training – wow! Trying to fight with a guy like Chuck Siani was not fun in any way, shape or form – he was so big and so tough. Later on, when he started teaching karate katas, this was terrific training as well. I loved this part of the training."

In our interview with him he said one thing many people do not know is that he was a tremendous dancer and he could really kick up a storm when it came to swing dancing.

Leroy went on to become on of the very best kata practitioners on the west coast, competing in many of Sensei Kim's famous Black Belt Only tournaments that were old school karate, to say the least.

Today, Rodriguez runs his school and his own organization called Shinkyu Shotokan USA. He is still training and learning and when you see him perform kata you will see how the true essence of karate training can improve your overall health. He looks like a man half his age when he takes to the floor.

Urbano Tejo

Urbano Tejo

Urbano Tejo made Shodan around 1965.

"Never forget who you are and where you came from."

Tejo started his training at 1819 Market Street in San Francisco, in 1961 under Professor Duke Moore and it was here he brought his three children with him to the learn the Martial Arts: Arturo, Fernando and Lenore. It was Lenore that went on to become a prize student of Sensei Kim's, with precision kata and passion for the Martial Arts. She continues this long standing family tradition today.

Urbano was one of the very few who was ever graded by Sensei Kim in Ju Jitsu. He opened up two dojos – one in San Francisco and another in Sacramento, at which Lenore taught, as well. Both schools were members of the Bu Toku Kai organization.

Ken Shockey

Born in 1939, Ken Shockey made Shodan in 1964.

"Say what you want about Richard Kim, we did learn plenty and he was an interesting and fascinating character."

Ken Shockey

He began his Martial Arts training in 1960 with the study of Judo and then started karate in 1962 and received his Black Belt in 1964. He received his nidan from Shobayashi Shorinryu, Master Eizo Shimabukuro, in 1966. Then in 1975, he received a 5th dan from Hidetaka Nishiyama's ITKF organization. He is presently ranked at Kyoshi 8th dan in the Dai Nippon Bu Toku Kai.

Ken started training with Sensei Kim around 1966 and continued training with Sensei Kim until the early 1990s when he chose to go his own way.

His school in Daly City California called Washinkan Dojo has many of Sensei Kim's old students still training with him.

Ken Shockey's knowledge of weapons kata, and openhand kata has always been looked at with great respect by all those who have known him over the years.

He knows well over 100 katas and that alone is an amazing feat just to be able to remember them all.

He is now the proud California representative of the Dai Nippon Bu Toku Kai under the direction of Mr T. Hamada.

These are Mr. Shockey's senior students: Herb Weiner, Peter Juliano, Louise Guerrero, Maria Garcia.

Chuck Siani

Chuck Siani

Siani made Shodan around 1965.

"His judo ground work was the best."

One of the absolute toughest and nicest guys to come out of the Chinese YMCA was Chuck Siani.

One of San Francisco's finest, Siani was a police officer along with Ed Geeter, and was one of the best and toughest fighters in the dojo. To the best of our knowledge, Siani never lost a karate match. He was always the man to beat.

Bald head, big mustache and strong body, and always a serious attitude...

no one wanted to fight Siani... it was just not fun.

He was also the one who took impeccable notes and even typed them up and shared them with many of us. Siani's notes have contributed enormously to this book.

His lovely wife, Roseamund, was the total opposite to Chuck as her flawless form was the envy of all.

Robert (Bung) "Mr. Lucky" Leong

Robert Leong

Born in 1923, Mr. Leong made Shodan in 1966.

"The thing I will never forget is when Sensei asked us to bring our dictionaries to class and he made us look up and cross out two words, 'TRY' and 'IMPOSSIBLE'. To this day, they are still crossed out of my dictionary."

Leong was Sensei's constant companion and traveling sidekick. To see Sensei and not see Leong was, indeed, a rare occasion. It was through Leong that Sensei would teach many of his lessons and it was also through Leong that we all knew our place in line.

A fellow merchant marine (Engine Department) Leong met Sensei in 1947 on a picket line. Sensei looked at him and said, "Go back to school kid." He continued training and traveling with Sensei right up to the end.

He became an international champion in open hand and weapons kata. It was his weapons kata, Chatan Yara No Kon, that forged his place in the competition ring.

When interviewed, all he could say was that he was the luckiest of us all, as it was he that Sensei would correct the most and it was because of this he changed his character. "I remember Sensei once saying to me," said Leong, "'it is easier to move a stream or a mountain then to change a man's own character.' This I will never forget."

He actually began training with Sensei Richard Kim in 1962. There was, and never has been, anyone who was as strong a supporter as Leong. He was most definitely Sensei's right-hand.

Cal Avila

Cal Avila

One of Sensei Kim's strong right arms during the late 1960s and early 1970s, Cal Avila was known for his strong techniques and his excellent kata practise. He actually began like many, by studying judo in 1959. He was a stickler for conditioning and insisted on being in top shape all the time.

"He was a stickler for basics," says Fred Jackaman, one of his first students who later trained with Sensei Kim.

Not only was Avila's dojo in a weight gym in the early days, but he also was a big time advocate of the makiwara.

He was located near Watsonville, California, where he taught many top martial artists. He left the Bu Toku Kai during the mid- to late-1970s to pursue his own training.

Lenore S. Tejo-Gaviola

Lenore S. Tejo-Gaviola

Born in 1948, Lenore made Shodan in 1966.

"I never realized how much both my father and Sensei meant to me until they were both gone."

She started Ju Jitsu training in San Francisco at the age of 14 years with Professor Duke Moore, and karate training with Hanshi Richard Kim until his passing in November 2001.

Lenore was one of the stalwarts at the Chinese YMCA dojo.

For 13 years she taught Ju Jitsu to adults and children for her father, Urbano S. Tejo, at his dojo in San Francisco and Sacramento and has been an assistant karate instructor for Martial Arts Way for the last 22 years.

Lenore was a member of the women's team kata from 1975-1992 and her individual kata performances were nothing short of beautiful. Lenore was most certainly one of Sensei Kim's pride and joy's.

She is now an assistant instructor with her husband Frank in Sacramento, California, where she is still teaching on a weekly basis.

Rod Sanford

Rod Sanford

Born in 1946, Sanford made Shodan in 1966.

"My family and I have dedicated our lives to preserving and teaching traditional Martial Arts as taught by O'Sensei Richard Kim."

Rod Sanford was studying Judo by 1960. By 1964, he had left Judo and was studying traditional Japanese Karate (Chito-Ryu). From 1965 into the '70s he also studied Kodenkan Ju-Jitsu under Master J. Chow-Hoon.

In the mid '60s, he joined the Zen Bei Bu Toku Kai and began to study Shorinji-Ryu under Professor Richard Kim at the San Francisco Chinese Y.M.C.A. Under Richard Kim, he studied Shorinji-Ryu Karate, Kobudo, Aiki-Jujutsu, T'ai Chi Chuan, Hsing Yi, P'a Kua and Chi Kung.

In the later part of 1967, Sanford began running a dojo under the watchful eye of his Sensei. For many years, he taught through various school and community centers. In 1980, he began to teach Martial Arts on a full-time basis and moved into his present 6,000 square foot dojo in Soquel, California.

In 1973, Sanford began to study Aikido and police tactics with Robert Koga. Sanford continued to study with Koga until the mid '90s. He has trained in Aikijujutsu under Soshi Siego Okamoto of the Daito-Ryu Aikijujutsu Roppokai, Japan and Soke Don Angier, successor of Yanagi-Ryu Aikijujutsu.

With Richard Kim's introduction, Sanford has trained in Goju-Ryu Karate with Tomoharu Kisaki and Morio Higaonna. He has trained in Shito-Ryu Karate with Kenei Mabuni and has studied Shotokan Karate with such greats as Hidetaka Nishiyama, Masatoshi Nakayama, Hiroshi Shirai, Keinosuke Enoeda, Takeshi Ohishi and Taiji Kase. He has also had the opportunity to train in Brazilian Jiu-Jitsu with members of the Gracie family.

After studying engineering and law enforcement in college, Sanford went on to study Vocational Education and Adult Learning at the University of California. He holds a Community College Instructor's credential. After graduating, Sanford joined the Santa Cruz Sheriff's Department. He received the rank of operations sergeant. While with the department he was a S.W.A.T.

 Always wear the best shoes you can afford. You will appreciate it in your later years.

team leader and was specially trained in dignitary protection. In 1983, he founded the Pacific Institute of Defensive Tactics. Through the Institute he teaches a wide range of police tactical programs and is a well known author on police tactics. In 1994, he was nominated for the Governor's Award for his contributions to law enforcement training in California.

Sanford now runs his dojo in Soquel with the help of his wife, Bedelia, and son, Sean. He and his staff offer traditional instruction in Shorinji-Ryu Karate-Do, Kobudo, T'ai Chi Chuan, Chi Kung and Aikijujutsu. He is assisted in his Karate programs by his son Sean and Dan Wakefield. He is assisted in his Aikijujutsu program by his wife, Bedelia. Lou Jemison runs his T'ai Chi Chuan program.

After Richard Kim's death in November of 2001, Sanford and other senior students of Sensei Kim pledged to continue Kim's teachings. Their vision is simple, to endeavor to make the world a better place by upholding, through teaching and practicing, the spiritual and physical traditions of Martial Arts training. Sanford is now the president of the Zen Bei Bu Toku Kai.

Mr. Sanford's senior students include Danny Wakefield.

Don Warrener

Born in 1948, Warrener made Shodan in 1968.

"Master Kim taught me Oriental culture, philosophy and psychology that I use every single day and every breathing minute. His impact on my life is only equaled by my parents who gave me life."

Don Warrener

Warrener began his karate training March 15, 1966, in Hamilton, Ontario, Canada under Benny Allen who also taught Wally Slocki, Teddy Martin and Tony Faceti.

He was promoted to shodan in 1968 by Benny Allen and the legendary Richard Kim of San Francisco, California. He won the Canadian Championship in 1968 and in 1971 won the Eastern Canadian Championships. In 1973, he broke the "Guinness World Book of Records" record for brick breaking.

In 1977, he was introduced by his Sensei, Richard Kim to Gogen "The Cat" Yamaguchi, who asked him to represent the Goju Kai in Canada, but he refused as his loyalty remained with Richard Kim. Although he did return to Tokyo on several occasions for training at the dojo of the "The Cat".

During the late 1970s he started the "Voice Of The Martial Arts Magazine" and "Masters Publication" now run by Annette Hellingrath. He also started to develop a system of teaching large numbers of students and school marketing which eventually developed into over 9,000 students by the late 1980s and over 32 professional schools, all in Canada. Many of these schools continue today and are some of the most profitable in the business.

At the base of the system was traditional karate which emphasized respect, compassion, and gratitude, which was the basis of the oldest Martial Arts organization in the world – the Dai Nippon Bu Toku Kai.

In 1985 he began the lengthy process of restoring a national monument and with the aid of his students restored the historic Hamilton Custom House (20,000 sq. feet) which was originally built by Queen Victoria. His purpose was to establish a Martial Arts college.

In 1993, he was asked to become the vice president of the World Karate Organization and eventually held the largest international tournament of the time in Canada with over 27 countries and 1,200 participants – over 700 of which were black belts.

Warrener has written well over 250 articles for virtually every magazine in the world and has also written six books in total and co-authored another six.

In 1997, he started to compete again and won the European and Pan American Championships in both forms and weapons forms in the Masters Division of the WKO.

Then in 1998, Warrener made a radical move and relocated to sunny California where he presently runs Rising Sun Productions with his partner, Isaac Florentine.

He presently is the Martial Arts advisor to Jean Claude Van Damme and is the President of his Official Web Site.

He continues to teach seminars around the world for his senior students in Canada: Phil McColl, Conroy Copeland, Tosha Lord, Tom Burtnik, David Turkoski, Dirk Gerlofs, Pat Lecomte and Vic Granic.

Fred Jackaman

Fred Jackaman

Jackaman made Shodan in 1968.

"I remember when Sensei said, 'fighting is not intellectual, it is emotional.'"

'Jackaman', as Sensei would always call him, began his training in 1964 under the guidance of Wallus Rumen and Cal Avila in Monterey, California.

An auto mechanic by trade, it was Jackaman who was one of the top fighters in the dojo, along with Siani, Geeter, Larkin and others, but it was that reverse punch he had mastered and his fighting spirit that were his trademarks.

His favorite form is either Arakaki Unsu or Wanquan.

"Wanquan is short and powerful, but I believe it is functional and suits my body style," says Fred. He learned both from Sensei Kim and has spent his Martial Arts career in training and perfecting them both.

A stickler for fundamentals, he strongly believes that basics and kata are the essence of karate. Like he says, "otherwise it is just street fighting."

Jackaman is now a 6th degree Renshi and trains at the Washinkan Dojo run by Mr. Ken Shockey.

Jim Larkin

Jim Larkin

Larkin made Shodan in 1969.

"Sensei Kim treated you like you allowed him to treat you."

Jim Larkin is, without a doubt, one of the nicest guys to ever come out of the Chinese YMCA. He was known for his superior fighting skills and he trained every Saturday morning with Sensei Kim. Not only was Jim an excellent fighter but he was and is a first class instructor, and his sons have become top fighters, as well.

He still teaches in the Bay area at inner city centers where he emphasizes Martial Arts that work, as his students have to fight for their lunch money.

He claims that although Sensei Kim's classes were not physically difficult they were much more intellectual and this made them invaluable, as he says he knew how to fight before he came to the Chinese YMCA.

It also made for great kata training and Sensei Kim's command of the English language made it much easier to train, as many other of the Japanese instructors were not as skilled in the English language as he was.

But after all is said and done there was no better story teller the Sensei Kim, he was the absolute very best.

Rosamund Siani

Rosamund Siani

Rosamund Siani made Shodan in 1969.

There were only a few who can say that they were on par with Rosamund Siani when it came to kata.

Her form was flawless and she was the front in the women's team kata that Sensei was so proud of. This team went on to place in many regional, national and international competitions.

Rosamund was the one who would also attain individual honors of the highest level.

Greg Mellor

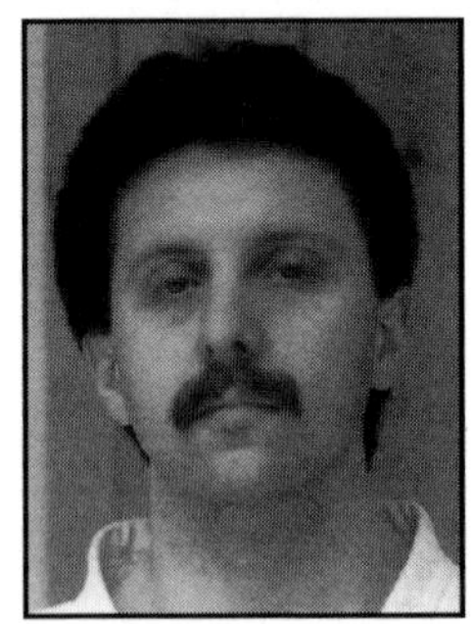

Greg Mellor

Born in 1955, Greg Mellor made Shodan in 1970.

"Sensei Kim was nothing short of incredible."

Greg Mellor began his study of judo at the age of 10 under long-time Judoka John Mills in Hamilton, Ontario, Canada.

In 1967, Mellor joined Benny Allen's Eastern Karate and began training with Benny Allen and Frank Wishart. He received his shodan from Sensei Kim in 1972.

In 1973 he attended one of Sensei Kim's seminars and a tournament in Hamilton and has since then been a student of Sensei Kim's, traveling the world with him as part of Sensei's entourage.

Considered by most Canadians to be the finest example of technique Canada has ever produced, Greg won more then his share of competitions in kata and in weapons kata.

He has been a full time instructor since the early 1970s and has produced some fine quality students. Mellor continues to teach the art that he learned from Sensei Kim in Hamilton, Canada.

Greg Mellor's senior students are Paul Benton, Paul Armstrong, Peter Lemmen, Robin Lemmen, Walter Baumann, Brian Cyr and Paul Altobelli.

Eileen Dennis

Eileen Dennis

Eileen Dennis made Shodan in 1970.

"I remember Sensei's jokes. He had the best jokes. I can't remember them there were so many."

She first met Sensei Kim in Hamilton, Ontario, at a tournament in 1973 when the Bu Toku Kai of Canada brought Sensei Kim in for a tournament and seminars.

Dennis was the acting secretary-treasurer at the time and was later put in charge of the Shorinji Ryu section in Canada by Sensei Kim.

Dennis began her training with Masaru Shintani in Grimsby, Ontario, in 1966, and then later became a student of Frank Wishart's and then a student of Sensei Kim's in 1972.

She ran her dojo in Grimsby for nearly 30 years before retiring from teaching.

Eileen was the driving force behind the summer camps in Guelph, Ontario, which she personally organized for Sensei Kim that so many Canadians attended for over 20 years. It was she who handled all the registrations as well as all the organization of the Shorinji section in Canada for so many years, acting as Sensei Kim's strong right arm in Canada.

She developed many students over the years, including Don Racine, Lisa Robinson and many more.

Antonio Molinar

Photo not available.

Born 1950, Molinar made Shodan around 1970.

He began his training in 1967. Molinar was, without a doubt, one of Sensei Kim's best kata performers. He, along with two of Sensei Kim's other top kata practitioners, competed for years in team kata and although they never won an ITKF world championship, many thought that they should have won in 1977 in Tokyo, Japan, when they did Yabu Chinto to absolute perfection.

Molinar's quality in kata and his over all knowledge of kata was tremendous to say the very least – not just in open hand, but also in weapons.

Molinar, along with Frank Gaviola, were the 'books of knowledge' when it came to the katas of Sensei Kim.

He taught for many years in the San Francisco Bay area but stopped teaching around 1996.

Ron Lok

Ron Lok made Shodan in 1970.

"Sensei (Kim) taught me my favorite kata, which is Kusanku Dai."

Ron Lok

He began training with Sensei at the Chinese YMCA in 1966 and became known as a quality martial artist.

In the 1970s he was a strong kata competitor and competed under Sensei Kim's name in Toronto, Buenes Aires, Germany and Japan.

A mechanical engineer by trade, he believes strongly that karate has many benefits like fitness, release of stress, and self defense.

Continuing his training at the Washinkan Dojo of Kyoshi Ken Shockey, Lok presently holds the rank of 6th dan Renshi.

Louis Jemison

Louis Jemison

Louis Jemison made Shodan in 1971.

"O'Sensei was a major influence on my life, from my 15th birthday until his death in 2001, and next to my parents there is no person that I feel more grateful to then O'Sensei Richard (Biggie) Kim."

Jemison began training with Rod Sanford in 1967. Within a few years, he moved to the San Francisco Bay area to attend the University of California at Berkeley. There he studied Oriental history and language. While attending UCB he began to study directly under O'Sensei Richard Kim at the Chinese YMCA in San Francisco.

Jemison continued to train directly under Kim until O'Sensei passed away in 2001. Jemison has extensive teaching experience in Martial Arts programs in San Francisco, Watsonville and Santa Cruz areas.

He also traveled extensively with Kim. Under Kim, he has studied Shorinji-Ryu Karate-Do, Kobudo (Okinawan and Japanese Weaponry), T'ai Chi Chuan, Chi Kong, Aiki, Martial Arts history, tradition and philosophy. Jemison has studied Goju-Ryu Karate under Master Tomoharu Kisaki, President of the Japan Karate-Do Goju-Ryu Yuishinkan and Master Morio Higaonna of the International Okinawan Goju-Ryu Karate Federation.

Jemison has studied under Master Kenei Mabuni, Soke of Shito-Ryu Karate, and he has studied Shotokan Karate under Masters Hidetaka Nishiyama, Masatoshi Nakayama, Hiroshi Shoji, Taiji Kase, Toru Yamaguchi, Hiroshi Shirai, Masaka Ueki, Hideki Okamoto, Keinosuke Enoeda and Professor Takeshi Ohishi.

He has also trained in Aikijujutsu with Soshi Siego Okamoto. Jemison has successfully completed the International Coaches and Judges courses through the International Traditional Karate Federation.

Jemison is known for his strong, powerful technique and his common sense logic in worldly matters.

Ed Geeter

Ed Geeter

Ed Geeter made Shodan around 1971.

"Follow in the footsteps of someone you respect, who has gone before you in the direction you want to go in life. You can go on your own but you are more likely to step on minefields. This was one of the hundreds of terrific lessons I learned from Sensei Kim."

Geeter began his training in 1968 under Richard Lee and was one of the best fighters at the Chinese YMCA. You might also say many of his techniques were road-tested.

A police officer, Geeter knew what tough was all about, as he defended the streets of San Francisco. He is now retired from the San Francisco Police Department. Geeter, along with two other officers, started the San Francisco Police Department Karate Team, which he is still very proud of. He competed with them in many of the Police Olympics around the world.

His first Sensei was Richard Lee but when Mr. Lee moved to Paris in 1974 he became a student of Sensei Kim's.

"I love the Sei Unchin kata," says Geeter, "as it is functional and suits my body style. Arakaki Unanku is more sophisticated but it is the same as Wanquan: strong, Goju-ryu style, strong stances and body dynamics, powerful movements, and quick inside stepping."

He is presently a 5th dan Renshi and trains at the Washinkan Dojo in Daly City, California.

Dr. Ray Castilonia

Ray Castilonia

Dr. Ray Castilonia made Shodan in 1972.

Castilonia, Kyoshi and founder of Aoinagi-ha Shito Ryu under O'Sensei Kim, was a true artist of life. He was a physician, earned an MD and PhD, was an avid mountaineer, a scuba diver, a certified mountain rescue team member, a college professor on environmental issues and a loyal son. But he considered himself, first and foremost, a martial artist.

Some highlights of Castilonia's diverse and complete Martial Arts history follows:

His initial introduction to traditional Martial Arts began in the art of Judo in 1957 thanks to his father who took him to a YMCA class.

In 1964, Castilonia's formal karate training began, learning Okinawan karate under the Genck brothers in Southern California.

In 1969, he trained under Del Saito in the Goshin Jitsu School in San Bernardino. The school was headquartered in Hawaii with Sensei Al Kahalekulu as chief instructor and Del Saito as the California representative. Because of the rigorous schedule imposed on Castilonia by his medical training, he would go to the dojo at 5:30 in the morning, where a bedraggled Sensei Saito would put him through the paces, sometimes falling asleep while Castilonia practiced.

Sensei Kahalekulu was Castilonia's first Shugyo Sensei and taught him many kata and lessons of life.

When Al Kahalekulu decided to stop actively teaching Martial Arts, Castilonia, along with Del Saito joined up with Chuzo Kotaka's organization(also based in Hawaii) and embraced the Shito-ryu style of karate.

On March 8, 1972, Castilonia received his first-degree black belt and the title of Sensei. He became assistant instructor at Saito's school and also began shito-ryu karate instruction at LLU.

In 1974, when Chuzo Kotaka would not renew his certification, Castilonia had no choice but to leave Del Saito and Kotaka's organization. He traveled to Hawaii once again and trained with Sensei James Miyaji. From 1974 until the early '90s, Castilonia returned to Hawaii and trained with Sensei Miyaji twice a year, often taking along several of his students to experience Sensei Miyaji's "moving Zen".

In 1975, through Sensei Miyaji, Castilonia was introduced to Richard Kim. Kim became Castilonia's primary instructor and Miyaji remained as his representative to the Zen Bei Bu Toku Kai.

This introduction sparked a 27-year relationship with Richard Kim that ended only at the death of Castilonia.

After a whole year of wearing a white belt, a series of challenging tests and tasks to evaluate his desire to learn, as well as his capability as a martial artist and student – including completing a research paper comparing Master Funakoshi with Master Itosu – Castilonia obtained the rank of Yondan (4th degree black belt) from Sensei Kim.

In Kim's words, "Castilonia was the first Bu Toku Kai member to break the barrier and beat the JKA in national competition!" He won first place in kata at the National Karate Championships, paving the way for many future Bu Toku Kai national and world champions, including several of Castilonia's own students.

His achievements in competition include a second place finish at the Pan American Karate Championships that brought international fame, glory and recognition to Mr. Kim's organization. Castilonia didn't care much for the "tournament scene" but because it was important to his Sensei he accepted the charge and took it all the way to the top.

In 1978, Castilonia established Aoinagi Karate-do at the Redlands Community Center, in Redlands California. In 1980 the organization blossomed into Willow Enterprises, a commercial school that was established in Redlands on Alabama Street and in its heyday had well over a hundred students.

Castilonia felt that teaching was his highest calling, and education a critical piece in one's personal development.

Dr. Castilonia's senior students include Paul Billimoria, Neville Billimoria, Cecil Cheung, Lee Carmean, Paul Schwartz, and Barbara Sedgwick-Billimoria.

(Thanks to Neville Billimoria for this information.)

Brian Ricci

Brian Ricci

Brian Ricci was born in 1950, and made Shodan in 1972.

"There is simply no one phrase that I can share with you as to the major impact he had on my life."

Brian's first interest in Martial Arts came as a result of watching movies. At the time, no one knew much about Martial Arts, but he knew he wanted to learn what he was seeing on film.

He began his training in 1965 with Peter Ventresca and he received his black belt in 1972. At 22 years of age he decided he wanted to learn more in depth about the Martial Arts so he wrote a letter to Richard Kim and word was sent back that he had been accepted as a student of Kim's. In July 1973, he quit his job and drove to San Francisco, California, and became a student of Kim's at the Chinese YMCA.

After many years, Ricci became an assistant instructor to Kim and in 2000, Kim awarded him a prestigious 7th dan.

Since the passing of Richard Kim, Ricci has continued his teacher's work in passing on the Martial Arts to the next generation of students. Many of the members in Kim's organization, the Zen Bei Bu Toku Kai International, are now training with him.

These are some of Brian Ricci's senior students: Edward Ricci, Brian Brandano (Asst. Instructor), Dennis Mann (Chief), William (Billyjack) Jakielaszek, and Ken Driver.

Frank Gaviola

Frank Gaviola made Shodan in 1972.

"Kata is the primary method of Traditional Martial Arts practice. It is a device to bring together the intuitive body and rational mind."

Frank Gaviola

Gaviola started Martial Arts training with Hanshi Richard Kim at the Chinese YMCA in, San Francisco, in the spring of 1968. He is currently teaching Martial Arts classes at Los Rios Community College Sacramento at the Folsom Lake campus and El Dorado campus; and operates his Martial Arts Way dojo at the Ballroom of Elk Grove in Elk Grove, California. Gaviola also teaches Tai Chi for Kaiser Permanente, YMCA Central Sacramento, Various State of California Agencies, Elk Grove Senior Center and Sacramento County Drug Court Rehabilitation Program and Elk Grove Unified School District-Adult Education.

Gaviola is well known as one of the best international kata competitors to ever be trained by Sensei Kim. His knowledge of kata and their details is second to none. If there was ever a collector of kata and the detail of kata that Sensei Kim taught it is Frank Gaviola.

He competed successfully from 1977-1996 and won many top honors around the world in team kata, individual kata and weapons kata.

Frank is undoubtedly one of Sensei Kim's top students and his skill in both kata and on the floor attest to this fact.

These are Mr. Gaviola's senior students: Rose Baldo, Patrick Barclay, Lonnie Francis, Edgar Sagun Sr., Kathleen Villegas, Frank Yuen Jr.

Dennis Farbatiuk

Dennis Farbatiuk

Dennis Farbatiuk made Shodan in 1960s and started training under Sensei in the early 1970s.

Farbatiuk began his training in karate in Detroit, Michigan, in the study of Okinawan Te. He then studied under Wado Ryu master Masaru Shintani in Hamilton, Ontario, Canada.

He met Richard Kim for the first time in the summer of 1972 and this would be the start of many trips to follow.

Dennis traveled extensively with Sensei Kim to Hawaii and France, and he made many personal trips to San Francisco to enhance his already wide range of karate knowledge.

A champion in tournaments in both kumite and kata in the mid 1960s, Farbatiuk's legacy is that of a strong, strong karate man who could fight toe-to-toe with anyone. Gifted with a huge, muscular body he was one of Sensei Kim's proudest students in Canada.

Now living in Vancouver, British Columbia, Canada he still practices his karate the way he was taught by Sensei Kim.

Dennis Farbatiuk's senior students include: Walter Bowman, Yulia De Wolfe, and Ralph Corvino.

Jean Chalamon

Jean Chalamon was born 1935, and made Shodan in 1975.

He began his training with judo, karate and kendo under Jim Alchek in 1958 and was strongly influenced by martial artists in France like Hiro Mochizuki, and Henry Plee.

Jean Chalamon

He was one of Richard Lee's earliest students when Lee moved to Paris in 1971, and when Lee went on his own in 1982, Chalamon stayed as Sensei Kim's representative for the Bu TokuKai in Europe.

A decorated war hero for the French Foreign Legion, Chalamon is an expert in hand-to-hand combat, as well as the katas of Sensei Kim and is excellent in his performance of both empty hand and traditional kobudo. He has also spent years training in Tai Chi and continues his own learning process in Tai Chi, one of Sensei Kim's morning rituals.

He has continued to help propagate Sensei Kim's teaching by organizing the Bu Toku Kai in France, Poland and Germany.

Chalamon brings Sensei Kim's senior students from America on a regular basis to teach and learn from at his summer camps.

Chalamon has written eight books on the katas of the Zen Bei Buto Ku Kai. They represent the most comprehensive work on the katas taught by Richard Kim during his illustrious career.

Jean Chalamon's senior students include: Dominique Germon, Max Bouton,Jean Michel Argant, Doan N'Guyen, and Michel Poultjian.

Lonnie Francis

Lonnie Francis

Lonnie Francis was born in 1959, and made Shodan in 1976.

Francis began training with Sensei Kim at the Chinatown YMCA dojo in 1970. He had first become a green belt under Frank and Lenore Gaviola.

His fighting expertise was first class all the way. In fact he was an alternate on the 1976 AAKF team while still a teenager and barely old enough to be on the adult team. As a fighter he never finished less then 3rd in any tournament in which he competed.

He also trained in Ju Jitsu at the Tejo Dojo under Lenore and Frank Gaviola.

Presently Lonnie runs his own dojo in San Francisco and specializes in teaching youth karate where he endeavors to pass along the traditions and technical excellence which he has developed from his teachers.

Yulia de Wolfe

Yulia de Wolfe

Yulia de Wolfe made Shodan in 1976.

de Wolfe began her training under Dennis Farbatiuk in 1973 in Hamilton, Canada, and later became a direct student of Sensei Kim's.

She also traveled the world with Sensei Kim as part of his entourage in France, all over the USA and Canada.

She was well known for her strength and skill in kata. Although she rarely competed, she was a top-notch practitioner.

She moved to Vancouver, British Columbia, in the 1980s and helped to organize the Bu Toku Kai in western Canada.

Rick Marshall

Rick Marshall

Rick Marshall was born 1946, and made Shodan in 1976.

In 1972, wanting something different, he joined Don Warrener's Martial Arts Academy. In 1975, holding the rank of brown belt he decided to travel to Japan and further his studies with Sensei Gogen Yamaguchi, who was the head of the Goju system in Japan. One year later he returned home as a Shodan and continued training under Warrener. Warrener had, by then, made a full commitment to the Bu Toku Kai organization under Richard Kim.

In 1978, after testing for Nidan, he moved to Parksville, British Columbia, and in 1979 began training in the local club. In 1980 he became a partner and in 1982 bought out his partner.

In 1983, he received his Sandan from O'Sensei Richard Kim, in 1990 became Yondan and in 1995 Godan.

In 1990 the University of Hawaii started an off-campus correspondence course in Martial Science called Polemikology. In March of 1995 he received his Masters Degree and in 1997 he received his Doctoral Degree in the field of Martial Science.

He continues to teach in Parksville, British Columbia.

Pete McHenry

Pete McHenry was born in 1953, and made Shodan in 1976.

"Sensei taught us that every class begins and ends with compassion, gratitude and respect. I have tried to cultivate this in every aspect of my life."

Pete McHenry

Pete McHenry was one of the best weapons and kata exponents of Sensei Kim's. His no-nonsense approach to training is something everyone admires and respects about Pete. He is one of the very few that has taken Sensei Kim's teachings and applied them to his every-day life.

He was a regular at the San Diego summer camps where Sensei would teach and was usually one of the first on the floor and the last off the floor.

His precision of the kata and mastery of them is something we all admire about him.

Pete's training began in Judo in Hawaii and has also trained in Tae Kwon Do, Ryu Kyu Kempo. Gracie Ju Jitsu, Tai Chi and Escrima.

Patrick McCarthy

Pat McCarthy was born in 1954, and made Yondan in 1978.

"Among tall trees, Richard Kim stood the tallest and provoked the pride of strong winds."

Patrick McCarthy

Although Pat did not start with Sensei Kim until 1978,

he earned his 4th dan straight away from Sensei Kim who obviously realized his talents and natural ability.

He started at the Saint John Judo club under Dutchie Schell in 1967 and went onto Kyokushin karate the following year under Adrian Gomes at the YMCA.

McCarthy's skill and knowledge have far succeeded many of Sensei Kim's senior students and, in fact, in a letter to Mr. Charles Goodin, Sensei Kim says that his two most advanced students were Peter Urban whom he deems an absolute genius and Pat McCarthy.

McCarthy has competed in all types of events and is now living in Australia but travels the world teaching Martial Arts. He travels at least 8 months a year and his seminars are packed to the brim.

An acclaimed author of several books, his most famous perhaps is his rendition of "The Bubishi", which he researched while he lived in Japan and Okinawa, where he stayed for nearly 10 years studying and learning with the old school instructors.

These are but some of Mr. McCarthy's senior students: Dirk Thesenvitz [German], Kurt Graham [NZ], Conrad Lee [England], Chris Mazzali [Oz], Steve McLellan [NZ], Ante Brannbacka [Finland], Per-Ivar Andersson [Sweden], Frank Barca [Oz], Olaf Krey [Germany], Don Ouellette [Oz], Richard Ouellette [Canada], Dudley Driscoll [Canada], Darrin Johnson [USA], Tyler West [USA], Jason Griffiths [Oz], and Hubert Laenen [Belgium].

Thousands of students trained with Sensei Kim over the years but in an attempt to protect those who actually did train with him from the fraudulent 'wannabes' who want to make the claim that they were his students, we have listed everyone we can think of that actually spent time training with him enough to be considered students, and not those who just took a few seminars with him.

These people, although we do not have bios on them, were students of his – most definitely:

Bill King, Dr. Murmane, Louis Di Piccari, Ron Forester, Raoul Castillo, Linda Castillo, Hamilton Williams, Ralph Corvino, Robert Saballa, Dr.

Herbert Weiner, Neville Billimoria, Paul Billimoria, CC Chung, Frank Yuen, Joe Papu, Sam Samurrai, Scott Greg, Kathy Greg, Kay Belle, Glee Miranda, Benny Abaka, David Benivideddas, Brian Conaughton, Terry Dumphy, Rick Atix, Ernie Wong, C. Lee, Joe Trent, Debbie Bilton, Selby Houseman, Joe Corcoran, Joe Fournier, Lynn Marquist, Andre Lefond, Bruce Fox, Jane Hedgepath, Patrick O'Neil, Naomi Larkin, Richard Fantiles, Claire Young, Dawn DeCunaha, David Kowalchuk, Maria Molinar, Tun Lee, Bob Polapos, Tamio Mansfield, Herbert Lee, John Vandenberg, Manuel Abuda, Benny Allen, and Bob Dalgleish.

The Last of the Real Samurai: Sokaku Takeda and Yoshida Kotaro

Yoshida's Teacher – Sokaku Takeda, 1859-1943

Sokaku was not a large man — he stood no more than 5 feet tall, but his eyes were darting and his techniques were, some say, at supernatural level. He was able to sense a person's past, present, and future even before being introduced. His students included a famous politician of the time Saigo Tsugumichi, and Hokushin Itto-ryu swordsman Shimoe Hidetaro, as well as military officers, martial artists, police officers and others.

Sokaku Takeda's official photo.

Takeda had three very important students who went on to claim fame in the Martial Arts arena. First, our own Yoshida Kotaro; second, Moreihei Ueshiba (who needs no introduction whatsoever), it was Yoshida Sensei who introduced Ueshiba to Takeda; and third, a young nine-year-old Korean who was the house boy (some say he was adopted) of Takeda,

Saigo Tsugumichi Saigo San was one of the most instrumental in the reorganization of the Dai Nippon Bu Toku Kai.

Courtesy Pat McCarthy www.society.webcentral.com.au/

O-Sensei taught a young Richard Kim in 1948 for 1 full year, 6 days a week from 6-9 every morning.

named Choi Young Sol (1904-1986).

It was Choi who founded Hapkido. He studied with Takeda from 1913 until his master died on April 25, 1943.

Mr. Choi was the founder of Hapkido, and was a student of Sokaku Takeda.

As a boy, Sokaku learned kenjutsu, bojutsu, sumo, and Daito-ryu from his father, and he also studied Ohno-ha Itto-ryu at the Yokikan dojo under Shibuya Toba.

In 1873, Sokaku traveled with his father to the dojo of his father's friend, swordmaster Sakakibara Kenkichi. He chose to stay on as a live-in student and totally immersed himself in the study of

Jikishinkage-ryu. While living here, he had opportunities to meet and train with the top swordsmen of the day, many of whom had formerly been members of the Tokugawa shogunate's Kobusho, the main Martial Arts school for the government's retainers. He studied hard and eventually mastered many different skills and weapons, including sword, staff, half-bow, short-staff, and throwing darts. He also received a license in the spear arts of the Hozoin-ryu.

Saigo Tanomo as a young man.

Tanomo became Shinto Priest Hoshina Chikanori

In 1875, he was on his way to help Saigo Takamori in the uprising against the new Meiji Government, but instead went to Osaka where he spent the next ten years as a guest in the Kyoshin Meichi-ryu dojo of swordmaster Momonoi Shunzo.

Sokaku learned Daito-ryu from his father Sokichi, but it was from Saigo Tanomo that he learned oshikiiuchi (secret palace arts of Ju Jitsu and sword fighting). After the Meiji Restoration in 1868, Saigo Tanomo had become a Shinto priest and taken the name Hoshina Chikanori.

Sokaku Takeda (bottom left), Yoshida Kotaro's teacher.

In 1875, Sokaku visited him at Tsutsukowake Shrine in Fukushima to study for the priesthood. When he was there, he received instruction in the arts of oshikiiuchi from Chikanori. Sokaku then decided not to become a priest, but he visited his mentor (Chikanori) many times, and under Chikanori's instruction is said to have perfected seemingly miraculous skills of understanding another's mind and thought, and to have grasped the true depths of oshikiiuchi.

On May 12, 1898, Chikanori presented Sokaku with a single poem. One translation of Chikanori's poem is that it compares the flow of a river to the flow

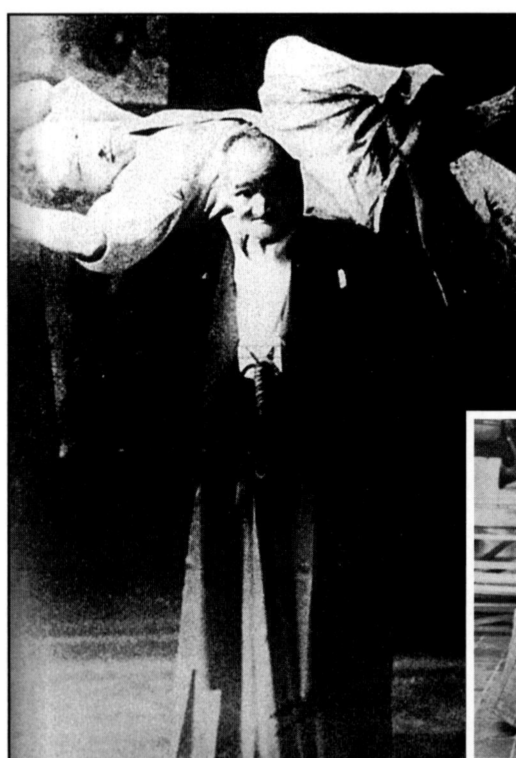

Sokaku (bottom left) and Yoshida – one of the very few photos with the two legends of Daito Ryu together.

of time. The beginning of the Meiji period brought about the end of the sword era. Therefore, it was time for Sokaku to pursue and make his way with jujutsu.

Above and inset, Sokaku Takeda as an old man was still very strong.

Sokaku Takeda seated with a group of senior Daito Ryu masters (seated 5th from left).

Yoshida Kotaro, 1886-1966

Yoshida Kotaro was a scholar – note the books in the background.

Yoshida Sensei began his training rather late in life, as he began when he was 29 years of age in 1915. He began under the direct tutelage of the legendary Sokaku Takeda in Hokkaido, in Shiragi Saburo Takeda Ryu Ju Jitsu.

Sokaku Takeda was so impressed with Yoshida's skill he even gave him a teaching license (Kyoju Dairi) which in those days was something very special.

Yoshida was a graduate of Tohoku Gakuin in Sendai (1906), Waseda University and an American University. He authored numerous books, operated a newspaper company and oversaw a private library.

Richard Kim with Yoshida Kotaro.

An interesting side note is a short story that Sensei Kim told us often. Once, when he visited Yoshida, he saw all the University diplomas on the wall and was very impressed with them.

Yoshida Sensei said to him, "Do not be impressed with these, they are only paper. It is the mind that counts, not certificates."

Although few are still alive that had actually seen him perform, there is much evidence that Yoshida Sensei was a master

Mas Oyama and Sensei were very good friends before he permanently returned to San Francisco in 1957.

Katsuyuki Kondo was the last full-time student Yoshida Sensei had.

beyond compare. His skill was acclaimed by such notables as Mas Oyama in his book "This Is Karate"; Katsuyuki Kondo, Yoshida taught Kondo in his later years (Kondo trained from 1963 to 1965 with him); and, our own Richard Kim.

He was a staunch right-wing activist and belonged to such ultra-nationalist organizations as the Genyosha (Black Ocean Society) which later became Kokuryu kai (Black Dragon Society). This group believed very much in the old ways of the samurai and, even though the samurai class was disbanded in the Meiji Restoration (January 3, 1868), it still operated but in the quiet. Yoshida was a member of this elite group and continued its ways and teachings until he passed away. Yoshida Sensei had obviously been strongly influenced by his teacher, Sokaku Takeda, who was prepared to go to battle against the new regime in 1875.

Also a member of this groups was Doshin So, founder of Shorinji

Doshin So was a priest, a Martial Arts master, and a spy for the Japanese during the Manchurian conflict .

Gogen Yamaguchi in Mawashi Uke posture, 1955. *Courtesy Hal Sharp.*

Mas Oyama and Richard Kim doing self defence. *Courtesy of Emil Farkas and The Beverley Hills Martial Arts Archives*

Richard Kim and Mas Oyama

Kempo. Although we have no proof, we also believe that other Martial Arts masters of that era, like Gogen Yamaguichi, Mas Oyama and Richard Kim were also members of this underground group of spies.

In his book, "The Cat", Yamaguchi talks in length about his involvement with spies in Manchuria. Oyama was in the Japanese Army and he, Richard Kim and Yamaguchi all became very good friends in the late 1940s. Both Richard Kim and Oyama became students of Yamaguchi and received their black belt in 1950 from him.

The Black Ocean Society was started in 1881 by a group of former samurai who had been suppressed during the Satsuma Rebellion of 1877. They became famous for their espionage and sabotage techniques, particularly in Russia, China and Manchuria in 1904-1905. They were especially active in the training of spies and agents.

The Black Dragon Society formed in 1901 was an offshoot of the Black Ocean Society (or Kokuryu Kai) and is said to have been of paramount importance in leading Japan into World War I.

Chiang Kai Sheck and Toyomo Mitsuro

A photo of Chiang Kai Sheck (Head of China prior to Mao Tse Tung's defeat of the Nationalists in 1949) and Toyomo Mitsuro, head of Black Dragon Society, taken in 1927 shows there was some sort of collusion between the two.

In fact, the Black Dragon Society was involved in several covert intelligence-gathering activities that included the USA prior to WWII.

Toyomo Mitsuro was also a member of the Dai Nippon Bu Toku Kai which, prior to the end of WWII, every martial artist belonged to – in fact, it had millions of members throughout Japan. It was shut down in 1946, as was the Black Dragon Society, by General Douglas MacArthur because the Dai Nippon Bu Toku Kai was deemed an ultra right wing organization which had a dangerous political influence on the Japanese society.

Yoshida Sensei passed away in the summer of 1966 in Hitachi Ibaragi Prefecture.

According to Sensei Kim, he had been injured and paralyzed on his left side during an accident when he ran his bicycle in front of a truck to save a young child's life. By diving in front of the truck on his bicycle, he forced the truck to turn and saved the life of the child but was seriously injured in the accident.

When Sensei Kim visited him in the hospital he said that when he looked at him with pity in his eyes, Yoshida Sensei sensed it and said, "Do not worry about this, as I will now have to operate on mind power, I will use the wireless system," and began laughing.

He lived with Sensei Richard Kim in Yokohama, in his house with his family, and this is when and where he taught Sensei Kim. He trained under

Mas Oyama and Richard Kim

Mas Oyama and Richard Kim

Yoshida Kotaro for seven years (according to Black Belt Magazine, June 1969). Sensei Kim often expounded on how difficult these years were under Yoshida. He was apparently tough to deal with and a real task master.

It was Sensei Kim who introduced his friend Mas Oyama, a Korean by birth, to Yoshida Sensei and he began training with Yoshida Sensei as well. In his book, “This Is Karate”, Oyama refers to him as his teacher and the greatest of them all. This now being hindsight, this was quite a compliment – having both Richard Kim and Mas Oyama calling him Sensei – so we know he must have been something very special.

Mas Oyama and Richard Kim

He was an eccentric in many ways according to Mas Oyama, and lived a life of poverty. His life’s work was reading, writing and the study of the Martial Arts. He once said that the Martial Arts were meant for human development physically, psychologically and for mental discipline and were not meant for gaining wealth or fame. Yoshida Sensei was most definitely from the old school of the Martial Arts, as he would not teach just anyone, no matter how much they paid him, unless their character was compatible with that of his.

Oyama, who apparently only trained a couple of years directly with Yoshida Sensei, was so impressed with Yoshida’s skills that he said in his book, “My teacher’s mastery of the arts can only be described as perfection and I fear that the readers of this book will only half believe me.” Yoshida Sensei taught him reverse locks, joint techniques, women’s self defense using a parasol and Jo Jitsu and Bo Jitsu techniques.

He tells how Yoshida Sensei could actually catch a fly with his chopsticks at will. He did it by constant practice (over 300,000 attempts) as he believed nothing was impossible. He at first caught a bee and then he tied the bee with a thread and continued practicing this until he was able to catch it at will with his chopsticks. He then caught a large fly, like a horse fly we suppose, and then he tied this up and practiced until he could catch it at will. Then came a regular fly in the winter months and finally a regular fly in the heat of summer.

Quite possibly this is where Sensei Kim came up with the idea of having us cross out two words in our dictionaries – “try” and “impossible”.

Although we have no proof of this, we again suspect that this is where

Yamaguchi Sensei with his crystal ball

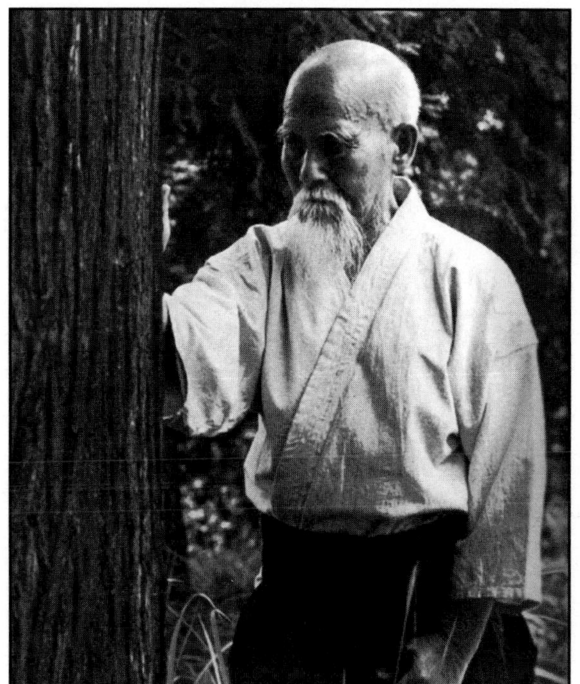

Also a student of Takeda, Ueshiba Sensei practiced the occult as well.

Sensei Kim developed his thirst for knowledge of hypnosis. He was a master of both direct and indirect hypnosis. (I personally saw him hypnotize over 200 people in less then 10 seconds in Britainne, France, while at a summer camp hosted by Richard Lee in 1985).

Yoshida Sensei was somewhat of an eccentric and his study of the occult was well known and documented, as was Yamaguchi Gogen's who loved his crystal ball. Ueshiba Moreihei was also a student of the occult and loved his crystal ball, as well. This is what makes us think that this interest in hypnosis came from Sokaku Takeda to Yoshida Kotaro to Sensei Kim.

Remember that Sensei Kim also trained with Yamaguchi Gogen and Moreihei Ueshiba, whose experience with the occult can be seen in videos and photos. Sensei Kim introduced his class to Dr. Milton Erickson, one of the world leaders in clinical hypnosis.

In Mas Oyama's book, he talks in length about

hypnosis and its relationship to the Martial Arts.

On more then one occasion, I personally saw Sensei Kim sitting down as he watched an individual who was on the other side of the room and then he began to explain everything about the individual and how 'it all made sense'. He watched the way the person walked and said, 'you can tell everything you need to know about a person by the way they walk'. He watched how they were dressed, watched the way they ate their food, watched their eyes, and anything else that was evident. He would explain things like if the man was well dressed he was probably well educated, or if he was sloppily dressed he was more then likely a factory worker. He would note things like which hand he used to eat with, and what he was eating. Whether he ate healthy or non healthy foods might dictate whether he was a martial artist or an athlete. He said he learned this in Japan and again we suspect he learned this from Yoshida Sensei. Yoshida was a spy for the Japanese during WWII, as well as in Manchuria, and was trained in these ways.

Yoshida Sensei's skill with all the traditional weapons of Japan was apparently unequalled and he was well known for his skill with the spear, sword, halbred, knife and shuriken as well as joint and muscle manipulation.

Yoshida received a teacher's license from Takeda and created his own style and a set of scrolls to go with the style. These scrolls contained the

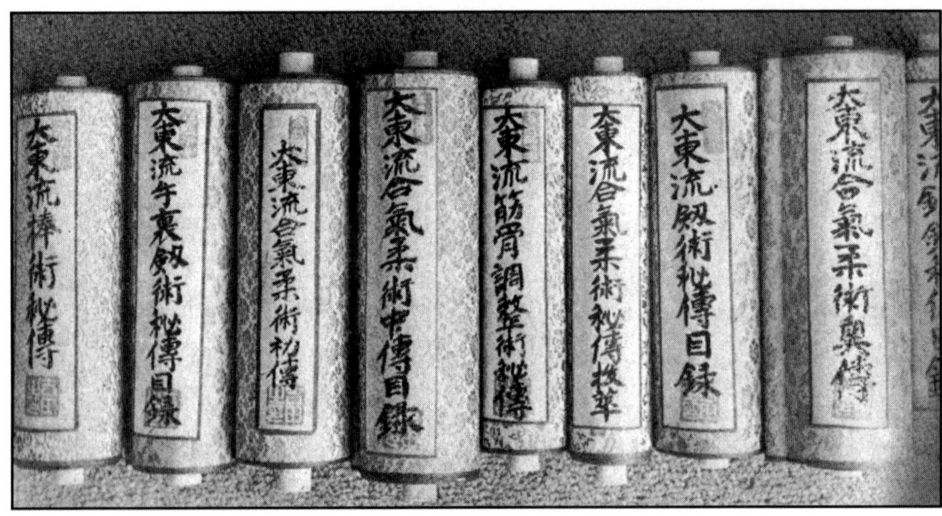

The scrolls of Daito Ryu Aiki Jitsu, which were given to Sensei Kim by Yoshida Kotaro in 1953.

secrets of Yoshida's Daito Ryu Aiki Jitsu. These scrolls are now in the possession of Mrs. Richard Kim (Sensei Kim's wife) and were seen by several of her followers as recent as Winter 2005.

The scrolls, shown on the previous page, are as follows, from left to right:

1. Daito Ryu Aiki Jitsu techniques with Bo and Jo. Signed Yoshida Kotaro.

2. Daito Ryu Aiki Jitsu techniques of Shuriken and throwing knives. Signed Yoshida Kotaro.

3. Daito Ryu Aiki Jitsu Techniques of Aiki #1. Signed Yoshida Kotaro.

4. Daito Ryu Aiki Jitsu Techniques of Aiki #2. Signed Yoshida Kotaro.

5. Daito Ryu Aiki Jitsu Techniques of Muscle Manipulation and Bone Adjustments. Signed Yoshida Kotaro.

6. Daito Ryu Aiki Jitsu Techniques of Aiki Judo throwing arts.
Signed Yoshida Kotaro.

7. Daito Ryu Aiki Jitsu Techniques of the Sword. Signed Yoshida Kotaro.

8. Daito Ryu Aiki Jitsu Techniques of Aiki Judo throwing arts. Signed Yoshida Kotaro.

9. Daito Ryu Aiki Jitsu – Can not see in the picture as it is cut off, but it is also signed by Yoshida Kotaro.

This photo of these scrolls was taken by George Dong for an article written in June 1969's Black Belt Magazine. It was taken in the apartment of Mr. Robert Leong. They were translated by Mr. Naito, a senior citizen in Los Angeles' Little Tokyo, and his assistant. These scrolls are signed by Yoshida Kotaro. There is no date on them in this picture. Apparently the date is inside the scrolls.

In the Black Belt article, Sensei Kim says that Yoshida sensei was the greatest Martial Arts master that Japan has produced since the Meiji Restoration 1868. Only those in the Bu Toku Kai and those who lived in Japan knew him, said Sensei Kim. It was Yoshida Sensei who ordered Sensei Kim to go and study with all the greats in the Tokyo area, including Ueshiba Moreihei. Sensei Kim personally told me that he trained everyday from 6:00 a.m. until about 9:00 a.m. with Ueshiba, in his home in Tokyo, for close to one year.

According to Mas Oyama, Yoshida Sensei's skill in Aiki, Sword fighting, judo and knife and shuriken throwing were unequalled. He never gave up the traditional dress and always wore kimono and carried an iron fan (tessen). In fact, it is reported in Frederick Lovret's, "Budo Jiten", that he actually killed a bear with his iron fan. This is also indicated in the notes of Sensei Kim's 'Six Lectures of Yoshida Sensei'.

Mas Oyama was given a teacher's license (Mokuroku certificate) from Yoshida Kotaro which is seen below. Although we have never seen the certificate that Yoshida gave Sensei Kim (as he never had a formal dojo) but we would assume that it was similar to the one Oyama received from him. In the article June 1969 Black Belt it does say that Sensei Kim did receive a certificate from Yoshida Kotaro. Kotaro also gave Sensei Kim an iron fan, which was one of his most valuable possessions from Yoshida Sensei who, according to Sensei Kim, had won 111 actual matches by using the fan.

Mas Oyama's Mokuroku certificate (teacher's license) from Yoshida Kotaro – the same one Sensei Kim was given by Kotaro. Courtesy Pat McCarthy www.society.webcentral.com.au/

Six Lectures of Yoshida Sensei

Following are six different lectures by Yoshida Sensei as told to Richard Kim, and by Richard Kim to his students.

Yoshida Kotaro Lecture by Richard Kim (2/27/1971)
Part One

If Yoshida Kotaro were living today, he would be anywhere between the ages of ninety-six to one-hundred years old. There are no records on him because he was a master spy. He was a man who lived simply, like most zen men, and had few possessions. Others, not knowing any better, might feel sorry for him, thinking he had a poor life, but he was rich in spirit. He taught only those people with whom he got along. When Mr. Kim last saw him, he was about eighty-two years old.

When Yoshida was thirteen years old, he went to a shrine every day to meditate. He did this for one hundred days. On the ninety-ninth or one hundredth day he was kneeling down, just about ready to get up and ring the shrine bell signifying the end of the period of meditation, when he dozed off. Someone was calling his name. He woke up and saw an old man standing in front of him. The man looked very old and had a white beard. He was dressed all in white with a medal I-Ching symbol sewn on his clothes. He was armed with a stick.

The old man knelt down on one knee in front of Yoshida, holding the stick vertically in one hand with the hand about eight inches from the top. He told Yoshida to attack him any way he could. (At this point in his life Yoshida's hair was not yet worn in the samurai style of having part of the head shaved and the rest tied back. Hair was not worn that way until you became a man by killing another man.) Yoshida drew his sword and tried to attack the old man, but when he did, the tsuba (the top eight inches of the stick representing the hilt of a sword) would grow in size closing the opening. The tsuba grew in size until he could hardly see the old man behind it. Finally, the old man said 'enough, that's very good'. He told Yoshida to think about what he saw.

Then Yoshida's mother called him. She had a meal all prepared at home to celebrate his one hundred day feat. When they got home, he asked for his father's sword, which was very famous. He took it out of the sheath and examined it, then put it back. He held the sheathed sword in his left hand, up against his side, and asked his mother to attack him. (Being a Martial Arts family, the mother had some training also.)

His mother said that there were two ways that she could attack him. One would be to attack his head and the other was to attack the hand that was holding the sword. What would be attacked in a fight would depend on the attacker's particular style of fencing.

Yoshida said that that was the way his father had died. Then he asked, 'suppose the tsuba grew so that it was several feet long, then you wouldn't be able to attack'. His mother said that was right. (His father had been killed before he could draw his sword.)

Yoshida's father thought that all the training in the use of the sword was a joke, not to be taken seriously. He studied it only because he belonged to a Martial Arts family and it was expected of him. He felt that because of the new contact with the west, and the subsequential effect on Japan's culture and way of life, dependency on the sword as a way of life was coming to an end. He was more of a scholar than a martial artist.

One night the father went to a party where he ate and drank a lot and had several women. When the party was over, the host sent a servant to escort him half way home, as was the custom of the time. By the time the two had reached approximately half way, which was near the edge of the forest, mist was forming along the ground. Off in the mist, the father saw what he thought was his servant standing in the middle of the road with his arms folded, so he dismissed his host's servant and went on ahead.

Getting closer to the man, he saw that the man's clothing was tied back with string in the manner of one about to fight. Then he realized that he had made a mistake. The man was a stranger whom he had never seen before. When the father tried to go around the man (Nitta Dengoro), the stranger stepped in front of him blocking his way. When he tried again, the same thing happened. It was then that the father saw the sword in the man's right hand that had been hidden by the folded arms. Finally, realizing that the man intended to attack him, the father made a mistake in strategy. He ran for the forest thinking that when he reached it, his rear would be safe and he would be able to hold off his attacker until his servant arrived. When he reached the forest, another man (Sakagami Shuzen) jumped out in front of him and cut his arm off, and then, giving a big kiai, cut him in the head.

The host's servant and his own, hearing the shout, ran to where he lay. He was able to tell them what happened before he died. Yoshida was thirteen at this time and this was the reason for his one hundred days of meditation.

Yoshida decided to try to find a spy school to study at. This was not an easy thing to do, for while every town has a least one Martial Arts school, there are few spy schools, and they don't advertise. Eventually, he found Takedo Sokaku's school which taught Daito-Ryu Aiki Jujitsu, including the art of being a spy. Sokaku agreed to accept Yoshida as a student. When he heard Yoshida's story about his father's death, he told him that the man who did it must have been very skillful because of the kind of stroke that he used. Sokaku also told him to forget about his revenge for the present.

Takeda Sokaku taught Yoshida principles rather than techniques, because a technique will only work under certain conditions whereas a principle can be applied to many different situations.

Yoshida had to learn to press out with his ki in order to be able to compete with the man who killed his father. The first thing that must be mastered for this is breath control. You must breathe in such a manner that if the teacher held a feather in front of your nose, it would not be moved by your breath. You must breathe with these syllables: a, um, aum. When you breathe in this manner, a certain part of the cosmic rays that are always penetrating your body can be absorbed and their energy sent to the skin. Being able to do this results in some physical changes to your body. These changes start from the marrow of your bones and proceeds outwards. The first change is an increase in the density of your bones.

To illustrate this, Mr. Kim told the following story: In 1948, an incident occurred to Mr. Kim which resulted in him being cut to the bone by a two foot bread knife. The doctors who examined him were amazed when they heard the story of what had happened because a normal man's bone would have been cut throughout, but his was merely nicked. Further tests revealed that his bones were on the average of three times denser than other men his age.

The following incident concerning Mr. Kim and Yoshida occurred in the winter of 1953. It had been snowing and the tree in Mr. Kim's courtyard was barren of leaves. It had five branches pointing up at the sky like fingers of a hand. When Yoshida saw this, he said that it was good luck and that they should go out and practice catching the cosmic rays. After a while they went inside and Mr. Kim was pressing a 220 pound barbell to see if he could use the cosmic energy to help lift the weight. As he was pressing the weight several times, his second wife's mother entered the room and when she saw what he was doing, she commented on what would happen to the floor if the weight fell. Mr. Kim lost his concentration and, not being a weightlifter per se, dropped the weight. It didn't hit the floor, but was suspended above the floor by Yoshida. When his mother-in-law saw that, she was no longer a skeptic.

Yoshida Kotaro Lecture by Richard Kim (3/6/1971)
Part Two

On Yoshida Kotaro.

When Yoshida was eighteen, he developed a sophisticated theory of values. (He had kufusuru at this age.) Simply, Yoshida's theory is as follows: Of the three great sufferings of mankind, namely desire, disease and death, desire comes first. Yoshida answered the question: Do you live to eat or eat to live? The man who works nine to five, five days a week, at a job he hates to do, to earn money to buy material things he desires and food to eat, lives to eat. The free man one who works if he wishes, at a job he likes and doesn't have many desires for material things, eats in order to stay alive.

Yoshida decided that the "ultimate" that everybody seeks is happiness. According to him, happiness has three prongs: gain, beauty, and love. Gain consists of material things, while beauty is the sensual pleasure derived from your gain, i.e. enjoyment of gourmet food or of a beautiful woman. Gain and beauty lie in the material world. Love is in the spiritual world and is your sharing of your gain and beauty with someone else. Few people can love. You must love to be able to protect yourself.

You must relax when you fight or else your muscles and tendons lock up the skeletal system with their tenseness. This will impede your strength. To relax you must relax your stomach and then your joints. This gives you true strength so that when attacked, you can explode from your stomach.

When you breathe out, imagine that the breath settles down to your stomach and that any excess goes down to your big toe. Then when you hit, at the moment of impact, you explode, relaxing immediately. In the kata you explode into the movements and relax between them.

All the above is what he developed at the age of eighteen years.

At the age of eighteen Yoshida was training in the mountains when he was approached by two men dressed in common clothes. One of them stood off to his left side while the one in front said, "Hey, boy! We notice by your dress that you are a samurai. Give us some money."

The man then applied nami-jujishime to Yoshida. (At this time in Japan's history, samurai were forbidden to carry their two swords because the Emperor feared they were likely to use them, which he didn't want. However, most samurai ignored the order and carried at least a knife in their waistband. Yoshida, who was dressed in fine samurai clothes, had on a silk waistband in which he carried a small knife.) As soon as the hold was applied to Yoshida's neck, he used the Daito-ryu escape of pushing the elbow to the ear and shoved the man to the side. Then, as he was shoving the man, he drew his knife and slashed his stomach. Slashing the first man and turning in one movement, he attacked and killed the second man to his side.

At first, Yoshida experienced a terrible feeling, for it was the first time he had killed, but soon there was an exaltation for he had killed in seconds two men who were going to rob him. His exaltation was short-lived, however, for when he dragged their bodies to the bushes at the side of the road, he was shocked to discover that the wooden swords they were carrying had extra long hilts like his. He thought that he was the first to discover that style.

Yoshida decided to stop for the night as it was getting late. He was near a farmhouse so he approached the gate and handed the attendant his letter of introduction. The letter, besides stating who he was and asking for hospitality, said that he had developed a completely different sword style. Although the farmer, his son, and his daughter had never heard of him, they decided to let him in because it was a dangerous area (mountain bandits).

When they saw him, they were shocked to find him so young. They wanted to know if his style worked and asked him if he had ever killed anyone. Yoshida replied that he had (the two he killed that morning). They then told him of the danger of being robbed by the mountain bandits in the area. It was then that Yoshida told them the story of what had happened earlier that day. They turned pale when they heard the description and the style of sword found on their bodies. It was a notorious gang and the farmer knew that they would seek revenge, so he rounded up all the outlying small farmers and stationed them in his compound.

The gang decided to attack that night rather than wait. There were fourteen of them, including their leader. They approached the front gate of the compound very late at night. Nine of them scaled the wall and crept up to the main house where they found the lights out and the door open and apparently unguarded. They decided that one man at a time would sneak in at three minute intervals. The first man entered and three minutes went by without a sound uttered except for a small hiss like a man breathing heavily. So the second man entered. Same thing. No sound except for the hiss. Finally, all had entered except the subleader in charge. After a while, he got very suspicious because there was no sounds of fighting nor any light or signal. He went up to the door and smelled. He could smell blood in the air but no fear, so he ran out and told the leader that something was funny. The leader didn't think it too strange. He said they must have killed someone and were probably enjoying themselves with the women. He told the subleader to go inside and check on them.

He went back to the door but got a very strange feeling so he didn't enter but instead felt the floor inside the door with his sword. There was a large hole just inside the door. He ran out to report it. (Yoshida had removed several floorboards just inside the door forming a deep pit. He stood to the side and cut the heads off the gang members as they entered and fell into the pit). As the subleader reached the wall, he was met by Yoshida standing in front of it with his sword in his sash and his left hand on the sheath. The subleader cut for his left arm and Yoshida blocked with the extra long hilt knocking the subleader's sword to the side and in one continuous motion drawing his sword with his palm (right) underneath and cutting the subleader's stomach.

Yoshida put on the subleader's clothes and went outside where he surprised the leader and his men, killing three of the remaining five, including the leader. The other two escaped (to fight another day) and spread the story of his skill.

The farmer invited Yoshida to stay a while, probably hoping to marry off his daughter to such a skilful man, but Yoshida had things to do.

The most important thing is complete relaxation before any exertion. There are two steps: (1) relaxation and softness, then bursting out from softness (explosion); (2) subconscious – if you tighten up your subconscious won't come out.

You must face your opponent as if you were in the gym practising. In the gym you know you won't get hurt so you are relaxed. Then the moment you go into action, your subconscious will come out.

Yoshida eventually killed Sagakama Shuzen, but not Nitta Dengoro, because he was Nitta and was blown up while trying to sabotage a train.

On Doihara Kenji.

Doihara Kenji was one of the greatest spies of all times. Unfortunately he was captured and executed by the Chinese.

Mr. Kim met his Chinese teacher in Shanghai. On Avenue Road directly across the street from the Marine barracks (Japanese) was the estate of Edward Hotung. All foreigners were interned except those on the Hotung estate because they were wealthy and paid not to be. The front gates of both the barracks and the estate faced each other so that the guard at the Marine gate was able to watch the estate also. However, after a while money turned his head away and they were free to come and go.

One day, while visiting the barracks with his brother-in-law who was the Japanese secret police, Mr. Kim observed Edward Hotung walking out the gate. Mr. Hotung had two wooden legs. When asked, his brother-in-law told Mr. Kim about them. Mr. Kim later became friends with Hotung's son, Eric, who told him about a Chinese man who was able to do incredible feats. Mr. Kim was skeptical when he first heard about the man, but his brother-in-law confirmed it. Mr. Kim promised Eric a pass if he would introduce him to the man which he later did.

Mr. Kim saw the following feats himself: The man push a boulder from a distance without physically touching it. He stood in a position similar to that of one in the soft form with his palms facing out straight ahead in front of his chest. When he moved his palms forward the boulder moved an equal distance. Another feat was killing mosquitoes. The man took off his upper garments and sat in a lotus position with his fist touching each other in front of his plexus. After meditating a while, he placed his palms together in the same position and "called" the mosquitoes to him. They swarmed all over him and bit him. After biting him they dropped down dead. The man ate a lot of arsenic compounds and was able to release into his bloodstream sufficient quantities to kill the mosquitoes without killing himself.

On Friends.

Once there was a stag who got very sick. So sick that he couldn't forage for food. He found a very green pasture that had running water so that he wouldn't have to move. When his friends heard about his infirmary, they all decided to visit him. As each one visited, they ate a little of his grass until soon he didn't have any more and he starved to death. Moral: Only a friend can trap you.

Yoshida Kotaro Lecture by Richard Kim (3/13/1971)
Part Three

To explain the statement: You must be able to love in order to protect yourself.

Why is a man aggressive? Society made him aggressive when it taught him the relationships that exist between men in society. Without these set relationships there can be no aggression. Witness animals. They don't kill except for food to eat. When they do fight, the loser usually runs away and without pursuit. Only man kills the loser. In modern society, aggression is represented by keeping up and surpassing the "Joneses" or by being "top dog", etc. Aggression provides the drive to win or to be the best.

There seems to be a paradox between a Buddhist's professed passivism and his ability to kill. However this can be explained. The martial artist seeks truth. But what is the truth? Is a woman who is forty but who says she is thirty-two telling the truth? Yes! She is telling the truth because her reason for saying it is true – she doesn't want to get older. What is true passivism? Is it the Quaker who tries to reason with a man who enters his house and starts breaking it up? No! The truly passive man is able to receive the energy exuding from the other and kill him with it – his own energy. It is passive because it is merciful.

You must know loss to know victory. You must be like water. If you pour water on the ground, it seeks the lowest level. If you can receive your opponent's energy (his suki), he becomes the lower level and the energy goes back in a circle and kills him. Like water flowing back to the lowest level, the ki flows back to him.

When you do the push and pull exercise, stand firm (brace) with the back leg. Step back if you are overpowered (his seven units to your three). In stepping back one step you are able to do anything to him because you are receiving his energy (his seven units become yours so that you have ten units momentarily). So in the exercise stand firm. The harder your opponent pushes, the harder you push. Take one step back if you must, then stand firm again.

Yoshida's philosophy at age thirty:

You have nine orifices: the eyes, ears, nostrils, mouth, rectum, and the urethra. That is your physical relationship with the external world (not counting the mind). It's sensory. These are called the external gates. To protect the external gates you use your appendages. Imagine a circle with a dot inside. The circle represents the body and the dot represents the mind (not the mind of thought but the original mind). The mind is the internal gate. This gate also has a protector – the intellect. The intellect is the protector that prevents you from knowing your original mind. The intellect identifies with the external gates. You must get through to the mind (samadhi). The mind is in internal turmoil except in samadhi when it is calm and the body is detached. In the sate of samadhi you see clearly, and everything is as it is. That is detachment – seeing everything in its proper perspective without colouring by the intellect. The intellect has as its ally the deluded mind. One result of the deluded mind would be when you see three women walking down the street and give a value to the one in the middle by saying that she is the prettiest. The man in samadhi would just see three women.

If you are fighting a person because of an argument in a bar, or because you are jumped in an alley, you are not detached but are instead emotionally involved. In the gym, you are detached because there is no animosity. You must fight as if you were in the gym.

A little later in his life (after thirty):

Everybody lives in his own world. In your own world you know best. Your world is for you. (When you love, you share your gain and beauty with another – you share your world.) You might have certain things in common with others – goals, hobbies, etc. However, everybody has at least two things in common: the ultimate desire – which is happiness – and the fear of death. (Because of the fear of death religions were formed.)

The only exaltation a martial artist may find in life is when he kills somebody who is trying to kill him.

A battle for Yoshida.

Sometime between the ages of thirty and thirty-three, Yoshida went to Manchuria where he developed these theories: there are many degrees (levels) of consciousness – sleep is a low level and being awake is a higher level.

While he was there, he was captured by Manchurian bandits. Accompanying him was another Japanese who worked for the Manchurian railway. He was a spy, as were most of the workers. The bandits observed Yoshida's stick and also his knife hidden in his waistband. In talking with one of his captors, Yoshida mentioned that he wasn't a spy. His captors said that that was too bad for, unfortunately for him, they killed all their prisoners.

Yoshida, being familiar with the bandit's customs, issued a challenge to them. If he won, he would be freed. The bandits accepted the challenge to them and agreed to a match to the death with one of their men. They kept him there for a week while they looked for their best men. Finally, after three weeks had gone by, their Chinese expert with the two broadswords arrived.

Yoshida had a week to prepare for the match in which they would only let him use the stick he had on him when he was captured. As he watched the expert practice whirling the two swords, he did his best to think of a defense... to no avail. He tried everything he had ever heard of doing to prepare himself: ate the right food, no drinking or women, standing on his head, etc.

Finally, he decided to practice what he preached and rely on his philosophy. He felt that it all came down to 'sitting'. Sitting, meaning not the physical act but having no thoughts in the mind, is the true essence of meditation. No thought means the eyes, the ears, everything flows with the air. When you are breathing, you are flowing with your environment. You must enjoy everything to the limit as if you are going to die at any time. If you are doing everything to its fullest, you "receive."

Seeing the expert practice, he decided that he must think of death as his friend (all your troubles and worries are over when you are dead) and he must not be worried about going inside the expert's reach. So when the time for the match came, he stood with the stick in his left hand. He decided that he must strike at the solar plexus with all his might (total concentration – no fear of death, it was his friend). He tightened up his rectum, took a deep breath and let it out slowly, then took a step back with his right foot, still holding the stick in his left hand at his side. When the expert came within range (he was coming down at Yoshida's head with one of the swords), he lunged forward with his right foot and poked him in the solar plexus deep, then twisted the stick and came down and out into a gedan kamai. The expert was dead.

Miscellaneous insights.

A woman can receive better than a man because she is more passive. That is why the Japanese don't like to see women in the Martial Arts.

Through your breath and mind you can send your own vibration (using your thought waves) – everyone's vibration is different. You must hit samadhi to do it.

If you can make your body vibrate, your blood vessels vibrate also and in so doing they clean themselves out (it takes about half an hour of vibration).

Yoshida's saying: A mouth has no virtue. The tongue has no bones.

Yoshida Kotaro Lecture by Richard Kim (3/20/1971)
Part Four

Another battle.

After winning the match with the bandit's champion, Yoshida was released. It was at this time that he started to form his theory of the 'cosmic circle' (whirling). It took him seventeen years to perfect it. During the Russo-Japanese war, he had either 105 or 111 matches to the death and he won them all. He felt that he was getting the whirl. Then he kufusurued while working on the cosmic circle and got the message.

Yoshida went back to Japan for a short time and while there, he saw his mother. When he told her about his discovery of the cosmic circle, she remarked that he had really seen life during his travels and that she was glad he had finally discovered the secret of whirling. She picked up a six foot naginata and told him to go out into the garden with her so that she could test him. They faced each other and she said lets see what you can do. She attacked with a downward blow to the head which he blocked. When the sticks met, she stepped back, switching hands as she did, and went into a left hosso kamai from which she immediately stepped forward with her rear leg and struck at his knee with all her might (a technique which no one had ever been able to block). He blocked it. His mother said to him, 'just a little more; you must perfect your cosmic circle'.

Yoshida went back to Manchuria. The Black Dragon Society found out about it and decided that they didn't want a magician to be there at this time (they considered Yoshida to be a magician) so they got the best man they could find, a champion, and sent him to Manchuria to challenge Yoshida to an old-fashioned duel with the sword. The match took place in autumn near the Korean border. When the two faced each other, Yoshida felt the ki and knew what he had to do. In his mind's eye, he saw how the challenger would die. The challenger was standing in a right hosso position when suddenly he stepped forward and gave a blow to Yoshida's head. By the time the blow was completed, he was dead. Yoshida had stepped forward and to the side of the downward directed blow, deflecting the sword arm with his right hand (which was holding a small knife) and pressing it further down as he kept going around to the rear of the challenger by stepping with his rear leg. As he did so, he brought up his right hand to the neck of the challenger and cut his throat as he circled behind him. This easy defeat of so good an opponent shocked Toyomo Mitsuro who had watched the match (and was connected with the Black Dragon Society), so he had Yoshida sent back to Japan where he then met with his most terrifying experience.

Yoshida was walking through a forest just outside of Tokyo to practice the sword when he heard the sound of a fast approaching horse. When the horse was close to him, although he felt that it was crowding him (forcing him off the road), he didn't look back. He felt nothing from the rider (no ki). He didn't want to look behind, though he thought that Toyomo had possibly sent him. The horse was almost on him and still he felt no force from the rider. As the horse passed him and nothing happened, Yoshida noticed that the rider was riding Mongolian style (no saddle) so he grabbed the rider's leg and pushed up to see what he would do. The rider jumped up as soon as his leg was touched, leaping over Yoshida and drawing his sword as he did, cutting Yoshida on the shoulder. Without thinking Yoshida also drew his sword and cut the rider on the hip while he was still in the air. When the rider landed, he immediately ran into the forest, limping as he did. Throughout the incident Yoshida hadn't felt anything from the man. He told his mother about it and she said that it could have been either an Igo or Koga man and that he must have met a magician. (Yoshida hadn't hit satori yet.)

Years later, Yoshida found his own cosmic circle. He had forgotten Shuzen Kakagami. There was a revival in Martial Arts after the invasion of China and the government was sending its men, including Yoshida, around the countryside to encourage its growth (they were twisting its philosophy in order to get people to fight China). Yoshida came across a village one day while on this mission at about 4 o'clock in the afternoon. He was broke, so he went to the tea shop to ask if there were any martial artists in the village (it was the custom for one martial artist to 'entertain' another who was on the road – and between meals). The proprietor of the shop told Yoshida that the greatest martial artist of them all was living there, that he was better than even the famous Yoshida Kotaro and that his name was Kashiwagi Tenta of Shinkage-ryu.

So Yoshida went to pay a visit to Tenta's home and when Tenta answered the door, he introduced himself. Tenta said that he had heard of Yoshida (although he hadn't met him) and invited him in. After they were seated and drinking saki, with the formalities over, Yoshida asked Tenta why he wasn't teaching. Tenta told him that he had had a terrifying experience one day while riding through the forest, and went on to tell about a magician, who without any warning, grabbed his leg and pushed as he was riding by. Yoshida said that it was him and showed Tenta the scar, telling him that he thought it was somebody sent to assassinate him. They both had a good laugh over the incident and then got drunk together. (Tenta experienced a small satore from the incident?)

Yoshida's philosophies.

Religion is based on two main things: The desire for happiness and the fear of death. Religions fall into two main groups: The first will give you happiness, but in a different world (heaven) It is escapist. Why go to another world? Why not have it here? The second says that happiness is a state of mind.

Martial arts philosophy says that it is bad to do good. It hurts both you and the person you are doing it for. (Mr. Kim then gave an example of what happened when he had helped somebody.)

When the martial artist feels pain, that is his hell; when he feels great in doing something well (ie. killing somebody who is trying to take your life), that is his heaven.

An act of aggression is when you make somebody feel inferior, not killing someone who is trying to kill you.

A man who is enlightened lives in a different world, not on the plane of normal man.

If you believe in a beginning to the universe, you will stay in the finite world and will never reach satori. The martial artist does not believe in a soul, per se. Life and death are two sides of a coin, you must live life now or you are the loser.

Yoshida Kotaro Lecture by Richard Kim (4/10/1971)
Part Five

On Mercy.

After leaving Kashiwagi Tenta's house, Yoshida was feeling good due to their drinking together. He went to a bar where he ordered some beer. As he was sitting quietly and enjoying his beer, a loud-mouthed racist military man entered and started raising hell over Japan's recent victory in its fight with Russia. The man was a racist who thought that because Japan beat Russia they could beat the whole white race. Yoshida realized that the man was potentially very dangerous to Japan's future and that he should do something. Yoshida caught his eye so the man walked over to where he was sitting and asked him what he was drinking. Yoshida replied beer. The man then asked the bartender what kind of beer he served to Yoshida and was furious to learn that it was a foreign brand. He called to Yoshida, asking 'don't you know that we just beat the blue-eyed devils?' Yoshida answered him by asking what was the matter with him. The man said that he felt like beating him up. Yoshida told him to go ahead. The man proceeded to beat up Yoshida until his nose bled, at which point the man stopped. Yoshida then asked if he felt better now. Then he left the bar. Yoshida was perfectly able to kill the man but instead gave him mercy. The man committed suicide several months later.

More of Yoshida's philosophy (developed through satori):

Love has an opposite – hate. Man is dichotomous by nature. If he loves, he also hates. They are two sides of the same coin.

Mercy in the Buddhist sense: Only mercy has no opposite; its the whole and encompasses all.

Mercy in the Christian sense: Mercy equals love.

Everyone has the Buddha nature; it just has to be developed by meditation (finding one's true self).

Everyone lives in his own world. If you impart love, you also hate. But not mercy. If you can impart mercy, you took a big step (since it is pure and has no opposite).

Yoshida went back to Manchuria for a while after he had kufusurued again and was carrying a small stick (cane-sized), he happened to come across another man on the same path as himself. What he saw coming towards him was just an old man carrying the same kind of stick that he was carrying. But he felt a strong ki radiating from him and knew that this old man was somebody, so he stepped aside and was going to attack him with his favorite technique, the dragon tail form. The old man never stopped walking and simply held his stick out in front of himself in a gedan position. Yoshida waited until he was closer but found that he couldn't move when he wanted to attack. He thought to himself that maybe he wasn't close enough. By then the old man was right next to him and simply pushed Yoshida's stick moving him aside and then kept right on walking.

Yoshida went back to his mother and told her what had happened. His mother took out her naginata and told Yoshida to attack her with his sword. He attacked his mother who dodged or avoided all his blows. Finally, she asked him if the man did this and proceeded to overwhelm Yoshida as if her ki were water overflowing a dam (not a bomb bursting). When he replied yes, she said that the man must have been Asari Matashichiro as he was the only person she knew who could do it. Yoshida wanted to know when he would be able to do it, but his mother said only when he finished his revenge mission because it was holding him back.

Yoshida later developed that ability and called it his second principle (the first being that you must relax, then burst out like a bomb exploding). This principle being that you overwhelm your opponent with your ki like water overflowing a dam. Yoshida said that everyone could develop this principle as everyone has the innate capacity.

Yoshida also said that man is dichotomous in that both violence and tranquility exist in him, no matter who he is. To overcome that violence you must know it and know the violence in you. (The two schools of thought are: The

 The reason you see zen priests begging for money is to show humility.

Christian or Sun Tzu school which believes that man is basically evil and the Helena or Buddha school which believes that man is basically good). The people who use the most violence are the people who don't know what violence is. The martial artist starts from the premise 'I can kill' and goes from there.

Fable – Story of the crows:

Once a year, the crows held a council whose function was to administer a test for manhood. This particular year, there were three would-be man-crows to take the test. The test was to answer the following questions: What is the most dangerous thing to a crow?

The first crow said; "An arrow is the most dangerous thing for it strikes without warning, silently." Everybody clapped at this wonderful answer and the council awarded the crow his manhood. There was much excitement among the crows for already one crow won his manhood this year.

The second crow then got up and gave this answer: "I think that the most dangerous thing is not the arrow, but the man behind the arrow with the bow because if he is an expert shot, you are in trouble!" At this, a tremendous clapping took place for such a marvellous answer. He, too, was awarded manhood. Everyone was hushed as the third and final crow got up to give his answer, for surely nothing could top the first two answers.

Then the third crow gave his answer: "Nonsense! The most dangerous thing to a crow isn't an arrow or an expert shot, its the greenhorn. When the bow of the expert goes twang, you know the arrow is coming straight at you and you can dodge, swerve, or duck out of the way, but when the bow of the greenhorn goes twang, you don't know what in hell to expect!" At this tumultuous whistling and cheering occurred and the crow was not only awarded manhood but was made chief.

Yoshida Kotaro Lecture by Richard Kim (4/17/1971)
Part Six

On Satori.

Mr. Kim met Yoshida in 1943. At that time Yoshida told him certain things that have just now been verified by western science (see Time Magazine, April 24 issue, "Man into Superman"). One of the ideas proposed in the article above was that the memory may be transmitted through eating the flesh of the animal (can be man?) in question. It is for this reason that yogis don't eat meat.

For everything that you study you must first have, ie. algebra for calculus. For reaching satori, you must know your body, from your big toe to your little finger. You start with your physical body, then go to your astral body and then, finally, to your cosmic energy.

Karate training is very authoritarian for a reason, that being that you can reach kufusuru that way. (Everybody has intuition. You can tell by your intuition that a particular student will stay with you.)

There was a man who achieved continuous satori. His name was either Dokyo or Dokuyo Eton and was the teacher of one of the most famous Rinzai sect (zen) monks by the name of Hakuin. Hakuin stayed with him only eight months before reaching satori. Eton was able to stay in the state of satori because every night he stayed in a cemetery meditating. At this time in his area there was a shortage of food and there were many wolves roaming about that would eat anything, dead or living, they were so famished. They would go up to Eton and sniff and lick his neck and body but were unable to do anything else to him.

If you try to find the purpose for life, you must go inside yourself, not outside. What you try to find is the truth. In satori you find your true self.

Fable: A jackdaw was watching an eagle foraging for food when all of a sudden the eagle swooped down and grabbed a lamb in its claws and carried it away. The jackdaw said to himself, "I'm an eagle. I can do it too!" When he tried it, his claws got stuck in the lamb's wool and he couldn't get free or lift the lamb. The farmer saw him and captured him, bringing him home. When the farmer got home, his son asked him what kind of bird it was. The farmer replied that if you ask the bird, he'll tell you he's an eagle, but we know him for what he is - a stupid jackdaw.

Moral? Don't be false, know who and what you are and live in reality.

The following is a true story that took place during Tokugawa Iemitsu's reign as shogun and is a major factor why women are discouraged to learn the Martial Arts (they have a greater capacity). Ii Naoto was the son of a high class samurai and was also due to to be married to a woman named Osada (it was an arranged marriage made by their parents). Then he discovered the joy of sexual intercourse and from that time spent most of his time in the red light district drinking and whoring. When he was married, he received a large dowry which he promptly spent in the red light district even though his wife was very attractive. He then told her to go to her father and bow to him, asking for more money. He said his girlfriend was waiting and it was her duty as a wife to satisfy her husband. So Osda went to her father and pleaded for money but her father refused. He heard the rumors concerning his son-in-law's behavior. Instead, he brought out a sword which he told his daughter had never been beaten in a fight. It was very famous and valuable. He told Osada to think about why he gave her the sword. She did.

When she returned home with the sword, Ii's eyes bugged out. He thought to himself about the money he would receive if he pawned it. But Osada said that she knew what was going through his mind and that there was a condition to his receiving the sword. The condition was that he had to beat her in a fight in which she would use the sword, then it was his. Ii agreed and they both went outside into the garden where they stood in their Kamai. Ii was thinking to himself that although she may be his equal (she was from a good school), she was after all only a woman and he would be able to wear her down eventually. So he attacked but she easily blocked and parried all his movements, forcing him further and further back until he lost his footing and fell in the pond. He was furious and started berating her for showing such disrespect towards him, her husband. Finally he up and left, going to the school of Yagyu Munenori where he studied the sword for a year. In all that time Osada never heard from him until one day he showed up and told her to get the sword and they would have a match.

Again they fought and again he was pushed back until he fell into the pond. His anger knew no bounds. He went back to Yagyu and studied approximately three more years until one day Yagyu told him that there was no more he could teach him. Yagyu said he wasn't even sure if he could hold his own against Ii and that Ii was probably the best around at that time. So again Ii went back but this time when he asked for a match against the sword, Osada told him that she had returned the sword and that now he was her equal. They were never beaten.

November 8, 1942, China declared war against the United States. Japan, in order to show the Nan-king government that everything was going well, sent a travelling show around the part of China that they controlled. Besides entertainers, the show included various martial artists, sumo wrestlers, etc. The martial artists put on matches and while the show was in Peking, a man by the name of Nitta went to the top.

Yoshida heard about it and made some inquiries in such a way that a match was arranged between him and Nitta. As soon as they faced each other, Yoshida realized that Nitta was not too skilful, so he fought the match with just enough effort to beat Nitta. He won by incapacitating Nitta's sword hand's thumb with a strike. Nitta, being vain, was happy to be able to put up what he thought was a good contest. Yoshida became friendly with him and then asked him if his name was Nitta Dengoro, to which he replied 'no' and also to the question if he had any relatives by that name. Yoshida showed him a picture that he drew when he was eighteen of Dokagami Shugen. Nitta recognized him and told Yoshida that he thought the man was in Shanghai now. Yoshida then asked another person who had knowledge of Shanghai's goings-on where Sakagami Shugen could be found and if he was still training. Yoshida learned that Sakagami was a spy for the Japanese government and that his style was Chugo-ryu. Armed with this new knowledge, Yoshida asked the person to accompany him to Shanghai.

Arriving in Shanghai, Yoshida went to where Sakagami practised and secretly watched him (he practised in the Japanese settlement which was across the Soochow river from the international settlement). As soon as he saw Sakagami, he intuitively knew how he would be attacked. Yoshida then arranged for a meeting with Sakagami who didn't know who he was. As was the custom, Yoshida went to the police (in this case the Kempei-tai, sort of like the German Gestapo of old) and told them of his mission of revenge for his father's death. They agreed to keep out of it.

Yoshida arrived at Sakagami's place wearing his long sword with the long tsuba and a short sword. He introduced himself to Sakagami and told him about that night long ago when his father was killed. Sakagami did not recall the incident since it had taken place several years earlier. However Sakagami did know he was going to have to fight for his life, so he made the first move. He jumped in close to Yoshida, who was standing with his left hand on the sheath of his sword tucked in his belt on the left side of his body, and placed his sword's tsuba on top of Yoshida's tsuba, while pressing down lightly. Sakagami had his left hand holding his sheath and his right hand holding his tsuba, while Yoshida had his right hand free and his left hand on his tsuba with his left thumb on the guard of his sword. Yoshida had foreseen the fact that he would be attacked in this manner.

This is what he saw in Sakagami's mind: 'In order to attack me my opponent must do one of three things. He can release his thumb from his guard; he can withdraw his sword; or he can use his right hand to draw away my sword in order to draw his own. In any event, I will attack with the dragon tail form when he makes his move.'

This is why Yoshida wore his short sword: When Sakagami placed his tsuba against Yoshida's and his eyes went to Yoshida's left thumb, Yoshida drew his short sword with his right hand and cut off Sakagami's sword arm. "That was for my father's arm," he said. Sakagami, unable to fight, started whirling, but Yoshida, being familiar with Chugo-ryu techniques, was able to strike the back of Sakagami's head killing him. (At this time, Sakagami was probably the most skillful man in technical excellence.)

Yoshida achieved satori three months later.

When Mr. Kim met Yoshida in 1943, Mr. Kim was attending a Jesuit University, St. John's. He was one of two foreigners attending at that time and was working on his master's thesis. Yoshida told him that it was so much toilet paper (degrees being useless – although Yoshida had a Ph.D from Tokyo University, one from Harvard, one from Princeton, and one another).

Yoshida said, what is the difference between modern man and man of, say, eight hundred years ago? The man of eight hundred years ago did not have the restriction caused by a strong intellect (not meaning intelligence, but ego). Technology and systematized knowledge (ie. that being taught in college) makes scientific proof satisfy the intellect but not the man 'himself' (your true self – your Buddha nature). The ancient man didn't have this to distract his intellect and so could realize his Buddha nature easier.

Breathing:

There is a trick to breathing correctly. Let's draw an imaginary circle and let it represent your total lung capacity. When you inhale, the circle fills completely. But when you exhale, there still is approximately one third of the circle filled. This is because of the nature of your lung tissue – that being it is made up of millions of tiny sacs that retain some air all the time. The normal person does not know how to breath how to use up all the available oxygen. Now when you inhale, you can't fill the already filled one third.

The way to learn how to breathe correctly is to breathe in cadence. Your heart is the cadence counter. You inhale eight counts, swallow, and hold for thirty-two counts, then exhale for sixteen counts. (You can use 4-36-8 if you find the other too difficult.)

To control your orgasm:

When you feel the point of orgasm approach, suck in your stomach, grit your teeth (curling your tongue up and back), tighten your anus, and send your ki into your penis. You won't orgasm and could service many women.

Yoshida Sensei's Philosophy

Yoshida Sensei was not just a Martial Arts master, he was a deep thinker and, as Mas Oyama said, his life revolved around the study of Martial Arts but he also was a learned man and scholar. His job, when he came back to Japan after the war, was to run a newspaper and he was also responsible for a very large library of books.

His life revolved around reading and writing and Martial Arts. That was all there was for him. He did develop several philosophies as well, and below we have some them.

Yoshida said: Scientists believe that: Rationality is at the centre of a man's life.

Superconscious is intuition. Conscious reason is rationality (domain of the intellect). Subconscious instinct is the level that animals function at.

The intellect rejects intuition because it wants proof. Intellect gives to the learning process; the learning process turns into memory; memory goes into the subconscious.

Descartes said, "I think, therefore I am." Because he said this, he is in the spiritual world without knowing it.

The game theory, originally from math, (Norbert Winner) is based on rationality. For instance two people play poker – one wins the pot and the other loses.

Consciousness for the average man starts when he wakes up until he falls asleep.

Playing the "master game", which is reaching toward satori or nirvana, causes your body chemistry to change. It affects the pituitary gland and prepares it for producing the chemical that causes enlightenment. It produces just the right amount for your body.

To reach satori you must overcome the problems and sufferings of mankind: 1) life itself; 2) old age; 3) disease; and 4) death. The best way is to know your body. Because when you hit satori, all knowledge is in your body. To do this though you must first develop attention (or concentration).

To a man in satori, a normal day consists of a blink of the eye (if that). Maybe the man who wrote the Genesis part of the Bible had satori and saw the 'days' march by. So, the literal meaning is not seven normal days; each day might be 77 billion years. Supposedly one period, of which there are four, lasts 500 trillion years.

Picture a circle. Inside the circle is yourself or the 'self', while the perimeter or shell of the circle represents the intellect. The intellect sees the phenomenal world through the physical senses only. 'Self' is existence, not individual existence, but existence per se. The intellect is individual existence (ego). What does this individual existence do? It is interested in 'I-ness' or 'mine-ness.' For instance, if your wife or child dies, you are sad because of 'mine-ness' – they belong to you, there was attraction. If your enemy dies, it means nothing to you because there is no sense of 'mine-ness' involved. So in existence, pain does not exist. Neither does fear (of death or of anything) and anxiety for your physical well-being or life because the 'self' is not concerned with either 'I-ness' or 'mine-ness' in regard to your physical body. 'Self' is knowledge and bliss is satori.

Once upon a time there was an old woman who was sewing when suddenly she dropped her needle. She got upset when she couldn't find it and called her neighbors for help. When the neighbors came, they saw the old woman searching in her garden for the needle. They too searched the garden to no avail. Finally, one of her neighbors asked the woman where she was standing when she dropped the needle. She replied that she was in her bedroom at the time. The neighbor asked if that was so, why was she looking in her garden for the needle. The woman replied that her eyes were really bad so she had to look where it was light.

Moral – for the intellect everything has to be sensual and logical and reason must prevail. You must go beyond this to intuition. The light in the garden represents the intellect while the dark of the bedroom represents the 'self' or the intuitive process.

The average person looks for the 'self' in the phenomenal world of the senses, but you must go inside to find your 'self.' You get knowledge through direct experience or realization (intuition – satori) and not through books or schools. To know pain, you must feel it yourself. So for realiza-

 Kensho is the martial arts term for satori or enlightenment.

tion (satori) you must pay the price. You pay the biggest price of all through devotion, sacrifice and above all, not moving from the path that the teacher sets for you – even one inch. The teacher has been there and therefore knows the way, you must let him be your guide.

The first thing that you must do in order to become enlightened is to rid yourself on 'mine-ness.' A man of satori (or one very close to it) becomes neutral because he is able to rid himself of 'mine-ness.' People go through stages, instinct: reflective action based on memory pattern (animals); reason or logic (most men), intuition: direct realization (some men).

No matter what you do, you are thinking in language (because you need the intellect and senses to deal with the phenomenal world), except in intuitive perception direct experience, where there is no language and where you are in bliss.

There is an Indian (Hindu) word for existence – Sat. When you can dream in Sat (existence), all knowledge is available to you. (The Ajapa sect would try to maintain Sat breathing until the last possible moment of consciousness.) There are three stages you go through in your practice of Sat. 1) Knowledge prior to memories; 2) Vision and psychic phenomenon; and, 3) Sat dreaming is realizing existence per se.

It's difficult for Western man to reach satori because of language.

Magazine Articles and Quotes

Over the years hundreds of magazine articles were written about Sensei Kim. In fact, so many, we chose to not put the entire collection of the articles in the book.

What we did was put in only some of the selected articles in their entirety and his quotes from many of the rest of the articles that go back to 1966.

Many of these same quotes were given over the years in his lectures.

The Wringer and the Press

If you were to take a statistical survey on the most unpleasant branch of the martial arts, especially in Kodokan judo, without fail the report would show that the most disagreeable aspect is being on the receiving end of strangleholds or chokes. Every judoka has gone through a phase of fear concerning these maneuvers, and that is why, for the most part, it is difficult to embrace groundwork as enthusiastically as the more spectacular standing work, where throws are the forte. If the martial arts purport to show the human body's fragility, no place is it more clearly demonstrated than in the strangleholds.

"Fear magnifies the technique," Sensei always said. "When the stranglehold is applied correctly, the recipient feels as if he is going to die. With a blow, throw, kick, chop – you name it – the receiver feels, mentally and emotionally, that he has a chance. But, if you choke a guy and he is not a skillful martial artist, he will panic. Make no bones about it: Shutoff the blood supply, or air, to the head, and a person will panic. If someone is choking you with a perfect technique, or near to it, fear will hasten the end. That is why all martial artists must practice strangleholds and get used to strangleholds; if not, they will panic if a strangle-hold is applied to them."

Sensei also said, "When a stranglehold is applied to you, you must keep calm, and that comes only through practice. There is no substitute."

If a skillful stranglehold is applied against a person, it is only a matter of seconds before dizziness sets in, and then the person will black out. If the stranglehold is continued for a few minutes, the person will die. It is the most terrifying technique in barehand self defense, because everyone fears "the noose."

Methods used in the martial arts are scientific, safe, and effective. There are many strangling methods, but when defending your life in a street encounter,the best method is the naked stranglehold, in which you use your hands and do not strangle with any part of the clothing. Sensei taught, "Because it does not need a hold or grip on clothing, the naked stranglehold is probably the only one that is useful in self defense during a life-and-death encounter."

If you know the principles of the "wringer and the press," you have it made in terms of martial arts holds, locks and strangleholds. If you develop a skill with the wringer and the press principles, it will stay with you far into old age, long after you have lost your ability to throw a person or knock him out. There is an old adage that, "when your legs go, you go", but fortunately, even when your legs have lost their spring, you can rest assured that the wringer and the press will stay with you until the end.

To become proficient in strangleholds, it is of prime importance that you have the ability to control an assailant on the ground, utilizing the press principle correctly and effectively. It is impossible to strangle an assailant if you cannot control him on the ground by proper holding.

"When an opponent is trying to escape from the press, it is the opportune time to strangle him," Sensei said, "because that is when he is wide open for the wringer." In fact, it is the only time. "The secrets of the martial arts evolved out of battlefield case analyses, where physically inferior men triumphed against what appeared to be insurmountable odds. Various martial arts schools carefully systematized and secretly taught how to turn an opponent's superior force to his disadvantage. However, irrespective of the many techniques devised, certain fundamental principles appeared which were universal, and formed the floor for all martial arts.

The stranglehold is the great equalizer: Anyone can strangle anyone. Sensei said, "Let a person, male or female, get you in a correctly applied stranglehold, and you are in trouble. If you have not had strangleholds applied to you, then it is 'bye-bye baby', because you will panic and struggle the wrong way, a sure road to pushing daisies." Sensei called the stranglehold a "wringer". He always used to call out, "Wring, keep on wringing, do not let up until there is submission." The difference between holding techniques as applied in a sporting event versus a street fight is a difference in philosophy. In a judo match, for example, a holding technique applied for 30 seconds scores a point and a win. The theory is that if you can hold a person for 30 seconds in a real fight, you can hold him indefinitely and nullify his effectiveness. That is essentially correct if you are fighting a mullet.

"Never, never practice the martial arts or self defense to fight an inferior opponent," Sensei always lectured. Instead, "practice to fight or defend against a superior opponent. Martial arts are not sports, with rules. Throw rules out the window; you are fighting for survival out there in the streets."

In the street, a holding or press technique sets up your opponent for the stranglehold or wringer, especially the naked stranglehold! In fact, you must execute your entry and takedown in a way that ensures that the opponent will be put in a position that enables you to use the naked stranglehold.

That is why when the age-old question was asked, of who would win in a fight between a boxer and a wrestler. "Between a boxer and wrestler of equal weight and abilities, I would have to put my money with the wrestler. The boxer's only chance is his first blow – if he can knock out the wrestler, which is a highly improbable situation. Statistical studies show that a professional boxer clinches an average of seven times in a three-minute round. A wrestler with the proper takedown and follow-up stranglehold will kill a boxer."

Most persons who have taken up boxing will use a left jab as an exploratory blow. If you are caught in an alley with a guy who comes at you with a left jab, you can slip, slide under, or block his jab with your right hand and hit him with a tackle, your left shoulder and left arm hitting his stomach as hard as you can. As you drive in, spin behind him, still holding his stomach area with your left hand, and wrap your right hand around his body from the back. You are now behind him. Place your right foot against the back of his right knee, push as hard as you can, crumpling his right leg, and bring him to the ground with you holding him from behind.

When you bring him to the ground, he will try to turn, to get up and escape from your hold; no matter what, he will struggle. As soon as you hit the ground, take your right hand and encircle his neck with your forearm, cutting into his neck like a vice – and this is the most important step: remember that the "steering wheel" of the body is the head. Place your head against his head, and push forward as hard as you can with your forearm cutting into his neck. As you push your head against his, forcing his head forward, your forearm will cut into his neck, shutting off blood supply and causing him to black out in a few seconds. You will have time to lock your left hand and your right hand together.In his panic. the opponent will give you time to do this. If you are experienced,you can do this in one motion. from entering, go-behind. and take-down to,strangle. Just a little practice is required.

The best part of wringer is that you do not have to be an expert. As Sensei always taught, "The punk or bully that tries to push you around or attack you will not have the patience or emotional capacity to take the martial arts and attain a high decree of efficiency. It does not work out that way because a blackbelt is just the first step on the road to mastery. So most likely the punk who attacks you is just a punk."

"I remember when I was teaching in Yokohama, Japan. One day, after a hard workout in judo and karate, the subject of the practicalities of principles in a street fight came up – especially against a jab. I made the class practice the takedown and stranglehold."

"This was during the Korean War and merchant ships of all nations were coming in and out of the port of Yokohama. Quite a few street fights took place in Yokohama, Chinatown and in Omarudani, a red-light district. Many a reputation was made or broken in those fights. There was one particular tanker seaman who had a fearsome reputation due to a few fights in the ring. Seamen,as a rule being better lovers than fighters, did not have a snowball's chance in hell, when our aggressor accosted them and challenged them to a fight. He never lost; he always set opponents up with a jab and knocked them out with a right cross. When he was drunk or feeling evil he picked on anybody."

"One night he picked on one of my students, a small Japanese man not more than 125 pounds soaking wet. This student of mine helped out as a handy man in one of the bar-restaurants in Yokohama, Chinatown. The way I heard it, when the champion threw his jab, the student slipped under, executed the take-down, and applied the stranglehold exactly as he had practiced it in the gym one session. The champion blacked out, and when he came to he was so embarrassed that he jumped ship and flew back to the United States, chastised by a man who had taken just one lesson in the wringer and the press."

On Childhood, War Years, Bushido, Kung Fu, Professional Boxing, and more...

Basically, the philosophy of the samurai was enlightenment. This is the conclusion that the martial arts masters and the samurai came to and which I learned in all the years I've been involved."

On a purely physical basis, there is no difference between man and animal. But man is different from the animal in that man is a spiritual person. Being a spiritual person, he needs philosophy.

My mother made me study martial arts. She thought that the martial arts could make a person learn respect. The way she put it, "The respect that one human being owes to another you can only learn in a combative environment." She felt that the tenets of the Japanese martial arts, being bushido, would make a person, at least, have respect for other human beings, and she felt that respect is the only achievement.

The martial arts are in an environment that's combative, but it is like being in the eye of a typhoon because it is highly philosophical. It's not fighting. Street fighting, on the other hand, is combative, but it is not philosophical.

I earned my first black belt in judo in 1941, but two years prior to that, I toured China and studied tai chi and pakua under Chien Chen Wa, that's how I pronounce it.

I also studied daito ryu jujitsu, and shorinji ryu kenpo karate. It was during this period, in fact, that I made a tour of the Orient with the express purpose of studying the different martial arts.

Japanese training is philosophical, diametrically opposed to the Chinese training, even though it may appear to be the same.

All the martial arts tell you that the first move is defensive – that's the premise of the martial arts. But the connotation takes in a very wide area. Most people, if you tell them their first move must be defensive, will wait for the enemy to hit and then counter. Now,with the Japanese samurai mentality, the fight starts when the issue or challenge comes up with an 'offensive defensive' move.

For example, suppose you and I get into an argument and you were the kung fu champion of Shanghai. We would argue, say, in a restaurant, and then we go out into the street. As soon as you square off, I hit you because the fight started in the restaurant. It is a defensive move but it looks like an offense and a lot of people cannot see that.

That is where the Japanese karate training – what I call true karate – has the advantage. A lot of people do not understand the semantics, for instance, of the karate man never delivering the first blow. Semantically, you would envision a karate man standing there waiting to respond to a blow. But once there is a challenge, the contact has begun and you defend with an offensive defense.

My only involvement with the hard style kung fu in China was six bouts with kung fu champs, and I knocked them all out. That was it. That's why I'm convinced that a combination of judo, Japanese karate and Chinese tai chi and pakua can take care of any hard-style kung fu people.

The kung fu people fight along one style – it's whatever particular school they follow, and they are not flexible. Their efficiency is so highly specialized, you have deficiencies because it is a very narrow field. The specialty calls for that. But I have found that the person who is a generalist has an advantage in a physical encounter.

You'd be surprised, in my experience, that the best fighters are the tai chi people. They can beat any of the hard-style kung fu schools if it came to the nitty-gritty because they and the pakua people are philosophically flexible. You see, they can extrapolate from any situation and even follow back on an attack that is being given out.

If it's done right, I think it will help classical karate. Contact karate does not step on traditional karate. Traditional karate is, just to use another expression, a different kind of animal.

Professional karate is not a martial art bushido and all. It's a sport like boxing, and it's a different arena, but not everybody can participate in it. But classical karate, anybody can engage in it, because you get taught respect and dignity of one human being over another. Also, it gives you some means of self defense in case your life is on the line. That's what it's meant for. It is not meant for some guy to go in the ring and be the Cassius Clay of karate.

Karate has changed in America and, probably, Japan, but the purist – a true karate man – is one that teaches his art exactly as those before him. Karate in America has changed because the styles have been simplified, but this is all on the physical level. Students we turn out may be high on a physical level, but if he moves to the sporting arena, which has wide appeal, he must not lose the philosophy. That is why we separate the amateur from the professional.

Richard "Biggie" Kim Biography

Richard "Biggie" Kim, 45, born in Hilo, Hawaii, attended the University of Hawaii and earned a degree in political science from St. John's University in Shanghai, China. World War II caught him in the Orient and he stayed there from 1941 to 1959, when he returned to San Francisco, California, to teach the martial arts at the Chinese YMCA and at his own school. He earned the rank of Kyoshi at the Dai Nippon Bu Toku Kai in Kyoto, Japan, and holds 7th Dan Black Belts in karate and ju-jitsu and a 4th-Dan in judo.

On Yamaguchi, Nishiyama, Norris, Hayashi, Yagi and Seagal

The interest in martial arts in South America is as great, if not greater, than in any other part of the world. Each country in South America has very strong karate roots, mostly with the (Shotokan–oriented) JKA (Japan Karate Association) or with shito-ryu.

Unfortunately, the people there who are taking karate are of the middle and upper classes. The poor people cannot take karate; they are far too poor to take lessons. In the United States and Canada, people from all walks of life take martial arts, even if they are working-class people. This is because the standard of living is very high.

When I hold seminars in South America, I stay completely on the physical level, mainly because of the language barrier and the fact I have to use an interpreter. I cannot gain access into what the people are actually thinking. There probably is interest in the philosophy, but there is no time for it.

"As the 1973 Black Belt instructor of the year, do you have opinions on what qualifications an individual should have before attempting to teach others martial arts?"

I am a traditionalist. I believe that if a person wants to teach and is totally in charge of the teaching, not under a senior, he should be at least a fourth dan (degree Black belt). This is because the fourth dan is a turning point in traditional karate. When a person is fourth dan, he can teach wherever he wants; he doesn't have to teach under the supervision of somebody.

It seems, however, that a fourth dan in one organization can be drastically different from a fourth dan in another organization.

Just as 12 inches is 12 inches everywhere, and 100 pounds is 100 pounds in any country, so should the criteria for martial arts be consistent, but is not because of so many different styles. The basic criteria should always be the same. If it is not the same, you will always have politics involved where a person gets a dan level through favor and not merit. If this problem was only confined to, say, the Japanese martial arts it would be an easy goal to overcome. But if you include the Korean and Chinese styles, their criteria is different. There will always be a controversy regarding ranks, because each country has caused standards to be different. The best way to judge the basic standard is to judge the time put in. The shodan (first degree black belt) is the hardest dan to get because before a person can get a shodan in Japanese karate system, not only is technical efficiency a requirement, but character is also important. The dan is given on character, so there should be a minimum requirement in my opinion. Although some people in one year can be just as skillful as a person who has taken karate five years, the former character may be lacking. For any sensei to really know a student, he has to have the student for at least three years. I saw recently that a seven-year-old girl got a shodan. That is impossible because she has not matured.

From my viewpoint, in the Western Hemisphere, outside of Japan, the finest karate instructor is Hidetaka Nishiyama. He is second to none. I have worked with Nishiyama Sensei and have watched the man in action. He is purely Japanese in his mentality. In my opinion, on a technical basis, Nishiyama Sensei is the best in Japanese karate. Teruo Hayashi of the shitoryu style is also an excellent teacher. As a demonstrator, he is almost second to none. His demonstrations are spectacular. Even now, when I am talking to Nishiyama and the JKA people, they say that as a demonstrator, Hayashi stands on top. Yagi Meitoku is an excellent goju ryu specialist. Also, I have to mention (the late) Gogen Yamaguchi. Another person, who is not too well known in the Western world, is Kinjo Hiroshi. He is second to none as a historian. For sheer physical power, not for karate the art itself per se, I knew Mas Oyama when he was in his prime, and I think he stood at the top in that area.

I personally know Chuck Norris; we performed together in Paris. He is an excellent instructor in his style. Not only is he an excellent instructor, he is also a gentleman, with an emphasis on the word gentle. That is the reason why he is so successful in the movie industry. He overcomes any lack in technical ability with sheer perseverance, and I've always had a high respect for him. With respect to Steven Seagal, I've never met him; I've only seen him in his movies. From what I I've heard, he trained in aikido, and from what I've read and if the accounts are correct, he must be skillful. It's hard to judge from the movies.

I will give Bruce Lee this credit: without him, the martial arts world would still be relegated to the background. He focused the world's attention onto the martial arts. That's probably his greatest contribution. Unfortunately, in my opinion as a martial artist, he never reached his potential. He died too young.

The word "sensei" was originally two Chinese characters. Sen means "ahead" and sei is "life". So a sensei is a person who has been on this earth longer than you, and so you follow his path. In the Orient, anyone who is educated and is ahead of you and teaches you something, he is a sensei. A sensei is a professional. He is a father figure. He is everything all rolled into one. He has gone through the minefield of life and so you follow him. He knows how you have suffered, for he has suffered the same himself. When we enter the dojo and perform the rei, the sensei goes down first and then, according to ranks, each person kneels down because the junior respects the senior. When the senior goes down and sees the junior go down after him, he has compassion, for he knows what it was like and he has been through that path. So the compassion and the respect meld together. A sensei is a leader, he is a professional. A sensei maximizes his knowledge. He realizes that he can learn something from every person he meets. He never stops learning. That is why the martial art sensei is the most difficult profession. The martial art sensei's learning never stops until to the beyond and meets God. Until that time, he is always trying to bring people along with him on his journey. That's a real complete sensei.

The Dragon Tail, The Eagle Wing, The Phoenix Beak

Do you ever get the impression that the world is full of violence? Well, judging by most of the news and other violent events coming to us from various sources, there is no doubt that making such a judgement is very close to being correct, one hundred percent even.

Sensei said, "The masters, in trying to solve this problem, come away with the inescapable conclusion that violence is kept under control by a greater force. What I mean is this, a person would not dare commit an act of violence on a person who could retaliate with the fury of an avenging angel. The price would be too high to pay."

In my years training in the martial arts, I had always been taught that violence is inherent in man. That, basically, until man got to wear the wings of an angel, he would follow the tenets of the god of war. What about the man who would turn the other cheek? Would it make the aggressor happier because he would have two cheeks to hit instead of one?

According to Sensei, the masters devised techniques of escape from the premises. In the end, these techniques are as myriad as the proliferation of schools that have sprung up since then, but the principles are universal and few. "Remember," Sensei always said, "Principles are the only thing. Anyone can practice techniques and perfect them, but to get into the principle, that is the secret and the road to mastery."

It all became clear to me one day as if I had hit enlightenment. Consider it, take the strongest man and the weakest man you can find. Stand them side by side, one strong as a bull and the other looking as if the wind could blow him over. The strong man appears invulnerable in comparison to the weaker, but on closer examination, using techniques the ancient masters used, both men are equally vulnerable with hardly an iota of difference between them.

That is how the principle of the dragon tail, the eagle wing and the phoenix beak came about. Man cannot strengthen his eyes and testicles against a strike. Those are the two places where muscular protection cannot happen. Fudo Myoo, the chief deity of the royal protectors of Buddhism, is known as the immovable, fierce-faced impartial judge, punisher of the devil and of all wickedness. He is usually depicted sitting in flames holding a rope in his left hand ready to bind evil. He also holds a sword in his right hand ready to kill evil. As far as I am concerned, Sensei was a reincarnation of Fudo Myoo.

"There are three principles involved in the dragon tail, the eagle wing and the phoenix beak," Sensei always remarked, "these are meant for those physically weaker, for women and for those who do not want to fight. It is a principle meant to help you get safely away. The masters knew that the dragon and the phoenix were mythical to most people, but in their observation of nature and when in deep meditation, the dragon and the phoenix became real. Therefore, they devised the principle of escape."

No one martial arts school can claim, with authority, that any particular technique sprang from their system. This is particularly true of the dragon tail, the eagle wing or the phoenix beak, which is embodied in all kata (forms) in all schools. This is the value of the kata, the language that the ancients used to transmit their secrets. If you ever had the impression that the world is full of morons, all you have to do is to listen to the claims made by various schools that such and such a technique is the sole property of their system. Unfortunately, morons do exist and such claims will always be made.

Since all masters, or most of them anyway, are geniuses, all of them once embroiled in a war or in a fight, came across the inescapable fact that the eyes and testicles were the best target areas. If a blow is properly delivered to either of these two areas it renders a person temporarily out of commission, great for a weaker person giving them enough time to escape. For a strong person there is plenty of time to deliver a follow-up coup de grace.

"Stand loose, the looser the better," Sensei cried out. "Relax and wait for the attacker to come within distance. Measure your distance carefully and at the right moment, strike! Use the knife edge of your hand – never your fist and as soon as you feel contact, keep on moving and get away."

I must have practised the technique a thousand times, both in kata and kumite. (All styles have one of the three principles embodied somewhere their advanced forms. Their posture, position, or name may be different, but the principle is the same. The principles are especially rigorously emphasized in weapons, because one false move could mean death.) The one element that stuck in my mind and made a lot of sense was the importance of being physically relaxed and mentally alert. Sensei said, "If you tense your body, or any part of your body preparatory to a strike or block, you will feel strong and believe that you will hit strong. But that is an incorrect belief, you are not doing it right. Always use the principle of the explosion and then the hit."

Suppose that you are trapped in an alley with someone threatening you with great bodily harm. If you choose not submit to his demands, what then? First, look around, check for a way to escape, then relax, draw a deep breath. As soon as your attacker comes within range, deliver either the dragon tail, the eagle wing or the beak of the phoenix, depending on the situation. Then, get away as fast as possible. This method is guaranteed to work. Although I cannot emphasize it too strongly that escape is crucial. Do not, I repeat, do not stay and watch your stricken attacker... you will more than likely lose the advantage of surprise and, most important, the time you need to get away.

Funakoshi Gichin, in his book 'Karate Do My Way of Life', wrote that when he was in his 80s, he was attacked by a young punk and used the dragon tail principle to subdue and hold the man until the police came. Since we are not all as learned as Funakoshi Gichin, caught in the same situation, we would better use this principle simply to get away safely.

The most effective techniques of physical self defense were developed on the battlefield, in mortal hand-to-hand combat, in one on one duels. The principles and techniques that evolved from that milieu arose out of the sword, such as the sword hand.

It is absolutely not necessary to harden the hands or strengthen the fingers, although if one did it, unquestionably the technique's application would be more devastating.

"Relax," Sensei said. "When your opponent comes towards you, step back, stay loose, and judge the distance. Stand with your left foot forward and your right foot back, lightly on your toes and watch your opponent's left foot. As soon as he steps hard on his left foot or steps forward, take a quick step with your right foot about three inches to the side of his foot; step diagonally and cross your left foot in back of your right foot so that your body turns away from your opponent. With your right hand, hit backwards and up into his groin area with the knife edge of your hand as hard as you can, preferably into his testicles. That, basically, is the dragon tail."

Sensei also told me that if the assailant is a southpaw, to just reverse the position and use the left hand instead. The dragon tail is especially effective against a powerful assailant. However, sometimes you meet an opponent who comes at you en garde, such as a boxer with his left hand extended in front preparing to jab. In that case, it is sometimes advisable to use the eagle wing if a jab is coming at you or the opponent is making feinting motions with his hands. Run in fast and execute what appears to be an X-block against the offending left hand or jab. Don't stop with the block; continue on with both your hands describing an arc like the spread of an eagle's wings. Plummet your hands downward and strike his testicles or lower groin with the palm of your left hand if you are moving diagonally outside of his left. If your move is sudden and swift, it is guaranteed to work without fail. You can only pull it off once, but once is usually enough if you are trapped and want to get away after temporarily negating your assailant's mobility.

The phoenix beak is meant for just one eye. It does not matter which eye, as long as you execute the beak strike quickly and decisively with the sole intent of getting away. Step back as far away as possible from your assailant and put your plan of action at the ready. Do not hesitate, as soon as your assailant comes within your distance, attack! With your right hand, strike under his left hand. If he jabs or holds his left hand in front of his face, hold your thumb and forefinger together as rigidly as possible and using the upper part of your hand in the section between your thumb and forefinger, strike as hard as you can at the juncture where the opponent's wrist joins his forearm. Keep on moving and strike one of his eyes as hard as you can. You can't miss. It always works once.

"In escape," Sensei always warned, "the mental attitude is of paramount importance. Be totally committed to the one act and then get away. Do not even look back to see the results. If you know you connected, you also know what the results will be. Don't try to be cute and stick around."

The Cosmic Punch

"A man knows no more to any purpose than he practices. Knowledge is not found,unsought, in heaven." ~Pollok

In the annals of unarmed combat, one argument has raged, is now raging, and will continue to rage as long as men get together and discuss the merits of which is the best kind of blow, and whether a left hook, right cross, straight right, uppercut, or a jab is superior. It has never been decided and probably never will as long as the arguments remain academic!

One day, I put the argument to Sensei. "Unarmed combat?" Sensei asked. "Yes," I said. "In a situation where no weapons are used and strictly with what nature gave us. What is the best blow to develop?"

"The cosmic punch!" Sensei replied. "Of all the blows which can be delivered by a human being against another, the 'cosmic punch' is the most effective. Don't get me wrong, any blow delivered properly and correctly has merit and can be very effective, but,the cosmic punch stands by itself."

Trembling with excitement, I waited, eager to pounce on each word that came out of Sensei's mouth.

He continued, "Suppose, just suppose, we were standing on the top of the highest mountain peak and threw a stone in three directions: one straight up over-head, one straight out level, and one straight down. Which one travels in the same original direction? The one straight down, right? The one that we threw straight up and the one that we threw straight out will fall backdown, but the one we threw down will continue down and not change direction. That is natural law."

"In other words, Sensei," I said, "what goes up must come down; we are talking about the law of gravity, are we not?"

"Yes. That is natural law, as I said," Sensei replied. "But, to utilize the law of gravity for physical self defense, that is the secret that few realize."

I ran through my mind everything that I had learned in the martial arts and its correlation to the law of gravity. Somehow, the gist eluded me. I could feel it but I could not put it into thought, much less into words.

Then Sensei said, "Do you know why Harigaya Sekiun was the greatest?"

And before I could answer, Sensei continued, "Sekiun utilized the law of gravity fully in his style of swordsmanship. He cut out all the frills and developed just one blow with his sword, the cosmic blow, and with it he became the greatest swordsman in Japanese history. Nothing fancy, no frills, just the cosmic movement."

I thought that I had learned quite a bit about Harigaya Sekiun, but, as they say, we learn something new every day, and I guess this was one of those days. Whatever it was, secrets always fascinated me, especially in the martial arts,and I waited.

Japanese history is full of stories of great swordsmen who caught the imagination of noted writers, and many such stories have found their way into the movies and television. The heroes of the Japanese sword are just as popular and well known to the average Japanese as the knights of the

Round Table or the Three Musketeers are with English-speaking people.

However, in the popular stories, none depict the adventures of Harigaya Sekiun; he is never shown on the celluloid of Japanese films, and if any mention is made of him, it barely covers one page or more. Whatever accounts may have been fictionalized for romantic reading have escaped the eyes of the general public.

According to Sensei, Harigaya Sekiun was too good for his own good. And to top it off, he was a man of Zen. The populace could not relate to him except for those who made the martial arts their way of life. Only to these lucky few, Harigaya Sekiun has come out of the pages of history to share his secrets.

One day, when Sekiun was over 60 years of age, he was in his garden pruning a tree. He was suddenly interrupted by loud voices, and he could distinguish the voice of his servant from those of the others in the argument. His servant was saying, "My master is busy, so please wait until I announce you."

"Wait nothing," one loud voice said. "My partner and I have come a long way and we are tired of the run-around."

Sekiun stopped pruning and called out, "Let them in."

His servant came out to the garden, followed by two men both wearing battle helmets. They were young, in their early 30s at the latest.

Both swaggered into the garden and stood braced arrogantly in front of Harigaya Sekiun. They peered at him and a flicker of surprise crossed their eyes.

"Why," the younger said, "you are an old man. Are you truly *the* Harigaya Sekiun?"

Sekiun, ignoring the rudeness, went back to his pruning. "Old man," the young one yelled out, "I am talking to you. We have heard of your mighty blow and do not believe it, and now that we have seen you, an old man, we believe more that our belief is right."

Sekiun said, "If you do not believe what you have heard, you can leave. It is not important as far as I am concerned. As you can see, I am an old man, as you say, so why bother?"

"You see this battle helmet, old man?" said one of the youths. "It is specially designed to take any kind of blow. Not believing in the stories that we have heard about you, we have come to test your blow. We hate to do this old man, but you know how it is; we have come along way and we have our reputation at stake," the speaker said.

"I cannot accept your challenge," Sekiun said, and kept on pruning. Both men left when they saw it was futile arguing with him, and in their ignorance broadcast all over town that the great Sekiun was afraid of them. After a period of time, it dawned on them that the townspeople did not believe them, and they went back to Sekiun.

"This is the second time we have come," both said.

"And this is the second time that I am asking you to leave," Sekiun answered.

The two went back to town and broadcast again the fact that the great Harigaya Sekiun had turned down their challenge to a match.

"He is afraid because he is old and washed up," they said.

"We do not believe you," the townspeople said. "Probably he does not want to kill you."

This remark so infuriated the young men that they both charged into Sekiun's residence and issued a challenge to the death.

"Well, if you insist, be sure that you have your helmet on, and be sure that you use a real sword so that you have a fighting chance. I shall use a wooden sword to make the match more equal," Sekiun said.

In the words of the elder of the two young men, "Sekiun faced my friend with a wooden sword in his hand, and as soon as they squared off, Sekiun hit my friend with a seemingly light tap on the helmet; to my surprise and shock, my friend, who is very powerful for his age, collapsed like a broken egg. He fell against a tree and blood was streaming from his mouth. When I went to pick him up, he was dead. What kind of man is Sekiun?"

What the man did not know was that Harigaya Sekiun had developed the cosmic blow; his sword had become the sword of Heavenly Reason; he had become one with the great ultimate (or great limit, taikyoku in Japanese, tai-chi in Chinese).

What Sensei said about Sekiun ran through my mind. In his early matches, Sekiun had quite a few close calls, and somehow managed to emerge unscathed. However, in doing so he came to realize one fundamental fact: A man who is not completely incapacitated in combat is still dangerous.

Once, when he was accosted by a ronin bent on making a name for him self as the greatest of the great, Sekiun delivered a classical cut to the body and the man fell dying. There was no doubt in Sekiun's mind that the seeker of fame and glory was finished; after all, every opponent prior to this one had never survived his cut.

Sekiun walked away from the scene. The dying ronin in his last gasp drew a shuriken and threw it at Sekiun. The shuriken struck Sekiun on the shoulder and as Sekiun spun around the ronin was dead.

"It was then," as Sekiun explained later to his students, "that I developed the cosmic blow. Never forget that as long as an opponent who is engaged in a life-and-death struggle is not completely out, he is still dangerous as long as he can draw a breath and has control of his senses. But conk a man on his head and drop him senseless, and that man is of no danger to you. That ronin who hit me with a shuriken would never have been able to do it if I had split his forehead and rendered him unconscious. If you happen to deliver a blow to any other part of his body and your opponent is dying, never, I repeat, never, take your eyes off him until it is safe."

Sekiun practiced all his blows from the jodan position. After his encounter with the shuriken-throwing opponent, Sekiun, through diligent practice, noticed that the most effective blow with the sword was the downward stroke to the top of the forehead.

As Sensei said, "If you stand and imagine a circle encompassing you as high as you can stretch your hand over-head and as low as you can bring your hands below your feet, the most force that you can generate is with your hands held straight overhead and striking down in that circle directly in front of you, from a jodan kamai straight down in front with full explosion. Divide that imaginary circle in four quarters, always holding your sword in a jodan position, and in delivery exploding downwards."

"I understand," I told Sensei. "But that is with the sword or weapon. What about empty hand combat? The cosmic punch as you said – what is the proper delivery?"

Sensei had me stand in a fighter's stance with my right hand placed lightly on my chest just above the solar plexus.

"Now," Sensei went on, "take it easy, relax, and throw your right hand as high as you can; throw upwards when your arm is fully extended; step forward with your left foot and you will notice that your hand starts downward. At the point where it is level with your face is the point of contact; that is where the explosion takes place."

I did what Sensei told me and it felt awkward. And I told Sensei so.

"Naturally, you feel awkward," Sensei replied. "I am showing you the mechanics of the blow. Now, coordinate it all in one movement. As soon as you throw your right hand, step in exploding; you will note that your right hand forms an arc, with you exploding at the exact moment your right hand is on the level with your face. Never, never tense, and use the explosion principle with the cosmic punch."

I cocked my right hand on my chest,threw my right in an arc, stepping in at the same time with my left foot as deeply as I could, and exploded as if I had a bomb in my lower abdomen with the explosion coming out of my right fist, which at this time came down in a circle right in front of my face level. It felt good. It reminded me of an overhand right – the type of right hand that Max Schmeling used to knock out Joe Louis the first time that they met.

But there was a difference: the explosion and the follow-through with the mind. It was more than mere mechanics; the boxer's overhand right may appear to be the same to an untrained eye, but, the martial artist simply uses his body and mind as an explosive device utilizing the forces of gravity for more impact. A true martial artist never tenses his body prior to any action, and simply explodes into an appropriate maneuver. And as Sekiun had discovered, the best is if you render an assailant unconscious. Then, there is no way he can come back at you.

"Don't get me wrong," Sensei had always taught. "Any blow that hurts an assailant or makes him believe that he can be hurt is effective. But show me, if you can, anything more effective than a knock out, anything more decisive. There is no debate when it comes to a clean knockout."

Sensei's words: "There is no debate when it comes to a clean knockout!", brought back vividly to me a story that I had read concerning the great black heavyweight, Sam Langford.

When Sam Langford was way past his prime, a group of Texans who believed that they had a future champion on their hands arranged a fight with Sam to take place in their state.

"Sam," his friends told him. "You are crazy to accept a fight like that. You haven't got a prayer. And, of all places, in Texas."

"Why the worry?" Sam answered. "My opponent is just a green kid and even at my age I can teach him a lesson on the art of boxing.

"That is not the point," Sam was told. "For insurance they have the referee in their pocket. It is known that the referees are so bad that a black man has not been able to win a fight in that part of the country."

"Have no fear," Sam said. "I carry my own referee!" And he held up his right fist. Sam chilled his opponent with a thunderous right hand, and no matter what the referee and the others did, the guy was out cold for 30 minutes. Sam was declared the winner. There was no debate.

Richard Kim: The Classical Man

By Don Warrener

I have been a student of Richard Kim since 1968 when I first received my shodan from him through my teacher at the time, Benny Allen. Since our first meeting, I knew he was not just another karate instructor who could punch and kick. The reason I have remained as a student with him is because I continue to learn from him. I went to the now famous Nishiyama summer camp in San Diego, which has been going on for over 35years, to both train and do an interview with Master Richard Kim, 10th dan in Shorinji ryu karate.

Q: *Where and when were you born?*

A: I was born on November 17, 1919, in Hilo, Hawaii. My mother was Japanese and my father was Korean. I began studying judo in 1925 when I was 6 years old under Tatsu Bata. My mother owned a hotel upstairs and down stairs was a Japanese club where judo was taught and she made me train.

Q: *When did you start karate?*

A: As a child, I went to watch a demonstration put on in 1927 by Yabu Kentsu and his assistant Sensei Arakaki at the Nuanu YMCA in Honolulu. Right after that, I began training with Yabu Kentsu who stayed in Hawaii for about a year, as I recall.

Q: *When did you get your shodan?*

A: I received my black belt from the Dai Nippon Bu Toku Kai.

Remember, before World War II they were the only organization who issued official dan rankings. There was no JKA or Kodokan in those days. These organizations only arose after World War II, when General MacArthur closed it down. He believed that the Bu Toku Kai was responsible for the war.

Q:*What style of karate did you teach?*

A: The style of karate I learned and taught was and is shorinji ryu karate, Yabu Kentsu's style of karate. This is why my kata are named like Yabu Chinto. Of course, over the years, I have refined the kata as karate in those early years was quite unsophisticated. There wasn't even any real names of styles in the early days – it was just called te. It wasn't until quite some time later that the word karate was even invented.

Q: *When did you leave Hawaii and move to Japan?*

A: I moved to Japan in 1939, and came back to the USA in 1959, after the war was over.

Q: *How did you become involved with the Bu Toku Kai?*

A: When I was in Japan and part of the Japanese military I was trained in the Busen as part of the Dai Nippon Bu Toku Kai, and it was there that I met Ohno Komo Sensei, a 10th dan in kendo. When I returned to the USA in 1959, he asked me to organize the Bu Toku Kai internationally, and I did so by teaching at the Chinese YMCA in San Francisco's Chinatown for years. I continued to organize the Bu Toku Kai until 1992 when Hamada took over.

Q: *Why did you never open a professional dojo?*

A: I never wanted to teach in mass. I always preferred to teach more on an individual or small group format. I preferred to encourage my students to run commercial dojos. I wanted to mix religion with martial arts because I really wanted to teach morality to the Western world and not just physical fighting. Some students did not understand this and they left because they wanted high dan ranks and I would not grant them-The highest dan rank I ever granted was a 6th dan which I gave to Brian Ricci in Boston and only within the last few years.

Q: *Did you have a problem going back to Japan when the war broke out?*

A: Not really, I had dual citizenship because I was born before 1924 and the Exclusions Act allowed me to have duel citizenship.

Q: *I understand that you are the inheritor of Menkyo Kaiden scrolls of Daito Ryu? Is this true and what can you tell us about Yoshida Kotaro?*

A: Yes, it is true. I was given the Menkyo Kaiden from Yoshida Sensei. He was a great martial artist. He went with Ueshiba to Hokkaido prior to World War II as part of a government program where individuals from each prefecture went there to help populate Hokkaido. While there, he trained with Sokaku Takeda and became the assistant instructor to him. Actually, he became the main instructor.

Q: *What were the main lessons you learned from him?*

A: I learned two main lessons from him. The first was that nothing is impossible and the second was before you become a thief or any other type of criminal you first become a liar; he stressed this lesson over and over and taught the importance of always telling the truth, no matter what.

Q: *What was the physical training like with him?*

A: It was very harsh but a different harsh than karate training. It was not kicking and punching but rather throwing and rolling around on the ground. We also did a great deal of work with swords and knives. The training was practical everyday and I became like an apprentice under him.

Q: *Who are some of the other great Masters you have met?*

A: Well, first comes to mind Yoshida Kotaro. He was the epitome of the word "master", technically, mentally, and spiritually. Ueshiba was another one of the great ones. In fact, I trained with Ueshiba for about a year every day from 6-9 a.m. Then, there was Sawai: he trained with Wang Xiang Zhay in China and became a master of the internal systems and, in fact, wrote a book called Tai Ki Kae. He was one of the most impressive people I ever met. Wang Xiang Zhay, his teacher, could actually just touch you and you would go flying. In fact, Sawai, who was a 5th dan from Kano himself and a 5th dan in kendo, once tried to hit Wang but only ended up on the short end of the stick and on his back. He even tried to hit him with a stick and could not. The first lesson with Wang was that we would just stand there for 3- 9 hours a day – of course, not all at one time – 30 minutes here and 30 minutes there. All he said to us was, "Just don't think."

Q: *Who did you learn your tai chi from?*

A: I trained with a man named Chen Chen Wan in China. The style of tai chi is an offshoot of the Yang style tai chi. In fact, if you saw them both side by side you would think them the same.

 The goal of life is to redirect Sha (negative energy) back to the giver.

Q: *Was there anyone else?*

A: I met a man in Hong Kong whose name was Charlie Tu Tai. He could do something no one else I have ever seen could do. He would let mosquitoes land on him and then using his powers they would fall off him dead. I never saw anything like this. I learned pa qua from him and he is the one who told me that no pa qua fighter had ever lost. Then there is Nishiyama Sensei who is alive today. He is the most knowledgeable man alive when it comes to Shotokan karate. No one is equal to him. Oh, yes, then Mas Oyama. He was excellent, as well. I remember that he, Sawai, and I were walking along discussing martial arts and Oyama hit this telephone pole and put his fist in to it at least 1/2 inch. He believed that nothing beat a good right hand. He and Kinjo used to come to my place in Yokohama at least once a week to train. I met Yamaguchi Gogen through Oyama – he, too, was very good.

Q: *You mentioned that Oyama believed that a good right hand is the best weapon. Do you believe that?*

A: Let me put it this way: the defect of karate is that they don't know how to use a good right hand like a boxer does. The good boxer will only use the right hand once he has feinted.

Q: *How much boxing did you do?*

A: I had 42 pro fights and became the champion of the Orient when I lived in Shanghai. I lived there for 5 years. I studied tai chi and pa qua as well when I lived in Shanghai.

Q: *In the early 1970s, you wrote a column called "The Classical Man", and got dubbed "The Martial Arts Historian." Why?*

A: I guess because I was the only one who was writing about the philosophy, psychology and the history of the martial arts at that time.

Q: *Why was the Dai Nippon Bu Toku Kai so influential?*

A: The Bu Toku Kai was the only body allowed to award dan ranks in martial arts. The Bu Toku Kai was mostly judo and the organization prior to and during WWII was the only organization and all others had to belong to it. After the war, it never regained its status or its recognition by the government. You might say it just isn't the same organization nowadays, as it was back then.

Q: *Why is it so difficult to get information from Chinese masters on the internal systems?*

A: Because of their culture. The master taught the student personally and this is the way the information was handed down – teacher to student – and in some ways, this is the best. The student would never leave the sensei because the teacher would always hold back one thing from the student and he wanted that one thing. Once in a while a great Chinese master came along, like General Yei Fei. He's the one who created the Eight Brocades of Silk and also the Superimpei kata. In fact, he created all the goju-ryu kata and also The Eight Gods Crossing The River. I think I am the only one who still teaches this form. But even Yei Fei fell victim to his own friend who turned on him and killed him.

Q: *Did you ever meet Gichin Funakoshi?*

A: Yes. I met him in 1957 at his final public performance. In fact, Bob Fazaro was there at the time and he performed in front of Funakoshi Sensei. Funakoshi was good but it was because of his ability to communicate with the Japanese that he was chosen to go to Japan and spread the art of karate. In fact,there were many more skillful masters like Miyagi, Yabu Kentsu and others – but Funakoshi was educated and therefore he was chosen to go. Most of the other masters only spoke Hogan, a dialect used in Okinawa.

Q: *If you were to suggest five books that every martial artist should have in their library, what would they be?*

A: Nishiyama's book would be number one for technical reference, it is excellent. Then I would choose both of my books, The Weaponless Warrior and The Classical Man. I think then I would suggest all of Donn Draeger's books and Jay Gluck's book.

Q: *Peter Urban – how and where did you meet him?*

A: I was teaching karate and judo at the Black Friars Gym in Yokohama and this guy, Smith, was punching a kid around in the ring. I stopped Smith and said, "what you wanna do that for?" He said the kid told him not to pull back so he let him have it. That kid was Peter Urban. Peter was one of the few men I have ever met in my life that had absolutely no fear – I saw that in his eyes that day. He became my student and then one day he asked if he could go train with Mas Oyama. Then he later became a disciple of Gogen Yamaguchi.

Q: *Is there anyone in America that you can think of that is on the right track of Budo?*

A: I am sure there are many, but two names quickly come to mind – Chuck Merriman and Chuck Norris.

Q: *Kobudo – How much value does weapons have in modern society?*

A: Weapons training is very important because it brings into focus the frailty of life. Without weapons, karate loses the concept of art and degenerates into a sport.

Q: *What is the difference between the Japanese students of karate and North American students of karate?*

A: Physically, North Americans are just as good as the Japanese, but the Western student lacks the morality and ethics that a Japanese student has. You know what I mean, Don; remember when Yamaguchi asked you to join his group and you deferred him back to me, your sensei? That is ethics and morality.

Q: *Why did you decide to move to San Francisco?*

A: That one is easy. The weather, it is perpetual spring and besides it is very cosmopolitan and there is a big Chinatown and a big Japan town.

Q: *Which martial art is superior?*

A: The Chinese martial arts are rich in tradition and the Japanese martial arts are deep in discipline. The Korean martial arts, although they do not like to admit it, are based on Japanese karate. In fact, in the beginning, their forms were Japanese kata but with Korean names. They do have very beautiful kicks, similar to the French, but all they did was incorporate their own kicking techniques with Japanese karate. What I am saying is that they do not have any history like the sword or spear, although they were exceptional in archery. But to give you a final answer, no one art is better than another. Mastery comes from the individual, not the style.

Q: *Is Japanese or Okinawan karate superior?*

A: Well first off, Okinawan karate is true karate – the Okinawans are much more traditional then the Japanese. But the Japanese, especially those like Nishiyama Sensei, have refined the Okinawan karate to what it is today.

Q: *What is your opinion of the belt ranking system?*

A: The Chinese started the belt system with the use of sashes and different colors, then judo and then karate followed. To be very honest, belts are just another means of bringing dollars into the dojo – it is another form of commercialism in the dojo. Unfortunately, it has been greatly abused here in the USA – nobody needs to be told this. Over the last 40 years the overall quality of a black belt degraded to the point where some instructors are selling their dan grades. In the Bu Toku Kai there was no belt system, there was only trainee, assistant instructor, instructor, and master.

Q: *In your opinion, what is a black belt?*

A: Shodan, in most traditional dojo, is three years minimum training. First to 4th dan is usually judged on a person's physical abilities, but 5th dan and above is judged on a man's character and whether he is a gentleman.

Q: *Why is karate not in the Olympics and tae kwon do is?*

A: It is political, as one of the heads of the Olympic committee is Korean and he had a great deal to do with it getting into the Olympics before karate. Also the karate groups are fractionalized and they are constantly fighting among each other.

Q: *How has martial arts changed before the boxer rebellion and after the boxer rebellion?*

A: The boxer rebellion of 1900 saw the loss of many great martial arts masters because they thought their chi could stop bullets. Obviously, they were wrong... bullets are a different type of weapon. The Okinawans in 1905-1906 lost the etiquette that was there prior to this – there was absolutely no commercialism before this point.

Q: *In martial arts we talk about the karate being physical, mental, and spiritual. What do we mean when we say it is spiritual?*

A: The roots of all Japanese martial arts is Buddhism, and in Buddhism we do not kill anything. Let me share a short story about this with you. There was a young boy and he was about to kill a cricket and the priest stopped him and said to him, "How important to you is your life?" The boy replied, "It is the most important thing to me." The priest then said to the boy, "It is just as important to the cricket."

Q: *If you could snap your fingers and change one thing in the martial arts, what would it be?*

A : Etiquette - simply etiquette.

Q: *It is now almost the year 2000, where would you like to see karate in the year 3000?*

A: First I would like to see it in the Olympics. Secondly, I would like to see it taught in every public school in the world.

Q: *Why the public schools?*

A: If karate were taught in public schools, crime would be cut drastically, as the students would learn respect.

Q: *At the beginning of the class, you often explain the purposes of the rei. Could you explain it?*

A: The first lesson in martial arts is respect, compassion, and gratitude. Every time you bow your head you are internalizing each of these words. You are showing respect to your seniors, and compassion for your juniors, as you know what they have gone through over the years because you, too, have gone through the same. Finally, you are showing gratitude for your country which you reap the benefits of every day, your parents who gave you life, and the friends who support you every day in your successes and in your failures. Finally, you revere God, as it is he who will decide what will happen to you.

The Circle of Power

Sensei and I were high in the mountains overlooking Yugawara. The air was crisp and we stood silently, breathing and enjoying the clean air.

Sensei broke the silence by saying softly, "Stand as if in attention," and I knew from the tone of his voice that special instruction was forthcoming.

"Now, step forward as if taking a walk," Sensei continued. "Raise your hands as if embracing someone, relax your shoulders, and bring your hands together with fingers outstretched about three to five inches apart. Now, concentrate on the area separating your forefingers and middle fingers."

It came to me in a flash. I as transported a few years back to Shanghai, China, and Jessefield Park. I was walking in a circle contemplating my fingertips. Then, after what seemed an eternity, I stopped and Chao Hsu Lai, a Taoist monk whom I met prior to World War II, instructed me in a posture that had not made sense to me then and did not make sense to me now. I never questioned him, because I had been taught that "all things come to him who waits." Anyway, that's what I was told.

So here I was in Yugawara, Japan, a far cry from wartime Shanghai. It was the same posture, but the instruction this time would be more explicit. Probably fate led me to this. I mentioned it to Sensei. He was not surprised.

Ultimate Secret

This posture," Sensei explained, "is the ultimate secret." Ultimate secret? All sorts of thoughts flitted through my mind. I wondered what he meant. I could not envision a secret in a seemingly simple posture as this.

"Have you ever wondered as to the seemingly boundless energy of the ancient samurai?" Sensei asked. "Well, the ancients discovered the secret of recharging the human battery without recourse to fancy frills, diets, and exercises.

As you are well aware, certain diets and exercises are unquestionably useful; however, since man is a spiritual creation, he must harmonize with the universe to get into reality and tap the power. Only then can disease and death be seen in proper perspective and hold no terror for the man who communes with the power through the secret circle.

I had heard that the sages of old had a secret that made them appear super normal, but I had always supposed the secret was locked in breath control. Even Sensei had stressed the importance of breath control, and the foundation of yoga was in the science of the breath.

"You must remember one thing," Sensei told me. "Man is apt to deny any phenomena that he cannot see, feel, hear, smell, or taste. Because power can be tapped through harmony with ether (the upper regions of space) and since the five senses cannot verify this, man as a general rule does not have faith in this secret and will discount it as being esoteric. But reality is reality whether it stimulates our five senses or not. That fact cannot change. This posture, combined with prayers or mantras can charge your batteries, revitalize you, cure your illnesses, and make you come into harmony with the great life force."

"What do you mean by mantras or prayers?" I asked.

"Mantras," Sensei explained, "are words which contain the essence of absolute truth. They are magical formulas that create wonders if a correct tone and posture is used. But it must be applied according to the rules. One thing for sure: In adversity, it gives you complete protection." In fact, he said, in many religions, especially Buddhism, the mantras are the only key to the great life force.

I remembered when I was a kid. In church, the preacher quoted from St. John, chapter 1, which describes Jesus Christ as "the Word": "In the beginning was the Word, and the Word was with God, and the Word was God ... In him was life; and the life was the light of men."

But I still could not grasp the connection between the mantras or prayers and the posture, the "circle of power", as Sensei called it. He then taught me the mantra of the prajna-pammita, explaining that it was the holiest of the holy among all the sutras. The prajna-paramita literature is comprised of 38 different books, written in India between 100 B.C. and A.D. 600. It is the path of transcendental wisdom. In Japanese, it is called the Hannya-Shingyo.

Electric Charge

After a long period of practice since that day in Japan, I have always felt good in a spiritual sort of way. No amount of adversity, and there has been plenty, has brought me down. Those that I have taught have told me the same thing. In the beginning, a sort of electric charge or tingling comes to the fingertips, then later a sort of pull, a force. Then, an ecstatic sort of vibration comes over you.

You must be careful not to think of any sort of breathing or method of breathing. Just breathe as usual. Do not try to empty out your mind. Just tell yourself, mentally, that you are a creation of God and as such you are free from delusion and disease.

If you are for some reason, on any particular day, nervous or troubled and cannot concentrate or calm down, use the mantra method to relax and take away anxiety.

Repeat the mantra at least three times, or as many times as you wish until you feel calm and your fingertips tingle or pull. Then go into "plus one," or positive thinking. Sensei always said, "there are two kinds of people, those who live in 'plus one,' and those who live in 'minus one.' Ninety percent of the people live in minus one they are the complainers and the losers. The very few who live in plus one have it made, because they have found happiness. There are many methods to plus one: however, the circle of power is unique because it helps everybody. It is beyond religion, creed, race, color, sex, or age. And it develops power."

Your positive thinking must go along lines somewhat like this: "I am a creation of God; I am created perfect, without sickness or disease; I am the 'real' man (or woman)." The perfect man is one who sees it as it is, without the blinders or "filtering systems" of language, society, or personal experience.

As you hold your posture, imagine strongly that life force enters through your fingertips and spreads all over your body. Your faith must well up in you and harmonize with the universe.

The mantra of the prajna-paramita is the highest mantra which makes one equal to "that which cannot be equaled." In absolute terms, everything is equal, but in relative terms, things are unequal. The mantra is the essence of truth itself and being the concentrated essence of the whole sutra is equal to the sutra itself. The mantra is: Tadyatha gate gate para-gate para-samgate bodhi sva-ha (going, going yonder; going yonder completed). In essence, it describes "going to the other shore," or reaching enlightenment. When you repeat the mantra, do not think; just feel with the heart.

Stay in your posture for five to 15 minutes, but not more than 20 minutes. Then close your palms together and stay in silent prayer, with feet together.

When you finish your silent prayer, rub your hands together as hard and as fast as you can for approximately 36 counts, and immediately take both of your hands and cover your face for a minute or so.

This circle of power makes one strong in physical and mental health, and also gives a spiritual foundation that can withstand the typhoons of misfortune and all demonic forces.

Stages of Kata – Mind, Body and Kinesic Energy

By Frank Gaviola
San Diego Summer Camp
Lecture courtesy of Martial Virtue Magazine

Kata is a device to bring together the physical body, intuitive awareness, and intellect to reveal and advance our hidden potential and overcome our weak points and deficiencies. Kata guides a person to cultivate a keen body, free of desultory emotions, and astute mind, devoid of errant thoughts. As in all serious studies into self knowledge, one must penetrate obscurities of the psyche. In the process, one comes to realize kata is a lifetime endeavor that advances the cultivation of three aspects of the human makeup: body, mind, and spirit. The junctures of beginner, coming of age, and adeptness differs for every individual, but a general guideline is as follows: Up to age 30, the student should develop their physical abilities to their maximum. From age 30 to 45, the student should develop mentally. After age 45, the student should turn their efforts to spiritual development.

San Francisco Bay is an historic golden gate of immigration and the wherefore of the city's Asian population. Resident townsfolk patronize commercial establishments of the Asian community and appreciate its cultural art forms. Smitten by the psychological verve and fighting dynamics of karate exhibitions, I took up martial arts at the San Francisco Chinese YMCA. From the spring of 1968 until the winter of his passing in 2001, I trained under the tutelage of Sensei Richard Kim. During those years, I had the opportunity to travel with Sensei, assist him in organizational business and benefit from his coaching to vie in national and international karate competition. His teaching was comprehensive beyond simply learning a system of fighting techniques. It was an education in the practical use of martial arts philosophy in the activities of daily life, because fighting skill alone does not engender the realization that when conflict takes place within the body and mind or outside them, it is always a battle against the self. In the Far Eastern sense, the martial arts engenders things that are of value for bringing the inner self nearer to perfection, for developing, craft skills and intellectual skills alike. Clarity of perception, attention to detail, and precision are essential to successful strategies in life because there is a correct way of doing everything to prevent error and discord.

For three thousand years of recorded history, East and West have been doing things with ideas and institutions that are often quite different, because Western philosophy is based on the intellect and Eastern philosophy is based on intuition. That is, the Occident favors working from the intellect to the body, whereas the Orient tends to work from the body to the intellect. Much of what Eastern esoteric traditions really teach is more like

Magazine Articles and Quotes

Over the years hundreds of magazine articles were written about Sensei Kim. In fact, so many, we chose to not put the entire collection of the articles in the book.

What we did was put in only some of the selected articles in their entirety and his quotes from many of the rest of the articles that go back to 1966.

Many of these same quotes were given over the years in his lectures.

The Wringer and the Press

If you were to take a statistical survey on the most unpleasant branch of the martial arts, especially in Kodokan judo, without fail the report would show that the most disagreeable aspect is being on the receiving end of strangleholds or chokes. Every judoka has gone through a phase of fear concerning these maneuvers, and that is why, for the most part, it is difficult to embrace groundwork as enthusiastically as the more spectacular standing work, where throws are the forte. If the martial arts purport to show the human body's fragility, no place is it more clearly demonstrated than in the strangleholds.

"Fear magnifies the technique," Sensei always said. "When the stranglehold is applied correctly, the recipient feels as if he is going to die. With a blow, throw, kick, chop – you name it – the receiver feels, mentally and emotionally, that he has a chance. But, if you choke a guy and he is not a skillful martial artist, he will panic. Make no bones about it: Shutoff the (kime). The union of limb and hip movements in tandem with breathing from the core center of the body engenders maximal efficiency. This constitutes the stage of Concentrative Merging.

Second Stage – The Body and Experience Unification

Kata is using the body as the focus of meditation. A preferred kata is one that is compatible with the practitioners temperament and body structure. Ideally, ones' favorite kata minimizes inhibitions that may hinder perceiving basic natural laws and principles embedded within the scheme of kata. Traditionally, there is no allowance for question and answer discussions in kata training. Consequently, the notion of uncritical acceptance can be a source of exasperation and misunderstanding for new comers to the seemingly stoic and evasive Eastern teaching method. In this sense, katas are likened to a Zen teaching method and its befuddling koan solving prerequisites, wherein the analytical calculating intellect is subordinated to insights and feelings that can only be born of actually doing the experience. Intuitive experience of the laws of nature furthers the control of the body which eventually effects the mind. Actions become unconscious without effort. Mastery of technique refines character.

Depth of knowledge means having a comprehensive grasp of the meaning in the choreographic inflections of kata because different kata accent selective combinations of neuro-muscular synchronicity in body dynamics. The initial stages of kata entails technique expressed from feelings at the core abdominal and hip area of the body, not form words expressed from the intellect and lips.

Various interpretations and applications may modify somewhat the outer appearance of a kata. Herein lies a primary reason for the diverse philosophical outlooks and stylish looks of different schools of martial arts.

Third Stage – Experience of the Wild Mind

Consciousness possesses an incessant cacophony of wild thoughts and emotions. Consequently, the immediate mind is often preoccupied by day dreams and lapses in attention. The aim of kinesic imagery is to sharpen one's meditative focus and intensify the clarity of immediate experience.

The concentration power indicative of kata expertise is directed toward eliminating discordant mental randomness. The adroit skill of psychokinesic imagery is to imagine oneself performing the movements of kata and experiencing the heightened sensations of actually doing the kata. This keen body consciousness confers responsiveness to mental lapses and furthers the ability to tame the wild mind. This is the stage of Experience the Wild Mind.

Fourth Stage – Experience the Intuitive Mind

The wellspring of introspective knowledge is inklings residing in the body. Wherein, one can distinguish intuitive mind from the intellect. At this level of proficiency, one's insight can grasp the esoteric principals of kata and absorb kata's scheme of ultra-efficiency. In a manner of speaking, one's awareness attains a keen sense of inferring the meaning of things not spoken and anticipating the outcome of causes not seen. In other words it is to be ahead of an action by grasping the intent before the action. This is preemptive self defense by foreknowledge and may not necessarily entail a physical encounter. It my involve insight about tactics which seek to nudge one into some sort of action. Often, doing nothing is more vital than doing something. Wisdom in the guise of happenstance interference is skill to evading and forestalling. This is the stage of Experience the Intuitive Mind.

Kata is a continuous flow. Transitions between techniques are not separate actions. As there is no separation between kata and the dynamics of daily life. Intent and action are as one, as kata movement are in natural accord with the wisdom of mind and body. Transitions in life are as meaningful as the goal and kata habituates "Right Now" as a main event feeling of life.

Fifth Stage – The Spirit and Concentrated Reflection

The desire for deeper understanding and spiritual awareness is innate in the soul of mankind. Advanced levels of meditation are usually thought of as the prime of the monastic calling. However, there are many levels and inflections of meditation that are within the mundane domain of layman and professional. Transcendent or non-conventional ways of life are not an exclusive path to wisdom and spirituality.

his stomach area with your left hand, and wrap your right hand around his body from the back. You are now behind him. Place your right foot against the back of his right knee, push as hard as you can, crumpling his right leg, and bring him to the ground with you holding him from behind.

When you bring him to the ground, he will try to turn, to get up and escape from your hold; no matter what, he will struggle. As soon as you hit the ground, take your right hand and encircle his neck with your forearm, cutting into his neck like a vice – and this is the most important step: remember that the "steering wheel" of the body is the head. Place your head against his head, and push forward as hard as you can with your forearm cutting into his neck. As you push your head against his, forcing his head forward, your forearm will cut into his neck, shutting off blood supply and causing him to black out in a few seconds. You will have time to lock your left hand and your right hand together.In his panic. the opponent will give you time to do this. If you are experienced,you can do this in one motion. from entering, go-behind. and take-down to,strangle. Just a little practice is required.

The best part of wringer is that you do not have to be an expert. As Sensei always taught, "The punk or bully that tries to push you around or attack you will not have the patience or emotional capacity to take the martial arts and attain a high decree of efficiency. It does not work out that way because a blackbelt is just the first step on the road to mastery. So most likely the punk who attacks you is just a punk."

"I remember when I was teaching in Yokohama, Japan. One day, after a hard workout in judo and karate, the subject of the practicalities of principles in a street fight came up – especially against a jab. I made the class practice the takedown and stranglehold."

"This was during the Korean War and merchant ships of all nations were coming in and out of the port of Yokohama. Quite a few street fights took place in Yokohama, Chinatown and in Omarudani, a red-light district. Many a reputation was made or broken in those fights. There was one particular tanker seaman who had a fearsome reputation due to a few fights in the ring. Seamen,as a rule being better lovers than fighters, did not have a snowball's chance in hell, when our aggressor accosted them and challenged them to a fight. He never lost; he always set opponents up with a jab and knocked them out with a right cross. When he was drunk or feeling evil he picked on anybody."

"One night he picked on one of my students, a small Japanese man not more than 125 pounds soaking wet. This student of mine helped out as a handy man in one of the bar-restaurants in Yokohama, Chinatown. The way I heard it, when the champion threw his jab, the student slipped under, executed the take-down, and applied the stranglehold exactly as he had practiced it in the gym one session. The champion blacked out, and when he came to he was so embarrassed that he jumped ship and flew back to the United States, chastised by a man who had taken just one lesson in the wringer and the press."

On Childhood, War Years, Bushido, Kung Fu, Professional Boxing, and more...

Basically, the philosophy of the samurai was enlightenment. This is the conclusion that the martial arts masters and the samurai came to and which I learned in all the years I've been involved."

On a purely physical basis, there is no difference between man and animal. But man is different from the animal in that man is a spiritual person. Being a spiritual person, he needs philosophy.

My mother made me study martial arts. She thought that the martial arts could make a person learn respect. The way she put it, "The respect that one human being owes to another you can only learn in a combative environment." She felt that the tenets of the Japanese martial arts, being bushido, would make a person, at least, have respect for other human beings, and she felt that respect is the only achievement.

The martial arts are in an environment that's combative, but it is like being in the eye of a typhoon because it is highly philosophical. It's not fighting. Street fighting, on the other hand, is combative, but it is not philosophical.

I earned my first black belt in judo in 1941, but two years prior to that, I toured China and studied tai chi and pakua under Chien Chen Wa, that's how I pronounce it.

that he can begin to apply the next stage of training, knowing when to "kime" or focus, etc. The muscles of the body are used to guide limbs toward its intended target and at a certain point, the muscles are contracted, stopping the motion in an instant and allowing the kinetic energy to be transferred into the target.

The actual thrusting power, which propels the arm or leg, is generated by the strong torquing action of the hips. This is a summation of joint forces or kime. The rotation of body segments gets the most of each joint resulting in a kime or focus. The tightening and relaxing of the correct muscles takes a tremendous amount of concentration and only in the kata can one learn to control his body to respond to his wishes and also exercise the same control over his breathing. This is when the value of the kata is realized.

Kiai helps to maximize body tension at the moment of impact. When the movements of a kata become so familiar that the kata can be practiced without hesitation or thinking, the mental relationship to both the body and the kinetic pattern will be released and a deep meditative awareness will develop. A mind-body awareness will be absorbed. An energy pattern will result in a controlled concentration.

Past studies have shown that practitioners of Zen and Yoga display an alpha wave (these waves are steady fluctuations reflecting electrical activity of the brain with a frequency of 8-13 cycles per second) activity during periods of meditation. A kata expert develops the alpha wave state in an active, or potentially active state. He is highly tuned to the totality of his surroundings a radical.awakening and directional awareness.

When confronted by an assailant, one who has reached this level immediately becomes tuned to and no longer feels apart from the surroundings, but at one with his environment. No thought, no emotions, such as anger or fear. The assailant is regarded as an extension of oneself. This is the quintessence of kata.

In traditional karate as practiced today in Okinawa and Japan, the kata repertoire described from Shorinji Ryu can be traced to two main trunks and a minor one A kata either comes from Shuri or Naha. and also to a minor degree from Tomari. The three localities are in Okinawa. As mentioned before, the main impetus to empty-hand kata came from Okinawa. One practices Shuri-Te, Naha-Te, or Tomari-Te. Some schools practice a mixture.

The first kata practiced in a school or ryu prior to 1905, when ltosu

Sensei composed the Pin-An (Heian) katas, were either Patsal or Seisan.

The traditional katas today are as follows:

Seisan – with two main streams – either Shurite seisan or Nahate seisan. Seisan literally means 13 japanese schools, notably Shotokan, call it Hangetsu.

Pin-An (Heinan) – 1,2,3,4,5. These katas were designed for school children in Okinawa. Pin an means peace, tranquility, a peaceful mind.

Naihanchi (Tekki) – 1,2,3. Sideways fighting (back against the wall); fighting on home ground with surreptitious steps.

Patsai (Bassai) – *to thrust asunder and breach a fortress*, has four distinctive types: that of Oyadorari, Matsumura, Matsumora and Itosu. Matsumora was from Tomaru. The oldest kata was Oyadornari.

Kushanku (Kanku) – named after the famous martial artist Kushanku also called Koshokun. The Japanese call it looking at the sky. Today, we have the Yara, Itosu (Dai and Sho) and the Shiho Kushanku.

Chinto (Gankaku) – *fighting to the East*; some claim it is a Chinese martial artist's name. There is the Yabu Matsumora and Itosu Chinto.

Wankan (Matsukaze) – *a king's crown; the pine tree wind.*

Wanshu – the prototype of the modern Empi – the swallow kata.

Wan do – *the king's way*. This Wankan and Wanshu are from China to Tomari, Okinawa.

Rohai or Lohai (Meikyo) – *the vision of a white hern or flamingo*; a clear mirror. Itosu Lohai 1,2.3; and Matsumora Lohai.

Jion, Jiin, Jitte – *temple sound, temple ground, and ten hands*. These three katas are typically Tomari-Te.

Chinte (Chinti) – *the winning hand*; although used in many styles, it is a Tomari-Te kata.

Ananku – *the light from the south*. A kata used quite extensively by the Shito Ryu.

Unssu – *Cloud hands.*

Sochiri – *The grand prize and fighting old man.*

Niseishi (Nijushiho) – *24 steps* – Neiseishi, Unssu, and Sochin belong to the Araki-Ha. Although all major schools now use these katas as they are very advanced, with many hidden techniques.

Useishi, Oseishi (Gojushiho) –- the ultimate kata in both Shuri-Te and Tomari-Te. It is the Phoenix kata with 54 steps. The Phoenix is the leg-

On Yamaguchi, Nishiyama, Norris, Hayashi, Yagi and Seagal

The interest in martial arts in South America is as great, if not greater, than in any other part of the world. Each country in South America has very strong karate roots, mostly with the (Shotokan–oriented) JKA (Japan Karate Association) or with shito-ryu.

Unfortunately, the people there who are taking karate are of the middle and upper classes. The poor people cannot take karate; they are far too poor to take lessons. In the United States and Canada, people from all walks of life take martial arts, even if they are working-class people. This is because the standard of living is very high.

When I hold seminars in South America, I stay completely on the physical level, mainly because of the language barrier and the fact I have to use an interpreter. I cannot gain access into what the people are actually thinking. There probably is interest in the philosophy, but there is no time for it.

"As the 1973 Black Belt instructor of the year, do you have opinions on what qualifications an individual should have before attempting to teach others martial arts?"

I am a traditionalist. I believe that if a person wants to teach and is totally in charge of the teaching, not under a senior, he should be at least a fourth dan (degree Black belt). This is because the fourth dan is a turning point in traditional karate. When a person is fourth dan, he can teach wherever he wants; he doesn't have to teach under the supervision of somebody.

It seems, however, that a fourth dan in one organization can be drastically different from a fourth dan in another organization.

Just as 12 inches is 12 inches everywhere, and 100 pounds is 100 pounds in any country, so should the criteria for martial arts be consistent, but is not because of so many different styles. The basic criteria should always be the same. If it is not the same, you will always have politics involved where a person gets a dan level through favor and not merit. If this problem was only confined to, say, the Japanese martial arts it would be an easy goal to overcome. But if you include the Korean and Chinese styles, their criteria is different. There will always be a controversy regarding ranks, because each country has caused standards to be different. The best way to judge the basic standard is to judge the time put in. The shodan (first degree black belt) is the hardest dan to get because before a person can get a shodan in Japanese karate system, not only is technical efficiency a requirement, but character is also important. The dan is given on character, so there should be a minimum requirement in my opinion. Although some people in one year can be just as skillful as a person who has taken karate five years, the former character may be lacking. For any sensei to really know a student, he has to have the student for at least three years. I saw recently that a seven-year-old girl got a shodan. That is impossible because she has not matured.

From my viewpoint, in the Western Hemisphere, outside of Japan, the finest karate instructor is Hidetaka Nishiyama. He is second to none. I have worked with Nishiyama Sensei and have watched the man in action. He is purely Japanese in his mentality. In my opinion, on a technical basis, Nishiyama Sensei is the best in Japanese karate. Teruo Hayashi of the shitoryu style is also an excellent teacher. As a demonstrator, he is almost second to none. His demonstrations are spectacular. Even now, when I am talking to Nishiyama and the JKA people, they say that as a demonstrator, Hayashi stands on top. Yagi Meitoku is an excellent goju ryu specialist. Also, I have to mention (the late) Gogen Yamaguchi. Another person, who is not too well known in the Western world, is Kinjo Hiroshi. He is second to none as a historian. For sheer physical power, not for karate the art itself per se, I knew Mas Oyama when he was in his prime, and I think he stood at the top in that area.

I personally know Chuck Norris; we performed together in Paris. He is an excellent instructor in his style. Not only is he an excellent instructor, he is also a gentleman, with an emphasis on the word gentle. That is the reason why he is so successful in the movie industry. He overcomes any lack in technical ability with sheer perseverance, and I've always had a high respect for him. With respect to Steven Seagal, I've never met him; I've only seen him in his movies. From what I I've heard, he trained in aikido, and from what I've read and if the accounts are correct, he must be bet – making the words – the vocabulary appears elementary.

The masters. knowing this, taught a selection of kata in sets of three or five in the case of children (the Pinan Katas were devised specifically for this purpose). Arakaki, for example, taught just three or five in the Niseishi, Sochin and Unsu. When one can. read, write, and speak a language, then one can exist in the particular society for which the language was meant to be.

25 Years a Student

By Don Warrener

Richard Kim is a man of contrasts. He is a stern taskmaster, yet a compassionate human being. He is known for his grueling morning workouts, yet his Tai Chi classes are so relaxing that they are meditation in motion! But one thing is for certain: anyone who has ever trained with this '20th Century Samurai' has come away from each class with a wealth of knowledge that only a true karate master can divulge. I received my shodan from Sensei Kim in 1968 and my fourth dan in 1978. 1 began to travel with him in 1973 and ended up seeing much of the world, as he taught in Paris, France; Toronto, Canada; San Francisco, California; Las Vegas, Nevada; Boston, Massachusetts; Kyoto, Japan, and other locations. Early on, I developed the habit of bringing a pen and notebook on these trips and recording much of what Sensei Kim had to share with me. The following are some of the questions I asked over the years, and the wisdom of his answers.

May 1973

Don Warrener: When we line up with the senior on our right and they bow first, is there any special significance to this?

Sensei Kim: Yes there is. This is where we practice respect, compassion, and gratitude.

We show respect for our seniors, compassion for our juniors and gratitude for our parents, our country, our teachers, our friends, and by all means, not least, our God, whoever we conceive Him to be.

May 1973

Don Warrener: What is the goal of a martial artist?

Sensei Kim: A goal is only a milestone. Martial artists should strive to develop a purpose. The ultimate purpose of a martial artist is to become an artist of life in all ways: physically, mentally and spiritually.

June 1976

Don Warrener: Why do most kata end on the same spot that they started?

Sensei Kim: This is very important from a philosophical point of view. When we come into life we enter with nothing and when we leave, we leave with nothing. In other words, by starting the kata and ending the kata on the same spot, we are physically realizing this important philosophical lesson. We learn from this that what we do when we are here on earth is very important; so no matter what it is that we do, we must always do our very best and give 100 percent all the time.

March 1977

Don Warrener: In fighting, are there different stages that we go through in our development?

Sensei Kim: Yes, there are several stages that we go through in our development. The first is: block, getaway. This is the lowest level, usually for white belts. The second is block, then counter. This is the level that we usually reach about green belt. It is very elementary, but far superior to those who have never trained. The third level is to block and counter simultaneously. This is the level that we reach around shodan and some, in fact most, never get beyond this level. The fourth level is to preempt the attack. This is the stage where you must try to feel your opponent and try to beat him to the attack; in other words, when he conceives the thought of punching or striking you. You don't wait for him to even move; you strike him first. The fifth level is where you are not there. At this stage you have learned the highest level of combat, and that is where there is no combat. You learn to avoid it before it even happens.

vation of nature and when in deep meditation, the dragon and the phoenix became real. Therefore, they devised the principle of escape."

No one martial arts school can claim, with authority, that any particular technique sprang from their system. This is particularly true of the dragon tail, the eagle wing or the phoenix beak, which is embodied in all kata (forms) in all schools. This is the value of the kata, the language that the ancients used to transmit their secrets. If you ever had the impression that the world is full of morons, all you have to do is to listen to the claims made by various schools that such and such a technique is the sole property of their system. Unfortunately, morons do exist and such claims will always be made.

Since all masters, or most of them anyway, are geniuses, all of them once embroiled in a war or in a fight, came across the inescapable fact that the eyes and testicles were the best target areas. If a blow is properly delivered to either of these two areas it renders a person temporarily out of commission, great for a weaker person giving them enough time to escape. For a strong person there is plenty of time to deliver a follow-up coup de grace.

"Stand loose, the looser the better," Sensei cried out. "Relax and wait for the attacker to come within distance. Measure your distance carefully and at the right moment, strike! Use the knife edge of your hand – never your fist and as soon as you feel contact, keep on moving and get away."

I must have practised the technique a thousand times, both in kata and kumite. (All styles have one of the three principles embodied somewhere their advanced forms. Their posture, position, or name may be different, but the principle is the same. The principles are especially rigorously emphasized in weapons, because one false move could mean death.) The one element that stuck in my mind and made a lot of sense was the importance of being physically relaxed and mentally alert. Sensei said, "If you tense your body, or any part of your body preparatory to a strike or block, you will feel strong and believe that you will hit strong. But that is an incorrect belief, you are not doing it right. Always use the principle of the explosion and then the hit."

Suppose that you are trapped in an alley with someone threatening you with great bodily harm. If you choose not submit to his demands, what then? First, look around, check for a way to escape, then relax, draw a deep breath. As soon as your attacker comes within range, deliver either the dragon tail, the eagle wing or the beak of the phoenix, depending on the situation. Then, get away as fast as possible. This method is guaranteed to work. Although I cannot emphasize it too strongly that escape is crucial. Do not, I repeat, do not stay and watch your stricken attacker... you will more than likely lose the advantage of surprise and, most important, the time you need to get away.

Funakoshi Gichin, in his book 'Karate Do My Way of Life', wrote that when he was in his 80s, he was attacked by a young punk and used the dragon tail principle to subdue and hold the man until the police came. Since we are not all as learned as Funakoshi Gichin, caught in the same situation, we would better use this principle simply to get away safely.

The most effective techniques of physical self defense were developed on the battlefield, in mortal hand-to-hand combat, in one on one duels. The principles and techniques that evolved from that milieu arose out of the sword, such as the sword hand.

It is absolutely not necessary to harden the hands or strengthen the fingers, although if one did it, unquestionably the technique's application would be more devastating.

"Relax," Sensei said. "When your opponent comes towards you, step back, stay loose, and judge the distance. Stand with your left foot forward and your right foot back, lightly on your toes and watch your opponent's left foot. As soon as he steps hard on his left foot or steps forward, take a quick step with your right foot about three inches to the side of his foot; step diagonally and cross your left foot in back of your right foot so that your body turns away from your opponent. With your right hand, hit backwards and up into his groin area with the knife edge of your hand as hard as you can, preferably into his testicles. That, basically, is the dragon tail."

Sensei also told me that if the assailant is a southpaw, to just reverse the position and use the left hand instead. The dragon tail is especially effective against a powerful assailant. However, sometimes you meet an opponent who comes at you en garde, such as a boxer with his left hand extended in front preparing to jab. In that case, it is sometimes advisable to use the eagle wing if a jab is coming at you or the opponent is making feinting motions with his hands. Run in fast and execute what appears to be an X-block against the offending left hand or jab. Don't stop with the block; continue on with both your hands describing an arc like the spread of an leave. It is just a matter of time, and after all, it is natural. The bear cub leaves its mother, as does the fawn leave the doe, so "the student leaves the sensei. It always hurts, but life is like a river: As we travel down it, we bounce between the banks of pleasure and pain, but we keep on going.

September 1983

Don Warrener: What is the main difference between Japanese and North American martial artists?

Sensei Kim: The main difference is that the Japanese student accepts unconditionally what the sensei says. The North American martial artist questions everything that is presented. This attitude can be seen more so in jiyu kumite matches where in the traditional ippon shobu type of kumite, a center referee can alone call a point, while in the non-traditional type of sparring, you must have three people out of five see, the point to get a point. The premise is that the North Americans come at the problem from the point of view that this way no one can be cheated as it takes two out of three. The Japanese come at the situation from the premise that everyone is honest and, therefore, the person with the best view should be able to call the point, and in most cases this is the referee.

November 1983

Don Warrener: I have always wondered why the crane, carp and cherry blossom were so important to the samurai. Can you explain?

Sensei Kim: You are correct; these three are very important to the samurai's way of thinking, each for a separate purpose. First, the crane. The crane is the only bird that can kill the mighty eagle; he climbs high above the eagle then he dives beak first and pierces the eagle from above, similar again to the samurai's way of thinking. One cut of the sword equal's one life, so it had better be your best stroke as it may be your Last.

When the carp is taken from the water and is about to have its head cut off, he will stop squirming and fighting like all the other fish do. In other words, it accepts death with dignity.

The cherry blossom is also one of the revered symbols of the samurai. The cherry blossom is the only bloom that will fall off the tree in full bloom. In other words, the cherry blossom accepts death when it is in its prime, another quality the samurai admired greatly.

 One of Sun Tzu's philosophies was to always leave an opening.

June 1984

Don Warrener: Can you explain the difference between kyo and jitsu?

Sensei Kim: These are states of mind that the samurai were aware of when they fought. This still applies today to jiyu kumite for the highly skilled fighters. Kyo literally means an opening, and jitsu means guarded. In other words, when your opponent is in kyo, he is psychologically open. He may have lost his focus or concentration or become too relaxed. When he is in jitsu he is like a coiled snake, ready to attack and his mind is sharp, focused, just waiting for you to make a mistake so he can charge in at you.

January 1986

Don Warrener: What are the character traits we as martial artists must guard against?

Sensei Kim: There are three traits we call the three poisons. They are ego, greed and anger.

June 1988

Don Warrener: How did the samurai decide whether or not to do something that he questioned in his mind as being right or wrong?

Sensei Kim: The samurai believed that there is no right way to do a wrong thing. He would test the deed with the three rules of the samurai which are: Is it fair? Is it ethical? Can you look yourself in the mirror after you have done it and still feel good about yourself?

June 1988

Don Warrener: What is your secret to retaining students for so many years?

Sensei Kim: As a teacher, you must satisfy the student with quality teaching, not just physically but also philosophically and psychologically.

March 1989

Don Warrener: What are the main differences between Japanese and Chinese martial artists?

Sensei Kim: The Japanese will teach everything they know in hopes of developing a student who someday will become superior to themselves. In doing this they realize that the only way a student can be superior to them is if they develop a student who is superior to them. The Chinese, on the other hand, never teach everything they know, as they always want to have a secret technique that nobody has been taught. The problem with this is that their art can go to the grave with them.

October 1990

Don Warrener: In the old days of the samurai, was there a caste system, and where did the samurai fit into this system?

Sensei Kim: There was most definitely a caste system in the days of the samurai. This lasted until 1867 when Japan emerged to the rest of the world. The highest was the nobility, followed by the samurai, then came the farmers, and then the businessmen followed by the poor.

June 1992

Don Warrener: What is the deep and real value of kata training?

Sensei Kim: The kata is the martial artist's path to enlightenment, or the silence behind sound. Kata is superior to jiyu kumite because in it you can strike with full force and you can kill your opponent in your mind. When we practice kata we should try to reach the alpha state of consciousness.

June 1992

Don Warrener: When we do a kata, what are the physical characteristics we must emphasize to seek its perfection ?

Sensei Kim: This is a good question. Let me outline several characteristics for you:

• Perform each technique as perfectly as you possibly can.

• When you do a technique, visualize you are applying each one.

• Use maximum speed or power as the move requires.

• When shifting, keep your center of gravity centered.

• Every stance must have stability and balance.

• You must keep your head straight and level; and at all times keep the same height.

• Keep your eyes focused and look to the next direction before you move.

• You must remember to make the combinations separate, yet run one into another.

• Move sharply and crisply from one move to another.

• Between each move you must relax and go soft. This adds to the sharpness of each move. When you perform a strike, make sure that you exhale always.

• The rhythm or pace of a kata depends on the application of the moves.

• The goal of a kata is to come back to the embuson (starting point), exactly where you started.

Wisdom and perception is what Sensei Richard Kim will, without a doubt, go down in the annals of karate for having. He will be remembered for his technical knowledge, but more so for his wisdom and perception, which only the great karate masters are able to develop.

"The Legend" Richard Kim – Karate's Guiding Light

Soft tradewinds were playing over Honolulu's Kapiolani Park that lazy Sunday afternoon. Clusters of people were scattered about, enjoying picnics, talking, having a few beers – some having a few too many.

There was excited chatter about Lee, the Korean school teacher who had put away six or seven burly Hawaiians when they attacked him on the way home from church. He had laid those boys out flat! Kicked them like a piledriver!

One little boy, who had seen it happen, described the fight in glowing detail to his parents. He watched his father's mood grow uglier with each beer, as the man eyed the Korean across the grass. With a sinking heart, the boy saw his father rise on unsteady feet and challenge Lee.

"Hey! I'm gonna give you people some entertainment!" he shouted, and lunged for the Korean. Two powerful blows to the chest, and the boy's father went down, his nose splattering blood over the startled onlookers.

He lurched to his feet, and as Lee moved in, the man lowered his head like a battering ram. With a roar, he crashed into the Korean, who dropped like a stone.

"Now that's the way to use your head," the father crowed. The fight was over before it had scarcely begun. But the boy was stunned, and his mother was not proud of the victory. She told the boy later: "You are going to learn to use your head, but not that way. You must learn the respect one human being owes another. You will learn to fight, but you will learn through the martial arts. You will learn to be a gentleman."

Thus, Richard Kim began his lifelong involvement with the martial arts because his mother firmly believed that respect is the only worthwhile achievement, and that it is best learned through the tenets of the Japanese code of bushido (the way of the warrior).

Because of his mother's foresight and staunch beliefs, Richard Kim stands in the world today as one of a handful of internationally recognized masters of the martial arts. One of those talented few who have become living legends. Yet, even in this select group, Kim stands apart from the rest because of his unique character, intellect, and personality. With a foot in both worlds, East and West, Richard Kim is today's classical man.

Growing up in Hawaii gave young Kim an understanding of Western ways, as well as an appreciation of his Japanese/Korean cultural heritage. Ethnic divisions existed in Honolulu in the early '30s, and there were plenty of territorial squabbles. Street fights helped Kim shape what he calls his "strategy." When he was only seven, he was frequently attacked by an older boy who considered himself a tough guy. Kim asked one of his first karate instructors, Arakaki, what to do. He was given some simple and sound advice.

"Strategy is what you need," his instructor told him. "Get him when he least expects it." So Kim waited one evening until the boy had finished stuffing himself at the dinner table, and then knocked on his door. The second the ruffian opened the door, Kim pounced on him like a cat, giving the bully a surprise that was not soon forgotten.

Strategy, and the concept of "Give it your best shot, it may be your only chance," are important lessons Arakaki gave his young student, and they are theories Kim still teaches his students today.

Kim's formal martial arts training began in judo at age six. A bit later, he studied his first karate with Kentsu Yabu and Arakaki. These learned men were only the forerunners in Kim's vast exposure to the martial arts greats of the time. Later, he would study with instructors Tachibana and Matsu in Honolulu, and train in China with Chao Hsu Lai (pa kua and shorinji-ryu kenpo) and Chen Chin Yuan (tai chi), plus a host of others whose names are unknown to most in the Western world. He absorbed all he could from the teachings of these men, beginning in Hawaii, then moving to the Orient. It was in Japan that he became a disciple of Kotaro Yoshida, who Kim considers an unsung genius of the martial arts.

From his earliest days, Kim has been a man of conviction and efficiency. He soon realized what was outdated and ineffective in the many techniques and styles he learned, discarding what he considered superfluous.

"The best offense disarms your opponent and defeats him quickly with a minimum of effort," Kim says. "It's the correct application of a technique that is important, not how many times you can do it."

This philosophy holds true for Kim today, and is the basis for his teachings in classes, seminars and clinics across North America and Europe. He teaches primarily shorinji ryu karate, which he learned and polished with a Taoist priest in Shanghai. He holds high black belt degrees in karate, judo, and aiki jujutsu, and is skilled in tai chi, pa kua, hsing-i, and numerous Okinawan and Japanese weapons.

It was during his course of study in the Orient that Kim was stranded in enemy territory by the onset of World War II. As a foreigner, his movements were restricted, so he plunged even deeper into his study of the samurai philosophy and the martial arts. Prior to World War II, Kim had been admitted to the prestigious Nippon Bu Toku Kai (Greater Japan Martial Virtues Association), and he attended classes and honed his skills at the Budo Semman Gakko in Kyoto, Japan.

Kim is as much a philosopher and historian as he is a martial arts instructor. Listening to him lecture, one cannot help but be amazed at the man's extraordinary knowledge and recall of dates, names, incidents and legends from across the centuries. Holder of a Ph.D. in Oriental philosophy, Kim has expanded his horizons to include world history, science, current events... just about everything his mind finds interesting. And he can relate it all, in several languages, in stories and vivid accounts to audiences around the world.

Opportunities to do just that arise often, as he serves as the international representative for the Bu Toku Kai in the U.S., Canada, France and the Philippines, and travels extensively in the course of his administrative duties. Kim's home base is a school in the San Francisco area, where he teaches and lectures, if you can believe it, free of charge.

So vast is his collection of tales and historical events that he has authored many columns and articles, plus three books: Kobudo – Weapons of Matsu Higa, The Weaponless Warrior and The Classical Man, which are must reads for anyone interested in authentic martial arts. They stand as stunning collections of priceless anecdotes and personal encounters with martial greats such as Kotaro Yoshida.

Yoshida's influence on Kim was profound. "Yoshida was the greatest martial artist I ever met," Kim asserts. "He was the shihan-hai (master teacher) in the (Sokaku) Takeda school, a master in all the arts. I believe that he was the greatest all around martial artist Japan has produced in the past 100 years. Mas Oyama feels as I do, Yoshida was his sensei (instructor), too. Oyama wrote a whole section on him in his book, "This Is Karate." Perhaps it was Yoshida who gave Kim his zest for life and lively sense of humor. Certainly he provided Kim with a host of interesting stories. There is no doubt of the reverence in which Kim holds his instructor... much of his book, "The Classical Man", reflects Yoshida's teachings or his influence.

Kim claims it was Yoshida's custom to dress in a kimono and carry a tessan (iron fan). The heavy fan came in handy on at least one occasion, Kim recalls.

"Sensei was in charge of a reclamation project many years ago in Hokkaido, a very mountainous country," he relates. "One New Year's, he was going home after a round of parties. He had had a few drinks and was feeling good. It was pitch dark on the trail, and he bumped into somebody he couldn't see. It was very cold there – it was winter-time – and the person had on a big fur coat. Well, the person made an aggressive move at Yoshida, so he sidestepped and thought, 'Boy, does this guy smell bad!' He hit the person right on the forehead with his tessan, but it took all his skill to land the blow. He heard the person go rolling down the mountainside, so he went on home. The next day it bothered him – he'd never met anyone so ferocious! So he went back up the mountain and discovered his opponent had been a bear! He had killed it with a single stroke from his iron fan."

There are more stories, and with the skill of a true raconteur, Kim tells them with freshness and vitality. For example, he recalls walking in Ikebukuro (a district of Tokyo) with Mas Oyama and an American friend, on their way to dinner.

"He (Oyama) looks like an ordinary man to me," the American said somewhat doubtfully to Kim. He had heard tales of Oyama's feats of strength, but here he saw a man – muscular, yes, but not so special looking. He had expected something more.

Kim laughed and asked, "What did you expect, King Kong?"

The two men chuckled a moment, and then stopped in their tracks as Oyama walked up to a telephone pole and swiftly landed a punch so powerful that the wood was indented with the mark of his fist.

"I saw it with my own eyes," Kim claims emphatically. "The pole was vibrating. My friend took one look and didn't say another word. I was surprised myself."

The story Oyama tells about Yoshida in his book is impressive in its simplicity. Oyama relates that his instructor was so quick that he could catch flies in midair with a pair of chop-sticks! Is it any wonder these men are in awe of Kotaro Yoshida? And yet, his is not one of the well known martial arts names outside Japan and the Bu Toku Kai. Kim does what he can to tell the world of his extraordinary teacher, and of other men of quality whom he feels the world has overlooked.

Kim learned his lessons well with Yoshida – seven long years of grueling and intensive training. Eventually, Kim was selected for the great honor and distinction of becoming the keeper of the menkyo kaiden, the ancient scrolls of the daito-ryu. As holder of the scrolls, he follows in the footsteps of Yoshida, Sokaku Takeda, and other great masters through the centuries, each of whom chose a worthy student to become his successor and carry on tradition.

This respect for tradition blends with a keen awareness of the present and is part of the complexity that is Richard Kim. To become an "artist of life" is the goal he urges for all of his students. Only a tiny fraction of them can ever achieve it; the artist of life holds complete control of everything in and around him or herself – total control of one's life. That is the ultimate goal in the Japanese martial arts. Trying to achieve it takes a lifetime.

In the words of Joe Trent, a longtime student of Kim's, the attempt to become an artist of life is a valuable lesson in itself.

Says Trent, "I've found my training with sensei Kim is not a temporary kind of thing. He serves as a guide, a leader along the path. What I've learned from him has helped me in every part of my life, and it helps me in my dealings with fellow human beings."

To understand Kim, one must realize the intensity of his convictions. A major point he makes to his students is that the prevalent idea of winning at all costs has no place in the martial arts; a concept some so-called martial artists would deny. Kim shows how you can win a battle effectively, but it is your attitude that is paramount. You must win the battle inside yourself first, he declares.

"Fear is the culprit," he states in his book, The Classical Man, "and what makes our training unique from other systems is that we put the emphasis on conquering fear, self, and ego. Defeating the opponent comes afterward."

This attitude is called aiuchi (mutual slaying). You may die, but you will take your opponent with you. You are ready to die, therefore all emotions fade away. It is one of the basic concepts taught to Bu Toku Kai students from the beginning of their training. Some systems impart this idea only to advanced students, or not at all.

Kim explains, "Say we are in a life-and-death match with each other. At the moment of actual confrontation, you may think, 'I can beat this guy, why should I die here? I'll win and go on my way.' That is the intellect taking over. The idea of letting go of life is too terrifying to think about. But that is the whole point! By not letting yourself think of death, you have lost your life.

"Our method of training is to face death with equanimity," Kim adds. "The martial artist, the samurai, reached deep down into his subconscious, and through imagination, re-structured his mind to view death as a passing phenomenon to the beyond, not to be feared, but to be welcomed as something natural to the scheme of things."

Even pain and anger can be handled without trauma in this manner, according to Kim, simply by mind control. He quotes Kotaro Yoshida: "Sensei told us that when emotion takes over, the body stiffens up, gets tense, and this exacerbates pain and fear. You've heard of freezing with fright? It's natural in the animal kingdom, and with men, too. The martial artist understands this and sets the stage for his opponent to be overcome with fear."

You can see this "psyching out" of opponents in the sports world quite frequently, the idea being play upon the enemy's fears, and eliminate your own.

Philosophy is obviously an integral part of Kim's message, and his life.

It is inseparable from the arts, as he sees them. But his views are flexible if need be. He has firm beliefs, and applies them to contemporary matters, because being a traditionalist does not mean rejecting innovation.

Today's sport karate is an example of Kim's flexibility. He believes it is a good thing for those who enjoy it, but he views it as a sport, not as karate, perse. It is only a game for fun and prizes. Traditional karate is a complete way of life that builds character, and the only game is of life and death.

The artist of life, like Richard Kim, strives to adhere to that traditionalist concept, and works always toward the state of mushin (selflessness), letting go of the idea that anything is permanent, including his own life. This concept can be extremely difficult for Westerners to grasp. They tend to get too hung up on the material world because of society's conditioning.

One good method to alter conditioned ways of thinking is meditation, according to Kim. He feels all of us are creatures of habits, some good, some bad, but all formed by need and all reinforced by repetition. It is Kim's conviction that meditation can rid you of all bad habits.

"You can call it praying, self-hypnosis, altered states of consciousness... you are simply going to the world inside, where anything is possible through the power of the mind," he says.

Visualization and imagination are the keys to controlling the mind. You can "think away" the bad habit. But you must truly believe the mind can overcome the habit, and go through the complete process of ridding yourself of it. How long it takes depends on the habit, the training, and how long you work at it.

Kim lectures on subjects like self-hypnosis, alpha waves, current events, political science – you name it. Liberally sprinkled throughout the facts are the never ending supply of stories, tossed in to emphasize or embellish a certain point. When he talks of letting go of the material world, he some times lightens the solemnity by telling about the time he was a millionaire. It happened when he was in China in the '40s, at the close of World War II. Japan had just surrendered, and there was general havoc in Shanghai. Everyone was desperately trying to get out of the city as soon as possible. People were milling about everywhere, there were fires in the streets, and chaos and confusion reigned.

Amidst the disorder, Kim came into possession of a suitcase containing two million Filipino pesos left behind by the fleeing Japanese, and was anxious to get away to a safe place with it. Because the power was out, he was forced to run down many flights of stairs to exit the tall building he was in, taking a good quarter-of-an-hour from top to bottom. He plunged into the crowded street with his precious suitcase only to be stopped by an American military officer, who shouted at him to halt.

After a brief discussion, the officer checked him out and said he could go, but when he saw all the pesos, he shrugged and told Kim, "You might as well throw that on the fire over there, that money is worthless now." So Kim reluctantly tossed the suitcase into the flames and watched his fortune disappear in the huge bonfire.

"You can imagine how I felt a few hours later," Kim laughs, "when I discovered that the pesos were still perfectly good, at two to one American dollars! I had been a millionaire, for at least 15 minutes!"

Kim is indeed a living example of what his students work toward. His influence has been tremendous on those who have been around him for any length of time. Robert Leong has been training with Kim for over 25 years, and serves as his assistant and fellow world traveler. Leong says he is almost completely different from the person he was before he met Kim.

"I started training with Sensei Kim, and have never left him. My training has never stopped," Leong says. "Because of him, my outlook on life is much different than it was years ago."

Kim reaches his students by insisting upon individual development. Kata (forms) is the primary path to self mastery of the individual according to Kim's teachings. He believes kata training is of foremost importance, and adherence to original form a must.

The masters who created the kata movements did so in a state of enlightenment, and it is the student's goal to practice repeatedly in an attempt to attain that same state of awareness. The original creators believed three years was the minimum amount of time to spend learning each kata. To those present-day karateka who clamor for "another kata," Kim chides them to remember, "Is it important to know more, or is it important to know better?"

"Kata teaches fighting skills and living skills at the same time," he insists." The aim of the kata is to make the individual one with the universe, attuned to the kata, attuned with himself. Sparring and self defense with partners are part of the instruction, but it is kata training that is most important.

 An organization falls apart from within, not from the outside.

The minute subtleties of championship form in kata performance are taught each summer by Kim to members of the All America Karate Federation (AAKF) kata team during the annual camp at the University of California at San Diego. Team members strive to perfect and ready themselves for world competition under his expert eye.

Hidetaka Nishiyama, AAKF chairman, is Kim's teaching counterpart at the summer camps, along with notable guest instructors. Kim has great admiration for Nishiyama, calling him "a tall tree in the karate forest." He sees Nishiyama as a truly dedicated martial artist, one whose life is "karate that was, karate that is, karate that will be, a rare man who teaches with blessing in his heart."

Teaching fills a major portion of Kim's life: seminars, weekly classes, lectures, etc. His life goal is to establish a college similar to that he attended in Japan. Organization for such a school has already begun, under the auspices of the Bu Toku Kai, and a search for a suitable site is under way. The curriculum will include academics, as well as the martial arts, insuring that graduates will be not only educated individuals, but also technically sound martial artists.

Volumes could be written expounding and recording the theories of Richard Kim, theories he has spent a lifetime constructing and evaluating, always listening, learning. Cataloging material to savor and share with audiences across two continents. His magnetism and presence affect all who come within his sphere. Instructor Rod Sanford, a sandan (third-degree black belt), reflects on his longtime association with Kim: "I've heard sensei Kim referred to as philosopher, scholar, historian and priest. To me, he's all that, and more... a man who has gone beyond teaching me the fighting arts and has taught me how to apply martial arts concepts to everyday living. He has taught me a way of life.

"He teaches that we should have love, respect and compassion for all our fellow human beings," Sanford adds, "that each of us are equal. And as I see him teach, I see the compassion that he has for all his students. I watch him make himself available to all his students, regardless of rank. He listens to their personal problems and opinions, then patiently guides them on the path. He teaches them to be individuals, to find strength within themselves. But most of all, he has taught me gratitude to my parents, to my friends, to my country, and to God. With all of this, I wonder how I can ever adequately thank the man."

Such statements are not unusual when Kim's students speak of him. From that determined little boy who would not let a bully defeat him, has come a gentleman in every sense of the word – today's classical man.

Of course, Kim himself learned from a number of fine gentlemen, including Kotaro Yoshida. Yoshida, who is perhaps best exemplified by Kim, told the following story to Kim and a group of students one rainy evening long ago. Kim has never forgotten its message.

"Suppose a master swordsman like Musashi Miyamoto and a Zen monk were here," Yoshida began, "and they decided to try to cut the rain with their skills. The question was put to Musashi and the monk how they would cope. Miyamoto said, 'I shall draw my sword, walk out, cut the rain, walk around where I made the cut, and not get wet.' He went out, ran in a circle, made his famous cut, and returned. The monk examined him and said, 'There is a drop of rain on your sleeve. Your magic was not enough.' So the monk went out, sat down, did zazen (seated meditation), and came back. 'You're soaking wet!' Miyamoto cried. 'I'm not wet in my mind,' was the monk's reply."

At this point, Yoshida explained that both men were possessed with "attachment." Miyamoto wanted to be the best swordsman who ever lived, and the monk wanted to achieve satori (enlightenment). Both were attached to their ambition. In their attachment, they forgot the meaning of life.

Richard Kim smiles as he recalls a student asking Yoshida, "What would you do, sensei?" Yoshida, without another word, got up, opened his umbrella, and walked out into the rain.

Oldster plugs "Karate Power"

Newspaper article, circa 1985

Richard Kim wants to strike a blow for karate as a sport. "There are still traditionalists in karate who don't believe in the sporting aspect of karate and I must admit that at first I was one of them," said Kim, who is the highest ranking black belt in North America. A San Franciscan who has been involved in the martial arts for 50 years.

"Let's just say I'm over 60," Kim is a ninth degree black belt in karate and fourth degree black belt in judo.

Although karate has its roots in the middle ages, it wasn't until about 1957 that karate developed a sporting aspect.

Many of the traditionalists rejected that, however, because karate as a sport, where punches are pulled, is diametrically opposed to karate as a martial art.

"One of my concerns then and even today is that in the sporting aspect of karate too much emphasis is placed on winning and consequently the philosophy of karate is lost," said Kim, who is 65 according to a press release.

"It's good to enter and nice to win, but we 'should be teaching that winning is not the overriding factor." Although he first opposed it, Kim has come around and believes the pluses far outweigh the minuses in karate as a sport.

"It has done a lot of good.It has given karate good exposure worldwide. It is a healthy development in the evolution of karate – a very necessary development."

"In the old days, before we had contests and tournaments, some people in Okinawa would abuse their skills and try to pick fights on the streets. In fact, there was a certain area of the city where you would walk with your Gi (karate out fit) on and that was a sign that you wanted to fight," said Kim. "it was a problem."

Exhibitions and contests are a way of life in karate now.

Although Kim is semi-retired – he still gives lectures throughout the world – he still has one more ambition.

"I would like to see karate included in the Olympics. The spirit of the Olympics is what we should be shooting for. I could retire happy if we were accepted. I know it's not right around the corner, but we'll keep working towards it.

Bu Toku kai Newsletter

March 1974

Frank Gaviola has come into his own as a kata champion of note. Recently in the University of California, Riverside, he defeated Kosugi and Ichiyamagi of Japan to take 1st place; during the eliminations he eliminated Iwakabe, a kata champion who took first place in the AAKF in 1970 and 1972. Until that date, Iwakabe had defeated the best in the Bu Toku kai, the likes of Leong, Molinar and others. Also at Las Vegas, Feb. 16, 1974, Gaviola took both kata and weapons championship against the best of several ryus, including Shotokan champions and Kung-Fu experts of the White Crane School.

Don Warrener, our Secretary in Canada and personal representative of Sensei Kim, holds the world championship in brick breaking. He has broken more bricks in a given period of time than any other living person and his world record is listed In the Guinness Book of Records; similar to a World Almanac. We believe his world records will stand for a long time and will not be topped as long as he is active.

James Miyaji reports that the Bu Toku Kai is now teaching at the Shingon teaching Shu temple at Haleiws. He is teaching a group of children under age of thirteen and we expect some day to see a champion among them.

Richard Lee reports that the Bu Toku Kai is now registered with the French authorities and if a Bu Toku Kai Instructor from another country should desire to teach in France, a great obstacle has been removed as far as getting a permit to teach. Permits to teach or work in France are not easy to come by and the Bu Toku Kai France has made it easy for qualified karate instructors certified by the Bu Toku Kai to obtain a permit. Richard Kim and others will make a trip to Paris in the near future and Richard Lee reports that both the Paris and Marseille branches are waiting for the visit.

Richard Kim, with assistance by Cal Avila, held a seminar for the Desert Karate Association at Palm Springs, California. The seminar was hosted by Summer Hardy, the President of the Desert Karate Association, an affiliate of the Japan Karate Association, and over one hundred students took part in the six hour seminar. Richard Kim taught for four hours and lectured for two hours interspersed between the rigorous teaching. As many of the students were Shotokan practitioners, the Bu Toku Kai methods and philosophy was something different and enthusiastically received. The kata Ananku was taught at the seminar as this kata was outside of the purview of Shotokan katas.

In our next newsletter, we will publish a list of the clubs in the East Coast of America that have been put on probation and of those who are no longer with the Bu Toku Kai in that region, mostly in New York.

The Ultra Secret

In this world of violence and aberrational behavior, purely physical self-defense may not be sufficient for all circumstances or conditions. What is the answer? Must we then support those who proclaim our right to bear arms? I once posed this question to Sensei.

"Unfortunately," Sensei said, "too much emphasis is placed on physical self-defense and the whole man is overlooked. Irrespective of how skillful a person becomes, physically there is always someone better. A challenge is always there. But if you become the ultra man, all challenges cease. And how do you become the ultra man? By mastering the circle of power and the ultra secret."

According to Sensei, the ultra secret is the key to the ultra man and perfect defense, because once one has mastered the ultra secret, all attacks and animosity cease. In plain words, we are all just a bundle of energy. It is energy that keeps us alive. Energy in its pure form just remains "inneutral," so to speak. Depending on our state of mind, the energy takes form and expresses itself through the mechanisms of love, hate, anger, sex, envy, jealousy, ambition, happiness, etc. If you look beyond the expression, you will see the source of pure energy. And if you are able to control the energy by returning it to the source from whence it sprang, you have become the ultra man: not through controlling an expression by stopping it which is merely delaying the eventual and more intense expression but by reuniting the energy with its source.

How do you do this? By meditating the way masters do: not by sitting down and contemplating the belly button, but by using the expressions of energy. The samurais who found the ultra secret use danger to meditate. They reasoned that anger was one of the strongest and most violent of the mechanisms that energy used for expression; by using the expression of anger to meditate, the masters found that they could go to the source and by reaching the source they found that anger subsided and pure energy welled up, giving you strength. You can meditate on any expression.

However, the energy that takes the form of white heat, such as anger, is the easiest to follow. This very simplicity also posed the most difficult obstacle, because the expression was always more satisfying than the meditation. It is easier to vent your rage than to follow your anger back to the source. That is why most people find it easier to meditate while sitting.

The masters meditated at any time. When an expression of energy asserted itself, a master took a deep breath and traced the energy back to the source. Those who kept pure energy at its source without giving it an escape mechanism felt humility and a peace of mind. Buddha and Jesus were examples on a universal scale. Oriental philosophy teaches us that we all have Buddha natures; according to Sensei, the ultra secret is the key to the Buddha nature in us.

When is the best time to meditate? At any time. The samurai meditated at all times. We are not talking of formal meditation under prescribed procedures; we are talking, of real meditations the way the enlightened did.

Any and all emotion can be used as the vehicle for meditation – to get to the source of pure energy before it took the form that was given by the mind.

The samurai used kata for meditation.

The true meaning and value of the kata have been lost in most martial arts schools. In fact, the ignorant have degraded it as classical deadwood. You will note that those who do not know the value and true purpose of kata always espouse the need for physical excellence. Without realizing that the true fight is with life itself. The man who conquers himself can easily conquer the outside because then no obstacle is too great.

If you do not nave the luxury of a martial arts sensei to lead the way, just use your moods to trace yourself back to the source. If you happen to be in the martial arts, you will realize that the kata adapt to different moods or evoke moods. So much the better, but if one does not know the martial arts, any emotion can show the way to the source and pure energy.

Do not think! Feel! If you think, you will check and stop; you will not be able to go to the source. The energy will take a different turn. Don't do anything with the energy; just feel and follow the energy back to where it comes from. If you succeed, you will know. That is real knowledge, universal knowledge – not the type of knowledge you learn in school, but the knowledge that has existed from the beginning. You just have to tap it.

The samurais who tapped this were not afraid to die.

What is the difference between academic knowledge and the knowledge that has always been there from the beginning?

The knowledge that you learn in school is public knowledge which you get from using your head and your intellect. You listen with your head and learn with your head. There is nothing wrong with it. Modern civilization could not function without the fruits of public knowledge. But it is limited, and not everybody in the world can access public knowledge. Many do not even know the three basics of reading, writing and arithmetic.

It is beyond debate that without public knowledge you cannot begin to know about the world around you. You would not even be able to read this magazine.It is important, and don't let anyone tell you different! But its main function is to tell you about the material world, the finite world; it cannot tell you about the real person in you, because that is real knowledge, universal knowledge.

Real knowledge is personal, private, and universal. It is private and personal because only you can discover the inner man in you. The method can be shown to you, but the discovery is yours and yours alone. Real knowledge is universal because every human being has the capacity to discover himself. It is not limited to any one race, religion, creed, or selected few. The samurais knew this. Those who succeeded became the ultra man.

How do you get to the knowledge that has been there from the beginning? "Do not listen with your head, but listen with your heart;" I must have heard that a thousand times from my sensei. Listen with your heart, feel with your heart, act with your heart. Especially when it comes to the fight.

Meditation will not be true meditation if you think with the head. By only thinking with the head, you simply postpone whatever emotion is trying to express itself as it wells up from the pure energy latent in you. By listening with the heart and feeling with the heart, you will be able to go inside and follow the method to the ultra secret. Only with the heart can compassion take over from suppression and reveal the true man.

What happens when you discover the real man? You will become humble and realize that you are more than physical, that you are a spiritual being, one with God; or as they say in the Orient, the Buddha in you will come out. Enlightenment.

Even if you do not reach enlightenment, the way will give you peace of mind and improve your physical capacity. After all, champions have more or less stumbled on some facet of the way. But unfortunately, it leaves them when they quit their game or sport.

With you, it will never leave; once you start on the way. You will remain there. The personal peace that you never realized you had will keep you there. The knowledge that has always been there from the beginning will take over.

The Mysterious Elegance of Okinawa Te

Okinawan karate is karate in its purest form.

Usually, when people speak of Okinawan and Japanese karate, they are thinking of the same thing. But only the physical part is the same, the exoteric part. The big difference between them is that Japanese added the samurai philosophy to the karate they learned from the Okinawan. That made their version quite distinct from the original. Of course, the Okinawans also had a type of zen, esoteric philosophy, but it was not thoroughly impregnated as it came to be in Japan.

Okinawan karate is different from Chinese kenpo, although its fountainhead is from China. Te as it was originally called, is purely physical.

Regardless of the style, whether it was goju from the city of Naha, shuri styles from Shuri,or Tomari-te, each style remained separate from the others. They never took ideas from each other, it was a very Chinese type of attitude. The Chinese are very conservative and traditional that way. That influence lived on in Okinawa, and to some extent in Japan, too."

"Despite some fierce resistance from ultra-nationalists, Gichin Funakoshi became the fountainhead of Japanese karate because, Funakoshi was a cultured and educated man. He could speak the Japanese language, and gave the Okinawan art the respectability it needed and deserved. He managed to overcome the prejudice against anything not-Japanese by presenting demonstrations at the universities. By gaining the support of the academic and professional classes, karate became firmly established.

Funakoshi's philosophy was that kata practice was more than sufficient to prepare oneself for times of need, and considered jiyu kumite (free-fighting) belittling to the art.

He brought just 16 kata with him to Japan, believing it would take a lifetime to master them. He chose the kata that were best suited for physical stress and self-defense. He took the specialty from each school,s o he was the first to mix the styles, in a very elementary degree.

Now, when you look at karate in Japan, it is eclectic – a little bit from here, a little bit from there. It is no longer pure. Perhaps it has developed into a superior form, if you want to use the word superior. Is taking the best from each school superior,compared to using the best from a single school? That's a philosophical question... are the best five better than the best one?

Once the Okinawan style gained a foothold in Japan, other masters came from the Ryukyu Islands to jump on the bandwagon, so to speak. Kenwa Mabuni brought his shito style, Chojun Miyagi introduced goju-ryu, plus Choki Motobu and others.

Kata is the heart of karate, all kata begin and end with defensive moves – *karate ni sente nashi* – never strike first, never strike in anger. Some people in America have forgotten this is a basic tenet of karate.

Some Americans have completely expanded the idea of combining styles, trying to find the one they think is best. But Americans have not succeeded in perfecting or refining their art, because they have neglected the philosophy. They look for what they believe to be the best, from a personal or subjective point of view. They might consider the best is what works in fighting with gloves on, or in kickboxing. There's nothing wrong with pro karate, or with kickboxing, but the emphasis there has become purely physical, and they have lost sight of the philosophical level. Not karate, per se. It's purely exoteric. Now, I feel that any art, to be complete, has to have both esoteric and exoteric components. It has to have the physical, and also the mental and spiritual, as well.

"I teach Japanese karate because it has these components. My background includes Chinese styles, my first teachers were Okinawan," Kim explained. "I believe that Japanese karate is a complete art."

In other words, when the art is complete, it practically becomes a religion because it is the total expansion of self. The martial artist comes to know that the human being is propelled by self interest. To overcome that self interest, you have to overcome the material world. We're all too hung up in the material world.

The religion of the martial arts is Buddhism because it accepts the fact that man's nature is violent and must be controlled. Looking only at the world outside, Western religions say, 'an eye for an eye, a tooth for a tooth.' That idea has caused a lot of trouble for mankind.

You have to recognize that what exists inside you, exists outside. For example: You wake up mad, nothing looks good all day, the coffee tastes terrible! But when you wake up feeling good, what a wonderful day! What delicious coffee! But, it's the same coffee.

You have to develop the world inside, and become an artist of life. That's the whole thrust and direction of the martial arts. Okinawa te was pure in the physical sense, but it lacked the completeness necessary for an artist of life. Once you become an artist of life, you see reality.

Everybody tends to believe that the world they see is the world that is. Not so. It's all emotions, formed by habits – good ones and bad ones. In the martial arts, we try to develop good habits. Meditation is the only way to get rid of bad habits. You must go to the world inside.

The samurai knew about this hundreds of years ago. Perhaps the terminology was different, but the technique was the same. They knew meditation was the only way to get to the world inside and cure themselves.

Meditation teaches you to control yourself and the outside world. You have peace of mind, and violence is no problem. The person who goes inside can handle any problem, because they can handle them selves. Once you reach into the world inside, the world outside is no problem. It's only a reflection."

Over 50 years of study qualifies Richard Kim as one of the most respected names in the martial arts world. He speaks eloquently, but it is his sense of humor and air of a raconteur that captures his listeners' attention. At seminars, camps, clinics, and classes throughout the world, he shares his wealth of knowledge.

"What is the difference between a man of Tao and a little man?"

"It is simple. When the little man receives his first dan, he can hardly wait to run home and shout at the top of his voice to tell everyone he made his first dan. Upon receiving his second dan, he will climb to the roof tops and shout to the people. Upon receiving his third dan, he will jump into his automobile and parade through town with horns blowing, telling one and all about his third dan."

"When a man of Tao receives his first dan, he will bow his head in gratitude. Upon receiving his second dan, he will bow his head and shoulders. Upon receiving his third dan, he will bow to the waist and quietly walk alongside the wall so that people will not see him or notice him."

"Funakoshi was a man of Tao, a humble man. He preached an essential humility that was rooted in the true perspective of things. He placed no emphasis on competitions, record breaking or championships. He placed emphasis on individual self perfection and he believed in the common decency and respect one human being owed to another."

The Ease of Power

1969

"If a person misses a hip type of throw, he can easily be countered as he comes out of it. With the ouchigari, there is no double movement like going in and turning the hips; the ouchigari is one, forward movement." There is no discussion on the subject; Kim has reached a conclusion and for him that is now law.

"Sawaii, who had been known to have participated in 105 fights in China and had won all of them, boasted only eight "secret" techniques."

"The correct application of any technique is what is important."

"There are many karatekas who believe in taking this form and that form to use in their total armament. To me, this is unnecessary. Call it the 'purist view' if you will, but if you learn just a few moves, and they are effective, that is all you really need."

"In those war years, I became very involved with the martial arts since I was not allowed to do anything else. In many ways, I cannot regret those years."

"Gogen Yamaguchi, in his prime, was the very best in goju ryu karate.

"Hirose Kinjo was a walking karate encyclopedia, capable of explaining any rule at any time and a man who had the widest knowledge of martial arts history."

"Minatoya, who lived with him in Yokohama, was the most outstanding man in the Shotokan karate kata."

"The greatest martial artist I met was Kotaru Yoshida, he was a master in all of the martial arts and I believe that in the last 100 years, he was the greatest, all-around artist Japan has produced. Unfortunately, only those in the Bu Toku Kai and Japanese sensei knew of him."

"If a person is going to train for a match, he must do some running."

"Get rid of the nonessential. Use only what is effective and rid yourself of what is ineffective."

"Karate begins where kempo ends. Both teach self defence, but kempo, as practiced in America, relies on technical efficiency; karate goes beyond excellence and strives for spiritual attainment. Karate is discipline. And in self-discipline a karate expert attains freedom. We talk very much these days about all kinds of freedom, political, economic, and otherwise, but these freedoms are not at all real. The real freedom is the freedom of self discipline, the awareness that a karate devotee develops as he progresses. A member of the human tribe should realize the simple dignity and respect one human being owes to another. When a man realizes this he is free in his inner life."

"In karate, we realize that training in detail technique is not to be neglected. But we must also emphasize the mind much more to strive for development of the empty mind (mu-shin)."

"Karate-do means the way of karate. Kempo is not concerned with the way (Do or Tao). We in karate place great emphasis on the realization of a

 Good habits go away, but bad habits stay because of resistance.

psychical state. A man cannot be a master without this realization. We, in karate, realize that a man has to go through a great amount of discipline for this, not only moral but highly spiritual. We fully realize that technical efficiency is a by-product of concentration."

"I have not seen a kempo meijin. I have seen a karate meijin. A meijin is a man who is more than an expert or specialist, he is one who has gone beyond the highest proficiency in his art. In karate the power one seeks to develop is the inner or intrinsical (ki) over the external or surface power (muscular). It is said that the internal power goes beyond that of the external power. The power of the ki is not a mystery but can be attained through discipline, deep concentration and hard work."

"The empty mindlessness (mushin) is important in self defense since the body moves automatically or instinctively with the situation. In self defense, one cannot afford the luxury of thinking, which is a time consuming element. He must meet the situation head-on or in some instances react beforehand. This, in fact, is a true essence of karate."

Decorum and the Dojo

I had to attend a funeral after morning practice at the training hall recently. No, I didn't kill anyone during training; the events weren't related. At least, I didn't think they were. Sitting at the funeral service, it occurred to me that a good many of the mourners did not know how to behave at such an occasion.

Some were dressed more appropriately for a game of touch football, others were hesitant about approaching the casket or unsure about expressing their condolences to the family. I have seen the same uncertainty of behavior at weddings, school commencements, and so on. Brides receive applause as if they are entertainers, and graduating seniors get howls and whistles along with their diplomas.

Some would argue that there's nothing wrong with such behavior; people are simply reacting naturally and just being themselves. But watching the discomfort of those at the funeral, I must disagree. They weren't behaving that way by choice; they simply did not know how to act.

It is one of the great curses of 20th-century mankind, and one that man has inflicted upon himself. By confusing formality with "snobbishness," decorum with arrogance, dignity with egalitarianism, we have disposed with etiquette and standards of behavior in nearly every facet of our lives. Perhaps we did get rid of the snobbishness with our preference for informality, but we have lost something else as well, haven't we?

We have lost a sense of decorum and dignity and, most importantly, we have lost the self-confidence, courtesy and respect for ourselves and others that are hallmarks of all worthwhile civilizations.

One of the most significant (and most overlooked) qualities of the traditional budo (warrior ways) is that they offer a method of rediscovering and recovering a sense of formality and all the good things that go with it.

At the dojo (training hall) that morning, I had bowed to the kamiza shrine to begin practice. I bowed to my fellow students. While we were practicing iaido (the art of drawing and cutting with the sword), we knew which foot to move first away or toward the shrine. We moved so that our weapons in their scabbards would not accidentally clash, and we avoided walking in front of others who were sitting or standing. There were a hundred actions in the dojo undertaken to meet the standards of correct etiquette-formality.

This behavior in no way interfered with our training. We weren't moving about like automatons. The perspiration was flowing; it was a tough workout. Moreover, the bulk of the manners we exercised, the demands of formality that training in a traditional dojo requires, were so subtle and integrated into our behavior that the uninformed visitor in all likelihood would not have even seen them being performed.

Some of our formalities, shared with generations of martial artists before us, have practical origins. Walking around a sword laying on the floor is courteous to its owner and safer than stepping over it. Other formalities, such as bowing to one another, encourage a sense of concern and appreciation for fellow practitioners. And still other conventions of dojo etiquette, such as our treatment of and behavior toward the school shrine, are reflective of the deep sense of the spiritual that pervades all serious budo training.

This kind of formality is very natural even though it must be acquired from careful and expert instruction. After doing it for some time, it becomes automatic; a reflex. Some may disagree. They may insist that latitudinarianism is more expressive of tolerance of the many different backgrounds and lifestyles represented in the dojo, that informality is conducive to a comfortable learning environment.

Maybe so. But some of the most skilled budoka (martial warriors) I have known, regardless of their backgrounds, have submitted themselves to the strict impositions of traditional dojo etiquette. They have learned well under quite formal circumstances. And they carry that sense of decorum and dignity with them when they leave the dojo. It isn't snobbishness or arrogance or egalitarianism. It is a calmness, a self assurance. Formality does not intimidate them, and they do not behave stiffly or unnaturally when it is necessary for them to maintain formality. Formality is apart of their everyday lives as the result of their dojo experience, and so it is part of their sense of one's true self.

One can obviously acquire this familiarity with formality without ever having studied the martial ways. But I wonder, can one be a budoka without it?

What is new in Kata?

What is new in kata? Is it good ?

The only significance, if any, would be of calisthenic value; from that viewpoint, any exercise is better than no exercise at all.

Only a meijin can create a kata. A meijin is one who has gone beyond the highest degrees of proficiency in his art. He is one who has achieved kensho. He is more than an expert or a specialist. There are no meijin in America and the last karate meijin was Funakoshi Gichin."

A unique method of religious practice with the aim of bringing the student to a direct intuitive realization of reality. It is meant for the body to be forged into a total instrument for realization of the 'Absolute Mind'.

Kata is not a manifestation of logical reasoning as Americans have superficially mistaken it to be. Kata brings the student by degrees, by complete transcendence, emancipation, total penetration and identical attainment to 'Do' or 'Tao'."

"Since the master cannot transmit his kensho, he uses kata to bring the student to the same state of 'illumination' he has attained."

Go No Sen – Master's Choice

The time will come when each one of us will look down that lonely road and meet his maker. Each one of us, sooner or later, will meet his death. All of us would rather have it later than sooner. No way to avoid this. In one of sensei's lectures he said: "Death is a total event. Very few of us ever give it serious thought. Until it is upon us then we get scared and regret we did not do more when we had the time. The samurai dealt with the prospect of death in great length."

The martial artist, the samurai, developed and trained himself to meet his death. According to sensei, "Grab life with your hands." The basis of martial arts is a challenge. Martial arts is serious business. It is not a game of checkers or hopscotch. On the field of battle, there is no second place winner. There is only one winner. From the first day I met sensei, he pounded this into my head.

Among the greatest samurai that ever lived were Harigaya Sekiun (1592-1662) and his student, Odagiri lchiun (1629-1706). According to Sekiun: "When two beings are locked in a fight to the death, each faces three situations on a technical and physical level."

The three are:

1) The superior one always kills the inferior one

2) The inferior one always loses

3) Equal ability results in mutual slaying (ai-uchi)

This is the physical law, the jungle law where might is right. Since we are all human beings and not animals, there must be a fourth principle or situation, that only belongs to the human race.

In the beginning, Harigaya Sekiun had mastered all technical knowledge and secrets of swordsmanship from his sensei, Ogasawara Genshin of the Shinkage-Ryu. However he was not satisfied with his accomplishments because on a technical level no one could go beyond the three situations or alternatives.

Harigaya Sekiun and his student Odagiri lchiun, who were probably the best that ever lived, developed a fourth alternative which they termed Ainuke (mutual escaping) instead of ai-uchi (mutual slaying). This alternative separated the human being from the animal and the law of the jungle. A martial artist, using ainuke, should develop his mental condition to such a degree that no one could defeat him, for by anticipating the opponent's thought and the attack, he would not fail. Then both participants would emerge alive and wiser. To Sekiun, highly developed spirituality, or freedom from fear and death when facing an opponent, was the exact point that a martial artist must arrive at to be called a true master of the art.

The difference between a technical master and a true master was the difference between night and day. To the true master, death was an inevitable conclusion, a thing that had to be met with total awareness. It was not calmly accepted (annihilistic approach), it was to be approached alertly and totally without fear.

When all is said and done, it can be seen that the quintessence of martial arts training, including Karate Do, is not to defeat an opponent in battle and take his life, but for that to be totally unnecessary. The most important thing in sporting events involving martial arts is the participation, and not winning or losing. Naturally, this concept does not equate well with the Western idea of winning at all cost. Winning at all costs puts a participant on the level of the first alternative, where the superior always wins. The day will come when one meets a superior opponent.

Before Harigaya Sekiun developed his style based on Ainuke, his Sensei Ogasawara Genshin of the Shinkage Ryu had always depended on Sen Sen Kachi (winning being ahead) or riding on your opponent's movement. This was one of three stages of effective relationships which occur in physical self-defense. The three stages in the martial arts, called "Sen", with three distinct levels depending upon the skill and development of the martial artist. The three levels are as follows:

1. Sen – the highest realm on a physical attack: able to defend against any attack, in a totally effective manner.

2. Go no Sen – Late comes Ahead (Atonosaki). Yagyu Jubei a legendary swordsman whose father founded the Yagyu Shinkage Ryu (Yagyu style of Shinkage Ryu) founded the concept of "Go no Sen." At this level of attack, "a martial artist deals with an attack just at the point of being initiated. The attack is stopped before it actually forms an attack". It is receiving the arc of thought mentally and hitting back. In Go no sen, your opponent always makes the first move physically and mentally, then your move, which comes after, is ahead of your opponent's physical move; hence, Late comes ahead. This is the stage of Masters of the art.

3. Sen no Sen – this is the level of Ainuke. It means that the martial artist stops the thought of attack the moment it occurs in the opponent and that the opponent thinks of something else. Therefore, there is no attack just a mutual passing through. This is a state generated only by the highest masters of the art and meditation. One must pass through the state of "Kensho" (looking into oneself) and into a higher state of enlightenment to achieve this state. This is the goal of all true Masters of the Art.

Elbows McFadden, The Old Noodle and a Girl's Knee

1995

THE OLD NOODLE

I was twelve when it happened! It was a fight that I will never forget! It is as vivid today as it was then. The Great Depression had hit and everybody was in a panic, except the Oriental population located in Honolulu. This was simply because they did not have much to begin with. With the exception of a few, most struggled to send their children to school for the education that they themselves did not get.

Life was a struggle. The annual Sunday School picnic at the Kapiolani Park in Waiki was a ray of sunshine, a small thing that made life more bearable. As kids, we all looked forward for that particular day. For the grown-ups it was a time to chew the fat, drink a little swipe (an alcohol brew made from pineapples), and forget the cares and woes of a hard work week.

My old man never said much. He was a loner and he did not care much for group gatherings. But he loved his family, and when picnic day came around he joined he fun.

This was also an era when many students from the Orient, especially from Japan and Korea, came to the Hawaiian islands to pursue an education. With the influx of students came an annual rotation of teachers in the Japanese or Korean languages. Most were gentlemen, they had to be, as the teaching profession is revered in the Orient. There was one Korean who taught his native language to meet expenses. He was known to everyone as a good teacher but I knew him as a mercurial person with an explosive temper.

"Spare the rod and spoil the child," not a saying taken to heart at a Korean, Japanese, or Chinese school. If anything, it was the other way around. Get out of line and down came the stick. A teacher's word was law! One day a bunch of toughs came to our school grounds and were raising hell. The Korean teacher came out and said, "You people have no business here on school grounds. We have children here. Why don't all of you go up the street to the Beretania playground instead of raising hell here."

The toughs started to leave but dragged their feet in doing so. The teacher's temper exploded. He charged out and pushed the leader, who turned and said, "Look 'yobo' ['Korean' in the Hawaiian pidgin language] you wanna get hurt? Watch your step or you get dis in da mouth." The others stopped leaving and started to laugh. The leader was shaking his fist in the teacher's face.

Without a word the teacher kicked the leader on the jaw, knocked him out cold. Before the others could recover from their surprise, the teacher continued with a kick to the chest, followed through with another kick that broke the tough's nose. The others ran for their lives.

The word got around and we discovered that we had the Korean champion in our midst. When I told my father he just smiled.

Later at the picnic, the teacher was the toast of the party. This time his tongue started wagging. After a little too much swipe, apparently he was more used to sake than this concoction, he started to get bellicose. In fairness to the teacher, most of the adults were slightly tipsy as well, including my father.

Then, as if in a dream, I saw the teacher and my father in a heated argument. I started to worry since I was familiar with the teacher's temper and his fighting ability. I went up to my father and tugged at his sleeve. He turned and said, "Don't worry; go back and enjoy the fun."

The argument continued. Suddenly the teacher lost his famous temper and let loose a kick. It caught my father on the chest and sent him back. The teacher kicked again and although my father partly avoided it, it drew blood. The teacher started dancing around getting ready for a finishing kick. My father faced him with his left hand extended in front of his face in line with the teacher's face.

I was into the rudiments of the martial arts by then, at the insistence of my mother. Street fights appeared savage to me, and now I was looking at one with my father as a participant. And to make matters worse, he was fighting the champion of Korea who had easily wiped out a bunch of Hawaiian toughs.

Somehow my father must have read my mind because he suddenly yelled out, "Don't worry! Look and learn because this is how it is done." While he was talking, the champion launched a kick. It seemed as if my father turned sideways and launched himself through the air like a battering ram. My father's head smashed into the teacher's face. I heard a sickening crunch and the next instant the teacher was on the ground out cold.

My father came to me and said, "As you can see, there is more than one way to use the old noodle. Ninety-nine times use it for learning, but there may come a time when you have to use it like this. It is brutal. One thing for sure: You do not need training. It is elementary."

In the years that have passed since that day, I have seen the 'Danish kiss' used in San Francisco, in Shanghai the 'Suez smash' and the 'Bombay butt' in Singapore, but stripped of all the fancy names, the plain old head butt is one of the oldest means of self defense. And as my father said, it requires no training.

ELBOWS McFADDEN

There once lived a fighter named Elbows McFadden. He never became a champion, but academic research will show that he was responsible in large measure for modern boxing rides and a shift in the style of fighting.

McFadden developed a peculiar knack of blocking with his elbows against a swing, and in the process hurt many a fighter. As a result, wild swings were taken out of the repertoire of fighters and short hooks used instead.

He used to step into a swing and catch the flailing arm with his elbows, causing temporary incapacitation in some, and severe damage in others. Nowadays, only karate practitioners use the elbow extensively and only for smashes in times of self defense.

Champ's Secret, the Honolulu waterfront in the '20s and '30s, produced some of the most awesome street fighters in the world at that time. The Pacific was not only a melting pot of the different races, but also of different martial arts combined with Western styles of fighting. Some of the fighters became legends equal to Paul Bunyan.

When I was a kid training in the martial arts, I heard about a no-holds-barred fighter who was second to none in the street. My uncle, who was the middleweight, light-heavyweight, and heavyweight amateur wrestling champion, used to say that he feared no man. When I asked him about this fighter, my uncle said, "He has something going for him that champions must have: plain old guts and supreme confidence. He also has something that nobody else has."

When I pressed my uncle, he introduced me to the champ. The champ did not impress me physically. Sure, he was a big man by Japanese standards, but he was dwarfed by the huge Polynesians who averaged about 250 pounds. I changed my mind when I saw his eyes. If ever I saw a human with the eyes of an eagle it was him. He looked at me and said, "Well, kid, what is it? Your uncle said that you had something on your mind."

Being a kid, I was not smart enough to observe protocol and was dumb enough to blurt out my innermost feelings and thoughts. "You don't look real tough to me," I answered back. "My uncle said that you have a secret. I want to know what it is."

The champ laughed. "Kid," he said, "there is no secret to street fighting. Just go in and smash. Ninety-nine out of one hundred people are scared anyway, so just go in and smash."

I was disappointed and puzzled.

Irrespective of what the sociologists say, growing up with all different races thrown together, many a fist fight developed. The big difference in Hawaii at that time was that after a fight the kids always shook hands. It was a way of getting to know one another, especially those of a different race and custom. The main reason my mother made me take up the martial arts was to instill in me the respect for the dignity of man.

I had my share of fights as a kid, and I always went in to smash and got smashed back in the process. I had many a bloody nose. Fortunately, I was always a little taller and usually managed to land the first blows, dishing out more than I took.

The champ smiled. "Kid," he said, "there is one thing, you must go in with the idea that you are going to die and that this will be your greatest fight, the samurai spirit, and you must go in with elbows and knees."

ELBOWS AND KNEES

The champ pointed out how the elbows are more impervious to injury than the fist, and much more damaging on delivery. He also said that the knee was a far more superior weapon than a kick. He pointed out that in every fight, in the street or ring, the contestants would clinch a perfect time for the knee.

He said, "If women learned how to use their head, elbow, and knee, men would think twice before attacking a woman."

In 1973, a woman student of mine was waiting for the train in one of the metro stations late at night. A huge man came up to her, grabbed her by the hand and started to drag her towards one of the exit passageways. At this particular time at night, unfortunately, no one was around. She had had jujitsu training and tried to apply a lock on the arm. The man was too strong and full of lust.

She suddenly remembered my lessons on the knee. She moved right in towards the assailant and came up with her knee as hard as she could. The man fell as if struck with a train and writhed on the ground. She left as quickly as she could, safe and sound.

The Big Three: Expansion, Contraction, Snap

Make no mistake about it, one thing's for sure: In the martial arts, you are going to spend about half your time perfecting the basics. It is like a building that looks beautiful but has no solid foundation – the slightest tremor and down it goes. A martial artist who has no solid basics will lose the first time that he is shaken up. Basics, basics, basics, that is the fundamental name of the game.

It all takes place in the box.

You must always stay loose, never tighten up, and, when you move, the contraction, expansion, and snap of the abdominal region will determine whether you hit, block or counter with maximum efficiency.

In a block any kind of block the expansion of the abdominal area like wise, will determine the maximization or minimization of the technique involved.

The snap of the abdominal muscles will also determine the effectiveness of flicking hits or blocks. Naturally, the rest of your body must stay relaxed except at the second of movement, and then use only the muscles that actually perform the work.

If you are tight before any kind of movement your performance will be hindered by the antagonistic muscles having to relax. Most of those who are in a hurry to learn sophisticated techniques overlook the basics or mistakenly believe that they have the basics down pat. There is no such thing! Mastery of the basics takes up most of the time required for mastery of any art. But it is worth it. And it can be interesting. With the exception of the few who are familiar with Asian culture, most students see the sensei's insistence on the horsestance for long periods of time as a waste, sheer nonsense. They do not realize that the stance was, is, and always will be meant to teach the pupil how to relax the antagonistic muscles, stay ready with the performance muscles, and use the abdominal area to generate all energy.

When they first practice the horsestance, students tighten up, complain, try to endure and suffer in the process. This goes on until the day when, to their relief, they learn the proper way to relax!

The body dynamics involved in the big three – expansion, contraction, and snap use all the scientific principles involved in what modern kinesiologists call the summation of joint forces.

Contraction, expansion, and snap deal with actually performing martial arts techniques – how to do – as opposed to body-building, conditioning, and motivating. The idea is to get the most from each part of the body involved in hitting, blocking, and moving.

The forces generated from each joint and segment of the body involved in the particular movement must be added together, so that no effort is wasted. Start with the biggest and follow through with the smallest.

Take a simple punch, for example. To maximize performance, the joint forces at the larger segments should precede those of the smaller segments. The punch actually starts at the abdomen, and in a fast, continuous motion, each segment follows – shoulder to upper arm, to forearm, and finally to the fist. The motion is progressive, although there is overlap.

Get the most out of each joint before moving on to the next.

The abdominal muscles must go through their complete range of motion before the shoulders start contracting for the punch, for example, and so on down the line. Punch straight in, and follow-through mentally, as well as physically. It appeared to that Sensei took an inordinately long time to teach us how to kick. He stressed the important difference between kicking with just the leg and kicking with the whole body. He said, "Most kick with the leg there is nothing wrong in kicking with the leg but if you want to maximize your effort, you must know how to kick with your body."

We students realized that all physical performance uses the same dynamic principles. The total effort must be concentrated in the one final point. If a part of the body that is connected with the whole performance is not used, or used poorly, then the end result suffers. You must subtract that much from the sum total. That is all there is to it.

Martial arts students who do not perfect their basics are performing at less than their capacity. In such cases, a complete restructuring must take place. They must be properly instructed in the full extension of body and self.

Death is a Constant Companion

"Now, punch with all of your might! Let the technique explode from within, as if there was a hand grenade going off inside your stomach. Ready...!"

"You must fight with feeling! I cannot even begin to emphasize that enough. It is of the utmost importance that you fight with feeling, not just for reason alone. When a fight begins, the reason why it started is no longer important. You must then deal with the here and now. That is why it is vital to draw from all of the resources of your being."

"Always remember, to the true martial artist the words 'try' and 'impossible' do not exist. When you make up your mind to do something, you must do it with everything you've got."

"When you are tired and feel that you cannot go on any longer, that is where true karate begins."

"In kata, you must train and learn how to respond to any given attack. You are learning principles, not just fighting techniques alone. In life there are three kinds of opponents that you will come up against. The inferior opponent, the equal opponent and the superior opponent. You must always train to meet the superior opponent; prepare yourself to bring him down!"

"In the Bushido philosophy of the martial arts you never lose in a fight – even in death!"

"Never be afraid to die! Death is always with us. It is an inevitable part of life itself. Death is our companion – not our enemy. The real challenge that we all must face is found in combatting life, not running from death."

"Remember, there is no rest in life. Rest is reserved only for those who have done all in their power to better themselves in life. We only find rest when we lay down our tasks of living and finally succumb to death."

"The students are allowed to either push or pull their opponents in order to break their balance. By practising this, one learns to understand the relationship with an opponent while struggling."

"The pinan shodan is the most basic of all the kata in karate. But at the same time, it is also the most difficult to do because one cannot cover up any weaknesses. Everything – power, speed, emphasis – must be co-ordinated in order to perform it correctly. Indeed, it is a great mental and spiritual exercise as well."

The Classical Man

By William Jakielaszek, courtesy of Martial Virtue Magazine

"Incredible that one man could have so much knowledge," said Ernie

Wong, a student of Sensei Kim's who studied at the legendary San Francisco YMCA in the early 1970s. For those who never had the good fortune to attend a lecture or seminar of O'Sensei's, it is difficult to explain the myriad of subjects of which Sensei Kim had knowledge. I'm not talking about a little bit of wisdom on each subject. Oh, no. When Sensei Kim lectured, he had a complete understanding of the matter.

Here is a brief synopsis of some of my notes taken at the various camps and seminars which I had the good fortune to attend. Please excuse my rambling style of writing, as my notes are not organized in any particular order, either chronologically or by subject matter. All quotes are attributable to O'Sensei Richard Kim: some are original, and others were favorites of his from a lifetime of study.

"Hug the tree."

Tai chi exercise. Visualize hugging the tree and feel the energy within. Then look up to the sky and rub your hands together 36 times and briskly rub your face as if washing it. "The face you see in the mirror will be the same one you see 20 years from now."

"Smell the battlefield."

When doing kata, during the yoi, feel the battle inside the form. Try and get to the point of living the fight within the form. Before the kata, program your mind by saying to yourself, "I am not afraid to die." The most dangerous opponent is one who is not afraid to die, and by constantly programming your mind you may be able to reach that point. This probably sounds quite violent, but remember, O'Sensei fought in the Second World War and had to live the life of the warrior. His survival depended on it. Also in today's society, we all too often hear of violent attacks, and as martial artists we must train to be able to defend our loved ones, and ourselves if necessary.

"How sweet it is."

A man is being chased by a tiger and is forced to jump off a very high cliff and grab on to a vine. As he is hanging on for dear life, the vine begins to slowly crack. About to plunge to his death the man notices a plump ripe grape hanging from the vine and picks it. It is by far the sweetest most delicious grape he has ever tasted. Don't wait until you're on death's doorstep to appreciate the many fruits that life has to offer.

"Ichi go, ichi i."

 To reach enlightenment you must go inside yourself. If you go outside there is a limit to where you can go.

Loosely translated, "One moment, One lifetime." Sensei's lesson, "You only have one life, from the womb to the tomb. Every second is the only second; you'll never get that second back. When you go to the beyond, go in saying, 'I wouldn't have changed a thing.'"

"What's inside the house?"

Spiritually, Sensei used the example of the politician who was careful to maintain an image of being a wholesome, church-going member of society. In actuality, he would sell his soul and his wife and children for his own political gain. Physically, Sensei used the example of the body builder who worked out for hours a day to create the image of the perfect body. However he never took time to take care of the internal mechanics and died at a fairly young age.

The Power of Positive Thinking

O'Sensei said, "If you think good thoughts you will bring good results. Bad thoughts bring bad results" Very simply stated, it's the power of positive thinking. O'Sensei believed in it, and taught it. In one of his lectures, he said, "Positive thinking causes solutions and negative thinking causes problems."

O'Sensei's prayer for everyday

"God grant me health, happiness, peace, love and the power of your holy light, today and forever." O'Sensei strongly believed in the power of prayer and often lectured on it.

"Do you see what you see?"

"Do you hear what you hear?"

And finally, this is the quote most often heard in the dojo. Usually, after he had demonstrated a technique and watched as we the students improperly tried to repeat the action. In life O'Sensei taught that most people see what they want to see and hear what they want to hear. "There is a big difference between hearing and listening," he would say."

This article does not begin to touch the tip of the iceberg of the amount of knowledge that O'Sensei shared. I will always be grateful to O'Sensei Richard Kim for all the lessons and all of his martial arts knowledge, which he gave so unselfishly. As Ernie Wong said, "Incredible that one man could have so much knowledge."

Incredible, indeed!

A 20th Century Samurai Warrior

By Don Warrener

Training directly under one of the greatest Karate masters who ever lived is not always a pleasant experience; as many who have trained under the tutelage of Hanshi Richard Kim have found out. Richard Kim is a stern taskmaster, yet a compassionate human being. He is known for his grueling morning workouts; yet, his Tai Chi classes are so relaxing they are meditation in motion! Richard Kim is a man of contradictions. Anyone who has ever trained with this 20th Century Samurai has come away with a wealth of knowledge that only a true Master of Karate can divulge.

He is the author of five books, the most famous of which is the "Classical Man". Other books penned by Master Kim include, "Weaponless Warrior" and a series of books on Kobudo.

There is never a dull moment when you are in one of Sensei's classes. He is not merely a Master of Karate but also a Master Instructor. He has the ability to blend his obvious passion for the Martial Arts with a sense of humor which makes for a light atmosphere that is very conducive to learning. During his class, he usually teaches kata or self defense techniques from Aiki Jitsu which he learned back in the 1940s; he will also teach Kobudo on occasion.

Richard Kim's Kobudo classes are always interesting and he has taught many of the top J.K.A. masters various weapons, like the Bo and Sai. Each weapons class starts with basics: the grip and hand exchanges. He then moves into teaching a wide range of weapons katas by Chatan Yara or those of Hama Higa. One is intensely aware of the great condition of this senior citizen. It is not uncommon to see him get down and do 75 perfect leg raises along with the class at the end of a workout.

Each class has an emphasis on basics. He believes that if the basics are good then the kata can become good and so can the kumite. When the sparring starts, you may find yourself facing opponents in their '60s or '70s, as his student range is 5 to 75. This, in itself, is an amazing feat when you consider he is able to capture the attention of such a wide range of age groups, all in the same lesson.

Every student looks forward to the end of the seminar. He always has a new story to tell, which teaches the morals and philosophy of the Martial Arts, in the format of an old Japanese wise tale.

One of my favorite stories is the one he tells about the scorpion and the turtle. The scorpion asks the turtle for a ride across the pond. The turtle says 'no' because the scorpion will sting and kill him. The scorpion finally convinces the turtle that he won't sting him because if he did he would die in the crossing of the pond. Yet, as they approach the opposite shore, just before getting off, the scorpion stings the turtle. As they both sink into the pond; the turtle, with his dying breath asks the scorpion, "Why did you do that?" The scorpion, as he makes it to shore, says, "What did you expect? I am a scorpion."

He teaches us that in life there are many scorpions. We, as Martial Artists, must be aware of them at all times. Our self defense skills are not just physical, they must also be mental self defense skills. A Martial Artist should strive to become an artist of life, which means perfection in all areas of life, not just physically.

Like most of the Masters of Old, most of his serious teaching is not even done on the mat. Either at breakfast or after class, the senior students go with the Sensei to a restaurant or to a quiet place where he can either begin or continue his lecturing. Sometimes, the evening lectures will go to 2 or 3 a.m. Students will be dozing off while Sensei is still lecturing up a storm. Richard Kim's youthfulness is ever present while in the dojo or after class.

His charisma and ability to relate to people through his stories is second-to-none. He has been called a Sensei's Sensei and for those who have been privileged enough to be in the presence of this great master of the "empty hand" they soon realize his real forte is the English language (and his ability to live life to the fullest).

Master Kim believes in practicing what he preaches. He explains, 'A samurai, whether he lived in the 1600s or in modern times, must learn to live life to its maximum. We, like the samurai of old, never know when this life could end. Therefore if one does live life to the fullest with no regrets, when we take our last breath of air we can look back at our life and see that we took from life that which we wanted rather than got from it that which was simply offered. "Remember," Sensei goes on to explain, "that second place means you lost."

Richard Kim's credentials are most impressive to those who understand traditional Karate. He is a 9th Dan from the highly prestigious Dai Nipping Bu Toku kai. He is also one the very few living graduates of the Budo Semman Gaku, which was a Martial Arts College in Japan, disbanded by General MacArthur after World War II. He is a Buddhist priest, and has Ph.D. from St. John's College in Shang Hai, as well as one from the University of Hawaii. He was voted "Sensei of the Year" by Black Belt Magazine in 1967 and 1973 became a member of the Black Belt Hall of Fame. His teachers included Yabu Kentsu for judo, Chen Chin Wuan for Tai Chi Chuan, Chac Hsu Lie for Pa Qua and Yoshida Kotaro whom he says taught him a wide variety of Martial Arts skills and an insurmountable amount of knowledge.

Richard Kim also was promoted by the Dai Nippon Bu Toku Kai to Hanshi, a very high position in the All Japan Military Virtue Organization.

He is a special individual who was raised in pre-War Japan and still has the understandable attitudes of someone of that era. His Martial Arts skills are unquestionable, but more importantly, he is a master when it comes to teaching his students the art of life from a samurai warrior's perspective.

I, for one, will be eternally grateful for the many lessons I have learned from Sensei Kim, even though some have been hard lessons. They have all been valuable lessons.

They say the greatest compliment any student can give a Sensei, is for the student to use the knowledge the Sensei has given him to make his own life a better life. By doing this, you make the Sensei's life even more fruitful; he knows that his time here on earth was of value and appreciated. I can say most sincerely that his lessons are used daily and will be passed on to the students of the future. Oss!

On the San Diego Summer Camp

"You know why we believe (classical) weapons training is still necessary? Because it brings into focus the essence of the martial arts. There is no second place winner. Your life can end in one stroke. Weapons training brings you to full awareness because you cannot make a mistake. In free-hand fighting, you know you're not going to die if you make a mistake. Not so with weapons."

"Say a student goes to the University of California at Berkeley instead of a small college, he may not get any smarter, but he gets more exposure to Nobel winners, baccalaureates, a bigger library. We may not be able to teach kata (forms) any better than Joe Blow up in Los Angeles, but the students get more exposure here. We are expanding their horizons. They learn things here they can't learn at the dojo."

"I get the satisfaction that every educator has – the more I give, the more I receive. I learn more everyday."

"This is an ultra-traditional karate camp. We don't use music with kata. Kata is not a dance. It's harder to perform kata without music, though. Imagine an ice skater not using music in her routine."

"But without tradition and custom, you have no root. As Aristotle once said: 'Tradition and custom have been around for so long, they must work."

"If there is a language spoken here, it is the language of the martial arts."

Self Mastery

"Kata training is the primary path to self-mastery."

"It is attitude, and not technique, that is paramount. Most important is winning the battle inside yourself. We put the emphasis on conquering fear, self, and ego – defeating the opponent comes afterward."

Let the Technique Explode

"Let the technique explode from within. You must fight with feeling. It is vital to draw from all of the resources of your being. To the true martial artist, the words try and impossible do not exist."

Chinese, Okinawan and Japanese Warriors

Sensei Kim would end each class with a samurai story that would depict some moral or life lesson. His storytelling abilities were nothing short of mesmerizing and although many have tried to emulate his skill few have succeeded.

We have found these stories that were meant for a book apparently, but were never published.

Harigaya Sekiun: "Sword of Heavenly Reason"

1970

You must free yourself of your intellect. The martial artist trains in the beginning for physical perfection (self-defense) and then for mushin (no-mind).

Harigaya Sekiun developed the 'Sword of Heavenly Reason'. If you don't think you've conquered your intellect, when you face your opponent then you have mushin. When you are approached by your opponent, he will feel your ki and feel anxiety if he has not achieved mushin. This will cause him to use his intellect in order to figure out a way to beat you. He might think, "I will fake to his head but upon his blocking attempt, I will cut his hand." When he does this, there will be a suki (an opening) and you will cut his hand without thought.

The first time that Harigaya stayed at Odagiri's house, Odagiri Ichion brought him one of the good looking local whores to sleep with. During the night, as Harigaya was having intercourse and approaching his climax, he felt a presence. It was Odagiri who chose this moment to test Harigaya by throwing a shuriken at him. Harigaya, without stopping his orgasm, reached up and caught the shuriken intended for him in the darkness.

The next morning Harigaya let Odagiri know that he knew it was him testing him. He told Odagiri that he had had his first lesson, to be aware of everything at all times, even during sexual orgasm. Odagiri practiced this over the following years with his favorite girl. It took him a long time to achieve it.

When Harigaya came back from his last trip to China, he asked for the girl that he had had that first night. Odagiri told him that she was old now and said that he would get a young pretty one instead. Harigaya insisted on the same girl, however. Odagiri had a hard time finding her but finally did and told her to go to Harigaya.

The girl was now a woman in her 50s, relatively well preserved; she carried her years well, a remarkable feat in itself for women did not last long in that profession.

Harigaya had sex with her. Afterward he realized that she had total serenity, unlike the first time. He asked her if she enjoyed sex better now or before when she was young. She replied that she enjoyed sex in her later years more because she wasn't afraid of becoming pregnant – she had reached menopause. This released her from her anxieties and gave her peace of mind.

It was then that Harigaya finally put together all his thoughts regarding sex. He said that for the sexual act to have any meaning (or spiritual communication), it must be done with total abandon, with no hidden fears or thoughts.

Genhachi Komatsu: Kyudo Specialist

Tanaguchi is a Japanese man in South America who founded the Universal Brotherhood. He is considered a saint by his followers since he has done miraculous things and is convinced that you can do ANYTHING with your body.

As a martial arts teacher, you'll find that some of your students will benefit from being an assistant instructor, etc. Some may complain about others when the going gets tough for them, forgetting the benefits they got from the martial arts. Genhachi Komatsu was one of them.

Genhachi was a rather obscure martial artist. He was a born samurai and specialized in archery. True to Japanese tradition, his older brother was the head of the dojo. Up to the age of eighteen, Genhachi helped his brother run the dojo and everything was good. His older brother made everything easy for him so he didn't realize what he had.

When Genhachi was eighteen, a scandal concerning graft broke. It happened in the town that Genhachi's family controlled. Japan didn't tolerate graft and they also believed that the head man was responsible for his subordinates, so parents were held responsible for their children. When word came from the Shogun that the brother, being head of the family, would be executed, naturally his family was disgraced.

Genhachi got mad at the injustice of it and ran away to a forest near a farm village. He gave up on people, decided to hell with them. He closed the gym when he ran away. When the villagers found out about this situation, they felt sorry for him and would leave food for him which he refused to eat most of the time. Although he was eighteen, he looked much older. He never bathed.

A widowed woman with a son, who found it difficult to remarry, got interested in Genhachi. Having heard his story she felt sorry for him. She was ten years older than him. She told him, "Genhachi! I want to talk to you."

"Who's there?" asked Genhachi.

"I'm a neighbor. I want to tell you something. I know your problem. You had it good and now you're feeling sorry for yourself; you think everybody let you down. Well, you can come out of it by having pride in yourself." She kept working on him this way.

But Genhachi wouldn't listen to her and refused to do anything, so she compromised him by sleeping with him. He couldn't understand why she had done it, after all, he was filthy, not having had a bath for two years. She told him that she did it to let him know he was a human being. Genhachi felt ashamed upon hearing that and straightened up and began to practice archery. He got pretty good at it.

Then one day, thieves came into the village and the woman asked Genhachi for help. Genhachi wanted to know why he should help, so she told him to show gratitude, after all, the villagers had helped him by giving food. Genhachi agreed and was able to capture the thieves by shooting their heels with his arrows. Word got around about Genhachi's skill and what he had done and he began to get jobs as a watchman and bodyguard.

When Genhachi was twenty-eight years old, the Shogun expunged his brother's record, since the original prosecutors had all died, reopened the case and found that his brother wasn't really the guilty party. When that happened, Genhachi went back home. The villagers told the woman that she wouldn't see him again, so she went back to her family.

Two years later a palaquin (a hand-carried carriage) stopped in front of her house and out stepped Genhachi. During the time he had been gone, he had given her his name by changing the records on their birth certificates, that was because she was of lower station than him.

Up to the age of sixty (at which time he retired) Genhachi taught archery. He would have his students shoot at a target which would be from 150 to 200 yards away. He had the ability to direct his students aim while watching them and without looking at the target. For instance he would say, "Move the bow up an inch; hold your breath; release the arrow now!" His students would hit the bull's eye every time. Genhachi knew just what corrections to tell his students.

Then one day, when he was about sixty years of age he made a mistake. He told his wife that he was going to quit teaching because he lost that ability, but she said that he could still do it; but he couldn't so he retired from teaching.

One day as Genhachi was shopping he came across some plates that he liked. They cost three ryo and since his eyesight was bad, he asked the shopkeeper: "Are there any flaws?"

"No." replied the shopkeeper.

"Are you sure?" asked Genhachi.

"Yes," said the shop keeper.

When he got home and showed them to his wife, his wife told him that that she noticed two tiny flaws in the plates. Genhachi took the plates back to the shopkeeper and showed him the two flaws, saying, "I'm returning these two plates because of the flaws but I want you to keep the money. I believe the best about people and I want to think that you didn't try to swindle me. That's why I want you to keep the money."

Genhachi was an odd person. He lived his own life and didn't let others influence him. He believed in the good in man. Another time he went to a merchant wanting to buy hachi. He asked him about it but the merchant couldn't explain, he just said: "Well, sometimes it's two ryo and sometimes three, depending."

Genhachi's wife thought that the merchant was trying to cheat him and said so but Genhachi said: "No. I'll pay three ryo." He tried to prove that the man was good. Word went around that Genhachi was an odd duck and consequently all the merchants started quoting him two prices with the same results – Genhachi always paid the higher price.

After a while the merchants became ashamed of themselves and so all got together and decided to return Genhachi's money. Genhachi actually received more money than he had paid.

Genhachi could have deceived his students but instead choose to quit when his ability started to leave him. He was a true believer in the adage: "It's what you are like when you're old that's important."

Ohno Sensei on Strength vs Technique

Ohno Kumao, a senior to Sensei Kim in the Bu Toku kai, said Ono Jiroemon Tadaaki was right. He had been observing a Judo championship in 1957, (the first world tournament), and a big man won. He was Japanese and won because of his strength. Ohno Kumao said that Japan would start losing in ten years if strength was all there was.

The following story illustrates the unimportance of strength.

There was a man by the name of Shirai Toru who made it a point to practice twice as hard as anybody else; if somebody did a stroke five hundred times, he would do it one thousand times. He was a pretty big man.

For fifty years he trained for great strength. When others tried to block him, he would shatter their bokken through strength alone.

When he was twenty-one he was the best student in his gym but his teacher wouldn't give him the inka because of his youth.

One day while Shirai was travelling around, looking to find other teachers, he met a man named Terada who was sixty-two years old at that time. Shirai told him what had happened and said that he was going to find a big man to train him so be would become the best in Japan.

Terada said, "Oh! Let's have a match."

Shirai agreed. Terada had a stick. Shirai had a sword. Terada was able to beat Shirai with his ki because when Shirai faced him, Terada was able to push him back with his ki. Shirai asked Terada how he was able to do this. Terada said that strength was unimportant, that you need only enough strength to hold up a sword and that's all. He recommended that if Shirai wanted to learn the secret, to go find a Shingon sect priest.

Shirai looked for, and found a priest. He watched him chant sutras, at the end of which the priest would hit a bell. He observed for two years. Eventually, he was able to see a surge of energy shoot out of the priest's hand and hit the bell. The priest would send all his ki from his hand the moment that he would hit the bell.

Shirai practised until he was able to put his ki into the end of his sword. He faced Terada again. Terada was now seventy-nine years old. Shirai lost the match. He had not realized that ki doesn't decrease with age but increases with practice. Shirai would never catch up with Terada because he had a head start.

Agena Tairagawa: The Small, Calm One

Agena, nicknamed 'Tairagawa' (the small, calm one), out of affection by the Okinawans, was born in 1870 in the tiny village of Gushikawa, Okinawa. He died in 1924 at the age of 54.

Agena was the first son of an upper middle class family, and as such he became one of the first non-noblemen to take up karate. Though only a commoner, he was affectionately referred to as a living bushi (Samurai Warrior). Prior to this you had to be either affluent or of nobility.

Despite his slight build and physical stature, he was obsessed with the thought of becoming a man of the 'iron fist' and 'steel fingers.' He pursued this objective with extreme dedication, eventually developing a fist like Thor's hammer. By the time he was thirty, he had a reputation for having a terrific fist.

Unlike most karate masters, Agena never opened a school, but instead continued working exclusively on his own fist and fingers until they were capable of performing incredible feats.

Gushikawa village was off the beaten path, but ended up being the location for one of his more colorful stories. It boasted a tree, which is still the topic of much conversation among the local residents. This tree first became famous around the turn of the century when one of its villagers, Agena, made history there.

On this particular day Agena was visiting his friend, Tengan Matsu, who knew that Agena had developed his hands to an extraordinary degree. Tengan opened a bottle of saki and after a few drinks said, "Agena, I'll make a bet with you. I bet I can rip off the bark of that tree faster than you can. The wager will be five pounds of meat. What do you say?"

"Aw, come on," replied Agena smiling. "Forget it. Drink up. It's a silly bet. You have as much chance as a snowball in hell."

"No, I'm serious," insisted Tengan. "But there is a condition. I use my chisel and you use your hands. After all, you are the man with the iron fist and steel fingers." Tengan smiled, feeling secure in the knowledge that even Agena would not take up such a bet.

Agena however, jumped up and said, "Get ready to buy me five pounds of top sirloin. I'm not asking for filet, just top sirloin." And he ran to the tree. Tengan followed with his chisel.

Tengan asked the village headmaster to referee, and on the mark, they started. Tengan looked at Agena wondering if he was drunk. He must be if he expect to beat the chisel, no matter how strong his hands were.

Agena repeatedly punched the tree with his fist, loosening the bark and ripping if off with his fingers. Punch, then rip, and the bark would come off in wide strips. Within two minutes, Agena had punched and ripped off an eight-foot strip, while Tengan had barely come down only one third of the way.

Tengan threw down his chisel, admitting defeat. By now the village people had heard what was happening and had gathered around the tree, amazed by Agena. Tengan went off to the market place, bought the meat and a few extra jugs of saki.

There is also a story featuring another Tengan, not Matsu. This Tengan worked in a bath house and had always wanted to see Agena in action before he died. One day as Agena was laying in his bath, Tengan approached him, telling him that he had dreamed about his death. He begged Agena to do something so that he could see him in action before he died. Agena agreed and asked him what it was he wanted to see. Tengan wanted to see his iron fist and steel fingers in action. Before Agena began, Tengan called for all the women, who were on the other side of the bath house wall, to witness the demonstration. When all was ready, Agena jumped up, giving one big kiai, and thrust his fingers right through the bath house wall. Tengan prospered when he began charging admission for all to see what Agena had done.

There are many episodes dealing with Agena and his steel fingers. He never hurt another human being, and when used for self defense he merely subdued his assailants rather that killing them.

No one knew for a long time that his teacher was Matsumura Sokon.

One day as Tengan and Agena walking through a village on their way home, they were seen by the local cooper. Recognizing the two men as strangers, the cooper began to practice his kata in an attempt to impress them. Tengan wasn't impressed however, and decided to teach the cooper a lesson. He went up and said, "I see you know karate. Well you must not be too good if you must use all those tools."

The cooper asked, "What do you mean? How else can you work with this material?"

Tengan replied, "In our village, we shape the bamboo with our hands."

"Of course," the cooper said "you are putting me on! Show me if you can."

Tengan, who was a big man, said, "To show you, I'll let the smallest and weakest of our village do it (pointing to Agena)."

So Agena walked over to a bamboo tree that was lying on the cooper's floor. He picked it up and rapidly stripped it of its branches with his fingers. Then he pounded it with his fist all the way down its length and ripped it in two. He finished by splitting it into smaller pieces with his chops.

The two of them then walked away leaving the dumbfounded cooper looking at the pieces of bamboo.

Agena had done it with the power of his mind – the ki.

Takeda Takachiya on Faith

Japan at one time did not have a national police force. If a man was murdered, the only way for his relatives to get justice was for them to find the killer and fight him. When caught, the murderer would be given a fair match, he would not be ambushed, for instance. The family would first have to register their grievance.

One day, a fourteen year old boy approached Odagiri and told him that his father had been killed, that he had been following the man who had committed the murder and had finally found him. (The boy had challenged the man and they were due to fight the next day.) At first, the boy didn't tell Odagiri that the match was set for the next day but simply asked Odagiri to teach him. Odagiri agreed, telling the boy that in three months he would be able to face the man. The boy then admitted that the fight was scheduled for the next day. Odagiri thought to himself that it was impossible to teach this kid enough in one day so that he would be able to beat the man.

Odagiri told the boy that he would tell him what to do and that he would have to do exactly what he was told. He said, "Tomorrow, before you reach the site of the match, take out your two swords. When you are twenty feet away from the man, yell out his name and charge, holding one of your swords in jodan (upper block position). When you reach him, jab at him with your other sword. You can't lose the match because I, Odagiri, told you how to win. Let's practice awhile to make sure you got it."

They practised awhile but the boy didn't really get it. Odagiri's heart went out to him. He told the boy that he was doing fine and that he was ready. He said, "Be sure to do exactly what I showed you tomorrow."

The boy had faith in Odagiri. He believed in him and in what he had told him. He did just as he was told. When he saw the man, he called his name and charged. Just as he reached him, he threw up one sword. At that point the man came down with his sword to hit the boy in the head. The boy just barely managed to block him, as he jabbed the man and killed him. Takeda turned out to be a very famous person.

Itosu Yasutsune (Ankoh): Naha vs Shuri

Sho Iku was the king of Okinawa at the time of Itosu's birth in the year 1830, in the town of Shuri, Okinawa. He died in 1915. The pronunciation of his name in Chinese is Ankoh. His father was a member of the nobility and had the rank of Shizoku.

When Itosu was seven years old, his father took him outside and tied him with a belt to a big pole stuck in the ground. The belt was long enough to allow two feet of free play between Itosu and the pole. His father would then pick up a bo and poke him with it. At first Itosu thought this was a game and would try to grab the bo. But when his father kept hitting him hard in the stomach and even on the head Itosu started to cry. It didn't matter, his father didn't let up. This became a daily occurrence and stopped only when Itosu got fighting mad. That was the day when his father saw a look in Itosu's eyes that seemed to say, "If I grab your stick – watch out!"

This is what his father had been waiting for. He told Itosu to meditate. Once, during this training a neighbor commented on how cruel it was. Itosu's father replied that it was a tough world and that he was trying to give his son fighting spirit. He predicted that his son's name would go down in history one day.

In 1846, (the father was forty-five years old and Itosu was sixteen), the father went to see Bushi Matsumura (Sokon) and asked him to teach his son. (Bushi means samurai.)

Matsumura wanted to have a look at him first. When he saw him, he said that he was too skinny. But when he looked in his eyes and saw his spirit, he changed his mind. Matsumura agreed to accept Itosu as his student, but told him that the martial arts is the toughest discipline to undertake. Itosu said that he understood and was still willing to go through with it.

Matsumura replied, 'you might agree now but it's the end that counts. It's easy to start in the martial arts, but when the going gets tough, its a different thing, you must stick with it.'

For the next eight years as Matsumura's student, Itosu got up at sunrise and began his training. He had to cook the rice, wash his teacher's back as well as perform other menial tasks. He couldn't sleep at night, because when he fell asleep, Matsumura would attack him with a stick and hit him. Because of his training, Itosu developed a terrific ki and the ability to perceive an oncoming attack from any direction, at any time. (During this period, the Chinese invited King Sho Iku to visit them, when he did, they kept him prisoner, replacing him with Sho Tai in Okinawa.)

One day Matsumura suggested that Itosu go and see the bullfights in Naha-no-kamaizoto. Itosu decided to go. While he was walking through town he saw a bull that had broken loose running through the streets. People were shouting in order to warn everyone. When the bull came upon Itosu it charged at him. Itosu managed to grab the bull by the horns and hold it. When the bull began to struggle, he pinned it down to the ground while the townspeople tied it up. Apparently, this was the very first time anybody had done that to a bull, and the people were very excited. They apologized about letting the bull get loose. In order to escape them, Itosu went to the red light district. He mingled in the crowd watching the bullfights, but because he towered above everybody else (he was six feet tall whereas the average Okinawan was only about five foot four), people noticed him and asked about him. When they found out that he was Itosu, a karate man from Shuri, they wondered if he could beat Tomoyose, the best fighter in Naha. (Naha and Shuri had different styles of karate. They were competitors, had different styles, similar to Goju versus Shotokan.)

Two years after the bull incident, Itosu was cooling off in the sea breeze on a hill near Naha (it gets very hot there), when he overheard two men talking. They were discussing the fact that Naha had the best fighters and that Shuri's fighters weren't too skilful. They were convinced that nobody could beat their champion, Tomoyose. Itosu approached them and asked who this Tomoyose was. They told him. Itosu went to Matsumura and told him that he wanted to fight Tomoyose. Matsumura agreed.

In the old days, the karate teachers frowned on fights between their students or between their students and others. A way to test yourself, which was okay with the teachers, was to go to the red light districts. You were bound to get into a fight with somebody over either a woman or something else. This kind of fight was acceptable. However there was one place in Okinawa that you could challenge the entire town and that was in Naha. Just outside of Naha was a big rock about three and a half feet high with a flat top. If you placed your clenched fist and arm upon it, it was viewed as a challenge and someone would defend the town's honor.

Itosu left for Naha to place his arm upon the rock. When he got there, there was already a fight going on. The fight was against a big man who was beating everybody. Itosu fought a severe fight with him and he won. He also fought and beat two others without too much trouble. He then said out loud, "What the hell is this! I thought Naha had the best fighters? No one here is any good."

A voice from the crowd said, "You haven't fought me yet." Itosu asked who was speaking. The man replied that he was Tomoyose, he walked over and put his arm upon the rock, issuing his challenge to Itosu. The two men stood facing each other, staring into each others' eyes. Itosu remembered what his teacher had taught him about attacking as soon as your opponent's eyes move. Itosu was watching Tomoyose's eyes. When he saw them move, he gave a big kiai and jumped at Tomoyose, striking him in the arm and breaking it. Itosu was now number one in Okinawa.

Itosu attained satori in 1903 and created the five pinans. He did this because the school children he taught (they were required to study karate in school), were having difficulty in learning the Seisan as their first form. The second form they usually learned was either the Patsai or the Wanshu, depending on the school. He took the movements of the Pinans from five main forms: Seisan, Patsai, Tensho, Nihanchi and Koshanku.

When he was seventy-five years old, Itosu was the head instructor for karate in the Okinawan school system. At this time, a man who had been the head of police in Kagashima, Japan, came to Okinawa to replace the island's chief of police. (The Japanese had finally been able to wrestle total control of Okinawa from the Chinese and had begun to replace the important officials of Okinawa, who had been either Chinese or Okinawan, with their own men.)

The new man had a fourth or fifth degree in Judo. He was very strong and the pride of Kano sensei. He was also a Bu Toku kai man, as was the entire Okinawan school board. (The school board members were all from Kagashima.) When he saw karate being taught, he was not impressed and ordered judo to be taught in the schools instead of karate. The Okinawans protested strongly, expounding the merits of Karate. The new police chief was adamant. He did issue an invitation to Itosu though, to fight him if karate was that so worthwhile. The Okinawans protested, Itosu was seventy-five years old after all. The police chief decided that they could pick someone to fight in his place. When Itosu heard of the challenge, he went to the school board and told them to let the police chief go to the red light district if he wanted to fight. In the end, Itosu accepted the match with reluctance.

Itosu didn't worry about himself, he was worrying about the police chief, he was afraid that he might hurt him.

Itosu wrote to all the karate men on the island, inviting them to the match to see real karate in action. He told them to watch close because the match wouldn't last more than a few seconds.

The day of the match arrived and everybody was at the school grounds. The police chief was waiting for Itosu in his judo gi. Itosu came walking out looking like a bear, almost as if he had stood in a horse stance too long. (In fact people thought that he was in a horse stance.)

When the police chief went to grab him, Itosu hit him in the stomach, knocking him out. The school board officials thought that Itosu had a weapon, they searched him, but found nothing. Itosu revived the police chief with katsu. (Fortunately he hadn't hit him using the technique in which you twist as you hit, rupturing the insides – a Cantonese corkscrew.)

Itosu told the crowd that today they had seen the power of karate and ki, he warned them not to use it. He asked the police chief if he wanted to continue, he did. The police chief tried to throw Itosu but couldn't do it, he was rooted to the ground. Itosu told him that he would release the ki and the police chief would then be able to throw him. It worked. Needless to say karate stayed in the curriculum.

Karate was seen in a bad light after that in Japan, because unfortunately several karate men went to Japan to commit political assassinations. One of the main reasons for Funakoshi's visits to Japan was to improve the image of karate (1972 and 1922).

The Chinese found out that it was possible to send your ki down into the ground like tree roots, making it impossible to be moved. The Okinawans learned it from the Chinese. This can be developed through the kata Sanchin.

When you punch physically, you explode from the stomach out to the end of your fist (the ki). But when you punch mentally, you imagine that your first goes through your opponent and explodes out the other side. This is how you practice the kata in order to develop the ki. When you can do this exercise well, you will be able to stop your blow at any point because your mind has already been there.

Itoman Bunkichi vs The Turtle

February 17, 1973

Bunkichi's teacher was Yada (not the same Yada from Chatan).

Bunkichi had an encounter with a man named Kame (turtle). Kame had his name because of his style, he fought with twin swords very low to the ground, springing up to attack – he'd learned it in China.

Kame wanted to challenge Bunkichi but Bunkichi always managed to avoid him. Kame came to the conclusion that it was because Bunkichi was half white. Kame knew that Bunkichi wasn't afraid. Kame's intellect figured that Bunkichi wanted to remain a deep mystery by not losing to anybody. The truth was, however that Bunkichi avoided Kame because he didn't want to hurt him in a fight since he knew that he could beat him.

Bunkichi's teacher told him that the best way of dealing with Kame was to humiliate him, along with giving him a good beating. Merely beating him wouldn't be enough since Kame might just train harder or simply shoot him in the back. Kame was physically as strong as Bunkichi.

Since Bunkichi ate a lot, he had may ways to obtain food. For one, he would go to a temple with a big bell, take it off its hanger, putting it down on the ground. (Takeda did this also.) Then, when the priest went to ring the bell, he would find it on the ground and have to ask some towns people to help him lift it back up.

These bells were so heavy that it normally required about 4 people to lift them.

At this point, Bunkichi would step up and volunteer to do it alone. When the town's people doubted his ability to do it alone, he would wager his services as a clean up man for one month against a good meal if he were successful.

Naturally, he would always win the bet since he was the one who took it off originally.

Pretty soon word spread about Bunkichi, so whenever he was in a town with a big temple bell, he was offered food before he could perform his trick. Kame also had this kind of strength so Bunkichi figured that the best way to humiliate him was to defeat him by using strength.

Finally Kame decided to attack Bunkichi. He started by following Bunkichi around with the idea of attacking him at his weakest moment. He followed Bunkichi into town where he saw him enter a brothel and shack up all night. Kame thought it best to wait until six or seven in the morning when Bunkichi would be tired from making love all night. When Bunkichi left the brothel early that morning, Kame decided that it would be even more desirable to attack Bunkichi after he ate a big meal so he followed him to a restaurant.

Bunkichi knew he was being followed so he arranged to stuff himself full of food. When Bunkichi came out, he knew what was on Kame's mind so he patted his full stomach and sighed. Bunkichi then walked away and picking out a high wall, leaned against it.

At this point Kame came out into the open and challenged Bunkichi. Kame always carried his twin swords with him but he took them off since he could see that Bunkichi had no weapons on him. Bunkichi accepted the challenge but stayed where he was, leaning up against the wall.

Kame figured that he was just tired so he decided to go for Bunkichi's stomach by using his head as a battering ram. He charged Bunkichi who at the last moment placed his hand against the wall and leaped up and over it. Kame knocked himself out against the wall.

Kame had a student by the name of Chung Duc Soo in the 1920s. Soo was always in trouble with the law but the police could never catch him because of his skill. Soo could elude his would-be captors by leaping over cars, walls, etc.

One time when they thought that they had him, he ran into a blind alley and at the last minute he escaped by jumping over the eleven foot high wall at the end of the alley.

This took place in Hawaii and the chief of police at that time was a man by the name of Duffy. Duffy made it a point of honor to catch Soo. Finally he was able to learn where Soo slept at night, underneath a church. The police surrounded the church and captured Soo. He was later tried, convicted and sentenced to hang. At that time, the law simply said to hang by the neck for fifteen minutes. For a normal man this was sufficient but when they hung Soo by his neck, his neck didn't break and he was smiling while he stared at Duffy. Thirteen minutes passed with no sign that Soo was suffocating so in desperation Duffy ran to Soo, jumped up, clinging to Soo' s legs. It was too much for Soo and he strangled.

Bunkichi had defeated Periera with his strength as well. He knew that in a crowd only eight men can attack you at a time. He would pick one out and attack him body and soul, disposing of him. After defeating four or five men in this manner, the rest of the attackers will usually disperse because they'll see that they can't handle you.

Ittosai Yanagi: Shuriken Hits the Peach

September 22, 1973

Public knowledge, information which is passed by word of mouth or script, is not important in relation to seeking and obtaining enlightenment.

Of course, in our society, public knowledge is important in regards to dealing with mundane affairs such as earning a living. Some people misconstrue a martial artist who says that public knowledge is unimportant. These people say, "A zen monk told me that public knowledge is unimportant so I won't go to school." What the zen monk meant was that it can't help you obtain enlightenment. All the knowledge in the world can't help with that. Public knowledge can be called second hand information, that is it comes from others, but it does help you exist in society.

The following incident shows how Ittosai achieved ki, and what steps he took to find universal knowledge, the knowledge of his self. One day as

Ittosai was walking in the mountains, an old man stepped out from the trees and said, "You cannot come into this area."

The old man had a staff (not a bo, but merely a staff for walking), and blocked Ittosai's path. Ittosai felt funny. He felt a powerful force coming from the old man and although it wasn't an evil force, it was pushing him powerfully.

Ittosai said, "Well I won't use this path. I'll go the other way." But even having said it, he felt funny. He was carrying two swords with real blades but his principal weapons were the two shuriken he had. Still feeling funny, he stepped back and told the old man, "I'll go down to the bottom of the hill and go up another way. "

The old man replied, "No! You're not permitted in this entire area." Ittosai tried to move but he still felt a force pushing against him. He was about fifteen feet away from the old man.

The man came towards him asking, "You want to attack me, don't you?"

Ittosai just looked at him, so the man said, "You're not skilful enough with the sword but you have another skill. Use your skill. It doesn't matter because I'm not your enemy, I'm your friend. Use your skill and try to kill me."

Ittosai judged the old man to be in his late seventies, he was slightly stooped. He decided to throw one of his shuriken but the old man just stuck out the end of his staff, impaling the end of the shuriken on it. It seemed that the old man knew exactly where the shuriken would land. The old man told Ittosai to throw another one, but Ittosai realized that it would be useless.

The old man said, ''What you did was to try to position me. Each person has a certain distance at which he never misses; it's just right for the shuriken or knife to flip over enough to hit point first. You had positioned yourself and all your vibrations (ki) gave away your position. So all I did was to stick out the end of my staff in front of me because I knew when and where you would throw it. Can you throw your shuriken at a moving target and hit it?"

When Ittosai replied negatively, the old man continued, ''You know why? It is because you don't now how to centre all your ki below your belly button (tanden). There's a way of centering it, then you must make it (ki) flow into whatever you're going to use, sword, shuriken, etc. The ki must flow from the tanden."

At this point the old man revealed that he was really a woman (a very great martial artist). It shocked Ittosai even more to find that a woman had defeated him. Before he could ask her anymore questions, she said, "Do you know why I live in the mountains?"

(It was the custom it that time not to initiate women into the martial arts, unless they were nobility and even then, they only learned the naginata for household defense. It was unheard of for a woman to go out and be a ronin, skilful with the sword or stick, that was because of the Buddhist philosophy in Japan at that time.)

She told Ittosai how to practice. "Do you know the momo? (Peach, in Japanese.) Get one and balance it on your finger looking at how it balances, then throw it into a fast moving stream where turbulence will sometimes cause the heavy part to tip to the top. When it tips, throw the shuriken. When you can throw and hit the peach, that' s when you will have it (ki in the tanden)."

Ittosai asked her how to do it. She said, '"You must do it from here (pointing to her tanden, two inches below the belly button). If you had thrown another shuriken at me, I would have captured it and that would have been it because you're not that good of a swordsman. You're good, but not good enough; I would have killed you with my stick." With that, Ittosai started practising the sword.

She also said that when women develop ki, they are more steady than men. She thought that it was because they were more emotional than men, thus it took more effort to be calm all the time and hold the ki in balance, so that when they finally did achieve it, they had terrific control.

She also told about the key that opens the door to private knowledge. With public knowledge the key is a college diploma. If you have one, you're recognized as knowledgeable. With private knowledge (universal knowledge) there is no such thing as a diploma. The one thing necessary in order to achieve private knowledge is so important that if you don't do it it'll make no difference what else you do you'll never achieve enlightenment – is meditation. You must meditate or else you'll never make it. Meditation is also prayer. If you pray and really believe, you'll produce a physical state similar to mediation.

Prayer has a calming effect and that is the process of meditation – calming the mind. Physiologically, the best position in which to meditate in is the lotus position. If you use a mantra or sutra when you meditate, it makes no difference if you don't know the meaning of it. For instance using NAMU YOHO RENGE KYO (the heart of the Lotus Sutra). The purpose of the mantra is to keep your mind in one place to help you achieve focus. It is a helping device to make your meditating easier as it aids in your concentration.

If you sat down and said to yourself, I am the greatest, I am the greatest, it would have the same effect as a mantra that you couldn't understand. It would settle down to your tanden the same but the difference is that if you know the meaning of it you might begin to argue with yourself. As in the case of the phrase, I am the greatest, you will begin to argue with yourself. So not having a meaning for the mantra will cause you not to fight as much, you will accept it. The Diamond Sutra is the sutra of emptiness and is the most suitable for martial artists.

In China, there was a school called the Tien Tai (in Japan it was Tendai). It was founded by a man named Tendai. He had a student who went to Japan and spread his teachings. Tendai achieved enlightenment in thirty years through chanting. The sutra he used was always on his mind. His student took about twenty years and then there was a man named Nichiren (a very controversial person), Nichiren is the man some Japanese claimed created the divine wind (kamikaze) that destroyed the invading Mongolian army (a great typhoon wiped out their fleet). He allegedly did this through chanting NAMU YOHO RENGE KYO. Nichiren had this ability. He could go on the mountain top or anywhere else and chant NAMU YOHO RENGE KYO very strongly and through it make the wind blow hard enough to knock down trees.

The Japanese government was afraid to kill him so they exiled him – but he came back. Finally he told them about a forthcoming invasion. He chanted NAMU YOHO RENGE KYO for fifty-three days.

It took him that long to gather enough energy to make the big typhoon come and destroy the Mongolians. This sect claimed that continued chanting of the sutra will bring you enlightenment, provided that you do it in a certain way over a prolonged time period (years).

In their temple in Japan (Sokogakai), the Lotus Sutra is chanted around the clock twenty-four hours a day. There is a terrific vibration coming out of the temple, has been for hundreds of years. The vibration moves down into a nearby valley, very strongly. They claim that an average person can get in touch with that vibration (tap its energy) by repeating NAMU MYOHO RENGE KYO.

Your body will act as an antenna and pick up the vibration. This

Japanese man living in Japan was doing a particular sutra which creates magic. He had doubts about it's power although he was doing it all the time. (Mr. Kim says that you must have this doubt. If you don't have it, that little bit of doubt, it's harder to train. Every body will reach the stage where they'll wonder whether or not the sutra will work for them.) So one day a crazy person, running amuck with a knife went straight for this man. The man thought he might as well do his magic, he was training all the time, so he made a sign called naomi as the crazy person went to chop him. The crazy guy froze. He couldn't move. The police were called and when they arrived, they figured they'd have to carry the crazy man away. The Japanese man told them to grab the crazy man's knife and with that he took off the spell by reciting a sutra. Needless to say the incident made the man a real believer in what he was doing.

Ittosai practised what the old woman taught him and one day while riding along the beach, a group of men forced him to stop his horse. There were nine of them, they surrounded him. The leader told him that he wouldn't be hurt but that he must surrender his weapons, clothes and money. He would be allowed to keep the horse. Ittosai knew that he could break through them with his horse, but two things bothered him, first, that they looked like dispossessed samurai and, second, that if word got out that he had fled he would be thought a coward. He felt it his duty to make a citizen's arrest and make it safer for society.

He didn't know how skilful they were, but he knew that the leader was just waiting for him to dismount. Ittosai knew that the moment he dismounted he would have a suki and could be attacked. He would be vulnerable and they could cut him down.

That would be the only time he would be so vulnerable. He had to think of something. The gang surrounded him so no matter which side he dismounted on they would attack him. So he grabbed the saddle horn and rose up as if to get off the horse, at a left forward diagonal (naomi) and as he did so, the person in that direction came towards him (probably the strongest swordsman). However instead of dismounting that way, he gave a sudden leap, jumping off one hundred and eighty degrees from it, landing at his right rear diagonal, as he did, he drew his sword cutting off the sword-hand of that man. He ended up killing six of them and severely injuring three. He realized then that he didn't have to depend on his shuriken and realized what the woman told him about the ki. Your ki surrounds you in an oval sphere and spins around you. You can feel it from your tanden and your tanden does the work.

He realized that she had been telling the truth because he had been able to get rid of nine samurai.

There was confirmation of this story. A man who thought a tobacco seller looked like a samurai commented on it to him. The seller admitted to being one. The man asked, "Why are you selling tobacco instead of being a man-at-arms?" The tobacco seller replied, "In the old days, I was young and rash and joined a band of ruffians. We used to make a hell of a good living waylaying people on the beach until one day we waylaid this certain person. This is the result, I lost my hand."

He held up the stump where his right hand used to be. This man then wrote about the incident and that's how they found out that Ittosai was just as skilful with the sword as he was with the shuriken.

Tomoe Gozen

Tomoe Gozen was a very famous general. She was the main figure in a certain lord's army and a thorn in the side of her enemies. Sixty-seven samurai, sent by her enemies, challenged her one by one to fight to the death. She won every match. Finally, a twenty-four year old general by the name of Shigetada, met her while they were both out riding. He grabbed her arm and said, "I hate to kill women, but the lord wants to see you so you better come along. He is going to divorce his wife and wants to make you his mistress."

She refused to go, but he wouldn't let go of her arm, so she hit it. He then let go, whereupon she grabbed his head and performed what is now known as daruma-gaeshi. She threw him off his horse and down to the ground. From this throw, which she devised on the spot, came the principle that the head is the steering wheel of the body.

The name Tomoe, is also the word for the buddhist's swastika symbol.

For some reason, possibly because of the imminent death of her lord, or possibly because he was going to leave her, she was going to commit suicide. She was all ready, kneeling down and set to cut her stomach, when Shigetada saw her and said, "What are you doing? You can't commit suicide, you don't have permission."

He didn't know what else to say in order to stop her, so he finally grabbed her around the neck with his left arm, choking her, grabbed her sword arm with his left hand. She just reached over with her left hand and grabbed his right hand which was holding her right hand, pulled it around her head to the left as she turned to the left, and applied sankajo technique. This is how the sankajo technique originated.

What a Wonderful Thing is Satori

Odagiri went on the road, in order to further his martial arts training. While on the road, he found a place to practice in the woods near a swamp. Overlooking the swamp was a fifteen foot high cliff. He would sit there and meditate. With him was Mikita Bungoro who had become his disciple and followed him wherever he went.

Odagiri ate only once a day at twilight, he hated to cook. He didn't believe in cooking, so Mikita would go into town, get the food, and prepare it, then bring it to Odagiri. By the time he was done, it would be twilight. One day, as Mikita was coming back with food, he saw two samurai on their knees, in front of Odagiri asking for a lesson, which meant of course that they wanted a match.

The two samurai were introducing themselves to Odagiri who was sitting in a lotus position not paying any attention to them. He didn't have his weapons with him during meditation. The two men were Inazu Magosaku and Doi Iinchiro.

Mikita was on the edge of the clearing, many feet away, but he felt that the samurai were going to attack Odagiri, and he started to reach for his sword. At this point Doi attacked Odagiri, a terrific downward blow to

Odagiri's head, the type of blow that is so hard, that if you missed you would lose your balance. All Odagiri did was to fall straight back, flat on his back, Doi lost his balance, falling over Odagiri and fifteen feet into the swamp behind him. Odagiri sat up, and was attacked by Inazu who slashed his left arm, not too deeply though. Odagiri went in after the slash, grabbing Inazu's short sword, pulling it out, killing him with it.

Inazu, realizing that he was done for, grabbed the short sword that was still in him, slashing it side to side, performing hara kiri. He then threw both his swords into the swamp so that Odagiri would not have access to them, because there was another samurai waiting in the bushes.

Mikita by this time had moved forward, sword drawn, when Odagiri felt a strong ki coming from the man in the bushes. He realized that Mikita would be no match for him and would be killed if he moved. He shouted to Mikita to stay where he was.

The samurai came out of the bushes and approached Odagiri. He looked very evil, one eye, the right, was wide open, the left eye closed. Odagiri was shaken to the very core by the man's evil aura.

The man attacked Odagiri with a terrific downward slash. Odagiri jumped back and felt his arm cut in the same place, only a little bit deeper. Both men stood looking at each other for a while. Blood slowly started trickling out of the closed left eye of the man. The man then told Odagiri his name, Sogo Korobyoe, excused himself and disappeared. Apparently when the man had slashed at Odagiri, Odagiri had jabbed his right hand into Sogo's eye. Odagiri had done this without thinking, it was the only weapon he had.

Twenty seven years had passed since he had fought Sogo Korobyoe. When Odagiri was in his eighties he was walking along a bridge (one of those curved bridges that span a small river) one day. It was raining and he had on a rain hat, the type of hat that comes down over your eyes so that you can just see the ground in front of you. When he got to the middle of the bridge he stopped when he saw a man standing at the end of it. The man said, "It's been twenty-seven years, Odagiri."

Odagiri hears evil in the voice. Upon closer inspection, he recognizes Sogo, still looking the same, one wide open right eye, one closed left eye, radiating more evil than ever. Odagiri could feel that Sogo was close to attaining mushin. Then Odagiri could hear people running. Although he couldn't see them because of his rain hat, he was able to count their footsteps, twenty-one people, eleven in front and ten in back of him.

Odagiri had no desire to kill Sogo's students. Sogo cut at Odagiri who stepped back just enough so that the sword cut through the rain hat, enabling Odagiri to see. At this point, the police arrived, blowing their whistles, etc. They observed Odagiri hit Sogo with some type of blow, killing him and then knocking down all twenty-one students. Getting closer, they saw that all twenty-one students had either an arm or a leg cut off but only Sogo was dead. Odagiri then walked off into the night and was never seen again.

What a Wonderful Thing is Satori

The following is another account of the value of satori. Odagiri had a fight with Kariwara Nogato who was the best in Odagiri's time. Nogato's technique was to come in fast with a terrific downward cutting stroke to the head, hoping that his opponent would step back. His strike came so quickly that nine out of ten people would step back so he would continue down to the ground where the blade would strike the ground and bounce up. He would then turn the blade over as he brought the blade up, slashing his opponent's jaw, killing him or breaking his jaw if he used a wooden sword. If his opponent blocked the downward blow, which was fast but possibly not enough to kill, he would then give the katsumi cut, bringing his sword around his head after being blocked, to a cut the opponent's side, killing him.

Odagiri thought to himself what a wonderful thing satori was because he could see all of the above coming. He could feel it in Nogato's mind. When Nogato came in with his attack, Odagiri stepped back, bringing his leg up, sustaining a small cut on his leg as he did so, then jumped up, striking Nogato on the head, killing him.

Odagiri's Secret

After fighting Chin 'The Frog' Odagiri had reached satori, and he had finally surpassed technical excellence.

He told Mikita (who later on became a famous man), that he would tell him a secret. He showed him a tatami with a black stripe on its edge and asked Mikita if he could walk along the edge without losing his balance.

Mikita said that he could, it was easy.

Odagiri next asked him, "What if the tatami were ten feet tall, could you still walk along the black edge?"

Mikita answered that it would be more difficult.

Odagiri asked, "Suppose the edge was ten miles long and went up to the top of a mountain (sloping up), could you still walk it?"

Mikita replied that his fear would make it very difficult.

Odagiri then wanted to know which would make it more dangerous, the height or his mind. Mikita decided the mind. Odagiri agreed, you must not fight with your mind, because you will feel fear, you must achieve mushin.

Odagiri on Self Doubt

Odagiri was a good carver, a skill that he had learned from Harigaya.

One day, while Odagiri was carving a bear, he noticed someone arguing with Mikita. This person wanted to teach Odagiri a lesson because he didn't think that Odagiri was as good as his teacher, Harigaya. The man wanted to challenge Odagiri. He looked rather unusual. On his back was a picture of a rising sun. He carried an eight foot staff with metal on each end, with knobs on the stick. The knobs were to prevent a sword from slipping down if he used the stick to deflect a sword blow. From his right shoulder down to his waist, he had the phrase, 'The best in the world.' On his left shoulder was his name, Mondo, and that he had had won one-hundred and one matches. In fact, he was the only man that Musashi did not beat.

Mondo faced Odagiri and challenged him to a match. Odagiri told him that he didn't think too much of him because any man who had a sign on him proclaiming himself to be the best in the world couldn't be too skilful, a skilful man didn't do things like that. Mondo told Odagiri that he had won one-hundred and one matches. At that, Odagiri remarked that if he went around dressed like that, he would have to be alert at all times for attacks. Mondo said that he was always aware, that he was ready even when he was sleeping. Mondo continued by saying that when he ate, he ate, when he slept he slept, he wasn't thinking about all kinds of things and worrying like other people when they slept, and dreamed.

Odagiri said that it was the same with him, when he ate, he ate, when he slept he slept. Odagiri knew that he could beat Mondo, although Mondo had achieved a certain kind of kensho.

Mondo proceeded to do his katas in front of Odagiri, slashing with the bo, stamping his feet, jabbing and yelling. Odagiri was thinking to himself that Mondo was trying to scare him, as if Odagiri was an animal to be frightened away. However this didn't bother Odagiri one bit and he asked Mondo to let him know when he was ready to fight. Mondo said he was ready, so they got in their kamai, facing each other.

Odagiri's only weapon was a stick he had been carving. Odagiri believed, as his teacher Harigaya did, that when you face an opponent, you don't fool around. Step to get in distance, and when you are in distance, strike. If you are in distance already, strike immediately. Mondo jabbed at Odagiri and when he did, Odagiri took a step forward, to the left, into a zenkutsu-dachi and knocked the staff away with the stick in his right hand. Then he grabbed the stick with both hands, moving in on Mondo, whirling the stick, hitting Mondo on the head with just enough force to knock him out.

Odagiri had killed many men in his life but for the first time he got a strange feeling standing over the unconscious body of Mondo. Then he realized what it was, Mondo was breathing slowly and evenly, ready to attack. Odagiri sensed that if he were to strike at Mondo, even though he was unconscious, Mondo would roll away or do something. (This was a defensive ki or kobu that Mondo had developed. He had trained himself to do kokyu breathing to revitalize himself after an attack.)

Odagiri shouted for Mondo to get up. Odagiri told him what he had developed was marvellous. Odagiri hadn't developed this technique yet. The two became fast friends.

Odagiri realized the importance of kufusuru (great self-doubt), after fighting with Mondo. The ego makes your mind a dictionary in that it separates you, the subject, from the object, which is reality. When you let loose an arrow, you become (or should become) the target so that there is no separation of subject and object, you and the target are one. He realized the importance of surpassing technical excellence and that reaching satori was superior.

Odagiri on Self Awareness

Self awareness is like a tea kettle resting on three legs: faith, tenacity and a great big ball of doubt. A great ball of doubt is ego pushed into a corner. For instance, if you have problems, and you are ready to commit suicide, you will feel that there is no hope, you will be in complete despair. When you reach this point in your training, you must break through; your martial arts teacher, sensing this, will help you. This is called kufusuru.

Odagiri knew he was going to die three days before it happened. (Although the exact age at which he died is not known, he was in his eighties.) Odagiri told his neighbors to visit his house in three days, when they did, they found him dead, sitting in a lotus position.

Odagiri was the son of a famous samurai who had a terrific temper. One day, the father got angry at Odagiri and threw a knife at him. Odagiri just moved his head, the knife missed and hit a tree behind him. This surprised the father, he didn't expect his son to have such skill. The father drew his short sword and threw that, too. Once again, Odagiri dodged the weapon easily. Odagiri was only twelve years old at the time and, of course, he thought he knew everything. He thought he had great skill, if his father, a famous samurai, couldn't hit him with a knife, or a sword, so he decided to leave home and live with his mother.

On the way to his mother's house, Odagiri happened to pass through a village where he noticed a posted challenge sign signed by Arima. Arima wanted everybody to know that he challenged anyone in the village to test his skill with a weapon of their choice. Odagiri crossed out a few words and wrote on the sign, "I accept, Odagiri."

Arima arranged the ground rules, where the match was to take place and when. At this point, Odagiri got scared because he was just a twelve year old kid, he began to realize what he had done. He went to a priest and told him everything, why he had left his father, and why he had accepted the challenge. The priest went to Arima telling him to take it easy on Odagiri, he was, after all, just a kid who didn't know what he was doing. Arima, being a man of good will, agreed with the priest. While Odagiri was walking to the appointed place, the priest continually told Odagiri to be sure to apologize to Arima so that he would go easy on him. Odagiri was becoming annoyed with the priest's repetition.

Arima couldn't back out of the match because he had publicly accepted the challenge, so when Odagiri faced Arima, Arima told him that it was okay, he didn't have to apologize. Odagiri got angry after Arima said that, and swung a club he picked up on the way, at Arima who was surprised by the kid. Odagiri's actions angered Arima and he went to draw his sword. Odagiri, was afraid now, and yelled, "Wait, let's wrestle."

Arima did not want to kill Odagiri and accepted.

Odagiri grabbed Arima's leg right away and threw him down. Arima hit his head on a rock when he fell and was dazed. He tried to sit up, he was dazed and angry and yelled, "You god damn kid!"

Odagiri was angry as well, and picked up the club again and hit Arima on the head, killing him. Odagiri looked at the body of Arima and asked himself, 'Is this how it feels to kill a man?' as he felt all these feelings going through him.

Odagiri did not reach satori until after the age of fifty.

The Samurai Who Ate, Drank and Made Merry

Odagiri had another story, a Taoist story.

A Duke had a fighting cock which he sent away to be trained. He saw the keeper ten days later and asked if his bird was ready. The keeper said, "No he isn't, he bristles up with anger when another fighting cock comes near, he's vain, he struts around, he's cocky."

The Duke said he'd wait another ten days. When he went back a second time, the keeper said that the cock was still not ready, that even when he sees the shadow of a different cock, or knows that there is a different cock nearby, he shows resentment and wants to fight.

Another ten days passed and the keeper said the cock was almost ready, but not quite, that when he heard the crowing of a different cock, he opened his eyes. Ten more days go by and the Duke learns that the cock is ready. The keeper says, "He's ready alright. When he hears the crowing of another cock or anything like it, he doesn't even bat an eye. He stays as still as a piece of wood. He is ready. This meant that the cock had absorbed all feelings and had found his own awareness.

One day, Odagiri was sitting on a stone, dozing, with his hands inside his kimono. The man sees him sitting there, asleep, and figures, "Gee! The great Odagiri! He's sleeping now. I'll test his ability. This guy surpassed his teacher, Harigaya." (The consensus of every skilful swordsman, then and now, is that there has never been a more skilful person than Odagiri, no matter what popular writing says about Yagyu or Musashi. Odagiri sought neither fame nor fortune because he believed that it would engulf him and he would lose his 'self'. The 'quieter' he was, the better, he thought.)

The man crept silently up behind Odagiri and hit him in the head with a wooden sword – a slight tap (he was skilful). Odagiri leaned away, avoiding the blow while he was sleeping. The man got scared. Odagiri had avoided his blow without waking up and was still snoring.

So the man thought to himself, 'Maybe he's half-awake. I'll attack him at four o'clock in the morning. I'll get him when he has had a good dinner and drinking at the bar.' (Some samurai felt that you had to refrain from women, good food, etc. but not Odagiri. Odagiri thought that we lived in two worlds – the external and the internal – and when you lived in the external world, you got the good things. The samurai who believed in asceticism found out, after they were dead, that they were wrong.)

That night, Odagiri ate a lot, drank more than he should have, and was seen staggering home by the man who wanted to attack him. He figured that this was a good time to strike. After Odagiri went to bed, the man waited until four in the mooring and pounded on Odagiri's door. He readied his bokken and waited for Odagiri to open the door.

Odagiri awoke and shouted out, "Who's there?"

The man shouted back, "Open up, I have a very important message for you from (it is unknown whose name he used)."

Odagiri slides the door open, while he's rubbing his eyes, totally hung over. Just as Odagiri starts to slide the door open, the man hits, Odagiri drops straight down causing the man to tumble over him. (Ueshiba used this same technique, it came from Odagiri.) When the man fell over Odagiri stood up and went back to bed.

This particular man joined Odagiri's school. He was a skilful swordsman in his own right, but he couldn't understand Odagiri's skill. He had reached his limit of technical excellence. He still figured that there had to be a way he could get hold of Odagiri – catch him unaware. He figured that he had to momaru Odagiri's mind (stop his mind).

One day, he saw Odagiri preparing his bath. Odagiri, being a poor man, prepared his own bath. The Japanese had bath routine – building the fire, boiling the water, then finally, entering the tub. Odagiri had everything that he wanted, he had his women, he ate and drank what he wanted and anytime someone wanted to fight him, all he had to do was turn around, hit them on the head, and knock them out. He didn't even have to kill them. He had satori – self-awareness, bliss. You don't need more than that.

Odagiri was bent over, poking the fire with a stick, trying to get it going for his bath water, he was completely absorbed in the task. The man could see his ki. It helped that he had conspired with some of the other students to make a lot of noise with their swords while practising nearby. Odagiri looked over at them, then went back to his fire, not noticing them anymore. The man snuck up behind Odagiri, gave one quick hit but was thrown down again. He never did figure out how Odagiri had done it, he knew that Odagiri had thrown him, even though he was still tending the fire.

When Odagiri was done with the fire, he told the man that he was finished at the school, the man's name was Hirayama, he was famous. Odagiri told him that he had reached his limit of technical efficiency and that if he, Odagiri, were not around, nobody in the area could beat him, maybe not even Yagyu, who hadn't reached self-awareness. He told Hirayama that he would like to see him in a match with Yagyu. Odagiri told Hirayama that the next time he attacked him, he might die – and then kicked him out of his school.

The Fox and the Badger

January 1970

The school of Mujushin-ken, (*sword of no abiding mind*), was founded by Odagiri. He believed that ken-jitsu should not be an art of killing, but one of disciplining the self as a moral being. The first requirement is to discard any desire to turn swordsmanship into a kind of entertainment or just a mere accomplishment, and to refrain from thinking about achieving victory over an opponent. Odagiri's system was characterized by natural techniques, a meekness of spirit, and the conviction that his style had no peers.

One day Harigaya asked Odagiri, "Did you have great ability when you were young? When I first met you as a youth, you had great skill."

Odagiri replied that he did not show great ability as a child, that he learned the sword for a reason. When he was a kid, a bunch of samurai dropped by his father's house one day and painted a picture of a tiger in a bamboo forest. Odagiri came by to take a look.

"Hey, kid, come over here. You look like a bright kid, can you rope this tiger?"

"Yes," replied Odagiri, "it's simple."

All the samurai laughed and said, "How are you going to rope that tiger, boy, that tiger is in a painting?"

Odagiri said, "I'll tell you what, you go into the bamboo grove, chase him towards me and I'll rope him when he comes out."

After Harigaya died, someone came by and told Odagiri that he didn't understand what Odagiri meant by meekness of spirit. This man had had a match the week before and almost died in it, he showed Odagiri a slight scar. Odagiri asked him what had gone wrong. The man said, "Well, I was watching my opponent's sword, we got closer and closer and I could tell what he was going to do, so I figured that I was going to beat him to the stroke. When I went in to strike, I was sucked in. If it wasn't for my dexterity, I would have been killed."

Odagiri replied, "The trouble with you is that you don't take into account the eyes. The eyes are not the mirror of the soul, as you might think. You have to achieve mushin for that. I'm going to tell you a story.

"There was a blind man who everybody played jokes on. One day, the blind man and some other people were on top of a mountain pass that had a steep gorge. The blind man was told to walk over a pole that crossed off the gorge, the blind man was unaware it was there. He stepped up on the pole and walked across the gorge, tapping his cane, without any fear at all.

After hearing this, the samurai said that anybody could do that. (The Japanese in those days believed in ghosts and the worst thing that could control a human being was thought to be the fox, kitsune, and the badger, tanuki. They were supposed to be monsters that could turn themselves into human form and control you. The fox usually became a woman and the badger became a man.) There was this one tanuki who got rid of every samurai coming up a certain mountain road. He would turn himself into all sorts of shapes, but when he met this blind guy and tried to capture his mind, he failed. He tried to enter the blind man's mind to control him but he couldn't because the blind man couldn't see and wasn't thinking, he was worrying about his next step and concentrating on tapping with his stick, his mind was on one track. So the tanuki stood in front of him changed himself into a giant tanuki and straddled the road in an attempt to scare the blind man. The blind man keeps tapping and hits the tanuki's balls with his cane.

The blind man feels a soft object, it won't go away, so he jabs it, he jabs the balls with his cane causing the tanuki to scream in pain and jump away.

'What the hell is the matter with this guy,' thinks the tanuki, 'can't he see that I'm blocking his way?' He didn't know that the man was blind. He had to enter a man through his eyes – the mirror of the soul. So he moves further away and changes himself into a dragon. He's breathing fire as the blind man approaches. The blind man feels the heat and using his cane hits the dragon's nose. It hurts the tanuki and he jumps away and gives up."

The message to the man was that sometimes when you face an opponent, if you focus your eyes on one spot and think 'I'm going to do this,' when you say 'I am' your opponent, if he has muju-shinken, he will hit you with his sword without thinking about it because muju-shinken is a mere extension of his stomach – his soul – he wouldn't have to do anything. If that person has mushin with you, what do you do? You both sit down and drink tea!

 Energy comes when you complete anything, uncompleted jobs drain energy.

Odagiri vs a White Tiger

One day, Odagiri responded to a summons from the Emperor. The emperor told Odagiri that he wanted him to have a match with Yagyu. (Yagyu was skilful and had incorporated zen into his swordsmanship.) Odagiri replied that he hated to embarrass Yagyu but, well, maybe he'd have a match, he agreed.

The day of the match arrived and both men appeared in the arena in front of the Emperor. Yagyu entered from one side and Odagiri from the other. Odagiri walked calmly, holding his sword, when Yagyu was about twenty feet away, Odagiri looked at Yagyu, turned at an angle and walked out of the arena – he just walked out.

The Emperor called Odagiri back and asked him why he had walked out. Odagiri said, "Yagyu is no match for me! Just ask Yagyu."

The Emperor did ask Yagyu if what Odagiri said was true. Yagyu replied, "I don't know. I have never met a man like him, it was as if there wasn't anyone there when he was walking up to me."

The Emperor asked Odagiri to continue the match but Odagiri said: "I would have to kill a man with Yagyu's skill. You don't want Yagyu dead. A chance will present itself that will test our skill." The Emperor agreed to wait.

One day, the King of Korea gave the Emperor a large tiger. The largest tigers in the world come from Korea. This particular tiger came from the White Mountains between Manchuria and Korea. The tiger arrived in his cage, growling fiercely, but he wouldn't turn around. The Emperor was watching and waiting for the tiger to turn around so that he could see the tiger's face. After a while, the Emperor called for Yagyu and told him to go into the cage and turn the tiger around, not to kill it, just to turn it around.

Yagyu took a look at the tiger. A boy near the cage asked if he should open the cage. Yagyu turned to the Emperor and said, "I can't do it. I'm just a human being. How can I turn this huge beast around." The tiger was very frightening due to his size and its fierce growling.

Odagiri happened to be passing by and heard the exchange. He approached the Emperor and said, "I'll show you why I didn't complete the match with Yagyu. I'll turn the tiger around for you."

The Emperor asked, "Will you?"

Odagiri replied, "Of course! This tiger is just an animal. He can't think, he's no match for a martial artist."

Odagiri told one of the retainers to hold his sword. The keeper opened the cage door and Odagiri entered, grabbed the tiger by the tail and gave one big yank, the tiger, screaming in pain, turned to look at Odagiri and stepped out of the cage facing the Emperor. Odagiri had beaten Yagyu.

Odagiri knew about the critical zone, the cura, that surrounds all living things, tigers included. The tiger had sensed Odagiri's critical zone, imprinting on Odagiri, but Odagiri, being a man of mushin, could turn off his aura. (That's why Yagyu couldn't sense him.) When Odagiri entered the cage, the tiger wasn't alarmed and he was able to pull his tail causing him to turn around. Lion and tiger trainers know and use this principle today. They control their animals by pressing towards, and slightly inside their critical zone, making them back up. They then stop the animal from attacking them by interposing a chair or object between themselves and the animal.

Ono Jiroemon Tadaaki: How He Got His Name

January 1970

Ono Jiroemon Tadaaki was a small man , only 5'2" tall. He was born in 1560 and died in 1628. When he was 15 years old, he met Ito Ittosai and stayed with him for five years, training in fencing. At the end of the five years they went on the road together. One day, they were passing a fishing village, when they heard a commotion. It was a group of men, one man facing off against about seventy-five fishermen. The man was very strong and had already knocked out twenty-two fishermen, but he was running out of wind and was now cornered. So Ito went up to the man and told him to get behind him. He turned to the fishermen and asked why they were ganging up on this man. The fishermen said that he was always getting angry, constantly fighting and sleeping with all the women. They had decided to teach him a lesson and cut his testicles off. Ito told them that he would be responsible for the man, took out some coins threw them in the air and when the fishermen went for the coins they were mollified.

The man was Ono Zenki, he was 5'11" and weighed 185 pounds. Both Ono and Zenki stayed with Ito for the next seven years. (Ono's name before he changed it was Tenzen.) Zenki later almost equalled Ito.

One day while at an inn, Ito called for Zenki to come to him. When Zenki entered the room, he was confronted by a screen made up of eight sections, which traversed the whole width of the room, leaving no room for a man to go past it. The screen was six or seven feet high, there was some space between the top of the screen and the ceiling. Zenki found no way around it, so he grabbed the top of the screen and leaped over it, landing on the floor on the other side where he saw Ito meditating in front of a shrine. Zenki called out, "I am here, Sensei. Did you want to see me?"

Ito told Zenki that he was going to pass the menkyo kaiden, (inka), which was a sword and scroll, the next morning at seven. It was to go to the winner of the match between him and Tensen. Zenki was thinking to himself that Ito might as well give him the inka now because in all their training, Zenki always beat the smaller Tensen. He knew that he would beat him again tomorrow. He agreed to the fight and left.

Ito then called Tenzen to come to his room. Tenzen opened the door and was also confronted by the screen and looked for a way around it. He also found no way around it and realized that it was nailed to the floor. He didn't jump completely over the screen, although he knew that he could, because he didn't know where his Sensei was and he was afraid that if he did that he might land on top of his head so he jumped on top of the screen. When Tenzen was perched on top of the screen, he looked for his sensei. He saw him meditating in front of a shrine. He called to him three times, receiving no answer, he jumped down and said, "Excuse me, I am entering the room."

Ito turned around and told Tenzen the same thing that he had told Zenki. Tensen knew that he was no match for Zenki and said, "Sensei, why don't you give him the scroll now, I can't beat him."

Ito told him, "Tenzen, you have been with me many years and you know that to succeed in the martial arts, you must pay the price. The price is that you must face death. You may die tomorrow but I want you to fight."

The battle was fought at Kogeno-ga-hara and was recorded by monks. This area was covered by a lot of scrubby brush and small trees. The night before the match, Ito sent a letter to both Tenzen and Zenki with just one sentence: *What you do tonight will determine your fate tomorrow.*

The next morning at seven thirty, a monk rang the bell. An out of breath Zenki ran up, panting, saying, "Gee I just made it. I ran two miles just to get here."

Ito asked Zenki what he had done the night before, Zenki replied that he had gotten into an argument with a samurai and felt that it was a good time to test his skill and had killed him. There was still blood dripping off his sword. There was no sign of Tenzen. zenki told Ito that he probably wouldn't show up, and that he might as well give him the inka. Ito replied that Tenzen would show. A monk rang the bell again at eight o'clock and from behind a bush stepped Tenzen dressed in his fighting gear and wearing a headband, (the headband had a little piece of metal inside it as protection against an omen cut), all ready to do battle, whereas Zenki just had his regular clothes on.

They faced each other. Tenzen knew that he was no match for Zenki and that he would have to try to win by distracting him. Tenzen held the blade pointed down, moving it in a small circle, hoping to distract Zenki and then strike him. They faced each other for half an hour, moving very slowly, circling each other, with neither one letting up on their guard or attacking.

Finally, Zenki was in a position where his back was to Ito, the moment this happened, he felt Ito's eyes boring into the back of his neck, it felt like a blow. Zenki realized that his teacher did not want him to win, but wanted Tenzen to win. At that moment, while he was thinking that, there was a suki and Tenzen attacked. He cut at Zenki twice, any other man would have gone down but Zenki was such a powerful man that he took the two cuts and sprang into action, blocking the next blow and knocking Tenzen to the ground. When Tenzen was on his knees with his sword pointing down, Zenki had his sword over his head and was just about to deliver the final blow when Tenzen saw a rat crawling on Zenki's stomach and just jabbed the rat, killing it.

There was no rat, it was all in Tenzen's mind, but in striking the rat he had of course struck Zenki, giving him a mortal wound. He sprang to Zenki to help him but the monks told him that there was no way of helping Zenki and that he only had an hour to live. They looked toward Ito, but he was gone. In his place was the inka – the sword and scroll. They took Zenki up to the monk's temple, Zenki told them not to worry about him, and also about feeling Ito's eyes on the back of his neck. He asked Tenzen to do him one favor, to take his first name as his name. Tenzen became Ono Jiroemon Tadaaki.

One thing I failed to mention was that when Tenzen was talking to his sensei about the match, the sensei was chiding him when Tenzen said that he didn't think that he could beat Zenki. The sensei told him that he must fight with hara, not intellect, to face death. Fight like you are catching rats. Tenzen was able to jump and grab a rat by the back of the neck and kill it just like the thirteen year old Takeda was able to do. So when he had the final fight and he pictured the rat, on Zenki's stomach, he jabbed the rat without thinking and that was the way he was able to kill Zenki. Up to that point, he had been using his intellect to try and suck Zenki in.

Gettan and the Mirror

If a champion may be defined as one who fights for another's rights or honor, then such a one was Tsuji Gettan. If a champion is a winner of first prize or place in competition, then we have to search in the sporting arena.

Tsuji Gettan was a champion of the first definition. He did not compete in the sporting arena. But then Gettan, who lived from 1647-1726 in old Japan, was a samurai who combined not only the art of the sword with Zen but scholarship, as well.

His writings were first class, a feat in itself, as most swordsmen in his era and the era before him could write well enough but not as scholars or academicians. Gettan could match his pen with the best, but we will never know how he would have fared if he had stuck to the pen and not sword.

Omori Sogen, a Zen monk and present day historian, who wrote 'Zen and the Sword' made a special trip to Kochi Prefecture to visit a museum where Gettan's artifacts were shown, and in his own account, came back speechless.

He had taken a first-hand look at the shinai that Tsuji Gettan had used. In his account, "What a master swordsman Gettan must have been. I noticed, and it put me in awe, that the only worn out part of the shinai was the striking part. Every other area of the shinai was as new. His skill must have been awesome!"

How fortunate it was for seekers of fame and glory, in his time, that Gettan cared less to be number one, but he used his skill when it came to helping the unfortunate. Once, after a long period of meditation in the mountains, he was one his way back home when the news came to him that seven ronins were terrorizing the people and established themselves as king of the walk.

When the mood struck them they would stroll slowly through town and woe to the unfortunate who would have the misfortune to block their way. As far as the bullies were concerned, it was always intentional. They demanded a respect that they themselves were incapable of giving.

Gettan ran smack into them. The ronins looked at him with surprise. "Do not use the whole street. There is room for plenty. Others want and have the right to use it," Gettan said.

The ronins stared at him. They saw that he had apparently come from the mountains as his clothes were in need of care and by the type of hat that he was wearing.

"Don't talk to us with your hat on. Take it off so we can see your face. Show some respect," one ronin yelled.

Gettan flung his hat and his hair sprang up in all directions, his eyes glared, and the ronins, shocked to see such a sight, broke ground and fled. One of them later said, 'I really thought I had seen Fudo Myoo, the chief of the royal protectors of Buddha, in all his righteous anger. It was too much for me! "

Gettan said, "Bullies are scared people who always live in secret fear. Out of fear, they band together and put on a show of strength. Break that shell and they will cry to heaven. It is a pity because they do not realize that life is a process of give and take. It is like being surrounded by mirrors – what you give shall return – the law of causation."

And he explained about the monkey who saw a reflection of himself in a mirror, and who, surprised at such an ugly apparition, painted the mirror with lipstick and rouge to beautify the apparition.

But, it was just as ugly. And the monkey got mad and the madder he got the uglier the apparition became.

He ran around the mirror in rage and finally it dawned on him that what he saw was a reflection, an illusion and he started to laugh. He looked in the mirror and the more he laughed, the more beautiful and happy the apparition became.

Ono Jiroemon and Three Kinds of People

January 1970

Tokugawa Iemitsu had an encounter with Ono during which Ono knocked him down after Iemitsu had attempted to kill Ono. Nothing was ever said about it afterwards.

Iemitsu, though, wanted to have Ono killed because of his rudeness. Obata suggested that this was not a good idea because you couldn't kill a famous man like Ono without starting people talking. Obata said that Iemitsu wouldn't be considered much of a man in the eyes of the people if this was known, since they already didn't care for him because of his homosexuality.

In the meantime, Ono was asked by the shogun to show him his technique. Ono agreed and got into his kamai and stood still for fifteen minutes, after which the shogun threw his fan in one quick motion. Most samurai would have been cut in half but Ono, was able to grab the lethal fan with one hand and lay it down without touching his sword. The shogun had been watching the sword and never saw it move.

Iemitsu loved the martial arts and had received the inka from Yagyu Tajomnikami, but he was vindictive and a schemer and had been jealous that Yagyu was the shogun's fencing teacher. He tricked Ono into having a match with Harigaya Sekiun. Iemitsu had heard of Harigaya's exceptional skill and arranged the match.

Ono was on time for the match. Harigaya was left-handed and thought left-handed (he was tricky). Ono later said of the match with Harigaya,

"When I faced him, I was impressed, he was a very big man, there was 'suki' and Harigaya attacked. The referee stopped the match immediately. I lost!"

Iemitsu was surprised by the match. It had been a strange one, it had seemed that Ono had never fought before. Iemitsu wanted to know why Ono had lost and asked him. Ono told him that there are two kinds of people – the one dollar people and the fifty cent people. He told Iemitsu that he was the fifty cent kind and that if he developed 'hara' to the best of his ability he would achieve his full fifty cents. He continued by saying that most people are nickels and pennies while Harigaya was clearly a dollar because he had satori. He told Iemitsu that he was better because he had to achieve his fifty cents, while a dollar person doesn't achieve anything. When you perfect your technical excellence you achieve your fifty cents. People like Harigaya came along only once in a hundred years.

Ono never did reach satori although he had 'kufusuru' (you are driven into a corner where you can't go any further, you want to give up but you don't and break through, a sort of second wind). If you achieve technical excellence you will beat all swordsmen, except someone like Harigaya.

Ono also said that there were three kinds of people, the fool who makes mistakes and never learns, the average man who makes mistakes once or twice but corrects them, and the genius who observes mistakes others make and doesn't make them himself.

Ono Jiroemon and Balance

January 1970

Ono was in his late fifties when he fought Harigaya Sekiun who was thirty-two years younger at the time, Sekiun was the only man Ono ever lost to.

One day, while Ono was waiting for a ferry which would take him across the straits leading from the mainland to an island, he heard a woman screaming. She was running towards their boat while a man, who looked like a fisherman, was chasing her. Although she was screaming for help, no one paid attention. As she got closer, Ono stepped out in front of her, letting her know that he would help and for her to get on the boat. The woman got on the boat and Ono followed. The fisherman also ran onto the boat and confronted Ono, asking him what he thought he was doing by interfering. Ono answered that he was helping the woman. The fisherman grabbed a harpoon while telling Ono that she was his woman and that he would do what he wanted with her.

The fisherman said, "Maybe you don't know who I am, I'm the best harpooner in this part of Japan! If you make one move for your sword, I'll throw this harpoon right through you."

The boat they were on was narrow and the sea was rough, Ono had his hand on the railing because the boat was rocking up and down. Ono was trying to get his balance while wondering what to do about being faced with an angry fisherman holding a harpoon ready to throw it at him. Ono realized that the man was as steady as a rock because he had 'hara' – balance from the stomach. The fisherman was still talking while Ono was fighting to regain his balance so he'd be able do something.

He said, "Well you may throw that harpoon, but you'd better be ready to pay the price."

The man threw the harpoon. The only thing that Ono was able to do was to flop back, which he did. The harpoon just missed Ono who jumped up, drew his sword, and cut the fisherman in half. Ono was very strict in this way, if anybody drew a sword against him – they were dead. He took this rule seriously.

The encounter troubled Ono because his balance had been so sadly lacking and he wanted to change that. He decided to ask a fisherman by the name of Senbei for help. Ono asked Senbei how to harpoon a fish and stay balanced.

Senbei replied that this took a long time to get right, because everything had to be taken into account, the movement of the water, the movement of the swimming fish, the clouds. He said that the key was to watch the fish intently and when your stomach (your hara), the fish, and your harpoon are one, you'll get a funny feeling, you'll sense it and when you get this feeling, throw the harpoon and you'll hit the fish.

Ono practiced for three years. At first he rarely hit any fish, gradually he got better until at the end of three years he never missed. He had also attained his balance which never failed him under any circumstances. Because of his superior balance, Ono was now able to beat a whole series of expert swordsmen.

The Roots of Daito Ryu

November 1970

Yoritomo and Yoshitsune (both of the Minamoto family). The roots of the Daito-ryu style started with these two people. Yoshitsune is very famous in Japanese history, while Yoritomo established the Kamakura shogunate. They were brothers. The story that follows is also a kabuki play now and was also made into a short movie by A. Kurosawa entitled 'They Who Tread On The Tiger's Tail.' The movie differs slightly.

There was a man by the name of Benkei who was very good with the naginata. He set himself a task – to fight a thousand fights, this is called Tameshi-giri. He stood on the goju bridge in Kyoto to perform his Tameshi-giri. Which means you fight a fight a day. For nine-hundred ninety-nine days he fought and won. On the last day, very few people came by the bridge. At the end of the day only one samurai passed. It was his last chance to finish his task. The man he saw was only seventeen years old. It was Yoshitsune.

Benkei stopped him and told him that he had to challenge him. Benkei was 6'2" tall. He told Yoshitsune about his task and Yoshitsune said, "Oh very well. Attack!"

Benkei attacked ferociously while Yoshitsune merely avoided, occasionally throwing him down by grabbing his naginata. Benkei attacked for several hours until finally he ran out of wind. Benkei realized the superiority and skill of Yoshitsune and asked to become his student. He said that he had been looking for a master for years and that he would follow Yoshitsune anywhere and everywhere.

Yoshitsune was a very good general who was popular with the people.

He won many battles, enabling his brother to establish the kamakura shogunate. Yoritomo started worrying about his brother's popularity and finally ordered him captured and put to death. Yoshitsune found out about this order and managed to escape. Yoritomo set up barriers all over Japan.

At one particular barrier called Ataka-no-saki, Benkei, Yoshitsune and their party attempted to pass but they were recognized by the captain at the barrier. The captain thought that one of the men might have been Yoshitsune but was only seventy per cent sure so he started to ask questions.

Benkei realized that the questioning was going bad so he went up behind Yoshitsune and hit him with his naginata knocking him down, yelling out as he did, "Stupid! How many times have I told you to be courteous to people." Benkei apologized for the rudeness and stupidity of what he called his servant. He hit Yoshitsune again several times.

When the soldiers saw this exchange they figured that they had made a mistake because Benkei would never hit his master. The captain called for the head man, who was the magistrate. The magistrate had known Yoshitsune since age eight. When he heard about Benkei hitting the man, he felt compassion, realizing what it meant to Benkei to have to hit his master. He told everybody that this couldn't be Yoshitsune since Benkei would never have hit him if it had been him.

The magistrate was curious about how far Benkei would go for his master, and decided to test him. He asked for Benkei's pass. Benkei reached into a sack and pulled out an order for groceries, reading it out loud just as if it were a pass. The way he read it, everyone 'knew' it had to be a pass so the magistrate let them go.

Yoshitsune and his followers reached Fort Koromoyawa, where they stayed for a while. Yoritomo ordered an attack on the men in the fort, where they were slowly whittled down until there was only a handful left. Benkei realized that he couldn't protect his master any longer, he had to give him a chance to escape to Korea.

The attackers called out: "Benkei, look at your kimono, it's falling apart."

They were teasing him, but it was true, the kimono was falling apart. The threads were loose, etc. Benkei was standing there with his arms outstretched and said: "Yes, this old kimono is tired, the threads have been here a long time."

Benkei was blocking the way while Yoshitsune escaped, they shot

Benkei from a distance, but he refused to fall down. They shot so many arrows into him that he looked like a pincushion, but still he wouldn't drop, and Yoshitsune made good his escape.

Takeda Takachiya: "One becomes Three"

One day Takeda was passing Sendai, a town near a river, when he saw an enclosure near the river surrounded by a solid high fence. There were people on the nearby hills trying to peer over the fence, but couldn't because of the surrounding trees. Fighting sounds could be heard from the compound. A man who was sitting near Takeda told him that the greatest of them all was in there teaching the ball and chain and that only students could enter, everybody else had to offer a challenge. To challenge the fighters you had to put up a sign stating that you wished to challenge them. You also had to agree not to hold anyone responsible if anything happened to you. The weapon was a seven foot chain with an iron ball on one end and a sickle on the other.

All of a sudden there was a ferocious yell from the enclosure, followed by silence. A couple of minutes later a man was carried out, his jaw had been ripped off. The man told Takeda that all of the challengers so far had come out feet first. Takeda told the man to be quiet for a moments, he then put his ear to the ground. Takeda could heard the footsteps of one of the fighters and started timing them with his breath until he found the rhythm and hence he knew how the chain was being whirled.

Takeda broke into the enclosure and saw somebody sitting in a chair dressed in a red kimono and someone else practising. One of the men stood up, a sickle in his hand, not seeing Takeda. The sickle had a pointed projection at the handle's end, a double edged sickle blade, a seven foot chain with an iron ball at the end attached to the sickle near the blade. Takeda saw him swinging it, and after timing it with his breath, knew that this was the person that he had originally timed.

Several students had observed Takeda break in but had been unable to stop him, Takeda had just pushed everybody aside. The man was still whirling the ball and chain, but all the students were looking at Takeda. The man sensed them and turned, finally seeing Takeda and demanding to know who he was. Takeda gave his name and the man said: "Do you know what you have done? You can't leave now! I'm going to have to kill you." Takeda replied: "Well, I guess I'll have to fight." The man told Takeda to pick any of the thirty students standing around, that any of them would kill him.

Takeda replied that as long as he was going to die, he might as well fight the best. He faced the man who was whirling the ball and chain. Takeda was still timing the ball and chain with his breath and the man could feel his ki. When he realized that somebody could do this (no one else had been able to), the man panicked and let the chain and ball loop down a little bit. When Takeda saw this, he knew he had him. The students also noticed that the chain and ball was looping down.

Takeda held his sword in the 'dragon tail' position (the sword is held towards the right rear diagonal). Pretty soon the ball was down, level to the man's waist, moving in an arc down to the waist in front, and up high over his head in the rear. Just at the right time, Takeda thrust out his sword, hitting the chain. The man was very skilful and threw the sickle but Takeda dropped flat on the ground, then ran in, cutting up with his sword, killing the man.

If he had turned and tried to leave, the students would have rushed him, the psychology of men is such that when you chase someone, you get stronger. Takeda ran towards the students, scattering them so that he could leave.

The Daito-ryu system teaches how to whirl the chain so that it can't be timed, thanks to Takeda Takachiya.

It took Takeda from the age of twenty-three to the age forty-five to achieve samadhi. He found out that the most difficult to achieve was kooki (self-control), to be able to concentrate at all times, a necessity to reach samadhi.

Yagyu Jubei: A Spy for the Tokugawa Regime

Jubei's father was the shogun's instructor, this meant that all the local lord's sons and the shogun's son, as well as Yagyu's sons, were playmates throughout their childhood. Over time it developed that Jubei became the scapegoat when it was really the shogun's son who made mistakes in the gym. (Yagyu couldn't chastise the shogun's son, so he chastised Jubei although everyone knew it was the shogun's son who was wrong.) Of course Jubei was bitter about this treatment. Even so, he and the shogun's son became fast friends.

Jubei died at the age of forty-four because his father sacrificed him by making him a spy. Jubei would ferret out any opposition to the Tokugawa regime by pretending to be crazy, thus inducing the opposition into confiding their plots to him. He would then kill them at night. There are two versions of how Jubei came to be a spy.

One version is that there was a samurai killing people at night. Jubei's father found out that it was the shogun doing it. He realized that somebody was going to have to stop him and that it would have to be him. So that day Yagyu called Jubei to him and gave him a lecture: "You know Jubei, there is another school of Shinkage-ryu similar to ours. Ours is called the Shadow because while others exhibit their art, we stay in the background." Of course, he was telling him about what he would have to do about the shogun.

Jubei got angry and called his father a fool. All the bitterness he had held back over the years came out and he said that if his father did this, it would be the end of the Yagyus and he left. That night, the father dressed up in old clothes and went to the river where he saw a peasant resting. He figured he'd make a good victim for the shogun so he hid nearby and waited. Sure enough the shogun came by, approached the peasant only to tell him to say his prayers before he would meet his maker, pulling out his sword as he did so.

Yagyu was just about to jump out to stop the shogun when someone came running out of the bushes and approached the shogun. Yagyu couldn't hear the conversation that followed but he did hear the shogun's sword clink against the sword blocking it. Suddenly the shogun was on the ground with the other person holding a sword to the shogun's neck saying: "Okay, you pray, because you are going to meet your maker."

The shogun shouted: "Stop! Stop! I'm the shogun." With this his retainers rushed up to help and the figure jumped into the river and swam away.

Yagyu went home wondering who the stranger was. He asked his servant if Jubei was in his bed. The servant replied that it was strange but Jubei had just come home with wet clothes and had asked if Yagyu was in bed. Yagyu realized that the shogun must have recognized Jubei. Yagyu went to talk to Jubei who admitted his involvement, and he knew that this was the end of his life as he knew it. He told his father that there were only two things that he could do, say that he had gone crazy or tell the truth.

The next day Iemitsu called Yagyu in front of him and he was in a rage: "Something terrible has happened. A terrible thing." He was ranting and raving. Yagyu asked him what had happened: "Have we been invaded? Gee it must be serious. There must have been an invasion or a rebellion for a shogun to say that something serious has happened."

Yagyu said: "Something terrible has happened to me, Jubei's gone crazy. I had to lock him up in a cage this afternoon, he's been attacking people!"

When the shogun heard this he was aghast because after all Jubei had been his lifelong friend. It calmed him down. No one really knows whether the shogun banished him to be a spy for the rest of his life or if Jubei did it on his own. His father sacrificed Jubei by not divulging the fact that someone had to stop the shogun from killing people and instead let Jubei be thought of as crazy.

Jubei was a genius, he didn't make mistakes because he observed other's mistakes. Jubei never made mistakes.

There are two versions of how Jubei came to lose the sight of one eye. The first is that Jubei and his father were arguing while walking in the garden. The father was really mad so he picked up a stone and threw it. Jubei had one eye that was stronger than the other, and since he didn't have time to avoid being hit, he turned and protected his good eye and was blinded in the other one.

The second version is that every time the shogun would make an error, the father would blame Jubei (the shogun would get the message). One day the father blinded Jubei for a certain error of the shogun.

Sun Tzu: Principles of War Fare

July 1973

A will maker noticed his King reading a book and asked him, "What kind of book is that?"

The King replied, "Oh its a book on philosophy written by the greatest philosopher who ever lived."

The will maker said, "Is that so! Well, I want to meet him."

"No. He's dead," replied the King.

The will maker chided the King by saying, "Well then the book isn't going to do you any good because you want to meet the man himself to really get his thoughts. Words will only let you grasp what you yourself know from within the realm of your experience. The interpretation of his words will be yours. When you meet the man, he may tell you something different from what you thought he had written."

This made the King mad. "What do you mean? If you don't explain to my satisfaction, I'll cut off your head!"

"Well, take me, for example," said the will maker. "Do you see this will that I'm making? I can teach this by using the words to anybody, like my son, for example, but the feel, that I cannot transmit. When I make a will, the product comes out just right. It's not too hard or too soft, but just right. I can put all the specifications down in writing for any person to follow those specifications and that person will get the feel of it. That's what I mean – you have to meet the man."

Sun Tzu's first principle of warfare: *You cannot use justice in warfare* (only in peace time). It's a very broad premise. If you are fighting for your life, you cannot use justice and say justice is on my side, so I will win. You may be wrong (on a scale of justice). If you are fighting for your life, you might get killed if you use justice, so do everything to win.

Sun Tzu's second principle of warfare: *In warfare you cannot have pity.* Warfare includes, person to person, persons to persons, person to society, etc. Also don't forget that you are fighting all the time – you are fighting life.

Both Sun Tzu and martial artists agree on this: If you must fight, never use a frontal attack, if somebody attacks you, never meet him head-on unless you are much stronger than the person, then you can beat him on a frontal attack. But even so, you must figure the consequences of doing so if you meet a person on a frontal attack and you are three times stronger, you'll damage him three times more than he damages you. You will still receive some damage even though you may put him away. Suffering that damage might weaken you so much that you won't be able to effectively fight your next opponent. The idea is to never meet in a frontal attack.

The philosophy behind this is: Don't fight if possible, always try to disengage and get away. If you get cornered and there's no way out (justice will then be on your side because society will not blame you, as you tried to get away), then you must fight back. Even if you are the weaker person, make the person pay the price. If you are the stronger person and you have that in mind, then it stands to reason that you will win. If you are weaker and make him pay the price, at least you will have the satisfaction of bringing him down with you. You cannot have pity when fighting for your life, the moment you do, you are going to lose your life.

Sun Tzu's first principle can be looked at from the point of view of a man-to-man fight in a street situation. If you are attacked on the street, don't think that you are in the right and the attacker is wrong for attacking you. God says might is with the right, (if you are a Christian). After you lose, although you may have been right, you are going to be dead.

This is human nature: If two men in a bar get in a fight and afterwards the loser goes to the washroom to get cleaned up, everybody will crowd around the winner slapping him on the back. They will tell the winner he was right, that the loser deserved it. They will do this without really knowing anything about who was right. The winner is always right.

Some of my students think along these lines when attending tournaments and it hinders them. (Everybody goes through this stage at one time.) They start to wonder how they look to the crowd. Then they try to impress the crowd or the judges because they are worried about their appearance. They forget about winning per se and try to impress people who can't possibly help them win. An experienced man concentrates only on the job at hand – winning. This is true of either fighting or kata contests.

Let's look at this from the point of view of a street situation: If you are in a street fight, (for whatever reason) and a crowd gathers around you, don't think about them. Suppose you have an opportunity to poke your opponent's eyes, or kick his groin and you are thinking of the crowd, you might second guess yourself. These people are not going to help you so forget about them.

Sun Tzu said that abiding by the rules in a contest, when it is not life and death, is fine, because your life is not in danger. But when it is you or him, the real thing, then you do everything to win.

In a sport like judo, you play for the attention of the judges and the referee. If you have the favor of the judges, you have an edge no matter how you look at it because you are dealing with human beings (they can't be totally objective). The judges can twist the rules anyway they want to.

Sun Tzu went on to say that you must practice your kata as if it were a question of life or death. The idea of life or death only exists within yourself because you are doing the kata by yourself. Your teacher cannot instill that in your mind – you must make it real to yourself. You must really feel this when you do the kata, you must also have zanshin. You must feel that your life is in danger and realize that there is only one winner.

The meaning of zanshin: After you hit your opponent and pin him down or hurt him badly, always react as if he might still have enough energy left to take your life. There is no second chance when you are dead.

Miscellaneous: Always respect your opponent's ability because he wouldn't be fighting you or challenging you unless he thought that he could win (in a real situation). The only thing that sports and the martial arts have in common is when it comes to fighting is the rei (bow). Bowing to your opponent is actually showing respect to yourself – you are coming to grips with yourself.

Kanbun Uechi: Founder of Uechi Ryu Karate

Uechi Kanbun was the founder of Uechi-ryu karate. Every other style of karate now in Japan came from Okinawa and originally from China to Okinawa. Uechi brought his art directly to Japan from China. Kanbun studied kempo in Funkein province, China.

The type of Chinese Kempo he studied was possibly Punawan Kua. When he went back to the Izu peninsula in Japan they laughed at him. The Izu samurai were very strong. So Uechi went to Okinawa, the Heartland of karate, and opened a school. Now his son Uechi Kanei is teaching in Okinawa.

The Spear

October 1971

There were six arts that the samurai studied: horsemanship, Jujitsu, bow and arrow, sword, spear and naginata.

The spear came into its own during 1615-1860. While there were several thousand sword-ryus, there were only 260 spear-ryus. Most people who learn the spear start by learning the stick first.

The most outstanding spear schools were those which were supported by Prefectures, for instance, Taneda, Kagamichi, Oshima, Muhen, Kikita or Saburi. The various spear styles all came from Naha, Japan, although they were influenced by the Tang Dynasty.

Gakuzenbo Inye was perhaps the greatest spear man in history, he represented Hozoin-ryu (the number one spear school outside of Daito-ryu), which was the ryu that the monks studied. Inye was a monk. His father had sent him to become a monk at a young age. When he was 43 Inye killed the twelve best spear men in Japan in one tournament. Matsunaga Danjo asked for a match with Inye.

Inye was fifteen, there was a big meeting of the monks. A monk by the name of Seishibo (an expert with the naginata), told the assembled monks that two monks up north had killed some sacred deer. Seishibo thought that they should be punished and the other monks were all in favor, including Kongobo (a short stick expert). So Seishibo and Kongobo led them to the monk's monastery to attack it.

Inye, listening to their plans, grabbed a short stick and decided to join them. He was stopped by the Bishop (the head monk of the monastery) who told Inye that he was there to learn the monkshood and to follow him to the chapel. Once inside the chapel, they began to chant the Lotus Sutra, which was very long. When Inye believed the Bishop to be involved in the Sutra, he started slowly backing away towards the door and then ran away.

The Bishop was aware of this but chose not to act. Inye took his short stick and ran to the battle.

As he approached, two monks ran away. One had a naginata and the other a bo. He didn't know that they were the men Seishibo was looking for but he jumped out in front of them anyway and hit the one carrying the bo on the shoulder as hard as he could, dropping him.

The monk said to Inye, "Good blow boy! You saw heaven but now you are going to see hell!"

With that the monk attacked, swinging his naginata in an arc towards Inye's head. Inye sidestepped and blocked with his stick, only to have it cut in half by the naginata. Pressed hard, no matter what Inye did, he couldn't get away. Finally Inye fell down, the monk standing over him, on his toes, preparing to swing his naginata over his head and down, to cut Inye's head in two. Suddenly the monk fell backwards with a sword in his back. Seishibo had seen the fight and being too far away to help just threw his sword.

The monk who had been hit on the shoulder, realizing his friend was dead, picked up the naginata with his left hand, (Inye had struck his right shoulder), and swung at Inye. Inye blocked and realizing that when faced with a superior opponent you must attack, he rushed in striking the monk in the head, killing him. Seishibo was impressed with Inye's performance and also with the fact that he had killed his first man at age fifteen.

When they got back to the monastery, the Bishop told Inye that he was being expelled because of his actions. Although the Bishop liked Inye, he had to let him go for his own good, Inye had to learn a lesson. Inye was shocked. He couldn't go home, his father would kill him. He asked the Bishop where he could go to finish his training. The Bishop suggested that he stay with Seishibo and Kongobo. They were glad to have him. Seishibo taught Inye the naginata, while Kongobo taught him the short stick. Inye stayed with them for six years. He would get up at three in the morning and train until six in the morning, then go back to sleep. Nobody trained as hard as Inye. At the end of those six years, he was as good as his teachers.

Because the Bishop was fond of Inye he kept a close eye on his progress. One day, he told Seishibo that he couldn't ask Inye to come back, but if Inye were to apologize he could accept him again. Seishibo passed the message on and told Inye he would have to leave, for there was nothing more that they could teach him. He suggested that Inye go to the

 An atheist cannot pray, but he can be prayed for.

Bishop and apologize, that he would forgive him and take him back. So Inye apologized, and asked to train fifty per cent in priestly matters. The Bishop agreed and suggested that to be a good martial artist, Inye must go to the temple and meditate in front of Buddha's statue.

One night, while meditating, Inye felt a terrific saki, it was coming from the doorway. He picked up his stick, moving to one side of the doorway. He asked who was there. A man replied, he was a stranger, wanting to visit the temple. Inye asked, "Why not just come in?" The man replied that there was a very strong ki coming from the temple keeping him out. The man then asked who else was inside and when Inye said that he was alone, the man didn't believe him.

When he came in, Inye saw an old man carrying a spear. Suddenly the man shouted, "Sorry boy!" and attacked Inye with a spear thrust. Inye immediately jumped aside, but when he landed he found the spear was up against his throat. The old man told Inye that this had been a test and that Inye was very good. Inye asked, "What do you mean? The spear was at my throat!"

The old man replied, "No one can avoid my thrust."

Inye asked the old man to teach him, but he refused fearing that he wasn't a good enough teacher. "If you want to learn, go see Kami-Iidzumi Ise-no-Kami. He is better than me," said the old man.

When Inye heard this, he thought to himself that maybe it was a fluke that the old man had beaten him, so he attacked. However, just as he tensed his arm in preparation to lift his stick, the spear was at his throat again, when he jumped back the spear was at his throat once again. The old man used his ability to 'receive' saki extremely well.

Inye asked the old man to stay the night to talk more, but the old man said no, sorry, turned and left the temple. Inye put down his stick and when he got to the door and looked out, the old man was gone. He ran up the road a ways, looked around but the old man couldn't be found. When Inye got back to the monastery, the Bishop told him that he had met a great martial artist and gave Inye permission to travel. Inye asked the Bishop how he knew, the Bishop replied, "I can see it in your face, you must find this old man!"

One variation of the spear is the halbred. It has a spear with a sickle attached to the bottom of the spear blade so that it can stab, hook and cut. The Hozoin-ryu used it. Hozoin-ryu techniques were passed down through poetry, with the verses teaching how to fight. Apparently poetry used in this manner was common.

Yamauchi Renshin Part 1

February 1971

No one knows exactly when Yamauchi Renshin was born or when he died. He lived around 1610-1700 and was born in the province of Bizon, Okayama prefecture, Japan. When he was young he went to Edo Saki (saki means before, so Edo Saki would be about two days before reaching Edo proper). He became a student of a man named Morooka. Morooka was a fine teacher who did not seek fame or fortune.

Morooka contracted leprosy when he was in his forties and all but three of his students ran away fearing they would also contract the disease. The three remaining students were Yamauchi Renshin, Kogumo Iwamasa and Megishi Tokkaku. (Renshin's nickname was Ishi.) These three men nursed Morooka as he got sicker and all three later received the inka, permission to teach.

Kogumo looked like a small bear. He was short and hairy, having a very powerful looking body, while Megishi was tall, six foot three and powerful. Megishi later became very famous.

Morooka and his students during this time lived in isolation on a mountain, uphill from a small village. One day in the early morning, Tokkaku and Renshin were washing out their teacher's bandages in a small stream on a hillside, so the villagers wouldn't see the bandages and get mad. Tokkaku stopped at one point and looked over in the direction of a temple, Katori Jinja, which was barely discernible. There appeared to be fog near it. Tokkaku called to Renshin and asked him what he thought was happening. Renshin said they were looking at fog. Tokkaku laughed and called him a country bumpkin (Renshin had never lived in a city) and told him, "I'm a city man and I know what's going on, it's not fog but deer. The thirsty deer are drinking too much water and exploding, causing the water to float up like mist." Renshin strained to see the deer although he knew that Tokkaku was teasing him.

Finally, Tokkaku stated that he would go and kill a deer for them to eat but Renshin objected. They had been given permission to live in the area only because they had promised not to poach. So instead, Tokkaku decided that he would go near Edo and buy medicine for their teacher. He went back to the house to prepare for the trip, where he found Kogumo busy sponging off Morooka's face which was so swollen with puss that he was almost blind. When Tokkaku told Morooka about the trip he was planning, Morooka told him that the three of them had sold too many of their clothes and belongings and he directed Kogumo to give his special sword to Tokkaku to sell.

Kogumo objected to selling his teacher's sword and even Tokkaku refused, saying that he still had some things left to sell. Morooka knew that Tokkaku was not planning on coming back and had wanted to give him this gift to help him get started. He was right – Tokkaku left and never came back.

Tokkaku ended up at a village close to Edo. He tried to make his appearance as odd as possible by dressing in weird clothes and tying his hair back in a ponytail. He was armed with a six sided bo that had serrated six inch metal tips. Arriving at the centre of the village, he posted a sign challenging everybody and anybody. He yelled out as loud as he could that he was the best in the world and then did a kata with the bo. After doing the kata he disappeared. His idea was that people would get curious about him, start talking and then come looking for him. When they didn't find him, they would get really get interested in challenging him.

Everything happened the way Tokkaku thought it would. When he went back to the village a month later, there were many people waiting to challenge him. He beat them all. All the lords and schools started sending their best men to fight him to no avail. Tokkaku was too good. When his fame had spread he started his own school. He called it Mijun-ryu. Among the more than five hundred students he gathered were several lords.

Four years from the opening date of his school Morooka died. Renshin and Iwamasa in the meantime had heard of his fame and decided to teach Tokkaku a lesson. Both Renshin and Iwamasa knew they could beat Tokkaku because he had not Kufusured. He had also not learned enough before he left. They did, however, not have any idea if Tokkaku had improved, or how much.

When Iwamasa arrived he had the problem of how to get Tokkaku to fight him. Tokkaku was now rich and famous and wouldn't fight just anybody. If he went directly to the gym, Tokkaku's students might try to kill him and there were too many of them to fight. If he put up a sign in the village, Tokkaku's students would see it and take it down.

Finally he got an idea. There was a bridge leading into the village, which was used by farmers to take their goods into town. If he posted the sign at dawn all the farmers would see it and word would get around. So Iwamasa printed his challenge on a wooden plaque and posted it near the bridge. He wrote that he was from the same school and was challenging Tokkaku for opening up a school using a name, other than his teacher's and if Tokkaku didn't fight, he didn't deserve his school or his fame. By the time Tokkaku's students got around to taking down the sign, the damage was done. The word had spread that a stranger with the same teacher as Tokkaku had challenged him to a duel on the bridge the next day.

Finally, Tokkaku himself heard about it. His four top students urged him to let them kill Iwamasa before the match but Tokkaku knew they were no match for Iwamasa and he refused them and prepared to fight the next day.

Tokkaku knew that he would have a difficult time surviving the match, for all had received the inka, and therefore were fairly equal in ability. How could he beat a man who was his equal and wanted to take his life? There was only a small margin of ability between them, so what would the deciding factor be?

If Iwamasa could face death – so could he. Tokkaku decided that having more guts was the answer. He must have more guts than Iwamasa so he went to a temple and meditated, making up his mind that he would have more guts.

The next day he chose the bo that he had used when he entered town because he realized that Iwamasa would pick up any old stick he came across for the fight. Tokkaku didn't want to use his sword against a stick because of his reputation. When he got to the bridge the police had cordoned off the bridge and the surrounding area was filled with spectators. The two fighters approached each other. To the untrained eye it appeared as if both men were completely relaxed, merely out for a stroll. However, the expert swordsmen realized there was no suki (opening for attack).

Both men stopped when they were six feet apart. Iwamasa began to chastise Tokkaku for being disrespectful to their teacher by opening up a school of a different name. As he was doing so, Tokkaku was thinking to himself that he must have the edge in guts, he must attack – he did.

Iwamasa avoided Tokkaku's ferocious attack until Tokkaku's bo came down and struck him on the head. He blocked with his short stick and pressed Tokkaku backwards. Tokkaku was forced back until he was up against the railing of the bridge. At this point, Tokkaku was leaning backwards half over the railing, Iwamasa then kicked Tokkaku's feet out from under him (gake), and as Tokkaku fell towards the water, he symbolically cut the railing in half with his short sword. Tokkaku was so embarrassed about his defeat that he took off all his clothes underwater and swam down river so that no one would see him. His top students, Kazama, Yamada, and Hanpeita and one other man met him when he got out of the water. They had brought a change of clothes for him, money and two swords in case he lost. (It was the custom for the winner to get all the possessions of the loser.) The men asked Tokkaku what they should do, whether or not to seek revenge, he said no, not to do anything that he would go to Kyoto to examine his soul. The top students, being very proficient, with over forty real matches each, decided to seek revenge. They looked all over but couldn't find Iwamasa, so they went back to the gym. When they got there they saw Iwamasa sitting out front. He had smashed the signs with the school's name on them. His students wanted to fight him but they couldn't attack, there was no suki, (opening), so Kazama knowing Iwamasa to be from the country and probably naive, decided to trick him. He bowed down and told Iwamasa that the gym and all the possessions of Tokkaku were now his since he beat their teacher in a fair fight and was now their teacher. The others followed his lead. They invited him inside and plied him with food and drink, hoping to get him drunk. They promised to get a woman in for the night and were very courteous to him.

Even when Iwamasa had his fill of saki, he presented no opening for attack so they set a trap. They told him that a bath had been prepared for him. (The bathhouse in a Japanese home is a small separate building made of wood.) This one was built with very thick walls and had a thick door. Iwamasa stopped at the door and looked in. He had brought his two swords with him. As he was relaxing in the tub, he thought to himself that maybe he was wrong in his suspicions and that the students were on the up and up.

After all they had been good to him with nothing indicating bad intentions.

Finally he was finished and as he stood up and started to get out of the tub, the ceiling opened up and boiling hot water poured down on him. Half-blinded he reached for his swords and ran for the door which was locked. He stepped back and then hit the door with all he had to no avail. Although the door had not opened the building shook so violently that the students ran to get anything they could to brace the door. They piled tatamis and furniture against the door forgetting all about their plan to poke spears through ports in the bathhouse walls.

Iwamasa managed to break through one of the walls, as he was still coming through it, half-blinded by the water and holding his sword, he was speared by the fourth of Tokkaku's top students (name unknown). As the student went to pull out the spear, Iwamasa grabbed it and pulled the spear violently into and through him in an effort to get the student closer. When the student, who was still struggling to pull out the spear was in range, Iwamasa drew his sword and cut him with one stroke across the stomach. They both fell down and died.

The others who had been watching were horrified. They had never seen anything like it.

A week passed. Renshin thought it odd that Iwamasa didn't report back but decided to wait a month, figuring he was enjoying his stay in the city. Two weeks later, a young boy of about seventeen showed up and asked for a lesson. His name was Mizutani. They went inside the dojo and each took up a bokken, then stood in their kamai.

Normally, the sword is held in one of seven standard positions, gedan, chudan, judan, right or left hossa, or right or left yoki uki monde. However, Mitzutani used none of these. Instead, he held the sword blade up and parallel to the floor at about an angle of seventy degrees from the side. When Renshin saw this he got mad because the kid had said he was not too skilful and here he was using an advanced technique taught at Morooka's school. Renshin demanded to know who had taught him. Mitzutani then admitted that he had really come to give Renshin a message about Iwamasa. He had seen the whole bathhouse incident with his own eyes and knew the names of those who did it and where they hid the body.

Renshin left for Edo Saki. When he arrived, no one noticed him since he appeared ordinary in every way. He went to the gym and challenged

Shigetada to a match and was accepted. The three remaining top students were mad because only about one-hundred of the original five-hundred students remained, the others leaving when Tokkaku lost the match. None of the students had ever seen or heard of Renshin before.

When Shigetada faced Renshin he knew that he was no ordinary swordsman. He felt no opening, so he finally charged in delivering a blow to Renshin's head. Renshin stepped to the side not even bothering to block up and around his head, hitting Shigatada on the side with what appeared to be a light blow (beat the count). Shigetada was dead. Yameda Hanpeita was next. When Yameda started to raise his sword to charge in, Renshin broke his hand, then poked him in the throat, killing him. Finally it was Kazama's turn. When he faced him and felt how strong Renshin was, he dropped down bowing and asked why Renshin, whom they did not know, wanted to kill them.

Renshin told him that he was the dojo brother of Iwamasa and that a witness stated that Kazama and the others had tricked and killed Iwamasa. Kazama, being very deceitful in character, said that he knew nothing of it and that he had only seen Iwamasa on the day of the match. He demanded to see the witness. Renshin told him that the witness was in a village two days journey away but that he would take him there.

So they left, with Kazama walking ahead of Renshin and although Kazama had his sword on, Renshin could still kill him before he could turn and draw. Only a very skilful man would guard a prisoner that way, instead of tying him up, Kazama could feel no way to escape.

They came to a river and got on a ferry. While on the ferry they ordered saki and Renshin asked Kazama what was going through his mind when they killed Iwamasa. Karamua replied that they were only seeking revenge for their master's defeat. Renshin scolded him saying that it was not the same thing, that Iwamasa and he had a legitimate reason for revenge and under the samurai code, they had not. He then asked Kazama to write his memoirs of the event.

By the time Kazama finished, the ferry was in the centre of the river. He told Renshin he was finished and put down his pen. Renshin was sitting opposite Kazama, and as he reached for his bottle of saki, Renshin attacked.

Everybody heard the splash, the ferry was turned around to look for Kazama. He was found dead, floating in the water with a slash across his stomach. Only a priest sitting nearby had seen what had happened, that Renshin had reached for his sword, drew it cutting Kazama in the same motion, putting it back in the sheath while Kazama was still in the air.

Yamauchi Renshin Part 2

Renshin went back to Edo-Saki to his dojo. The kid, Mizutani, who told him about Kogumo, was waiting for him. He wondered how the three felt when they faced Renshin because they knew they were no match for Kogumo, who was Renshin's equal.

A man came to the gym and asked Renshin for a match. (A lesson is a friendly contact with a wooden sword and is not to the death. A match is a dual to the death with a sword.) The man's name was Terado Jukuchi, a student of Tokkaku. His purpose was to seek revenge for his teacher's disgrace. Renshin accepted his request and stood facing Terado with only a wooden sword. From the manner in which Terado stood it was obvious that he had total disregard for his life. (He stood with one foot forward with the sword on his right shoulder with the blade pointing straight to the rear and parallel to the ground.) The position he was in was a suicide position in that it wasn't designed for defense but for counter attack. What could Renshin do? Any move he made to strike Terado would also place him in a position to be struck and Terado didn't seem to care if he died. So Renshin did the only thing possible, he attacked his sword. He stepped in and out, found the spot approximately eight inches from the hilt of Terado's sword and knocked it out of his hands, followed it up with a strike to the head, killing him.

In the year 1659, approximately February 20th, (in the dead winter) at midnight, Yata Oribe, a shinto priest, got up out of bed to go to the bathroom (in Japanese houses the bathroom is a separate building). He felt strange. He felt that someone was on the grounds of the temple. Then he heard water splashing. He looked around and saw a naked man who was an average type of person, nondescript looking. He was pouring ice cold water from the well with a bucket over his head. Oribe watched the man from the veranda. The man appeared to be in his thirties and had his hair tied back with a ribbon. Oribe counted twenty-one buckets of water before the man stopped and put on his clothes and sat down to meditate. The priest watched for half an hour at which point the man stopped his meditation and left.

The next night, the priest wondered if the man would come back, so he stayed up watching for him. He did show up. That night Oribe saw that he had brought swords. The man came back and repeated the same process for a total of 21 days. On the twenty-first night, the priest dressed in a white robe, complete with a short swords. Oribe figured from the number of buckets of water the man poured over himself each night, that this was the last night he would show up. That night the man completed the same routine but in the end he took off his sandals, and barefoot went through the seven main positions of kamai with the sword, then he smiled. As the man started to leave, the priest called to him to ask him why he came to a Shinto temple rather than to a kashima or katori temple, (these were temples of war). The man answered that he wanted to find his own secret.

The priest had prepared drinks and food that night and invited the man to have a party with him. After they had something to drink and had eaten they made small talk, the priest said that he saw a man do the seven positions of the sword and then smile. He asked him what he had discovered. The man said he had developed spiritual and physical excellence (technical ability) and the third quality – strategy.

He said, "When I smiled, the answer had come to me."

He refused to tell the priest what the answer was. The priest thought that the man had reached kensho and told him so, but the man said no, he had not. The man told him what most samurai high up in ability have a strong ki, especially if they had killed someone or fought a severe battle.

"I want to overcome that strong ki. You claim that I reached kensho who are you?" asked the man. The priest told him that his family had had some martial arts ability. The man went onto say that the Gods of War gave him only technical excellence. He said, "I must find the real me. What I found was the pressing advantage." (When you're pressed you can die. When pressed your solar plexus closes and you can be hurt there.) The priest asked again, "What did you discover?"

The man told Oribe to take out his sword and face him. The man held only a stick in the chudan position. As the priest watched the man's stick became bigger and bigger. The priest saw him fading into darkness and then just as suddenly the priest gave a kiai. The man told the priest that he had a strong ki. The man was Yamauchi Renshin. (The four greatest swordsmen and Yoshida Kotaro had mastered the fading techniques.)

The Kuroda family is famous in Japanese history (they developed ninjas). Kuroda loved warfare. He had two students who were very good, they were Hiyoshida and Asakutsu, the leaders for his style. Asakutsu was 51 years old, six feet tall and very strong. He had performed in front of the Emperor and impressed him so much that he was given a scroll (this is very extraordinary).

Hiyoshida was also good and had killed many men. At this time the samurai going to war were laughing at dojo practice. They were doing the real thing fighting to the death and thought that men who just practised in a gym were wasting their time. One of these men, Chikare (36 years old) was of the opinion that training means nothing, you must have guts for the real thing. He discussed his opinions with Asakutsu who thought that a lot depended on conditions, place and time. Chikare wasn't impressed with that answer, he thought that those men, (samurai going to war), killed mostly farmers and that he made short shift of them.

At a party held by Kuroda, all the samurai gathered there laughed at the gym practice. Chikare pulled out a small tree from the ground and held it up challenging everyone there to face him in a fight. Hiyoshida accepted the challenge with nothing more than a small eighteen inch stick. Chikare never failed to win a fight when he used his technique of giving a big kiai and then coming down on his opponent's head through any block his opponent might attempt. If he missed, he would step in immediately and poke. When he did this to Hiyoshida, Hiyoshida side-stepped and knocked down the tree and tapped Chikare on the head. Chikare admitted defeat, while Kuroda shook his head.

Six of Hiyoshida's men (his servants), murdered someone and escaped. Hiyoshida, being only a martial art's teacher, had to go after them. They were not his students, just employees, in other words, in battle they might carry his weapons and gear and only occasionally fight, but they were tough. Hiyoshida caught up to the men at a mountain pass. When they saw him, the men realized what he was there for.

They decided to surround him and attack, and if only one of them survived, they didn't care, they figured he was only one man, they were six men, so they had a chance. When Hiyoshida reached the men they suggested he could just leave and say that he couldn't find them. But Hiyoshida wanted to hear their story. After all, there were two sides to every story and since he couldn't hear the dead man's version, he would hear the servant's story. One man stepped a little way in front of the others to tell the story and when he did Hiyoshida immediately killed him. The other men became enraged and chased Hiyoshida when he ran away. Some of the men were faster than the others, so eventually they were spread out from each other. The more they chased him, the braver they became. Unfortunately for the fastest man, he didn't realize that he was also the closest to Hiyoshida and away from the others. Hiyoshida turned and killed him. He did the same for all the rest, except one man, whom he brought back alive.

Everyone applauded Hiyoshida's skill, he was a hero. Kuroda said that Hiyoshida's strategy would fail, that fame leads to trouble, and sure enough, five years later Hiyoshida got in trouble with a minister and was executed.

Asakutsu decided to leave and told Kuroda to give his possessions to any one he desired. Kuroda was mad because he wanted Asakutsu to serve him like he had served his father, but Asakutsu insisted on going. He changed his name to Juin and went to pray to his father. Juin was sixty years old when he left.

Juin approached a house in Edo-saki and asked for Yamauchi Renshin. The man who answered the door looked to be between thirty-two and thirty-five years old. He replied that he was Yamauchi Renshin. Juin insisted that the man he was looking for would be in his sixties. Renshin replied that he must mean his father, who had died several years ago. So Renshin Jr. invited Juin in, saying, "You look old and tired, let me give you a tub of water to rest your feet." Juin asked how the father had died and the son told the following story.

"My father was the greatest in Japan, but people were very superstitious. A giant sea turtle was killing and eating all the fish and scaring away all the rest of the fish from the area the fisherman nearby usually fished in. Several fisherman had tried to kill the turtle but lost their lives trying. The fisherman then asked several samurai to kill the turtle. Some of them swam out with nothing but a knife between their teeth. They were all killed. Because of Renshin's fame, he was approached by the farmers for help. He agreed to help since he felt pity for them. He took along a bow and arrow and stood on the shore waiting for the turtle. When it appeared, he shot at it hitting it in the head. The turtle went under the water and never appeared again. Soon the fish came back and Renshin was a hero."

Later Yamauchi Renshin Jr. went back to see his teacher's grave. While he was at a temple, he saw an arrow stuck in a wall. Upon asking the priest about it, he learned that the arrow was found in the head of a giant turtle washed up on the shore. He was shown the carcass of the turtle, he pushed it with his foot to test its weight, he felt a painful prick in his foot from the shell. He knew he was going to die from it and asked to be buried next to his teacher and Kogumo. Three days later he was dead.

After hearing the full story Juin said, "It goes to show you that you must find your soul and not seek fame or technical excellence or you will suffer all your life." Juin was actually Tokkaku.

Miscellaneous facts: Tokkaku's school was named Mijin-ryu, the school of the small particles, because he felt that life is like a small particle. To overcome, it he would have to expand his material gains. He found out later that he was wrong.

Morooka taught Toda-ryu and Daito-ryu.

It was said of Miyamoto Musashi, "*He is a swordsman among pirates, but a pirate among swordsmen.*"

Matsumura Sokon: Okinawan Karate Legend

Sokon was born around the year 1786 and died in 1892. He was the fourth son in his family. During his lifetime he served four different emperors and was given the name of Bushi Matsumura by Emperor Shoko (meaning Samurai Matsumura), when he was 14 or 16 years old. Sokon's father was friends with Sakugawa and asked him several times to teach his sons karate. Sakugawa refused each time he was asked because of Matsumura's reputation for being a hot-head. Finally Sakugawa agreed to see Sokon to decide whether or not to accept him as a student (Sakugawa was 85 years old at the time). When Sokon arrived, Sakugawa told him that he looked for two things in a student, his personality and his character. To that end the training would be very severe with many scoldings. Sokon became his student and later was made his Shihan-dai (right hand man).

In 1816 Sokon went into the service of the Emperor, his title was Chikudon. (K. Sakugawa was a Peichin, a rank just below nobility.) In 1818, Sokon married Yonamine Chiru, the marriage had been arranged by their respective parents.

Everyone wondered who was the better fighter because she was from a famous fighting family. One day while sweeping the floor, Yonamine was seen by two townsmen using one hand to effortlessly pick up an eighty-eight pound rice basket. The story spread and people wondered if Sokon was as strong as his wife. This bothered Sokon but he did nothing about it.

One night while he and his wife were attending a party, Sokon sent her home early as he had his eye on another woman. It was close to midnight and as Yonamine was walking home she was accosted by three men who thought they would have some fun with her. She fought them, knocking them all out and tied them up together with her obi while they were unconscious. Then, being near a temple, she placed a very heavy temple pole on top of them so that they couldn't move and then continued on her way.

By the time Sokon was ready to leave for home he was very drunk. As he was walking by the temple he heard moaning sounds. He soon discovered the three men tied up. He released them, asking what had happened. All the men would say was that somebody beat them up. Sokon continued home unconsciously retaining the obi. In the morning when he saw the obi in the light he was shocked to find that he was holding his wife's obi. He surmised what had taken place and decided to test his wife's skill.

On July 9, 1826, (when he was thirty), he arranged a party and made excuses for sending his wife there alone. Later that night he disguised himself in different clothes, painted his face and used stuffing to look heavier and waited in ambush for her. When she approached, he jumped out in front of her and gave a tremendous punch which she avoided by jumping back and out of the way. He continued the attack and she eventually knocked him out. When he woke up, he was horrified, even more so when she didn't even mention the incident when he got home.

The incident bothered Sokon so much that he finally decided to ask

Sakugawa's advice. He asked if it was possible for his wife to defeat a man in combat. Sakugawa said yes and stated that that was the reason women weren't allowed to train in the martial arts. Sokon went onto say that this had happened to him, although it was with a woman that he tried to get fresh with. Sokon had lost because he didn't know how to fight against a woman. He told Sokon that no matter how good a woman is as a fighter, she will always try to protect her breasts. To be hit there, will cause loss of equilibrium and therefore allow defeat.

Armed with this new knowledge, Sokon again arranged a party for his wife to attend without him. Once again he disguised himself and waited in ambush for her. When his wife, on her way home, passed him, he jumped out and started attacking her. Sokon wasn't able to land a decisive blow for a while until at last an opening presented itself to him to hit her breast. When he hit her, she lost her equilibrium as Sakugawa had predicted, Sokon was then able to knock her out. He quickly ran home, cleaned up and pretended to be drinking saki when his wife arrived home. She went up to him and congratulated him on being able to defeat her and told him that he could now beat anybody. (Maybe she let him beat her!)

One day the King decided to check on the rumors he had heard of corruption among his officials. He dressed as a commoner and toured the countryside with Sokon as a bodyguard. Sokon dressed as a farmer armed with only a short stick. One day while the two were walking on the beach one day when they heard a girl screaming from a clump of palm trees nearby. (Okinawa is a semitropical country.) The King ordered Sokon to check what was happening. What Sokon found was a Japanese man, dressed in the attire of a Satsuma clan samurai, trying to rape an Okinawan girl. (The Japanese had an agreement with the Chinese order to prevent continual fighting among themselves over trading rights. The agreement was that they would alternate trading with the Okinawans and when it was one's turn, the other would take down their signs and stay indoors out of sight. The Satsuma clan was the Japanese clan that had been given trading rights with Okinawans by the Shogun, they were strong fighters. In other words Okinawa was considered to be neutral territory. This went on until Japan defeated China. Okinawa was forced to pay tribute to both countries.)

As an Okinawan, Sokon was in a bad position with the Japanese, therefore, if he wanted to avoid serious trouble he had to be careful. So, thinking fast, he approached the Japanese and bowed, saying, "Oh samurai, please forgive me, she is my daughter and will be married soon. Please refrain so that she will be pure for her new husband."

The Japanese was furious that a common Okinawan farmer was talking to him in such a manner, but he nevertheless agreed. He said, "Okay, but I must kill you because you saw my face and may tell people, embarrassing me."

With that he drew his sword and attacked Sokon who managed to avoid his blows with difficulty because of his opponent's skill. He was forced to use his stick. He struck the samurai's shin and when he went down, followed up with a strike to the head, crushing the man's head and killing him.

Another time, they were walking along a road when they came upon an eighty-two year old man crying into a dirty towel. The King asked Sokon to find out why the old man was crying. When Sokon asked him, the old man told him that the head official was corrupt. In order to be allowed to fish, he had to give the official thirty caddis of fish in order to be allowed to fish, (a caddi is a measurement of about 1 1/2 pounds) for three days running. He said that it was bad enough for an old man like himself to have to pay, since it was hard for him to fish, but on top of that they had given him a dirty towel. (It was the custom to acknowledge the receipt of these payments with towels, a clean towel represented a large payment and a dirty towel a small payment.)

When the King heard this, he went up to the old man and told him what to do. The King told the old man to divide the fish into two piles, the best fish in one pile for the officials and the worst in the other pile for the King.

The next day the old man did what the King suggested. When the officials saw what he had done, they told the head official who came out and told the old man that he was a good taxpayer and gave him two clean towels. When the King head about this, he was furious and wrote a letter to the official asking him to resign without explanation. The official couldn't see a reason to resign, so he refused. The King got back to the official and told him that if he didn't resign, he would have a match with Sokon in two weeks at dusk. The official agreed. The official's name was Oihara.

Oihara and Sokon met at dusk on the agreed date. Oihara was armed with a pair of sais, Sokon had a small stick. They fought for fifteen minutes during which time Sokon was hard pressed to defend against Oihara's attack. Oihara was very skilful in the use of the sais. (Sokon didn't know what school he was from.) He continually pressed the attack forcing Sokon to retreat. Finally, with his arms getting numb from blocking, Sokon had to use his weapons. Fortunately for him, he was carrying his sickles tied to his belt (he didn't always carry them). He drew his sickles and was able to knock one of Oihara's sai out of his hand. Oihara continued to press Sokon, he figured that he might die, so he attacked, hitting Oihara's weapon arm, cutting it off. Oihara ran away and was never seen again. This had been Sokon's hardest fight.

At the finish of the fight, Sokon picked up Oihara's sais, tied them in his handkerchief and went to a bar to have a drink. In the bar, the serving girl noticed the blood on his handkerchief and commented on it. Sokon told her about the fight and told her that anybody who had been through what he had been through, would have taken the bloody sais as well.

It is an established fact that Sokon faced a bull in unarmed combat and won. There are two versions as to how this occurred. In both versions the match came about because of the King. He had written the beginning of a poem and asked several members of his court to finish it, in order to test them. He became incensed at their work, drew his sword and then chased everybody. Everybody ran away except Sokon who just stood calmly. The King asked Sokon why he didn't run away. Sokon replied that he had sworn to obey his King and if the King wished to kill him, he would not resist in any way. The King decided not to kill Sokon, instead he would have to fight a bull unarmed. The bull had been given to the King as a gift by a foreign dignitary. Sokon, of course, accepted and this is where the two stories differ.

The first story tells of Sokon facing the bull in the arena located in the village of Shuri. When the bull was released, it saw Sokon and ran to within a few feet of him, stopping and pawing the ground in preparation to charge. Sokon, never having fought a match of this kind before, decided to take the initiative, so while the bull was still pawing the ground, he ran to its side and hit there. When the bull turned to face Sokon, he hit it on the nose as hard as he could and jumped to the other side. The bull turned to face him again and this time Sokon poked it in the eye, the bull, totally bewildered, turned and ran. Everyone cheered.

The second story has Sokon becoming friendly with the bull's keeper, who is flattered that a man with Sokon's reputation would befriend him. He readily agrees to Sokon's request to be left alone with the bull for a few minutes each night and to keeping these visits a secret.

Each night, for several nights, Sokon visited the bull dressed in his armor and stabbed his nose with a sharp, pointed, iron-ribbed fan. He poked the bull's nose repeatedly with the fan. The bull couldn't move since he was tied down and could only struggle in vain to escape the torture. For the first week, the bull tried its best to get to Sokon, which was not possible. After a few days, the bull just cringed, whimpered and tried to get away whenever it saw Sokon, it was terrified of him.

The day of the match came and the bull was released into the ring. Sokon, dressed in his armor strode into the ring. The bull took one look at him, turned tail and ran like hell out of the ring. The audience cheered madly at their hero who had only to stare at a bull to defeat it.

Karate Sakugawa had as his top student, besides Sokon, a man named Iwa Ason (Chinese). Ason had two or three students but never systematized his style and as a consequence didn't survive in history like Sokon who had organized the Shorin-ryu style. Ason developed a good student by the name of Itsushi, but unfortunately his art died.

Sokon had four top students, Yasuzato and Itosu who eventually both taught Funakoshi, Chien (none of his forms survived), and Tawata (who was famous for the sai). Sokon trained until the day he died.

Bokuden: "The Test"

This lecture deals with a tournament that took place in the early part of the 16th Century. The winners of two previous tournaments were to meet at this tournament, to be held before the Emperor. The first tournament had been held in Hosokawa, which was the old name for the City of Kyoto. It determined who would represent Hosokawa before the Emperor, the contestants had been narrowed down to five.

The first contestants were Okamoto Mikawado, 47, the second Yoshioka Shineamon, 40, the third Maebara Chikuzen-no-kami, 39, the fourth Ochiai Torazaemon, 31, and the fifth, Arar Jibushoyu, 28.

The second tournament was held in Koshima and its field of contestants had been narrowed down to seven. The first being Bizen Matsumoti, 44, the second Iizaki Wakasa-no-kami, 41, the third Ogano Echizen-no-kami 37, the fourth, Kabuto Gyobu, 35, the fifth Nukaga Ginosuke, 31, the sixth, Matsucka Hyogonosuku, 29, and the seventh Urabe Sukegoro, 23.

Urabe was supposed to fight Ogano the next day. That night before the fight Urabe went into the Japanese latrine, as he closed the door and had his back to it, he felt an air of death (saki) he turned around and just as he did, a sword cut through the door (it being made of thin wooded strips and rice paper), cutting off his right arm. By the time Urabe opened the door, the assassin was gone, so Urabe was unable to fight. He had the match postponed until he found a replacement. Urabe sent for his brother, Bokuden, who later became a very famous martial artist, in fact, the teacher of Miyamoto Musashi.

Bokuden arrived for the match and the same thing happened to him. The night before the tournament, he went into the latrine, closed the door behind him and then he felt the saki. He was more sensitive to this feeling than his brother had been, although he was a year younger, and therefore, as he felt the sword coming he was able to avoid the attack. By the time he flung the door open, the assassin was too far away for him to see his face, however, he threw a shuriken, and saw it hit the assassin in the leg.

The next day when Bokuden stood in front his opponent, he challenged Ogano to see his leg, telling him that he had been attacked the previous night and had nicked his assassin in the leg. Of course Ogano refused, because he was the assassin. Bokuden said that if Ogano didn't show him his leg, he would demand a real sword instead of the wooden sword. Ogano agreed to use real blades. Bokuden beat Ogano. All the others were beaten except for Bizen, who was a very skilled man with over one hundred battles under his belt. Bokuden faced Bizen and in the attack that followed Bizen broke Bokuden's sword (wooden), but Bokuden, knowing the rules very well called for a point of order. This meant that he could challenge Bizen to a wrestling match, bare hands no weapons. Bizen accepted and although Bokuden was not as skilled, Bokuden's stamina enabled him to win, so although Bizen won the sword match, he lost the wrestling match.

 Diet: 60% fruit and vegetables; 20% carbohydrates; 20% meat protein.

The officials were going to let him represent Koshima. But Bizen, realizing that in Kyoto, Okamoto Mikawado, being the eldest and most experienced, would probably win, the same sort of thing might happen (there might be a point of order) and Bokuden might beat him on the point of order, he asked for Bokuden to represent Koshima.

It turned out as Bizen had thought. Okamoto won in Kyoto and faced Bokuden before the Emperor. During the match, both swords were broken and Bokuden asked for a point of order. He beat Okamoto because of his superior stamina.

The next day, Bokuden visited the judge from the match as a matter of courtesy and the judge gave him the following advice, "There is more to the martial arts than technical excellence alone. You should train your mind as you train your arm."

As the judge was saying this, Bokuden said to himself, "What a stupid old guy he is. I beat Bizon and Okamoto with my right arm. I don't need anything else."

It so happened that Bokuden became employed by a lord and was due to be in a battle, his first battle. Never having been in a battle before, he sought the advice of Bizen as to what he should do. Bizen's only advice was, "You will be all right in the battle if you can see the small hole in your opponent's helmet." (All Japanese helmets had a very tiny hold right in the top for the purpose of letting air in and out for circulation.) Of course, Bokuden did not know what Bizen was talking about.

The day of the battle came and Bokuden and everyone else was on horseback. Bokuden thought back to what Bizen had said and looked around and saw that everybody had his head down and spear out, charging the enemy. He noticed that when he looked at his opponent, he discovered that he couldn't see the hole. When he sat upright he found that he could then see the hole very clearly. He then realized what Bizen was talking about and became calm and cleared his mind and was able to see the hole in his opponent's helmet, since the opponent was also sitting upright. His opponent was a very skilful man.

Later on, after Bokuden became famous, he had a test that he gave to his students, he would stand with his right arm raised out at shoulder length while holding on to a short stick. Now each student was supposed to strike the stick as hard as he could. When they hit the stick, Bokuden's arm wouldn't move, or even tremor. There was a man, however, named Kami Iidzumi-no-kami Hidetsuna, who had a student by the name of Harigaya Sekiun. Kami asked Bokuden to test Harigaya Sekiun, Bokuden consented.

Harigaya faced Bokuden and made a stroke just as if he were practising the stroke slowly. He hit Bokuden with the wooded sword, Bokuden felt the shock down to his small toe. As Bokuden was hit, he couldn't feel any saki coming from Harigaya because Harigaya had mushin (the reason for the lack of saki).

The purpose of the above story is to show the level of Bokuden versus Harigaya. Harigaya was far superior to Bokuden who was about the most famous martial artist in popular Japanese history. Harigaya was able to shake Bokuden in the test, thus demonstrating his superiority.

Harigaya's advice to his students was this, when you are fighting for your life, don't use your eyes because they will deceive you. The blind man wasn't afraid of the tanuki because he didn't see it. Fear is what prevents you from reaching satori. In other words, if you are in a fight and you start thinking, or you start looking at your opponent through your eyes, you will start to intellectualize and then you will want to live, you are looking for ways to live (maybe I'll fake him and when he goes for the fake, I'll cut him and I'll win, I won't have to die). So this fear, at the back of your mind, caused by your intellect seeing through your eyes is what prevents you from reaching satori. In other words, you want to make up your mind to die with your opponent, that's the first step – mutual death. Charge right in. You don't lose to your opponent, you both die. Then, later on, when you have mastered this, he dies instead and you live.

Self-awareness (satori) rests on three principles: faith – belief in your own ability and skill; tenacity – never give up no matter what happens, practice, practice, let nothing interfere; and the third and most important principle (and what only a martial artist has), is self-doubt, if your teacher says you have reached the top, you must have doubt and think that you can go further – you must try to. You must be pushed to the depths of despair and break through to reach satori. This is kufusuru or satori.

Chosin Chibana: Karate Legend

Chosin Chibana was born on June 5th, 1885. He did not complete high school, so it is highly unusual that he received Kyoshi, since one of the requirements is that you must have an M.A. in at least one field. In 1957, he received the degree of Hanchi from the Bu Toku kai (Dai Nippon).

When he was 15 years old, he started studying karate from Itosu and continued for 15 years. At the age of 35, he opened his own gym, which later became very famous. In the summer, students would go to Okinawa from Japan to study with Chosin. In 1956, he formed the Okinawan Karate Organization and became its first president.

He had two major beliefs, the first was that you must never, never change your kata. You can teach variations to your students (because of their body structure, for instance), but never change the kata that you learned from your teacher. This shows devotion to your teacher.

The second is that you must teach somebody younger than you. One of your students will strive for Kufusuru. Chosin also felt that karate was not a sport, but a way of life.

He received the Okinawan Times Award and became the first karate person to be honored in this way. In 1961, he quit the organization he had formed to found Shorin-ryu Karate Kyohan. He broke away from his original organization because of internal politics. He became the president of the new organization and died at the age of 82.

Terada Soyu: Trained Only the Kata

Terada died in 1825 at the age of 82. He was a good example of a man who trained only in kata and to face death in practice (meaning that he imagined that he was facing a superior man who wanted his life and every movement that he made was his last).

A martial artist trains so that he can stand alone. You die alone when you die – nobody dies with you. If you know that you can face death emotionally (not intellectually), you will be able to read your opponent's mind. You'll never develop that kind of perception however unless you reach myo or develop the ability to face death.

Ono Jiroemon Tadaaki had a student by the name of Nakanishi.

Nakanishi was the first to develop and use the split bamboo shinai. When he did, Ono kicked him out, but he later relented. However, he told Nakanishi that since he didn't teach it in his school, he, Nakanishi, would have to call the style by another name. The style became Nakanishi-Ha Itto-ryu, and at his time there erupted a considerable controversy over sparring with the bamboo shinai versus just kata training alone.

In Soyu's time, the argument again raged. Proponents of Nakanishi-Ha Itto-ryu said that to determine a winner you must actually make contact. They would wear protective equipment and contest with split bamboo shinai's making full contact. The referee would make a distinctive sound.

They felt sparring was a more effective way of improving one's skill than the old school thought of doing just kata. Of course the old school, the classical style of training, felt that sparring wasn't necessary at all. They were considered old-fashioned.

Terada was approached one day by somebody who asked him his opinion on the controversy. He replied that he didn't know as he had never had any experience in using the split bamboo shinai in that type of match. The best was to pick a champion from each school of thought and have a match but he thought that kata training was sufficient to prepare for a match to the death.

A tournament was arranged between the two schools of thought. With Terada as a participant in it for the old school. The old school were saying: "Just wait until these guys face a man whose sword has become part of him and they see the flames of his ki shoot out the shinai." The other side said: "Just wait until these old-timers get hit for the first time."

The match was witnessed and recorded by Chiba Shusaku who was in his twenties at the time.

Here is his account of what happened:

The contestants were divided into two lines with the old school on one side and the new school on the other.

First to fight was Terada and he was to face the champion of the new school. The others were paired off down the line and were to fight after Terada. Some of the others from the old school were worried. Terada was offered protection to wear but he refused saying that "I have never used that so I don't want it now but you can use all you want."

All the old school refused protection. Terada was in his late 60s or early 70s at this time.

When the champion and Terada finally faced each other for the match, the champion thought to himself: "Well, he's just an old man so I won't hurt him. I'll just tap him on the head." But Terada told him after he had thought that: "I know what your thinking – you think I'm an old man. Well the moment you strike for my head I'll break your arm."

This happened to be the counter for that kind of attack. Terada had spoken aloud so everybody had heard him. The champion grew alarmed at the idea that Terada might be able to read his mind so he decided to attack with a fake to the head first, then suddenly switch and strike Terada's side. Right after he thought that, Terada said aloud: "When you attempt to hit my side, I'll poke your throat." Now the champion knew that Terada could perceive his intentions so he dropped his shinai. Terada won the match without throwing a blow. It was the same with all the others.

Chiba said in his diary: "I spoke to all the losers. When I watched Terada in action, I realized the value of the kata. Before, I thought it old-fashioned.

If you have myo and somebody wants to hurt or kill you, you will feel his intentions. You can only do it if you can face death (emotionally). The intellect cannot feel so it can't detect an intended attack. Eventually you'll come across a kata that you like a lot. Do it often in the manner described below and you'll be able to accomplish the above.

Actually you need no special kata but one that you like – you'll have a certain feel for and it will be easier. For instance, you may use the first Pinan: On the first move as you turn and block down with gedan-barai, you must FEEL as if this was your last move on earth before you died. You accept your death but make up your mind that in the last move you have, you'll at least break your opponent's leg with your block. You must believe that your next move is your last and if you can do every move of the kata like that, you solve the secret of the kata that you're doing (each kata has it's own secret).

Be sure that it is not an intellectual belief but an emotional one.

A martial artist develops a large sensitive critical zone because he has conquered his fear of death. Also a martial artist tries to develop his magnetic field since the magnetic field is more powerful than an electric field.

Before you can achieve a higher level of awareness you must die a zen death – you must die emotionally in full control of your facilities.

Because conquering your fear of death can be a lifelong task, the samurai developed a short step by answering the question: How can I develop dignity or class outside of conquering the fear of death? Their answer was to first start by controlling their hunger. That's the reason they might be starving from hunger but refuse a meal from someone, claiming that they just had a big meal and make their point by pulling out a toothpick and picking their teeth.

A martial artist overcomes the easy things first – hunger for instance. If you can, then you will be able to conquer your desire for more money or material things. Then you go inside and conquer your fear of death.

Takeda Takachiya and the Ninja

November 1970

When Takeda Takachiya was 23 years old, he met a ninja who was 62. The ninja told him that there are seven precepts that you must master to be a samurai (this later became the Daito-ryu code).

1) I have no parents; heaven and earth are my parents;
2) I have no home; my home is in my tanden;
3) I have no life and death; my breath is my life and death;
4) I have no law; self protection is my law;
5) I have no principles; adaptability is my principle;
6) I have no talent; wit is my talent;
7) I have no sword; mushin is my sword.

The second precept is concerned with the question: *Who am I?*

The ninja invited Takeda to try and move his sword which was just held out straight. For three days, Takeda tried to move the ninjas sword but couldn't. On the third day, the ninja told him to come wearing a do (side protector).

Takeda was thinking to himself, "How can I move him?"

He got the idea of rushing right in and tripping him. So he tried it and did trip the ninja. He couldn't help smiling at finally getting him. The ninja had rolled over, taking the fall. He told Takeda, "You're thinking that you have beaten me but look at your do." He looked down at his do and took it off, discovering that three of the inner bamboo ribs had been broken. He refused to admit that it was the ninja's doing, saying that they must have been broken beforehand.

He went home and a cousin of his who was studying the sword saw the do and said, "This man must be very good. This blow would have killed you." Takeda then realized the skill of the ninja and so went back to apologize. The ninja told him that he must learn muji – means no word. Muji must come in your mind – no word must come in your mind. The samurai teach in silence.

Takeda-practiced for 20 years trying to understand muji, to no avail. The next time the ninja practiced with Takeda he held the sword facing Takeda and by advancing a step at a time, pushed Takeda back to the wall. There was nothing Takeda could do but retreat for some reason. At the end of the week, he pushed Takeda out of the gym and closed the door.

Takeda went to see a monk and told him the story of what had happened. The monk and Takeda (now in his 40s) went to a circus. There they saw a women balancing on a ball. There was nothing in her mind; by looking at the expression on her face you could see that. If there had been anything on her mind, she would have fallen. It took all her concentration to stay on the ball. The monk told Takeda to look at the woman's face:

"There's nothing on her face. You are like the woman when she jumps off the ball and her expression goes back to normal. In the gym, you concentrate but stop when you leave it. You must not – you are your 'meditation' when you leave the gym or end your exercise."

Takeda thought that the monk was right.

The next day, he went to the gym and again the ninja pushed him out of the gym again. Takeda went home where he meditated on the feeling that he had felt in the gym and was able to reach enlightenment. He reached enlightenment at the age of 45.

The next day he again went to the gym and the ninja smiled when he saw him. Ninja said, "Now you know what muji is."

The ninja went on to tell Takeda that he has found out that when you face your opponent, your mind precedes your action, but you overwhelm your opponent with it (he's talking about the ki).

Saito Denti-bo Founded Tendo-Ryu, 1487

Saito founded Tendo-ryu and died at the age of 38, in 1487. The following story took place towards the end of his life.

Unfortunately for Saito, he forgot the most basic lesson In the martial arts to avoid trouble. One of his teachers was Bokuden. Bokuden was the type of man who, if he saw trouble, avoided it. He avoided it physically, for if he sensed that there was going to be trouble he didn't go to that place but took a round about way (see a previous story about Bokuden and the horse).

Saito's skill was so great after he formed his school that he went to Kyoto and he managed to be one of the very few men in Japanese history who demonstrated in front of the emperor. In order to do it he utilized all the martial art principles that he had learned. He used them in his everyday life, even politics and so managed to demonstrate for the emperor. He was so pleased with Saito's skill that he gave him the name of Ide Handan Denti-bo. The Handan meant something akin to a special agent. He could go all around and see that law and order was kept in the country.

When Saito got back to his hometown after performing in front of the Emperor, all the martial art students in the area from the different dojos started attending his school to learn from him because of his skill.

Eventually, he lost his balance. He forgot everything that he learned in the martial arts. He became cocky. He was a monk and as such was supposed to shave his head everyday but now for the first time he refused. The head of the temple said to himself: ""He lost sight of Buddha".

Although it could never be authenticated, there were stories going around that maybe he had used magic to gain the audience with the Emperor.

Saito lived in the time of all the greats and the most famous fighters like Miyamoto Musashi, Hozoin Inye, etc. and he had never fought any of them and yet managed the audience.

Everyone knew how good the others were but how could they judge Saito who never fought them. Still, Saito was considered to be one of the best in his day (in technical skill). It could have been his reputation of his skill that spread, plus the fact that the monks were like public relations men spreading his fame – after all he was a monk himself.

When Saito talked to people and demonstrated, they were convinced that he was the best – he didn't have to fight any matches. Musashi had to fight 63 matches to the death to prove his skill.

Thus the students flocked to his school. When Saito refused to shave his head (which is a sign showing that you're taking away your vanity) he let his hair grow a little bit. The head monk said, "Saito is possessed by the devil." He may not have been possessed by the devil but what he did certainly made people think. Instead of dressing very plainly in a simple black frock like the rest of the monks did, Saito wore a leather coat with feathers sticking out of his hair. It was noticed that his eyebrows started growing upwards, and combined with the feathers in his hair that looked like horns, he began to look like a devil. Although he bragged about how good he was, there was no doubt that he was skillful.

The lord in Saito's home town was a very skillful swordsman and he had a large school. They both trained in the same place so the lord began losing students to Saito. When that happened some of the lord's top students started saying around, "Saito really isn't too much. Nobody has seen his skill in combat. Sure, he performed in front of the Emperor but maybe he used magic, maybe the devil got him in front of the Emperor. His magic was what got the Emperor's favor. He's nothing."

Well it came to Saito's ear. It was then that Saito made his first step down. He issued a challenge. "If you think that I'm not skillful because I have not fought a lot of men like Musashi and all of them, you're wrong. It's because I'm so skillful, I don't want to kill anybody. My skill is that great. You are the shi-handai for the lord but you're like a kid compared to me. If you want to fight me, I'll fight you, but on one condition: that it's shinken shobu. Then the real value of a man comes out." According to the books Saito was grinning devilishly as he said it.

The shi-handai, who was a very skillful person, accepted. When they faced each other. The man made one move and he was dead. Saito killed him right away with no problem. Then people realized that Saito actually was skillful. He could live up to his mouth, a rare thing as braggarts usually can't.

After the match Saito said, " You see! It's a good thing that Musashi and the others don't challenge me. I really don't want to kill anybody despite my skill, I don't talk or go in the sporting arena and use the wooden sword with a judge who tells who won. Not me. When someone faces me, he has to go down to hell and I'm gonna put him there."

The father of the shi-handai went to the lord after his son was killed and said, "Well, what are you going to do with a person like that?"

The lord replied, " Saito must be possessed by the devil. He's always bragging. The only way to fight him is to use the same strategy he uses, all is fair in love and war; you have to overcome him on an equal basis." That's all the lord would say.

So the father challenged Saito to a match. Saito asked what the terms of the match were and the father replied, "Well, we'll meet at a temple." Making mention of a certain pine tree (It was in Akashi, Japan. The people had planted a pine tree there which is still standing today.) "We will both have two seconds to make sure that there is fair play."

Saito agreed, saying, "I'm sorry. You're going down to hell, you haven't a chance with me but if you want to, that's okay with me, but I'll give you a chance to refuse the match. I don't want to have to kill both the son then the father."

But the father said, "Never mind. We'll see who goes to hell."

The morning of the match came and Saito took a spear with him. Everybody was surprised, "Saito, you're a swordsman, so how come you are using a spear?"

Saito replied, " A martial artist is a martial artist. He is skillful in anything he handles be it swords, spears, bows and arrows, hand and feet, or what have you. I'm just as good with the spear. I'll send anybody to hell. There's no difference in the skill because a martial artist is a well rounded individual. So I'm going to show the world my skill because nobody thought that I could use this."

He was bragging like hell as he was walking to the temple with his two sec-

 Body language regarding lying: You can tell someone is lying by the flickering of the eyes.

onds who really adored him. They were his shi-handais, his two top students.

When they arrived at the temple, the father was not there, so his students said, "Where's your opponent?"

"Probably he's scared," replied Saito, "but I'll wait an hour."

So he sat down under the pine tree.

After fifteen minutes, they heard a lot of noise so Saito sent his students to see what was making the noise from the nearby plains. One of the students came back and said, "Sensei, the man has taken unfair advantage of you. He's coming with thirty bo men and ten horsemen. What's the reason for that?"

Saito replied, "Well, it looks like they came to kill me. They came for a match."

The students suggested that they run away, but Saito said, "No, that's all right. Before I die they will see my skill. I couldn't prove it by just killing one boy. They came to kill me so both of you go back home."

The students wanted to stay but he ordered them three times to go, when they didn't he told them to watch from the hill.

"Watch how a real man dies." he said. Saito knew what would happen when thirty bo men and ten of the best horsemen showed up. (One of whom had the same name as him – Saito. That man, whose full name was Saito Honsan, wrote about him.)

Saito walked away from the pine tree and over to the temple, standing with his back to the temple so that nobody could attack him from the rear. He stood waiting with his spear in his hands. When they advanced, Saito Honsan said, "You know, you just killed a young boy. There's no doubt that you're skilful but the funny thing is that you do look like the devil. How come you have that spear?"

Saito said, "Never mind. You people have come here to kill me. Watch how a real man dies. Lets' see your skill."

Honsan said, "If you can ward off my arrow, you are truly skilful." So saying, he shot an arrow at Saito who had no problem knocking it away. The same thing happened with the second and third arrows shot at him. All the time he was being shot at Saito was advancing, so Honsan told his men, "If we shoot at him one by one, there is no way of hitting him so let's shoot in volleys."

They shot in volleys of three, four men at a time. Saito knocked down the arrows. They shot in volleys of six but still Saito was able to knock them all down. Then Honsan said, "Lets shoot at once in volleys of ten."

Saito knew then that the game was up, so he said, "Stop!" He walked back to the temple and said, "You god damned cowards, watch how a real man dies." They shot him full of arrows but Saito never fell down, just stood there. Eventually they carried him over to the pine tree and left him standing there.

One of the mistakes that Saito made, according to Honsan, was that he showed his skill by knocking down the first arrow so easily. If Saito had used strategy instead he could have pretended to have trouble by barely warding off the arrow, possibly being slightly wounded in the process. Then they would have figured that they could handle him one by one with honor, and before they realized it, Saito could have been among them, chopping them down. But instead he so easily knocked down Honsan's arrow that they were surprised. Then he did the same to the volleys of three and six. How can you cope with a guy like that? Fill the air with volleys of arrows so he can't possibly get them all. By then Saito knew his fate and stood near the temple. Only two men in history were able to die like he did – Saito and Benkei.

The moral might be that you have to pay the price in the martial arts. The better a real martial artist becomes, the more humble he should become. If Saito had listened to the head priest and shaved his head and been humble, he would not have provoked the pride of winds. The tallest tree – the type of enemies you make, depend upon your mouth. If you use your mouth only for eating you will never get into trouble. Every time you talk you get into trouble.

If you train well and properly in the martial arts and you happen to approach somebody on the street who is in a murderous rage, wanting to shoot somebody, you can avoid him because you will be able to sense his vibrations. Maybe all it would take to set the guy off would be for somebody to look at him. He might ask, "What are you looking at?" and shoot you down.

That's the reason why, when a man who was looking for a real master, never looked for technical efficiency alone, and no matter how skilful a man was, it wouldn't be enough to qualify him as a potential Sensei. However, when they did find a real master, they were usually disappointed for he would make them stay on just one technique for a very long time. The more they practised that one thing, the more tedious it became – it was the equivalent to the koan used by some schools of zen (verbal riddle). By doing a kata long enough, you discover a lot of things you never realized before such as a wrong position of your body when doing a certain more.

Your memory is contained not only in your brain but throughout your entire body. Every muscle has memory ability, so that if you train in a kata over and over again the way your Sensei tells you to, you are making your muscle memory complete – not just the intellectual part of you.

Since every part of your body has memory, for instance your finger, if you make a move using that finger and you're off position slightly, your finger will feel it. Through the kata you begin to feel your own vibrations and can then tap muscle memory. So if you are near somebody hostile, his vibrations will throw you out of harmony and you sense the danger and avoid it. Only a real master can bring that out in you – the skill you develop is beyond technical efficiency.

Never be satisfied with the performance of your kata – think of satisfying your sensei. That will be your goal and if you accomplish it, you got it.

Agena: Hands and Fingers of Steel

Born in Gushikawa, Okinawa, a small village. He was a very small person, around 130 lbs when he was full grown. Born into an upper middle class family but when he was very young he decided that he was going to train in the martial arts.

In these times you had to be of nobility in order to train in the martial arts completely. Agena was the first exception. He devoted all his energy to build up an iron fist and iron fingers. Mentally, he believed he could do this and developed this through a proper mental state. His sensei was Matsumura Sokon.

Tengan Matsu a friend of Agena's got him drunk one afternoon. Tengan pointed to a tree and said. "I bet I can beat you in taking the bark off that tree?" Agena said Tengan was crazy to make such a bet. Tengan said there was one condition though, he would use a hammer and chisel.

The two agreed on the bet and set five pounds of meat as the prize. Agena stated he would settle for sirloin. Tengan got the village head to officiate the contest. Agena punched the bark with his fist to loosen it up and then tore it off with his bare hands in large strips. He stripped off 8 feet of bark. Tengan had removed only a third of this on the other side of the tree. This tree is still famous.

Agena's name, Tairagwaa means "small" – Taira. It is a name of affection given to him by the villagers. In Okinawa at this time, common people took the name of the village that they were born in. Only noble people had surnames.

A different Tengan, Tengan Matsu, worked in a Japanese bath house. His job was to make the fires and clean up. At this point in time bath houses were not divided in the villages, only in the cities. Later they became divided in both.

Tengan always wanted to see Agena in action. It became his life-long dream. Tengan had a dream and believed he would die soon. So he told Agena he would like to see some demonstration of his skill as a Meijin before he (Tengan) died. Agena consented. Tengan called 25 to 30 women into the men's side of the bathhouse to observe the demonstration. Everyone was naked. Agena stood up, struck out at the wall dividing the men's from the women's side, then sat down with his back to everyone. Tengan felt that Agena might be embarrassed because the women were present. Tengan asked what had happened. Agena pointed to the wall. There were holes in the wall from Agena's fingers. The wall boards were nailed on from the women's side yet the force of the strike did not knock them loose.

Tengan and the women went around telling everyone. Many people came to see the bathhouse wall in disbelief. Tengan, an entrepreneur, charged to see the wall and made a large sum of money. The bathhouse was destroyed during the WWII.

Agena never killed anyone in combat, as he always subdued them. He often traveled with Tengan. Often they were way laid by enemies. Tengan said Agena never killed any of these people.

One evening Tengan and Agena passed by a barrelmakers in a small village. The barrelmaker stopped work when the two strangers walked past. Tengan told the barrelmaker that in their village, Gushikawa, they did not use tools to make the bamboo barrels. Tengan said they used their hands instead of chisels and sickles and used the tools only for the finish work.

The barrelmaker called out the other villagers and then said Tengan would have to show them or the villagers would not let them pass. Tengan was a large man while Agena was very small. Tengan told the barrelmaker that he would not only demonstrate but that he would have the weakest man of Gushikawa do it. The barrelmaker said he would reward them with enough sake to get them drunk for a week if they could do what they claimed. Tengan asked for some bamboo, a large piece, maybe four to five inches in diameter. Tengan handed the bamboo to Agena. He crushed it with his grip, then smashed a second piece with his hand. The villagers asked Agena to teach them the art but Agena refused. The art was possibly lost with the death of Agena although some at the Dai Nippon Bu Toku Kai say the art may be still practiced by some Chinese. Possibly by some Chinese women.

Agena's hands were not developed or deformed. In fact they were small and soft looking, almost like a woman's hands.

Sadayu Ichimori on a Mountain Path

January 1972

Ichimori lived about three hundred years ago and came from the province of Bizen. By the time he was twenty-seven years old, he had mastered Kyokushin-ryu and had received the 'inka'. (Kyokushin-ryu is a combination of Daito-ryu and Toda-ryu).

At the time of the following true story ichimori was working for a small lord by the name of Ikeda. Ichimori had a mild case of skin trouble, so he occasionally visited hot springs as soaking in them was good for his skin.

This particular hot spring that he was going to was way up a mountain and the path at one point was wide enough for only one person at a time, with the mountain on one side and a sheer drop on the other side Also, the path was curved so it was not possible to see ahead to check if someone was coming, so the local custom called for anyone coming down the path to yell loudly thus warning anyone going up the path. When you heard this you would stop at a niche that had been carved in the side of the mountain and wait for the person coming down to pass.

Ichimori was walking up this narrow part of the path, followed by his servant, when he heard somebody singing He thought nothing of it and continued on his way up. When he got around the bend, he saw a cow being driven by a farmer behind it. So there they were: the farmer, the cow, Ichimori and his servant,with no room-for anyone to pass.

The farmer called out to Ichimori "Hey samurai! Didn't you hear me singing?"

"Yes," replied Ichimori. "But I thought nothing of it.

"Well you were supposed to wait back at the niche until my cow and I passed". Now, you both will have to turn around and go back to the niche so we can pass."

At this time a monk, who had walked up the path came upon them. Seeing him, the farmer got upset. "Now see what you have done, samurai! Traffic is all backed up."

"Don't be upset," Ichimori told the farmer. "My servant and the monk can go to the niche and I will go around you."

Upon hearing this, the monk said "I'll follow you samurai" to which Ichimori objected, saying "But you won't be able to do what I am going to do!"

But the monk insisted and so Ichimori sprang up on the cow, touching lightly, and then over it and the farmer, landing on the other side of them (it took great skill to jump on the cow without causing it to lose it's balance).

When Ichimori turned around to look for the monk, he was confronted by him. The monk had jumped over both the cow and the farmer without touching either of them. The monk, applauding Ichimori's skill, asked for his name, and when Ichimori gave it, he said "Well, you're famous, no wonder."

Ichimori returned the question and when he heard that the monk's name was Karasuyama Eian, he dropped to the ground and bowed low, asking Eian to forgive his rudeness. (Eian mastered the Kyoro-ryu art of stick fighting – an art having had all its students achieving at least enlightenment. Eian had his own ideas about stick fighting, consequently his art differed from the others which were mostly based on the Hozoin-ryu-style.)

Eian learned that Ichimori was going to the hot springs also, he said that he would accompany him. At the springs after they had registered at the inn and were both lying in the mineral bath, Ichimori asked why Eian was there. Eian replied that he was only human and therefore had frustrations like others so he soaked in the baths to prevent piles (the Japanese believe that frustrations can cause piles).

Meanwhile the innkeeper, a deceitful man who considered himself an expert swordfighter, was examining the register in order to determine who was using a false name (many samurai, if they were famous, used false names while traveling so as not to be bothered by curiosity seekers). When he found one who turned out to be a famous swordsman he would challenge them to a contest in such a way that they couldn't honorably refuse.

The innkeeper was suspicious of Ichimori so he approached Ichimori's servant and said "You know your master doesn't appear to be a common samurai. I'll bet he's famous.'

The servant replied "That's right. He's really Sadayu Ichimori." Hearing this and recognizing the name, the innkeeper later on challenged Ichimori to a contest with wooden swords. Ichimori was forced to accept and the match is set for the next day at a nearby place. Unknown to Ichimori, the innkeeper had previously prepared many pitfalls in the ground by digging holes and covering them over with grass. After they paced each other and started the contest, the innkeeper moved off to the left at which Ichimori moved to the right. Then the innkeeper retreated and moved off to the right at which Ichimori advanced and moved to the left. Suddenly Ichimori stepped into a pitfall and stumbled, whereupon the innkeeper attacked, winning the match. Eian who was watching told the innkeeper that he probably wouldn't be able to defeat Ichimori in real combat although if they had been using real blades then, he would have killed Ichimori when he stumbled.

Later when Eian and Ichimori were drinking tea together, Ichimori remarked that no one would be able to avoid the pitfalls. Eian took exception to this, telling Ichimori that the purpose of the martial arts was to achieve myo, samadhi, and satori, and having achieved any of these, it would be possible to avoid such pitfalls.

Ichimori didn't believe it, so Eian let it leak out who he really was. Ichimori was large for a Japanese, being 5'9" at 170 pounds, whereas Eian was only average build, dressed in ragged but clean clothes, so the innkeeper had never given Eian a thought until he found out who he really was. The innkeeper then challenged Eian to a contest with wooden swords the next day at a different place than previously thought. This new place had been prepared with more and even trickery pitfalls than the other.

When they fought, no matter how the innkeeper moved, he could not cause Eian to fall into a trap. Finally, the innkeeper got exasperated and Eian figured that it was time for the match to end. Eian did the Hawk Wing technique, defeating the innkeeper.

When it was over, Ichimori couldn't contain himself and so asked Eian what he had done in order to avoid the traps. Eian replied that he had become the innkeeper and so was able to know his every thought. He explained that when you achieve either myo, samadhi, or satori, you can read your opponent's mind, making it simple to beat even the best.

Ichimori became Eian's student but it took him many years to master the Wing technique because Eian did not formally instruct him, but would visit him occasionally or send another of his students to check Ichimori's progress.

Ono Jiroemon Tadaaki's Teacher was Ittosai

He was born in 1560 and died November 10, 1629. He came from the village of Mikogami which had only nine houses. Even today it has only nine houses as there is only enough farmable land to support this number of households. Mikogami lies in the county of Awa-gun in the prefecture of Chiba-ken.

Ono's grandfather was a samurai by the name of Toichi-Hyobu-Nokami. He was exiled from Mieken for some offense. Instead of being killed however, he had to agree to disappear from the face of the earth so he moved to Mikogami and changed his name to Iwanami and became a farmer. He gave his grandsons farmer's names. Iwanami had three grandsons. The first two were all right; they studied their lessons and behaved normally but the third one was entirely different. He was Ono (he was originally given a farmer's name, Tenzen Mikogami, but he changed it after killing Ono Zenki).

Ono wouldn't study and was always chasing squirrels. When Ono was seven, his grandfather saw him chase a squirrel up a tree. When the squirrel ran out to the end of the branch, Ono followed and stood staring at it. Just then the branch broke and while the squirrel jumped to another branch. Ono fell to the ground landing on his feet.

Observing this, the grandfather decided that Ono would be a martial artist because he didn't think of the consequences of his actions.

A priest by the name of Iido was the head of Ishido Temple that was a couple of hundred miles away. Iido would visit Mikogami village once a year. One year, as Iido was visiting, Ono's grandfather asked the priest to take Ono back to the temple with him to live. He wanted the priest to discipline Ono's mind and the priest agreed to it.

Ono's duties in the temple included serving guests their meals. One day, Ono (who was ten to twelve years old at the time) was serving tea and sweet pickles to a visiting samurai by the name of Maebara Yagoro. After he had put down the tray and stepped back he noticed a large rat crouched down near the pickles. The samurai knew the rat was going to jump and grab the pickles, but so did Ono. As the samurai was going to chase the rat away, he felt the boy. He looked at Ono and saw his concentration and so he sat still. Just as the rat jumped for the pickles, Ono sprang into action and grabbed the rat with his left hand at the back of its neck as it landed at the pickles. He broke the rat's neck and threw it on the floor, apologizing for the disturbance.

The samurai was impressed with Ono and decided to teach Ono the sword even though Ono was left handed. When Iido came back, the samurai asked about the Ono's background,, so Iido told him about Ono's samurai grandfather.

Then Iido remembered that he seen the samurai thirty-five years ago when the samurai was only eighteen years old. At that time the samurai had cut down a tree and floated down the river. As he left, he shouted to the priest: "When you see me again, I'll be famous." So Iido asked him if he had become famous. The samurai replied that he was known as Ittosai Ito Kagehisa.

Iido was taken aback.

Ittosai had been spending the night in a whorehouse and was having his sixth round with the girl he was with. The bed was covered by a mosquito net.

Because he was a martial artist, even though he was in the middle of sex, he heard a small noise. He felt the girl stiffen beneath him and so knew that he was going to be attacked. He grabbed his sword just as three men attacked.

The first came straight for him and cut down through the net just nicking Ittosai on the forehead. Ittosai cut up, killing the first man, cut the net as he spun around low and close to the floor and cut off the foot of the second man. As he finished the second man, the third, horrified at the quick defeat of his companions, jumped from the window. When Ittosai reached the window, he saw that the third man had accidentally killed himself by impaling himself on a picket fence.

After this incident Itto-sai decided that to live a long time you should never make enemies.

Odagiri vs "The Frog"

When 'The Frog' fought, he would assume a stance like a deep zenkutsu dachi, with his body leaning down and forward with both of his swords extended straight out to the sides. Then he would jump up in the air at you and as he was coming down, he would give a terrific cut down and to the side, cutting the head. This is how he won all his matches.

One day Odagiri received a challenge which read, "This is The Frog. I challenge you, Odagiri, to a match. You are like a frog yourself. You think you are the greatest when actually you are like a frog at the bottom of a well who looks up at the top of the well. Seeing just a small circle of sky, and says this is the world. Odagiri you are just a small frog in a small pond. I'm going to kill you. So Odagiri let us two frogs fight."

Odagiri knew the reputation of 'The Frog' when he accepted the challenge.

'The Frog' wrote back: " Let's fight in your garden."

'The Frog' appeared dressed in a green suit with black spots in order to blend in with the green foliage in the garden. He went through all his katas and sword cuts, etc. in front of Odagiri. Odagiri realized that he was no match for 'The Frog' with a sword. So he grabbed a spear. This surprised 'The Frog', but Odagiri said: "Well you challenged me and I'm going to use this spear."

'The Frog' faced Odagiri and went into his special stance at which time Odagiri put the point of the spear directly in line with the frog's nose. No matter how the frog moved – to the side, back, or forward – Odagiri kept the spear aligned with his nose. Then suddenly Odagiri gave two quick short jabs and put out 'The Frog's' eyes.

He told 'The Frog', I don't know how you are going to live in the world now, but you are not going be scooping out any more brains."

Odagiri's lesson was the same as that in previous lecture. When fighting for your life, don't use your eyes because they will deceive you. Odagiri said that if you want to find yourself your true self, you must realize that the world is obscured by dust. By this he meant, of course, the filters of your intellect, language, logic, and cultural taboos which, taken together, are called cultural relativism. He said that you must see without seeing. In other words, you must perceive, you must be aware, without using your eyes. Close your eyes and you will see clearer because you won't be using these filters. You must knock down the egocentric barrier which is the barrier caused by your intellect.

The main lesson that we get from Odagiri is that you must think of the three points to break down this barrier.

The three types of opponent's that you can meet: the inferior man, the equal, and your superior. Of course, there is no need to train for the inferior man for by definition, you are better already. The equal man is not much problem. It's the superior man that you must train for. Maybe he's bigger or quicker or more skillful than you. Possibly he knows more techniques. This is the man you must always expect to meet and must train for. When you face him you must say to yourself, 'well, he's superior; he'll probably kill me; the odds are with him, but if I attack and kill him, then I have not lost, for he is the superior of us and should have killed me without losing his own life.' This is called Ai-uchi and when you can achieve this state of mind (mutual death), you will not be afraid. This is what you must strive for.

Odagiri's Philosophy

How can a man see his own soul? On the verge of death you can. Trying to find a way to circumvent death is useless. Death is actually your friend.

Your troubles are over when you're dead. No more worries about earning a living or about your wife nagging you, going to work, etc. You should welcome death.

Odagiri found an old skull. 'Let me talk to you,' he said. 'You and I know the score, you have found your friend.'

The man who conquers life knows when he will die. You must realize that life is a challenge; you must take it in your hands and hold it saying, 'I have you life. The ending is the beginning.'

For instance when you face a man in mortal combat and you go in, that's the last step, the beginning of the fight. You either die or he dies. So make it your last step. Attack with no thought of any fear of death, and strike.

Muhen Ryu and Hozoin Ryu Spear

Ohuchi Muhen founded the spear as an art. He was born in the province of Yokote-gun in Ohuchimura village. Muhen-ryu Spear School was named after him.

Muhen was a fisherman who speared his fish with a sharp bamboo spear. He would spear them and lift them up and out of the water. When his village was invaded one day, he speared the invaders in the leg and when they fell down, he speared them in the throat. He became famous because of this technique. His style was very unorthodox as most people would spear their opponent's head or body whereas he would go for the legs first then the torso or head. His challengers soon began taking their legs away when attacked by him but he would then whip the spear up from the ground and cut their eyes or neck. He developed the spear into a fine art. He had no protection as he was, after all, just a simple fisherman not a samurai.

Inye, a priest of the Hozoin temple, known as all Hozoin priests were for the spear, wanted to beat Muhen-ryu. Inye made all the priests study the spear. He meditated and practiced breathing exercises (he reached satori eventually).

One day while practicing, he saw the moon (crescent shaped) shining in the water and got the idea for a new spear. He developed it (only the

Japanese have a spear shaped in this manner and formed what was called Hozoin-Ryu – thought by the public to be the best spear school ever – they didn't know of Daito-ryu of course). There are only nine spear schools in Japan: Hozoin, Tanedo, Kaga, Michi, Oshima, Huden, Muhen, Hikite, and Saburi. There were several shapes of spears (yari): Su-yari, Magariyari, and Hozoin-yari.

Liu Bi: Three Strategies of Warfare

Prior to leaving his village, Liu Bi wrote to the governor, Liu En. Kwan delivered the letter personally, explaining to the governor that they – the three sworn brothers – had formed their group in order to fight the Yellow Turbans (ribbons) and that all the men were volunteers. The governor was impressed and told Kwan that he would greet and welcome Liu Bi's arrival.

The man who fights the hardest is the fanatic, not the mercenary. The mercenary will only fight as hard as he was paid and will quit when he feels it's not worth the money. Liu Bi knew this – that the fanatic was the toughest opponent to fight because he didn't care if he dies. That was why he told the men that they wouldn't be paid.

Kwan had one request of the governor before he left and that was a pardon for his younger brother, Cho-hi. He explained the circumstances of Cho-hi's killing of the guards and so the governor agreed to a pardon.

Kwan returned and told Liu Bi of the governor's words.

The governor introduced the three to Chao Ching, one of his generals who was fighting against a particular general of the yellow turbans, and explained the situation to them.

It seemed that Chao Ching was stumped about how to attack this general and his 5000 men who were entrenched in a castle on the top of a hill. It was a war of attrition. Liu En asked Liu Bi's help.

Upon arriving at the battleground and seeing the terrain, Liu Bi drew a picture to study. The castle's position was impregnable. Chao Ching and his men had been there two years already. While thinking about how to attack the castle, Liu Bi remembered the words of his teacher (the old Man) "You must get your opponent off balance (talking about warfare, not hand-to-hand combat). A way of doing it is to make your opponent proud of himself. He will lose his intellectual balance, then you can win."

The next day, Liu Bi assembled his men and approached the castle. Getting close, he yelled out to those inside, "Your general is the most fantastic person. He is known for his prowess as a fighter even way down south. He is the kind of man that would fight one-to-one with me, winner take all."

Then, a few minutes later, the gates burst open and the general came riding out hard. "You're right!" he shouted. "I don't need all these men in the castle, I will fight you myself, winner take all, But look at your men; they're ragged. I've never seen such ragged men. They look like they haven't eaten for a week. Come into the castle first with me, and I'll give a feast and give you women."

Liu Bi replied, "I know that you're a good fighter but I heard that you're sneaky, so sneaky that you can crawl under a snake's belly. I don't think that it can be done, but they say you've done it many times already. How can I trust you?"

With that the general became furious and charged his horse straight for Liu Bi.

Cho-hi stepped out of the ranks with his halberd saying, "I won't let your ghost roam these plains!" He cleaved the general's head with perfect timing as the general rode by.

The battle was over. Liu Bi and his men returned to governor Liu En's place. The governor gave them a party that lasted for three days with all the food and women he and the men desired. Alter three days, Cho-hi approached Liu Bi and said, "You know what your teacher said, 'two days a guest; three days a pest.'"

Liu Bi agreed with this, but said, "What can I do? He has been treating us good. I can't be so rude and ask to leave."

Liu Bi's problem was solved when the governor sent for him.

The governor told Liu Bi of a place to the south that had a lot of swamp land and a town that was being besieged by 50,000 yellow turbans under a great general. He asked Liu Bi to help their forces, telling Liu Bi that he would give him 500 additional men. Liu Bi agreed and left with 700 men, counting his own. This was to be Liu Bi's first great battle,

He saw the terrain, which was swampy and where the battle had raged for three years already. He asked Kwan what he thought and Kwan replied,"There's no specific leader this time. It's the same as before."

The situation was this: a walled town was surrounded by the yellow turban forces. There was a great swamp between the yellow turbans and the attacking government troops. The battle had raged back and forth across this swamp with first one side winning and gaining ground and then the other.

Liu Bi thought that attack was the best defense and without realizing it, his pride was to bring him his first defeat although he would go on to eventually win the battle.

Liu Bi went to see the general in charge of the government forces (his name was not recorded in history because of the way he treated Liu Bi). The general looked over Liu Bi's ragged army. He had heard of how Liu Bi had defeated the other yellow turban general and felt that it was not a good test of Liu Bi's army, consequently he treated Liu Bi quite coolly. He gave Liu Bi and his men the worst place and made them do menial chores.

After taking this for awhile, Liu Bi decided to show up the general, so he gathered his men and attacked the enemy head on. He and his men were beaten badly, however, and they were pushed way back. The Yellow Turbans were laughing at them and hurling insults as Liu Bi's men retreated.

Later, Liu Bi admitted that his pride caused him to attack the enemy rashly and that he should have known better. He then decided to use a type of strategy against the enemy known as "the horns of the buffalo!"

So he went to the general with the following proposition, "I'm going to stake all on my strategy. If I do it and win, I will retire and won't bother you again. To accomplish my plan, I will need five thousand men from you."

The general went along with Liu Bi and gave him the men he needed.

Liu Bi divided the men up, giving one thousand to Cho-hi, one thousand to Kwan, and taking three thousand for himself to command. For twenty-four hours prior to the attack, Liu Bi's men sounded horns and trumpets in an attempt to unnerve the enemy (The Chinese used this tactic to scare their opponents).

When Liu Bi was ready to attack, he had Cho-hi's group head off to the left and out of sight, with Kwan's group heading off to the right and out of sight. He then attacked with his three thousand men, fanning out like an upside down umbrella, attacking the enemy on a broad front. As they attacked, they sounded certain sounds having the color red (each sound has a color).

They charged the enemy but right after making contact, they fell back feigning defeat and dropping their weapons. The enemy charged after them, scattering their forces. At this time, both Cho-hi's and Kwan's groups rushed in and picked up Liu Bi's dropped weapons and attacked the enemy's flanks and rear. It was dusk by now and the enemies forces were dispersed.

Liu Bi's men then defeated the enemy in detail, attacking all who wore yellow ribbons in their hair (that being how the Yellow Turbans distinguished themselves at night). When the enemy realized what was happening, they sounded a different horn, to retreat. The general's forces in the town heard it and rushed out together with Liu Bi's men and they finished off the remaining yellow turbans.

The governor couldn't do enough for Liu Bi after this great victory. He threw a terrific feast that lasted five days. Cho-hi was in heaven. "This is the way to live! To fight and win and then to celebrate. When I was a common soldier, I had to steal women, now they come to me."

But Kwan told him that there was, more to life than just that.

After the feast, the governor again asked their help. He said that this time the terrain was solid, having lots of plain with tall grasses. The bandits had attacked the government forces with sixty-five thousand men. Again, Liu Bi agreed to help. The governor gave him fifteen thousand men.

Liu Bi went to the general in charge but the general wanted no part of Liu Bi and refused his help. Liu Bi asked a colonel how the fight was going and the colonel replied that the yellow turbans were fighting Guerrilla-style, using the tall grasses to hide in. He said that the turbans wouldn't stand and fight so the only way to beat them was to either entrap them and wipe them out or convert them to the government's side. They had sent out pamphlets in an attempt to convert the turbans, but the only result was that it made them fight more.

Liu Bi thought over what his teacher had told him: "When you fight with large groups, you must use the terrain to your advantage. Looking out over the tall grass, he got an idea to use fire against the turbans. Each of his men was given a flammable liquid and assigned twelve places to douse with it. Liu Bi's idea was to circle the hiding place of the turbans with fire. Timing the lighting of it with the time of the lung. (The time of the lung is

3-5 am and at this time the lungs are at their greatest energy, thus a man attacked then would either fight hard or become terrified, with the latter most probable.

At the sound of the trumpets, Liu Bi's men lit the fires and attacked. Liu Bi dispersed the turbans but unfortunately they had an escape route to the south. As the turbans fled, Liu Bi heard the sound of fighting and to his surprise observed them being attacked by soldiers carrying red banners. They were led by a man dressed all in red and riding a red horse.

As soon as he was able, Liu Bi rode over to the general and saw a man about the same age as him, with a thin face, whiskers, and slanted eyes. When Liu Bi asked why he had helped, the man replied "I'm Chao-cho, the fifteenth descendant of the king (Liu Bi's kingdom) a first son, and the state minister of Wei. The strategy that you used against the Yellow Turbans was fantastic. I studied all the tactics and strategy ever used but I never thought to attack by the principles of yang and yin.

Chao-cho later became Emperor of one of the three kingdoms that were later formed. His son (an only son) later defeated Liu Bi's son.

Kyan: Small Man, Big Power

Kyan's sensei was Matsumura Sokon (Bushi). Matsumura was the only man in Japanese history to be named Bushi. He received the title right on the spot after he had fought the bull. Kyan had a top student who carried on his line by the name of Arakaki Ankichi, who taught people like Nagamine Shoshin. Omine is one of Nagamine's top students and is teaching presently in San Bruno. Theirs is an ancient Chinese style.

Kyan was a small man 5'2" tall and weighting about 115 lb. He was thin. He developed such strong will power that he could do the unbendable arm feat while totally relaxed. While there are many leverage gimmicks that apparently can be used, such as insert all your mind into your triceps, Kyan used none of them. He just flowed his ki from his tanden to his fingertips while all his muscles remained relaxed. They couldn't even move his arm and if they moved him hard enough his whole body would move but not his arm relative to his body.

They could never understand how he did it. Once they asked him and he replied, "It's all in the mind being very secretive (he taught Chinese style – always holding back a little from each student) he never explained it fully. He never told them how to flow the ki from the tanden into the arm and have complete control.

When he stood, it was as if he were rooted to the ground. If several people tried to push him, the longer roots would extend into the around. It is claimed that skillful martial artists are able to send their ki through their feet and into the ground like roots of a tree so that they cannot be moved. This is especially true of Tai Chi and Pa Kua practitioners as they do it all the time. They say that a great master can extend his roots 12 to 18 inches while a fourth dan in the old days should have been able to do it at least 3 inches.

Unless you're very skillful, however, digging roots into the ground isn't a good defense against karate man because you're just a stationary target then. The more you stay solid on the ground, the more relaxed you must be, because if you're tight, although you think you have strength because you have an external feel, there is actually little strength at all. If you're relaxed, your body is like an unclogged pipe and your ki can flow. Tension causes blockage of the ki. Tension is caused by stress and where does stress exist? It exists only in the mind. Stress will make you feel anxious and thus certain muscles will tighten up. That's the reason why you feel good after a massage – it's relaxing. A skillful man has no hard muscular armament on his body.

Mr. Kim mentioned the Japanese Lt. from Nakano spy school who recently was discovered and convinced to give up in the Philippines. The man had been fighting WWII for over thirty years. Mr Kim said that only a man who did one thing for a long period of time could have the frame of mind of that Lt. enabling him to last for so long. He had a set pattern to his life, everything was the same from day to day. He always ate at the same time, afternoon nap for 3 hours, then food at night.

One of the requirements in the Nakano school is that you walk in a circle like the zen monks do (not Pa Kua style) over and over again until, even if there's a slight current when you're walking you can feel it. This exercise enabled you to feel the environment around you very sensitively. They get so sensitive that they can tell whether or not the floor has been

 When you correct an error in personality all your strength intensifies.

swept recently without looking and before stepping down. They develop a sense of physical acuteness with anything that has to do with outside of themselves. This is part of Oriental philosophy: You master outside yourself after mastering that within yourself. Mr. Kim said that he wasn't able to enter the Nakano spy school because he is one half-Korean but that he did go to a school that was almost as good in Shanghai college.

Kyan believed that a student must practice the Seisan kata for seven years before advancing to a different kata. The Seisan is the prototype of Tai Chi, the original Tai Chi had thirteen steps like the Seisan kata does.

Kyan's theory was that doing the Seisan softly (not like the hard Goju breath) developed your ki of course that portion of the which deals with engagement and disengagement you do with an explosion – explode and step, explode and step.

Kyan trained like this. He would do the Seisan near an object, such as a table and he would have somebody suddenly make a loud noise. Upon hearing the noise, he would suddenly jump backwards and land on the top of the object. (This part may be partly a story, as it's not authenticated). Apparently by doing the kata like this, he was able to build up a lot of energy and release it explosively in a jump upon, hearing the noise. That's the way you are supposed to train in Tai Chi.

There is a bridge in Kadena, Okinawa, where Kyan taught and rumors were that he would float under the bridge in a boat and wait for a noise from above, at which he would suddenly jump up backwards and land on the top (people claimed to have witnessed this). It was a jump of about six feet at least. Nobody thought it possible to jump backwards higher than a man could jump forwards, so although several people have done it forwards, it wasn't until modern day high jumpers started breaking world records with the Fosbury Flop, that Kyan's jump was believed. High jumpers take a running start whereas Kyan stood still. (Mr. Kim saw the bridge and said that from an intellectual standpoint, it was hard to believe that it could be done.)

If you can get to the point where you are able to completely place your mind in your tanden and leave it there and from there send it out – if you can really do it without any outside thought – that's it, you got it and can then do anything. Achieving this is in the realm possibility for everybody.

The tanden is the center of your physical balance.

There are two ways of going about achieving that control. One way is by means of physical movement, ie. the katas. The kata is an aid. This is one of the best ways: When doing a kata, every movement that you do in the kata, whether it be hard or soft kata, should come from the tanden. When you're standing, you try to bring all of your mind down to your tanden even if it takes a conscious effort and any movement that you make, it's the tanden that does it. When you hit or block, imagine and feel that it's the tanden hitting or blocking; it's the tanden advancing or returning.

When you do that, you will find that from your tanden up, your body is very loose and relaxed because your tanden is doing all the movement regardless of what your hands are doing (That's the reason why they say a style is soft). The so called internal systems came from the external system. The originator of the internal system realized that the only way to relax was to make soft movements. Thus actually it's a case of terminology there is no such thing as hard or soft styles; it's the same thing. They mean them hard style if a person does a lot of things that use external strength.)

So if for instance you're doing the two hand push, you're not pushing with your hands, you're pushing with the tanden and the hands are only like the infantry dispersing and taking action. To reiterate: if you're blocking down, the tanden is blocking down, all the action has to be from tanden with the hands and legs only appendages of the tanden moving.

In the beginning the action of the tanden has to be a very conscious effort but the more you move with the tanden, the more you'll find out the shoulders, head and spine are always erect. Even if you're doing the move from Tai Chi, snake creeps down, (some people do it wrong their bodies are bent whereas the head spine and shoulders should be perpendicular to the floor always in the move) if only the tanden is moving, you will find that the head spine and shoulders are straight. Then when it doesn't take any conscious physical effort, all the explosion will come from the tanden. The mind will control the explosion and after that your whole body will be exploding because your whole body is your mind – even your fingertips. (When you cut off part of your finger tips you're cutting off part of your mind. Every cell in your body has a memory western scientists know this.)

What is satori? According to Western science, we use only 5%of our brain capacity. The other 95% is a mystery to them, as they don't know its function. The 5% that we do use, however, has to do completely with the intellect.

When you achieve satori, or have a burst of intuition (the Rosicrucians say 'a glimpse into eternity'), the intellect gives way momentarily and suddenly, for one split-second, there is a break through into the other 95% and you find the answer to something that had been bothering you, or have a glimpse of some knowledge one of your ancestors had in the past or maybe in your future. Every time that you hit it, the flash of intuition gets deeper and there's no end to it.

It can hit any section or all of the brain. This flash has to do with private knowledge to know thyself. There's something to do with your life or somebody's life that has to do with knowledge.

Orientals measure a person's advancement, spiritually, on a scale of one thousand chakras. A normal man is only five on the scale and the higher animals maybe two or three. Only Buddha is alleged to have hit one thousand, to have opened all the petals of the thousand petalled lotus. Jesus hit 777 while Moses was above 800.

Inye vs Taizen and the Art of Emptying Out

October 1971

The old man's name (see previous lecture on Inye) was Narita Taizen Dayu Morinhaid.

In the martial arts you must polish up your strength, so you can pick a weapon that's suitable to you. One that you like and enjoy. The weapon must be compatible with you. Similarly be sure to go into the profession or endeavor that is compatible with your nature.

The intellectual mind is only a small part of your " real " mind and deals only with public knowledge. You must find your original mind by reaching satori so that all real knowledge will be yours. The intellect is necessary in order to cope with the mundane world.

To find your original mind you must meditate. What's meditation? It's not just zazen, but also "When you eat, you eat." That is informal meditation that you should be doing continuously 24 hours a day.

You must live the moment totally, with all your being.

Some people make a mistake of worrying what they look like when they perform a kata or fight. You must not. You must have ichinen (One pointedness). Do the kata or fight like you do it when your practicing it alone.

Now the Story.

Inye went from Nara to Kyoto looking for the old man (Taizen) he went to all the temples. While he was in the 1000 and 1st temple, the goddess of mercy, he saw Taizen walk in. Taizen was curious at seeing Inye in this particular temple since he knew that Inye was of another sect. Inye told him that he had been looking all over for him since the time they had last met and Taizen had disappeared. In the meantime Inye had studied from all the masters that he had heard about. Inye said that he had been practising the spear, stick and the sword and that the spear felt best to him. He desired to learn from Taizen.

Taizen told him to go to the east hall where he would watch Inye perform with the spear so that he could see if it was "alive" in his hands. After watching, Taizen taught him the best kata that he knew including the poem that went with it. Thrust the spear, strike with the hook, and pull the sickle. Taizen told him that he must "get it" – not just the literal meaning – if he wanted to really understand the spear. In order to learn the spear, Inye practiced for two hours.

After he learned the kata, Taizen told him to go and see Kami Iidzumi ise no kami Hidetsuna. Kami was able to stop Takeda's army and although he was a famous swordsman, he was also a very skillful spearman. After telling Inye this, he disappeared again.

Kami gave Inye three poems to master and also this advice "if your dreaming of something and suddenly another dream enters, try to recapture your original dream."

In answer to Inye's question as to how to do it, Kami said, "You must do it in your waking moments. Then do the kata and achieve ichinen in the kata. Thereafter when you dream, stay with the first dream. "So during your waking moments when your thinking of something and another thought intrudes, try to recapture your original thought" said Kami again.

Inye stayed with Kami until he was 31 years old. At this time the bishop of the hozoin temple died and he became the head of the temple and so had to return.

One day as Inye was reading, he felt a terrific force, as if Taizen had walked in. He stood up, looked around, and then saw him. Taizen said that he had come because he wanted a match with Inye. Inye agreed so they both went out to the courtyard and got into their respective kamais (fighting postures). Inye "emptied out" himself and all of a sudden Taizen said " stop you won the match" He told Inye that no one in Japan could beat him with the spear. Inye couldn't understand however why Taizen, admitted defeat as no blows had been struck. Taizen replied that he had realized then that Inye was the slight better of them both and that they both could beat Kami.

After the match, Inye invited Taizen to eat badger meat with him. Taizen kidded him about the meat. Taizen said, "In my mind, I didn't eat meat, I eat prana. My body eats the meat."

In the sutra, I discovered that the yang represented the masculine and is the physical aspect (mechanics) of the art (techniques), while the yin represents the feminine and is the spiritual energy that comes out – the ki or prana.

The yang is the outer part of the human being the body while the yin is the inner part. Everybody is yin on the inside.

Why did Taizen lose to Inye? When Taizen faced Inye, the yang meant nothing because in "empty out" Inye caused the yin to burst through.

Taizen asked Inye what he would do with the poems and told him not to write them down. Thus, the poems were not written down until 1924 when the Japanese government began building up it's military strength.

Higashionna Kanryo Rips Opponent's Cheeks Off

The Okinawan pronunciation is Higaonna. There is a Higashionna East and West in martial arts literature, and both were living at the same time. Higashionna Kanryo is West.

Kanryo died in 1915 at the age of 75. He was born in either 1840 of 1841, depending on which system of age was used to figure that he was 75 years at the time of his death (Japanese children are one year old on the day of their birth).

At the age of 17, Kanryo was working for an Okinawan tea merchant who had taken him in (Kanryo was an orphan) and made him, more or less, his son. The merchant did a lot of trading with China, often making trips there, especially to the province of Fukien. During one trip, the merchant was robbed by some of the numerous bandits. He told Kanryo about it when he got back and suggested that Kanryo accompany him on his next trip. Kanryo agreed to go.

When they arrived in China, Kanryo observed the merchant talking to a Chinese man with whom the merchant had had frequent dealings. After talking awhile, the merchant approached Kanryo and said that the Chinese man had agreed to let Kanryo live with him awhile in order to teach him the trade. As a bonus, Kanryo could study with the Chinese man's fighting class (he had his own style). Kanryo had studied Naha-te, one of the three styles of karate in Okinawa (the other two were Shuri te and Tomari-Te).

When Kanryo observed the class, he saw fighting such as he never saw before. The Chinese master said, 'why not learn it?', so Kanryo started and from then on, practiced every day.

The merchant returned to China two years later and asked the Chinese man how Kanryo was doing in the art. The man was not satisfied with the amount that Kanryo had learned and so told the merchant that he would like him to stay maybe five years longer. The merchant agreed but Kanryo ended up staying 18 more years until he was 37 years old.

Finally, the Chinese master told him that he better go home since he had stayed most of his life there already. Prior to coming home Kanryo had become the best in the class. Just before Kanryo was due to go home, the Chinese master took him on a three month tour to see the rest of China. While on the trip, they met a bandit. The Chinese master arranged with the bandit that if he fought with his student (Kanryo) and won, the Chinese master would give him not only their money, but their clothes too, and on top of that the Chinese master would pay tribute to him.

The bandit, looking at the small Okinawan, agreed to fight, with the understanding that he would leave them alone if he lost the fight. So the two fought until Kanryo managed to do a certain ripping technique he learned from the Chinese master (Fukien fighting style has a lot of ripping techniques) and ripped off the cheek of the bandit, holding it in his hand. The bandit took one look at his cheek in Kanryo's hand and ran for his life.

Kanryo went back to Okinawa and eventually taught the art of Miyagi Chojun who was from Naha.

One of the things Kanryo could do (which he and learned from the Chinese master) was to stand on top of a table with ropes tied around his ankles. Men would then pull on the ropes but wouldn't be able to move him. (He could send his ki into the ground like the roots of a tree).

Odagiri Ichiun and Perception

When Odagiri ran away to escape owing the nickels and the pennies, he would often change his name to Katagiri Kudon. Odagiri practised his sword kata every day. There were two types of thought concerning sword training techniques, one school believed in doing the kata while the other believed that you had to have contact. The proponent of contact training with wooden swords, was Shinai Toru, of Jitte-Shinkage-ryu. Shinai used both hand and head guards during practice, of course. Odagiri believed in the kata.

Iemitsu arranged a match between the two in an effort to settle the controversy. On the day of the match, Odagiri stood with his sword held in one hand out in front. His opponent, Shinai, was standing in his protective gear. To begin with, they just stood facing each other, Shinai started thinking to himself, 'Well I'll just go in and hit him in the head.'

Just then Odagiri said, "When you hit at my head, I'm going to hit your side." Shinai was alarmed and thought to himself, 'Gee, I'd better try to trick him. I'll fake to his head, then I'll hit him on the hand.'

Odagiri said, "As soon as you hit for my head, I will hit your throat."

Shinai realized that no matter what he did, Odagiri would read his thoughts and he was powerless against him. He lost the match.

Odagiri taught his students that when you have two people, you have three conditions. 1) Your opponent, 2) you, and 3) perception. These three points can be represented by the ying and the yang symbol. You at one end of the circle, your opponent at the other end, and the 'S' shaped curve connecting the two of you. The arrows flowing around clockwise represent perception. The thoughts of your opponent flow around the circumference of the circle and only spiritual training will teach you to sense. You will then be able to sense any thought your opponent has – it will flow to you. Only people who practice kata will develop this perception. Shinai's school of thought used a similar idea (they were the technical efficiency believers who said that you must have contact). Theirs was a triangle, one corner being you, the other corner your opponent, and the third perception.

There are approximately two thousand seven hundred koans of which the following is one: "Oshin." "Hai!" "Oshin." "Hai!"

This might be difficult to understand unless you have trained in kata. If Odagiri's information is understood, then so is the koan. At the first call of Oshin, the student automatically responds to his name being called by his master. The second time, he is wondering what his teacher wants. The third time he anticipates his teacher's call. He is at this point his teacher's equal or better.

An analogy of the koan in karate would be as follows: the teacher strikes and the student blocks – the student blocks without thinking, the second time, the teacher strikes and the student blocks – the student thinks to himself that maybe there is another way to block. He's also thinking of other things besides doing the block, the third time, the teacher strikes and the student blocks – he's done it so many times that he blocks automatically without thinking so that he's free to look around to see how others are doing it, he anticipates the strike.

Odagiri's students asked him if he could anticipate an attack at any time. He gave them permission to attack him any time they wished, while sleeping, eating or whatever. He promised that if any of them caught him unaware, that that student would receive the menkyo kaiden. Nobody succeeded, expect for one student.

One day, Odagiri was watching the cherry blossoms falling while he was urinating in the river. One student thought that this would be the perfect time to catch Odagiri. Since he was probably thinking about how pretty the cherry blossoms were, it was the perfect set up. The student ran up behind Odagiri, just as he was going to push him into the river, Odagiri spun around and the student fell into the river while Odagiri continued to piss.

Next, the student decided that if Odagiri's intellect was absorbed, that this could provide an opportunity to attack him successfully. The student engaged Odagiri in a game of Go. At one point, Odagiri was stuck for a move since this student was very good at the game. Odagiri was thinking hard about his next move, the student decided this was a perfect time to strike. His hand was under the board, clenched into a fist ready to strike when he heard Odagiri say, "You'd better learn how to make a fist."

Odagiri told the student that when he reached kensho, he would be able to feel any saki (air of attack) and have that perception.

Four years later, the student devised a very complicated move in Go. During a game with Odagiri, the student decided that at a certain point when Odagiri was about to touch a stone, he would attack without thinking. The complicated move came up and Odagiri was just about to touch the stone when the student threw a terrific punch at him. Odagiri fell back and grabbed the student's hand. The student had nothing on his mind but Odagiri was still able to detect the attack.

The student finally realized the importance of kata.

Miyamoto Musashi's Match with Muso Gonosuki

September 1973

It was said that Miyamoto Musashi could tell when something was amiss with a person, that he could feel his enemies, and knew when a person's ki was strange. He would be careful around people if their vibrations were not normal.

Musashi was staying in Akashi, Japan, which is right below Kobe, almost exactly in the middle of Honshu. One day, while he was sculpting a figure of Buddha from a piece of wood, his servant came running out to the courtyard shouting at the top of his voice, "He has come! He has come!"

Musashi looked at him and asked, "Who has come?"

Replied the servant, "The great one, the great one has come!"

"Calm down now, and tell me who has come," said Musashi and stopped sculpting. "Muso Gonosuki, the great one has come," answered his servant.

"What do you mean?" asked Musashi.

"He is outside with eight of his students, standing behind him like a platoon," replied the servant.

Musashi told his servant to show everyone into the house. A big man, about six foot one or two, entered first. He was very large for a Japanese. It was summer time and Gonosuki was wearing a large silken coat emblazoned on the back with a red rising sun. Across the front of the coat was written (in conji) 'Heiho Tenkai Ichi' which means, "The Greatest Strategist Under Heaven' and 'Nippon Kaizan Shingon Muso Gonosuki' (Kaizan means a type of mountain that can't be moved. Gonosuki meditated on one). Both statements were written big and bold and glittered in gold. In fact, history books, when referring to Gonosuki, said that he glittered when he walked.

Gonosuki was a student of Katori Shinto Ryu at the time. He had had many matches in Tokyo, and prior to meeting Musashi, had never lost one. He had fought all kinds of people, armed with all kinds of weapons and was famous all over Japan.

Gonosuki told Musashi, "I was on my way to Kyushu when I heard that you were here, so I stopped by."

Musashi said, "So you are Muso Gonosuki."

All eight of Gonosuki's students were about the same size as him, six footers. They were standing in line like a squad of soldiers with four on one side of him and four on the other. The shi-handai was holding a big fancy case containing a very valuable weapon.

Musashi said, "Relax, relax," but Gonosuki said, "No. You know I saw your father's art in the sword. It was a very good style and I heard that you, Musashi, have improved on your father." (The connotation was that Musashi's father was good but that he had beaten him.) "I would like to see the changes you made and the improvements you have accomplished." (He was asking for a match.)

Musashi said, "Well, if you saw my father's style, it isn't necessary for you to see my style because it's the same except for a few changes here and there, there's not much difference. You don't have to see my style."

Gonosuki insisted. Musashi said, "Well, okay, if you insist."

He went back into the courtyard, still holding the stick he had been sculpting.

Gonosuki told his student to bring him his case and removed a big wooden sword from it, very fancy, featuring a polished band of steel which ran all the way underneath it. He stood facing, Musashi who said, "I see that your strategy is the best under heaven. My heiho (strategy) is to defend against any attack you wish to make. Attack me at will, if my defense is not good enough, you penetrate it." (Those words were written on his silk coat, which he hadn't taken off.)

Gonosuki didn't say one word, he just attacked. He was bigger than Musashi and attacked with all his strength, but Musashi just deflected his attack. No matter what Gonosuki did, Musashi was able to deflect it. This surprised Gonosuki's students who were watching. Finally Gonosuki used his best technique, his favorite, and whatever it was, he fooled Musashi who duelled the wrong way, so that Gonosuki struck Musashi's sleeve where it was hanging down from his arm, as Musashi moved.

At that point Gonosuki shouted, "I've scored a point! That's it!" and he walked away. (He was a character.) "I've scored a hit, a hit!" All his students jumped up.

But Musashi demanded, "What do you mean a hit? You just touched my sleeve underneath my arm. You want to know what a hit is? I will show you!" He attacked. (This account was in Gonosuki's memoirs not Musashi's.)

Gonosuki wrote that he never saw anything like it, the stick seemed to be alive and he couldn't think, so he just retreated. As long as he couldn't think, he was all right, he was blocking the blows. Then the thought entered his mind that he had a chance to turn Musashi's attack into a defense. With that he had created a kyo (gap or opening) and had a thought, Musashi tapped him under the arm, on his sleeve in the same place, with the exact same stroke that Gonosuki had used on him. Musashi shouted, "See! That's not a hit."

Gonosuki realized that Musashi had tapped his sleeve without he himself realizing it, (because his thought had made a kyo), he looked down at his arm in surprise, just then Musashi hit him on the forehead, knocking him out.

When Gonosuki fell down, Musashi turned to Gonosuki's students and said, "He's not hurt, just a little bruised ego. Tell him when he wakes up that clothes do not change the skin. Now take him away."

History goes on to say that Gonosuki continued down to Kyushu and that after three or five years of meditating in the mountains, not eating meat, etc. he achieved satori. He devised his four foot two inch stick and developed his own style, Shindo Muso Ryu. The story goes on to say that he met Musashi again in later years and defeated him in a match but spared his life because Musashi had let him live.

(Mr. Kim doesn't believe this part because he read one of Musashi's original manuscripts and nowhere in it did Musashi say that he ever lost a match.)

Question: How can you talk and not have kyo? (Referring to Musashi talking to Gonosuki after hitting him on the sleeve.)

Answer: It did not matter if Musashi talked then because Gonosuki had had kyo, he was so surprised when Musashi said, 'that's not a hit', that he looked at his sleeve and then it didn't matter if Musashi had hit him on the head or not because it was too much for him. He was surprised because he realized in his mind then, that he had not hit Musashi, but he had just touched his sleeve and that Musashi had done the same thing to him without he, himself, realizing it until Musashi had said so.

There are ways of psyching out your opponent so as to create kyo in his mind. While fighting, talk to your opponent – insult him. While he wants to answer your insults, he's thinking, as he answers – hit him. When you answer your opponent you are creating your own kyo.

A modern strategy to use nowadays, since we generally fight without weapons, is to talk while fighting, or just before, then the moment your opponent wants to answer – hit him. While he's answering you, he is not fighting for a split second, he is thinking, so in that split second there's a gap in his awareness. You cannot talk to somebody who is ready to attack you or else you'll have kyo and you may get caught unaware.

Choki Motobu

September 1971

Choki Motobu was one of the greats in karate. His nickname, 'monkey', came about because of his amazing ability to jump. He went to Hawaii to visit, but was not allowed to land (there are several versions as to why he was not allowed). One version has it that there was a big fight with the immigration personnel. It seems that Choki was born of a very rich family, high in nobility, he was also a huge man. He was almost like a king in Okinawa, he was so rich. He never worked a day in his life and never attended school. In fact, he never learned to read or write. He thought money would take care of everything. His friends who trained in karate never had to work either since Choki ended up supporting them. These circumstances tended to bring out arrogance not easy to ignore. A man this rich tended to look down on people who had to work for a living. Add to that the fact that the immigration personnel probably looked down on Okinawans and it is easy to see how a fight may have started. (When Choki was beaten by Yabu Kentsu, he 'awoke' so to speak, and realized the error of his ways.)

In 1919, Choki went to Japan, although it wasn't until 1922 that his big interest in karate developed because of Funakoshi's visit. At the time he was in Japan there was a big German fighter who was cleaning up against his weaker Oriental opponents. (Fighters who were getting old or who were not too skilful would go to Japan and fight to pick up some easy money against less capable opponents.) Choki was introduced to a Japanese man by the name of Yamaguchi who was very impressed with Choki's great wealth. He told Choki that he had never met a man so rich and one who could do the things that he could because of that wealth. Choki thought, from the way he was talking, that he needed money, so he offered him some. Yamaguchi told Choki about the German fighter and also mentioned that there was karate in Tokyo which Choki was surprised to hear about.

Choki paid Yamaguchi's train fare and together they went to Tokyo where they saw the German take on all the members of a very good judo team. The German was dressed in trunks and had gloves on, while the Japanese were dressed in judo gis. He beat them all. Choki watched it all with interest. After the last match, the German issued a challenge but nobody accepted, so Choki jumped up and accepted the challenge.

During the previous matches, Yamaguchi had been teasing Choki about the level of karate in Okinawa. The audience wondered who this Okinawan was. Yamaguchi tried to stop Choki from fighting, he didn't know that Choki was quite accomplished in karate. Choki didn't have a gi so one of the Japanese gave him his. Choki told the German that he didn't want to use gloves and this pleased the German, who rubbed his hands in anticipation. They squared off and started the first round. During this round, Choki was feeling the German out by jumping back and forth, side to side, like a monkey, in order to avoid the German's jabs, which he deflected by watching the German's eyes. (His eyes would move just before he would jab.)

During the second round, the German went all out and attacked with a barrage of blows, while Choki kept running around him. Finally, the German got mad and threw a right 'hay maker' which Choki avoided by stepping to the side and blocking with his right hand. He then stepped around behind the man, hitting the German in the back of the head with his left hand. He then faced the German, knocking him down and then proceeded to choke him, although the German was by this time unconscious. The referee came over and told Choki that he shouldn't have choked the German, since he was already unconscious but by Choki's way of thinking, a fight was a fight and anything goes.

Lectures on Philosophy and Psychology of The Martial Arts

Sensei Kim would often sit down and lecture us on various topics from Buddhism to positive thinking and visualization or the history of martial arts.

His early morning or late night table talks were something else, as he would sit and lecture us sometimes for 4 or 5 hours non-stop. When some would fall a sleep he would all of a sudden tell something funny and everyone would laugh and the student would wake up in the middle of the lecture. Then we would all laugh at the student who had fallen asleep.

He would often lecture us in bars, on trains, in cars, in restaurants or in hotel lobbies – it didn't matter where or who was listening. There has never been a man who could capture the attention of students the way Sensei could in one of these lecture sessions. He was awesome and always totally fascinating.

The Traditionalist

Most karateka subscribe to the position that a karateka should never be the first to attack; not only from a moral standpoint, but as a martial arts principle as well. However, unavoidable situations may arise in a man's lifetime when he is called upon to demonstrate his skill.

Under such circumstances, the best possible offense is a good defense warding off an attack. Self-defense means the ability to stop your opponent or assailant on the spot. So, the measure of your self-defense techniques starts when you hit your opponent with your best shot. If your best shot gives your opponent the giggles, you haven't got much of a self-defense.

Of course, the well-trained martial artist does not have to attack an untrained opponent at all, much less drop him on the spot. It's possible to be faced by someone who is past the point of verbal argument or reason, in which case, instead of attacking you should concentrate on a defense which would effectively block the attack and place you in a position to counterattack if you had to.

When it comes to defending against the hooligan or punk, however, if your best shot doesn't stop him, you're in trouble. So don't forget the bomb!

My sensei relates this story: Some time ago there lived in Shuri two Ishimines. One, who was from Shuri-no-Akahira, was known as Akahira no Ishimine, and the other, from Shuri-no-Gibo, was called Gibo no Ishimine.

Although Gibo no Ishimine was six years younger than Akahira no Ishimine, he was very cocky about his reputation as a skilled karate fighter. One day, as he was walking along a stone wall, he bumped into Akahira no Ishimine.

"I hear you are practicing every day and your reputation as a fighter is spreading," Akahira stopped him. "Let me give you a word of advice, one Ishimine to another. Self-defense is two spokes to a wheel..."But Gibo no Ishimine was not listening. He was bored with the elder's incessant chattering and finally blurted out, "Can you give me a lesson?"

Akahira smiled and faced his eager opponent. He blocked and feinted as the younger man continued to throw blow after blow. Gradually, he began pushing Gibo against the stone wall. The youngster finally realized what,Akahira was trying to teach him: It is difficult to overpower a truly skilled karate man by any form of direct body attack.

Gibo no Ishimine bowed his head in apology as the wiser Ishimine walked away.

Ichiren: "Single-mindedness"

The Martial Arts are Universal because they deal with the Self.
ICHIREN: Singleness of Purpose.

A passion or faith that all Martial Artists must have.

Lesson of Inye the Spear Master:
1. You must have singleness of purpose.
2. You have to expect failures sometimes.
3. When you have failure, don't build a case against yourself.

Must-have Ichiren.
1. Go into the endeavor you like, the one that is compatible with your nature.
2. Meditation. Live in the moment totally.

The First Step Toward Awareness:
1. You must know every part of your body.
2. You must be able to control every part of your body.

"It is slavery to live in the mind if it is not part of the body.'

A Further Step Towards Awareness:

One of the most important things in the Martial Arts is, once your Sensei teaches you and you don't understand admit that you don't understand and ask for clarification.

A Martial Artist behaves truly to himself. A man who is master of himself – an artist of life – behaves truly to himself. (This becomes true love.) He loves his fellow man and believes all men deserve respect. A Martial Artist lives for the moment.

A Martial Artist must develop mental pressing from the tanden. Press out at the opponent. First you must learn breath control – and then catch cosmic energy. Breathe out on the syllables "Aum". First the density of the bones changes. This change begins in the marrow and works out.

The way to teach a person not to kill is to train him to kill quickly and efficiently.

Poem taught by Kami Iidzumi Hidetsuna, called 'Ise-no-Kami':
If you are thinking (dreaming) of something,
And another dream interposes on the first dream,

You must be able to return to the first dream.
Stay with the first dream.
When you sleep.
Your intellect sleeps.

Why learn so many katas? As you train in the Martial Arts you will become one of two things. You may hit Kufusuru and become an artist of life and have self awareness or you may become a teacher; then you will need the katas to give public knowledge. You will eventually learn one kata that particularly suits you. This kata will help you achieve awareness.

The Samurai Way of Developing Mushin

To develop mushin and therefore their ki, the samurai learned to face the problem of death. They started with the concept of Aiuchi – mutual death. You don't lose to a superior opponent if you both die. He loses because you would have lost anyway because of his superiority. At this point when you are about to die, there is no thought (satori), this is what you strive for – no thought.

Types of Auras

Every person has an aura. A person with some control of the tandem or a normal person, has the greatest width of the oval shape of the aura protruding from his stomach (horizontally). A person who uses his head a lot (an intellectual), has a pear shaped aura with the largest measurement appearing around his head. A person who thinks with his stomach has an aura which looks like a flat disc, protruding horizontally in all directions.

Enlightenment Through Breathing

The internal system: The universe can be divided into two parts: the finite or the Intellectual aspect (relative) and the infinite. There is a sharp dividing line between the two and in crossing it, you reach satori (kensho is the martial arts term) enlightenment.

The road up the mountain (mastery of the art) is long, but if you get part way up before stopping in our system, at least you have a by product of self defense. There are many ways up the mountain: yoga, zen, martial arts, Sufism, etc. Control of your breath is the quickest, pure concentration the longest and hardest with karate (performing the kata) in the middle level of difficulty.

The top of the mountain is satori (enlightenment, kensho), an awareness of reality, of knowing yourself. Ordinary reality is seen through the filter of the intellect which parts an interpretation on it, shades it so to speak. An example of this is language.

A man thinks according to his language. If you speak in a different language from somebody, you therefore think in a different way. The phrase “red like a rose” may mean something different to people of different language backgrounds. An American may think one shade or hue, an Oriental another, etc. (a man who speaks more than one language has an advantage). Because the word for an object is different in each language; they also have a different meaning (although not necessarily radically different), therefore each man sees and thinks in a different way. The more languages you now (as good as your primary one), the more ways you see things and the more true your reality is. However as long as you have an intellect, you can never see true reality because of the filter effect – unless of course you reach satori.

Satori (kensho or enlightenment) is the absence of intellect. Therefore to reach if you must do away with it a zen death. The intellect will fight you all the way because intellectualizing is a well learned and very ingrained process.

The dividing line between the finite world and the infinite world represents the breaking down of the intellect - death. It is a breaking point at which will become stuck before crossing. An analogy is running: when you get tired, if you continue running without stopping, you will reach a second wind and you will then feel as if you could run all day. When you cross the dividing line, you will see logic in what was before illogical (everything will make sense, for instance the zen koans) and your body and mind will become one.

The Oriental believes that everything that has composition decomposes except the soul. They believe that the soul is always there. When you believe this, you realize that the soul is immortal and therefore you are not afraid of death (mushin is the term). This is the first level.

They also believe that life is suffering because man fears three things: death, disease, and desire. Desire is the worst to suffer and it is the block of the intellect. Suffering can be overcome by reaching enlightenment, then you won't suffer the three Ds.

The Oriental believes that everything that has composition, that has physical attributes decomposes, except the soul.

In Oriental philosophy life is breath. From the first breath you take as a newborn baby to your last gasp before you die. They measure time by the passing of your breaths. To prolong your life you must breathe right (control your breath). By controlling your breath you can still your intellect and eventually draw on the energy of the cosmos.

The following breath control exercises aide in breaking down the intellect:

Inhale four counts, hold for 1, then exhale 8, repeat. Each count is one heartbeat. The best position to do this exercise is the lotus or half-lotus. Be sure to use stomach breathing only and not chest breathing (is the best breathing for these exercises the so called yoga complete breath?) Repeat the exercise 10 times.

Make a fist with your right hand but straighten our your thumb and little finger. Block off your left nostril with your little finger and inhale through your right nostril 8 counts. Pinch off both nostrils with your thumb and little finger and hold your breath 12 counts. Swallow on the first count that you hold in order to lock your glottis. Release your left nostril and exhale through it 12 counts. Then inhale through your left nostril while still blocking off your right nostril with your thumb for 8 counts. Pinch together your two nostrils as you swallow and hold for 2 counts. Release your thumb from your right nostril and exhale 12 counts. Repeat at least 10 times. Each count is one heartbeat. All breathing is done through the nostrils.

The easy way to meditate is by use of the breath. A device in meditation to help concentrate is to use the count in the breathing exercises or you can inhale 7, hold one (swallow), exhale 7, then hold one before inhaling 7 again, etc.

The Orientals believe that the solar plexus is a storage battery for the ki. Breathing correctly charges it up with ki from the air. Beginners should do the breathing exercises at least 20 times – advanced persons should practice more.

Breathing through your nostrils regulates body heat. One nostril (the right) absorbs heat and the other (the left) radiates heat.

When doing breathing exercises, imagine vividly (and feel strongly) that you're sucking the energy (ki) out of the air when inhaling and that when exhaling, you're sending it through out your body.

When you can control your breath well and can get your body to vibrate, you will be able to cure headaches.

If you can spend a lot of time in meditation, you need not do the breathing. However, breathing can shorten the time needed to break down the intellect and a valuable by-product of it is good health.

One road to kensho is to use the kata Patsai-dai with correct breathing (there are 22 counts – moves made to breaths). Because the Patsai-dai is an internal kata (literally meaning breaking through), you can break down the intellect with it.

Kyo (Space – Empty – Cavity)

How does kyo come about in combat?

Until a man becomes one with himself, his intellect is involved in an attack that he is making. This causes him to be defending in his mind and he will say to himself, "What if I miss? What shall I do?"

When that part emerges the intellect takes over just as it does when you attack and are not one with yourself, kyo is created. These blind spots in your awareness gaps are called kyo.

In the JKA for fourth dan examination you must explain what kyo is and be able to demonstrate it against an attacking person.

Usually shodans or nidans have lots of kyo. Of course you will only be successful if you are able to feel it.

The Value of Sutras

The most important thing in the martial arts is to do away with fear, even if you are facing your death. When you achieve it, you have what the Japanese call mushin. If you do the sutra of emptiness, you can do away with fear.

The great pyramids were built on that part of the world where the energy hitting the earth is at it's greatest strength.

The Shingon sect of Buddhist practitioners were able to control the wind (as could Nichiren although he used the lotus sutra) and thunder by the use of certain body positions. For you to invoke the kundalini forces you must do certain postures.

Question: Why can't a person invoke these forces by playing tennis or swimming, etc.?

Answer: Because by staying in these postures for a period of time, your body becomes like a magnet and attracts the ki or energy.

You can only magnetize yourself in certain postures. It is possible to get into certain postures and feel what you think is the energy but it may be only body electricity. When you change the configuration of your body, you also change the body currents and that might be what you feel and think is the energy (ki).

The main thing, according to the Shingon sect, is the incantation for chasing away your bad luck. If you chase away your bad luck, then everything will be good for you. But what is good for you may not be good for somebody else, and vise-versa, so the thing that counts is to keep away your bad luck.

Always speak incantations or sutra in a monotone. Get the intonation right and don't slur the separate words together. Do it until you feel the vibration begin in your tanden. The vibration is the important thing and the sutras and incantations build and develops it in your tanden.

Have a spot all your own that you use whenever you meditate, etc. The incantation NO MA KU SAN MAN DA BA ZA RA DAN KAN invokes the power of fire so it necessary to always do it in front of a fire. A candle flame is okay but incense is just as effective and smells good besides. Stare at the tip of the burning ember on the incense stick. Fire is considered the eternal purifier.

When doing the kokyu breath (a type of sutra sound) and exhaling with the "sat" sound, be sure to constrict your sphincter muscles as you exhale (as if you weren't letting any energy come out your anus). The energy is supposed to go up your spine and out your third eye.

You can read people's mind through your third eye if you develop it very carefully. You can tell when somebody is lying because the skin in the middle of your forehead, (behind which lies the third eye) will feel itchy or as if you were just staring.

The Japanese have a saying. The man who lies will eventually become a thief.

Ten Character Traits

In life there are several negative character traits that need to be realized and then need to be corrected as a Sensei it is your job to recognize these character traits in your students and then point them out to your students who must make the changes in themselves. Remember, 'change a man against his will, he is of the same opinion still', was a quote we heard so many times.

Natural Againster: This is the person that no matter what he finds fault or error in it. Let us say he is talking to someone and they say "isn't it a great day today" the natural againster will say "yeah, but it's going to rain tomorrow". Or if someone says isn't that John Smith over their he would say no that is Mr. Smith. He just has to be right no matter what this is the natural againster.

Sometimes Winner: This person is the one who kind of accepts life's ups and downs and he wins sometimes and loses sometimes and no matter what he just keeps going not trying to change the losses into wins.

Loser: The loser is of course the worst character trait. He is the one that finds fault with absolutely everything in the world no matter what it is. If he gets a bowl of ice cream he would complain about the flavor of it. If he won a car he would complain about having to pay the taxes on it. He is the loser and his life will just never work.

Winner: He is the one that finds the good in everything if it rains he says it will make the plants grow. If someone steals something he will say well he probably needed it more then me. The problem with this is that life does have bad things in it as well as good things.

Treadmill Traveler: This person many of us know these types and they are the ones who go through life and just seem to go nowhere at all. Today is just like yesterday and tomorrow will be just like today.

The Taker: This person just simply takes and is thankful but never gives back in any way shape or form he simply does not understand the law of karma and that is that you get what you give in life and eventually his house of cards will fall down.

Oversized Shoes: This person invariably gets in way over his head and tries to do things that never work out because he just does not have the talent for the big job or he takes on some one out of his class. Then he wonders why things do not work out for him.

Self Destroyer: This is one of the worst traits any one can ever have. This person is the type that no matter what he must be a victim and a loser so even when something is going perfect he will jump in a sabotage the event just so he can say you see I was right I am a loser and he will be a loser.

Hidden Revolutionary: This person is the type who always takes up a cause that is against the odds and is trying to change the world to see things the way they see things. Although this is not always such a bad thing it is a waste of time in many cases.

The martial artist is none of the above he is different. He sees the world for what it really is. It is bad and evil at times and it is good and positive at times.

It was Jesus Christ who said to John The Baptist when asked what is the secret of life and Jesus said, “Do you see what you see and do you hear what you hear? This is the secret of life”.

The End

I asked Sensei Kim once, “When is a person considered a real jerk”.

He said that when a person resorts to physical violence, that it is when he can be considered to be a real jerk.

He then went on to say there is only one way to deal with a real jerk.

Simply say to them:

1. Do not ever talk to me again.
2. Don’t ever mention my name again.
3. Don’t ever look me in the eye again.

“Simply put, you totally eliminate or as one of by best students, Peter Urban, said, you evaporate them from your mind as fast as you possibly can. You do the exact same thing to them as you have asked them to do to you.”

1. You never mention their names again.
2. You never speak to them again.
3. You never look them in the eye again.

It is over. Period.

Kata

By Louis Jemison, from a lecture by Sensei Kim

One day a student of archery was practicing by himself in the dojo. He thought, 'I shall eliminate the first movement' (that of stretching the hand upward prior to pulling the bow) 'and just shoot the arrows as fast as I can. The sensei is not in the dojo now, and he cannot insist that I perform all the movements as he always does. He is such a stickler on the complete kata. I'm glad he is not here. The kata is not really that important.'

Then the student took two arrows and shot them as fast as he could eliminating the first movement of the kata. He hit the bulls eye, the student was pleased with himself. As he was congratulating himself his Sensei, who had been in the library adjoining the dojo came in and admonished the student for eliminating the first movement.

The sensei, a Zen Master, knew what the student had done without being in the dojo. The sensei told him, "Practicing must be maintained the same at all times, even if no one is watching or supervising. One must practice for one's self. You are not practicing for me or for society, you are practicing for yourself - for your self-improvement and awareness. If you eliminate or add movements to the kata, you are cheating yourself, not me.

The elimination or addition of movements in a kata shows disrespect to the style or school.

The kata teaches fighting and living skills at the same time. The aim of the kata is to make the individual one with the universe. As he tunes in with the kata, he is in tune with himself, and the universe in the end.

Kata achievement requires blood, sweat and tears. A student used to spend 3 years on one kata. Three years on one kata produced the awareness of what the kata meant. The kata is karate and karate is the kata.

Kata, the formal patterns are the backbone of karate training. They develop form, style, balance, speed, and control. As with all other practices in karate, kata trains the individual in “zanshin” (alertness in mind and body).

Kata consists of a series of defensive and offensive techniques against multiple imaginary opponents. The person performing kata must always be aware of what each movement means. While kata may look like a formal ritual dance with set forms, it differs in that the person doing a kata is always aware of what his imaginary opponents might be doing. In the end he should be prepared for the unexpected attack.

In the kata, you must train and learn how to respond to any given attack. You are learning principles, not just fighting techniques alone.In life there are three kinds of opponents that you will come up against. The inferior opponent, the equal opponent, and the superior opponent. You must always train to meet the superior opponent: prepare yourself to bring him down.

The pinan shodan is the most basic of all the kata in karate. But at the same time, it is also the most difficult to do because one cannot cover up any weaknesses. Everything - power, speed, must be coordinated in order to perform it correctly. It is a great mental and spiritual exercise.

The kata is stylized form derived from, but not identical with,combat movements made by a man fighting against four or more opponents simultaneously. Every movement in kata has a specific purpose. Such as an attack, block, or throw against a definite move by an imaginary opponent. The kata develops; balance, grace, breath control, speed,agility, flexibility, reflex strength and mental attitude.

The Difference between Eastern and Western Philosophy

The basic difference between the West and East philosophically is that the West’s concept is by postulation (based on mathematics and Aristotelian logic) whereas the East uses intuition rather than intellectualization.

So what has the concept of postulation created as far as philosophy deals with religion? It has created an anthropomorphic god. Eastern man however, because he uses intuition and delves inside himself, does not see evidence of a mechanistic god. In him god exists all over – there's a basic harmony in the universe – yang and yin; there's always an opposing faction.

Logic dictates that if there's an anthropomorphic god, then there must be an anthropomorphic devil who opposes him or else there would be all good in the word (which there isn't). Thus, Eastern man tries to find "the answer" himself by delving inside his mind (original mind). Western man tries to find the answer outside himself through science. That is the answer to the meaning of life, it is what they're looking for.

Of course a martial artist needs postulation in order to deal with the mundane world but in order to discover him self it's not enough because it hits the ceiling with the intellect. Postulation is a function of the intellect because only it can be logical, discriminating, and deal with empirical evidence. The intellect demands proof. Even if a Western man has a gut feeling that there's a devil, his intellect will want evidence "show me the devil."

Seeing the movie The Exorcist one will make apprehension although the intellect will still try to figure it out. That same intellect will admit to a god but for some strange reason, not to a devil.

Practically without exception people study karate in the beginning in order to learn how to defend themselves. When they meet the concept of intuition as the sensei attempts to explain the real reason for the kata and what it does for you, they can't make sense of it. The only sense that it makes to them is as a root way of dealing with particular attacks (because their intellect is functioning). Your intellect will say: "Well, maybe this won't work because what the sensei says doesn't make sense – the kata is too stylized (for example). I have my own ideas." You start questioning, then you doubt that there is such a thing as illumination (satori).

The doubt is an intellectual doubt and it must exist for you to reach satori (curiously enough). Even Eastern man has it although they tend to completely accept everything that their teachers tell them – they take everything as the gospel truth.

You must do what the sensei tells you to do because he's been there. It's analogous to a squid crossing a minefield. The first man who makes it across leaves footsteps that the others can follow. If they do exactly as him, they will make it. They can go their own way but they take the chance of stepping on a mine and being blown-up. If you follow your sensei, you should achieve myo. Your intellect may say: "I can discover my own way."

 Pai Fu Yeng introduced the five fists.

You can but how long will it take and at what risk do you put yourself in.

This leads to the obvious questions. What method or approach do you use to get your students to accept your teachings? How do you start? There are many ways but this is how the Orientals start. Usually from the time when you're young, they tell you certain stories. They don't go over the children's heads because children have an empty cup. Your cup must be empty in order for you to learn.

This story illustrates that idea. An intellectual type visited a well-known zen priest in order to learn about zen. However, every time the priest tried to explain something the intellectual would interrupt him. Finally, in exasperation he decided to serve tea. When he poured the tea into the intellectual's cup, he filled it up to the brim and continued until he was spilling on to the floor. The intellectual looked on in amusement until overcome with curiosity he asked why the priest continued pouring into a full cup. The priest replied that he was like the cup – he was so full of his own ideas that he couldn't learn.

The following is an example of a story told to youngsters. An Emperor of China heard that a very famous master of the martial arts was in town so he sent his prime minister to invite the master to the castle where he was to be given the red carpet treatment. The prime minister found out the address and had somebody take him. The minister was surprised that they came to the worst part of the town where prostitution, gambling, and crime in general was rampant.

The street that the master lived on seemed to be the worst in the section so the minister was thinking that there must be a mistake in the address, a man like that couldn't be living in that kind of place. But since it was the only address that they had, they went down the street checking house numbers, finally coming to the last house on the street which was very shabby. The house looked like only beggars could be living in it.

A man was in front of the house pulling up weeds and in general puttering around. The minister asked him if they had the right address and the man affirmed it. Since he was dressed poorly, the minister thought him to be a servant so he asked him if his master was in, naming the man that he was seeking. The man wanted to know why he was being sought out so the minister told him of the invitation to the palace. He said that the emperor wanted to give the master all the fame and recognition that he deserved since he was such a quiet person and so skillful.

The man replied: "Oh. Well when he comes back I'll tell him about it. I think he's coming back tomorrow morning."

"Will you tell him?" asked the minister. "Here's the address and this will gain him audience with the Emperor." With that he left and when he returned to the castle, the Emperor asked him if he was successful.

The minister said: 'No, but believe me, I think that we had the wrong address." He then proceeded to tell the emperor about the condition of the house and that area. He told of seeing the shabbily dressed man out in front and his answer to his question about the master. When the emperor heard about the man, he asked what he looked like. The minister described him after which the emperor said: "You stupid fool. That was him. Go back and grab him tomorrow and bring him here." When the prime minister went back, the master was gone.

The purpose of this story is to teach humility. This famous man in any other non-Oriental society would have grabbed at fame and recognition. Fame and name has it's price to pay, it doesn't mean that the martial artist doesn't want it, but the moment you accept it you must be willing to pay the price that goes with it. For example people will pester and bother you. However you must keep that basic humility.

You might ask: If I only delve in Oriental philosophy and it doesn't bring name and fame, what does it bring? What will the concept of intuition bring the practitioner? It gives you something that only belongs to you self knowledge because there are two kinds of knowledge:

1. Public: schools, libraries, news media, and other people are it's sources; it's second hand knowledge

2. Private: whereas public knowledge doesn't tell you about yourself, private knowledge belongs only to you because you cannot transmit it to others but at the same time it's universal because every living being has the capability to achieve it (enlightenment or satori). But only you can discover yourself.

Western man devised the concept of empathy. They say that they can empathize with you: "I know how you feel now that your wife died."

But they don't know how you feel. You might be happy as hell on the inside and outwardly presenting a sad facade. With private knowledge only you know how you feel nobody else. When you discover yourself, only you know that. You could tell somebody but they can understand only

 Tiger fist- jumping, power from waist.

within the confines of verbal communication it's not 100% accurate except between those who have reached satori, they will know. When you reach satori, your sensei will know because he's there with you.

Train Until You Drop

In the martial arts you must have a teacher because he will teach you to reach kufusuru. He will drive you into a corner by making you train until you drop or else putting you into situations that are so tough that you want to quit or die. This is necessary in order to achieve satori.

Human Nature

Iemitsu started the caste system in Japan and also started the modern dojo – the building built specifically for practice of the martial arts only.

Iemitsu was willing to give Odagiri a fief of 10,000 kokyu and Odagiri's students told him to take it because he could use it however he wanted - in other words for the people. Odagiri wasn't really interested in it for himself. His students convinced him and Odagiri agreed to be Iemitsu's master. When he went to see Iemitsu, he saw the politics. They wouldn't let him help the people. The politics was as follows: Yagyu was jealous of Odagiri's position or what his position would be if Odagiri accepted the fief so he set Iemitsu against Odagiri in a subtle way. When Iemitsu learned that Odagiri was willing to accept the fief, Yagyu said to Iemitsu: "Oh. I won't tell you why he wants it."

Naturally this made him curious to ask Yagyu, who told him that Odagiri wanted the people to benefit, in other words to give the people riches. Iemitsu thought that that was okay, that there was nothing wrong with it. But Yagyu told him about the time that he had met Odagiri in a match where Odagiri had defeated him, but it was a peculiar kind of defeat. He also said that he had seen Odagiri on the street that day. At first he didn't recognize him, but when he recognized Odagiri, Odagiri turned off down a side street. Yagyu said that he had a strange compulsion to turn off the other way, which he did. Yagyu told Iemitsu that Odagiri had the art of no art – he was like a snake, which can paralyze a bird. When his opponent's faced him they lost all their art and couldn't do anything. Iemitsu didn't believe it, he didn't believe that Odagiri had this power.

So a match was arranged with Yagyu as the referee. Of course they didn't want any first rate swordsmen killed so they used second-raters. Odagiri agreed to meet anyone. On the way to the match, he picked up a branch. The shogun had all of the men lined up and he asked Odagiri who he wanted to fight. Odagiri said that he would fight these thirty and that he would beat them all in thirty minutes.

Odagiri faced the first man who had his sword out. The man couldn't do anything, Odagiri projected his ki and they all backed up when he approached. After several of them had gone through this, he ordered them to attack. But even when they attacked him, they couldn't do anything, he just knocked their weapons aside. Then Iemitsu realized that what Yagyu had said was right. Iemitsu came up with an excuse not to give Odagiri the fief.

The lesson to be learned from this is: If you become good, watch out because someone will try to cut you down to size because of human nature.

Live in the Now

One of Sensei's favorite topics as we would gather around a table in a bar either late at night or around the breakfast table early in the morning was that of living in the NOW!

He would often talk or shall I say lecture us on how we can not change what has happened good or bad in our lives up to this point in time. Also

 Snake fist - inner breathing (big in Tai Chi).

how we can only predict the future and even though we may believe strongly that one thing or another will happen we can not be absolutely sure that this one thing will happen or not.

The only thing that we can count on is right now.

This is why it is so important for us to live in the now not the past or the future.

"When we drink this beer right now, it is the best beer I have ever drank," he would say. Or, "this is the absolute best bacon and eggs I have ever had," or, "this is the best trip I have ever been on".

He lived totally in the now. This way he never had regrets.

"The samurai," he would say, "would wake up in the morning look up at the sky and say, 'ah this is a beautiful day to die', whether they would or they would not die today."

Ten Precepts of Buddhism

The 10 precepts of Buddhism are:

Do not murder
Do not steal
Do not sleep with your friend's wife.
Do not lie.
Do not use profanity
Do not use two tongues.
Do not elaborate.
Do not let greed overtake you.
Do not let anger overtake you.
Use wisdom.

Kata Part 2

Step one: Before you start your kata take a deep breath and exhale out, doing the finger meditation exercise for a few minutes. When you feel your fingers start to repulse each other, begin your kata (the pinan shodan is good), doing it very slowly and flowing with your breath as you concentrate on the color orange, you should feel a terrific surge of energy coming up from the round and entering your spine.

Step two: This time you do the kata gather up energy (being sure to relax completely- start with your shoulders and work downward, relaxing your body) and then explode out into each movement. The energy should come out from the bottom of your feet to the base of your spine.

Step three: This time perform the kata by breathing in and looking your opponent in the eye (don't take your eyes off of his). Fight your opponent. Do the moves of the kata in the specified combinations.

Step four: Go back and repeat step one before finishing your practice. If you also meditate, you will develop energy through the kata (if done as described above) faster than somebody who just practices T'ai Chi Chuan.

By continued practice you might someday have your real teacher (spiritual) speak to you from over your left shoulder as your walking, training or etc. It is your higher self (high level). In order to make contact you must not have the following emotions in your mind anger, hate, or jealousy. These three emotions form a barrier between your low self (subconscious) and your high self (spirit body).

Facts on The Takeda Clan

Aizu in the Fukushima prefecture is the main island in Honshu. Ono Jiroemon Tadaaki was born here. This is also the birthplace of the Takeda family. Takeda Shingen was the man who codified the Aiki system. He fought with Uesugi Kenshin, (who was a homosexual), for twenty years over who was going to rule Japan. Both men lost in the end to the Tokugawa family. Both men shaved their heads and became monks near the end of their fight. It is believed that both men achieved satori.

Takeda Shingen started the ninja system. Shingen's younger brother, Nobuchiyo was turned against the war by his father and his mother (who was but one of sixty wives). He ran away to Kuroda to escape all the warfare. Nobuchiyo taught the clan aiki which he learned from his father.

The Power of Prayer

All Mighty God, the budo fudo, all the deities and all the spirits of my ancestors thank you very much for this food. ~ This was Sensei Kim's prayer before every meal.

The initial purpose of meditation or prayer is to focus your attention on the now. The power of prayer or meditation will help you discover the miraculous power that is within us all right now. The point of power is in the present, right now, not tomorrow.

Regular practice is important, not how long you do it, but doing it regularly. Our minds are like computers, once in the hard drive it stays for as long as the drive is around. Our brain does what we tell it to do, what we program it to do.

We are in command. We are made in the image of God in our mind. We are all equal in spirit and mind. Our thoughts and mental images determine how we behave. If we want to change how we feel we must change our thoughts and mental images. To change the programming, you must issue new commands to the mental computer.

The oldest type of mind power is the prayer.

The Training of the Samurai

Whoever laid down the precepts of the martial arts realized that the man who has developed mushin can face death right on the battlefield. Mushin being a state in which you're free of any fear and have reached a certain level of awareness. It's the man who wants to live who shifts his mind and is full of kyo (Kyo translated means un guarded). That kind of man's mind becomes cunning and tries to win by technique or trickery. A cunning mind is full of kyo.

Everyone has done things absent mindedly that's what happens when you're calculating in a fight. You have done the thing absent mindedly because your intellect has taken things for granted and is thinking. There's a cleavage between thoughts.

The samurai tunes in with you and the moment a cleavage begins he attacks you. If you have a mind like a mirror you cannot have cleavage.

A man like Jesus must have been able to sense the cleavage because of his great ability although he wasn't a martial artist. If he were sitting in front of' you and you wanted to strike him, he would know. He might let you hit him but he would know it was coming. That doesn't mean that he would read your mind but he would know your intention. He could receive all kinds of vibrations because he didn't form any opinions.

The moment you form an opinion you're already blind. If you form an opinion, that's a prejudice and a prejudice is blind because you cannot see the other side of the story. If you can look at a thing without forming an opinion, you have formed some sort of an open mind and are that much closer to seeing true reality. A scientist would say that you had an objective mind. If you look at it subjectively by saying well, I know what it is. Then you're blind already.

If you had to face a samurai in a fight to the death, he would just wait for you to get scared and when you did, there would be a cleavage in your mind kyo at which time he would strike. In other words he would hit you at your blind spot when your mind was shifting. If you're thinking to yourself: I'm going to do this or I'm going to try this, in between those thoughts there are small stoppages (kyo) although it's only for a split second.

If you remain calm and do not think, then you'll be like a mirror you'll pick up everything and reflect it accurately, but if you think, your mind will shift allowing your opponent to strike you in that blind spot (kyo). The samurai trained completely for that ability.

The samurai have trained themselves to accept death so his mind reflects like a mirror. The reflections are equal because the mind doesn't form an opinion. The mirror doesn't favor any reflection. If there were a nice looking girl in it, it doesn't concentrate on her to the exclusion of other things and neither would a man trained as a samurai who had a mind like that.

The samurai train for this, hours per day. He wants a reflection of the shift in your mind's attention (only the intellect has attention). The moment your attention shifts he strikes simultaneously and you might not even realize you were hit.

Few people know about kyo and that thoughts cause the mind's attention to shift. You will have no kyo if you don't think, thus you can't be caught in that manner. Very few people reach that level, but when they do, you cannot attack them successfully even from the back.

Although few samurai make it, in trying to reach that level where they would have an open mind, at least they overcome the fear of death. Thus a samurai is a formidable opponent, one that must be killed in order to beat him. That quality mushin will in itself overcome someone else's technical efficiency.

He Who Seeks a Compliment Finds Truth!

"The truth rarely makes a person happy," my sensei was saying, "it ought to but it does not."

He was talking and waving his spear for emphasis. Sweat was running down my brow and every once in a while I had to wipe my face to prevent the sweat from getting in my eyes. As uncomfortable as I was physically, I was much more uncomfortable mentally and squirming inside. I looked at my friend, Seki, and, felt sorry that he had come to this. But it was inevitable, the way it happened.

He was a student of Shinkage-Ryu and bragged about his prowess with the spear. He was a very pleasant person. Often we took a cup together. It was when he was in his cups that he was always seeking a compliment about how great he was with the spear. The patrons at the bars we frequented enjoyed his hospitality and agreed with him that he was the greatest. The better he felt he more money he shelled out.

One day Seki found out that Yoshida Kotaro was staying at my house. He could hardly control his excitement. Seki grabbed my hand almost spilling my beer. He shouted, "Why didn't you tell me that the greatest martial artist of all, Yoshida Kotaro, is staying at your place? I must meet him."

"Why?" I asked. "You are studying another ryu and your teacher is very good." But he interrupted. His words gushed forth.

"If Yoshida sensei should see how skillful I am and acknowledge it, I am made. You are my friend. Please introduce me."

That is how I brought Seki to my house. That is how we came to learn that truth does not make people happy, especially for a martial artist who thinks he is the greatest – drinking in a bar, yes, but facing a master, no!

Sensei Kotaro was not in when I brought Seki home, so we went into the front yard and went through our warming up exercises while we waited for the sensei to come back. After an hour or so sensei returned. I took him aside and told him about Seki. "Reality is hard to take," sensei responded. "In the make-believe world of the bars, truth fits the pocket book and becomes twisted. It is better for your friend to stay there."

Seki heard him and prostrating himself, and said "Onegai, itashimasu" which means please teach me. "Let your friend have your spear, if he wants the truth, he shall have it today." Seki, smiling, grabbed my spear and went into a kamae.

"Excuse me," sensei said, and thrust his spear towards Seki.

Seki gave a big jump but the spear was at his throat. "I was just testing you" sensei continued. "Now get ready," and he thrust again. No matter what Seki did the spear was always at his throat. Finally he backed up against the fence and could not move at all.

I felt sorry for Seki and looked around to see if anyone was watching. There was no one around. I felt better. I liked Seki, and knowing him I knew that a few beers would fix him up and restore his spirits. My sensei then told us this tale.

"There were times when Mercury, between errands on Olympus, yearned to know whether he still was held in high esteem by mankind. So one day, disguising himself as a traveler, he visited a sculptor's studio. Walking about among the many statues displayed there, he pointed to an image of Jupiter. "How much are your asking for this odd piece?" he asked.

"I will let you have that one cheap" replied the sculptor. "It is one of our less popular numbers. One drachma." Mercury laughed in his sleeve. Then he asked: "How much for this Stout lady here?" The sculptor said: "Oh, that one is Juno. I have to get a little more for females."

Mercury's eye now caught sight of an image of himself. Thinking that as messenger of the gods and source of all commercial gain his image would command a gratifyingly high price, he said: "I see you have a very handsome statue there of Mercury how high do you value that excellent likeness?"

"Well," replied the sculptor, "I am willing to make you a bargain. If you will pay me the price I quoted to you on the other two statues, I will throw this one in free."

An Overview of All Kata Forms

After the subjugation of the Ryukyu islands by the Japanese in the 17th century, all martial arts weapons of any sort were banned. The double prohibition only served to sharpen the ingenuity of the Okinawan martial artists. Drawing a veil of utmost secrecy around themselves, they continued the practice they called "Te", which had the unobtrusive meaning of hand.

For almost 300 years, the Okinawans developed an unadulterated form of empty hand fighting. Styles varied from region to region, but remained unaffected by outside influences.it was during this 300 year period that the two major styles, Naha-Te and Shuri-Te, and one minor style, Tomari-Te, developed.

Naha-Te would become Goju-Ryu and Shuri-Te became shorin-Ryu. From the Shorin-Ryu in Okinawa came the modern styles in Japan of Shorinji-Ryu, Shoto-Kan, Wado-Ryu and Shito-Ryu. From the Okinawan Goju-Ryu, we have in Japan the Goju-Ryu and the Goju-Kai. These make up most of the major karate styles in Japan today.

"An Overview of all Kata Forms", gives a brief description of the katas of Shuri-Te and Tomari-Te and of Naha-Te. Below we list the traditional Okinawan katas:

SEISAN: with two main streams, either Shurite Seisan or Nahate Seisan. Seisan literally means 13. Japanese schools, notably Shotokan call it Hangetsu.

PING-AN (HEI-AN): 1,2,3,4,5, katas were designed for schoolchildren in Okinawa. Ping-An means peace, tranquillity, a peaceful mind.

NAIHACHI (TEKKI): 1,2,3, sideways fighting (back against the wall) fighting on home ground with surreptitious steps.

PATSAI (BASSAI): to thrust asunder and breach a fortress,has four distinctive types: that of Oyadomari, Matsumura,Matsumora and Itosu. Matsumura was from Tomari. The oldest kata was oyadomari.

KUSHANKU (KANKU): named after the famous martial artist Kushanku. The Japanese call it looking at the sky. Today we have the Yara, Itosu (Dai and Sho) and the Shiho Kushanku.

CHINTO (GANKAKU): fighting to the East; some claim it is a Chinese martial artist's name. There is the Yabu, Matsumora and Itosu Chinto.

WANKAN (MATSUKAZE): king's crown, The pine tree wind.

WANSHU: the prototype of the modern Empi the swallow kata. The king's way. This kata, Wankan and Wanshu are from China to Tomari, Okinawa.

RORAI or LOHAI (MEIKYO): the vision of a white heron or flamingo, a clear mirror. Itosu 1,2,3, and Matsumora Lohai.

JION, JITTE, JIIN: temple sound, temple ground, and ten hands. These katas are typically Tomari-Te.

CHINTE (CHINTI): the winning hand; although used in many styles, it is a Tomari-Te kata.

ANANKU: the light from the south. A kata used extensively by Shito-Ryu.

UNSSU: cloud hands.

SOCHIN: the grand prize and fighting old man.

NIESEISHI (NIJUSHIHO): 24 steps. Nieseishi, Unssu and Sochin belong to the Arakaki-Ha. Although all major schools now use these katas as they are very advanced, with many hidden techniques.

USEISHI (OOSEISHI or GOJUSHIHO): the ultimate kata in both Shuri-Te and Tomari-Te. It is the Phoenix kata with 54steps. The Phoenix is the legendary bird that arises out of the ashes every thousand years and eats dragons for breakfast – as the legend goes.

NIPIAPO: 28 steps. A kata used to combat Nieseishi.

PAPUREN: 6 steps at a time. Designed for positional and oblique attack.

HAKUCHO: 100 birds, A swarming attack and defense.

AOYAGI (SEIRYU): green willow kata used quite extensively by the Shindo-Jinen Ryu founded by Konishi.

The katas presented above came primarily from Shuri-Te and Tomari-Te. We shall now present those that came from Naha-Te. It should be noted that the katas, as in China,represented symbolic fighting styles of animals, reptiles,mythical creatures, and deities; however, the Naha-Te katas and especially the Go-Ju-Ryu katas stress a Tiger and Dragon lineage.

SANCHIN: three battles, three steps forward. Miyagi Chojun created this kata as one of two basic katas for his ryu. As Go-Ju means hard (go) and soft (ju), t-he Sanchin represents the (go) kata. It is a very difficult kata to master, using only fundamentals and not using techniques per se. It was designed to perfect coordination between mind and body,using sanchin-dachi and basic hand movements. A self-training method to tighten muscles, coordinating breathing with mind control. The emphasis is on power training and perfection. It is said that it takes seven years minimum to perfect this kata.

TENSHO: turning palm and change of hands grip The Tensho represents the (ju) kata of Go-Ju Ryu. It is soft and hides the fighting spirit below the surface, whereas,the Sanchin shows outward physical power. A very defensive kata using the open hand, with circular movements, blocking,trapping and utilizing the opponent's power against him. A kata designed to take advantage of an opponent's weakness.

GEKISAI: 1 and 2, Attack and smash. Miyagi Chojun, after World War II, created this kata. In the beginning, this kata was practiced only with an open hand. This kata was designed to introduce fundamental attacks, stances, and three basic blocks, namely, jodan, chudan, and gedan.

SAIFA (MOTOMO YABURU): the final breaking point, destroy,defeat, greatly, the maximum. This kata changes from fundamental to complex techniques. A proper flow. It does not begin with defense only but starts with combination techniques. It also has reverse techniques.

SEIUCHIN: the storm within the calm, Also known as the tiger kata. Usually this kata is taught at the Ikkyu level.It is a difficult kata to master even for black belts. Until one obtains Ni-Dan, this is the main kata to practice. The shiko-dachi is emphasized, as well as hand techniques more than leg. There are 50 techniques in this kata with at least half attacking.

SANSEIRU: 36. This is the dragon kata, using very strong attacking techniques. There are 39 techniques in this kata with 36 of the techniques in attack formations with seven kicks.

SEISAN: 13. Advanced tiger techniques from Seiuchin. Although advanced from Seiuchin, it looks easier to perform. The emphasis is the open hand with 56 techniques in all, utilization of speed and a concentration on small techniques.

SEIPA (SEIPPA): 18 cupful. A dragon kata with half of the techniques of Sanseiru but an emphasis on reverse techniques and breaking.

KURURUNFA: come, stop, defeat, holding your ground and stay the waves. A number 17, this kata originated in China and was modified in Okinawa. This kata is a San-Dan kata. it utilizes takedowns, breaking the arms and throwing. Before one can be a Sensei, this kata must be mastered.

SHISOCHIN: the kata of 4 fighting monks. A number 19. Only the Go-Ju of Miyagi Chojun uses this kata. The other Naha-Te schools do not use it.

SUPAREMPEI (PEICHURIN): This kata is the most advanced kata in Naha-Te. All techniques of Naha-Te are in this kata, 108steps. This is the creation of General Yue Fei during the Tang Dynasty and both Shuri-Te and Naha-Te used this kata,However, after Miyagi Chojun returned from Shanghai, he modified this kata without taking out the essence. The modification was only in the directional movement. Therefore if one should see Peichurin performed and Suparempei performed, he would see a directional difference but not a change of postures.

The Most Important Lesson

Courtesy of Martial Virtue Magazine

Many of his classes would start with a lecture and end with a lecture as Sensei Kim's classes were always more cerebral then physical although at time they could become physically very hard on us.

But one his favorite ways to start a class especially if it was in front of a new bunch of students who had never been to his class before was his lecture on "The most important lesson you will ever learn in martial arts".

"When we start our classes" he would say "we always line up with the senior on the right and the junior on the left and when we bow our heads at the beginning of each class we are practicing three very important words to the martial artist. RESPECT, COMPASSION AND GRATITUDE this is the code upon which all martial arts are based.

When we bow our heads it should be with sincerity and not just a physical action and what we are saying with our bodies is that when we bow our heads or raise our heads or when we kneel down always the senior (sempai) goes first and then the junior (cohei) follows as this demonstrates physical acceptance of your position in the dojo of either being the senior or the junior I am showing respect for my seniors. At the exact same time I am demonstrating compassion for the juniors. I am not saying oh I am sorry for you because you're a green belt and I am a brown belt but what I am saying is I accept the responsibility of making sure you will learn the martial arts and I as your senior accept this responsibility. On the other hand when the junior bows his head and moves after the sensei he is physically saying I accept the role of cohei or junior.

The third thing that you are saying with your body when you bow is that you are grateful.

Grateful for 4 things:

1. For your parents who gave you life,

2. Your friends who you can go to when you have a problem.

3. Your country as it is your countries that make so much possible whether it be th roads or the police or the fireman who save lives every single day.

4. The fourth and the most important is your God as it is he will ultimately decide on whether your sold is saved or goes to hell.

Sensei would often then just recap. "Now remember: Respect, Compassion and Gratitude. Never forget this."

And he would then begin the class.

Q & A on Zanchin, Kata, Meditation and More

Question: What is the value of the kata?

Answer: Practising kata is enough because it teaches you to cope with fear. The most important aspect in a fight is your own apprehension - your fear. Kumite, punching and kicking exercises, and tournaments only sharpen your physical skills, they don't help you conquer your fear. Through kata you come to grips with yourself. You may be skilful, but if you are scared, all the training in the world isn't going to do you any good.

Question: Should you always imagine an opponent in front of you? If not, then when should you?

Answer: All katas start with a defensive movement. Prior to making that defensive movement, just stand still, meditate, lower your breath (bring it down to your tanden). Open your eyes and imagine your enemy. Your enemy then makes the first move (which all exists only in your mind) which suits the first movement of your kata, you then reply with the first move. He is in front of you either all the time or else other enemies are. If you don't use an imaginary opponent, you wont be able to master gathering the force in your mind.

The process goes this way: First you think about it – in the beginning it has to be intellect. You imagine an opponent attacking you. Then, after you are able to see the opponent every time, you must feel the enemy make a move in your mind before he actually does. That is how you develop the sense of anticipation. But it must not be an intellectual anticipation, rather it must be felt from the tanden (experienced there).

Everyone has been really scared a least once in their lives, so you know the first thing that happens is that your bowels, from anus up, tighten. If you get too scared, your anus muscles let loose and you will defecate in your pants. Thus the first thing that you must learn to control is your bowels (stomach region) – your tanden.

When an untrained man faces death, the first thing that happens (on the physical level) is that there is a terrific outpouring of adrenaline. Then the person will do one of two things without thinking. He will turn and run, he'll run like mad. Or he my freeze and not be able to do anything. Untrained people in a dangerous situation either run or freeze, which prevents them from doing anything else.

However a trained man, even one that had his senses knocked out (senses have to do with the intellect) (like a pro fighter in the ring, who was knocked out on his feet) will do what he was trained to do, it's deep down inside him. Through proper kata training, of ingraining fighting on your subconscious mind, you will fight without thinking, which is what you must do when you fight.

If you have never participated in a real fight before, you are going to be apprehensive. The thing that will snap you out of your apprehension is the first blow you'll receive. After you are hit, you'll be all right because you'll know it's serious. As long as you are not hit, the apprehension will stay with you, unless you are a real professional. However, with enough kata training, put in the same situation, you will react to your training.

Question: Is it necessary to know the meaning of every move in the kata you perform?

Answer: It is preferable. Some yoga teachers teach you a meaningless mantra (sound) to use in your meditation. The mantra has meaning for you in the intellectual sense. They don't go into a long philosophical discussion of it's meaning, so to you it's just mumbo jumbo. However the meaning is in the sound. By concentrating on the mantra, superfluous thoughts won't distract you so easily and with practice they can be excluded. Also, the sound sends vibrations throughout your body if you are doing it right. So the mantra has meaning in the total sense but it doesn't have it in the intellectual sense.

If you are doing a kata and visualizing an enemy, you will visualize your own type of defense. So if you don't know all the meanings of the moves in a kata, it's all right because the ancient katas were devised on magic principles. On the other hand if the kata you are doing had been made up without rhyme or reason, that's different.

Question: Can you explain Zanchin more for us?

Answer: Zanchin – it is spiritual mental alertness. If you have dealt your opponent a deadly blow, you stay alert so that his soul won't hurt you. When you kill a person, you assume that the soul will leave his body so you must be mentally aware, in order not to be harmed by him in the event that he tries to take over your body with his soul. When a person is killed, you must be sure that he won't be able to attack you spiritually.

A martial artist is a black magician or one who practices the lower arts, sometimes commits suicide against you. Supposing you have an avowed enemy who is practising black magic and has developed the ability of possession, he may seek you out in order to get into a fight with you (this happened in the old days). If you kill him and have no zanshin and just walk away, he will take over your body.

So always assume that you are facing a black magician who will try to take over your body the moment he has been killed. When you kill him, have zanshin, then your ki will keep his spirit away.

Orientals believe that if you don't kill an animal the right way, one which releases the soul immediately, the animal dies resentful, thus making the meat taste bad. In practising the kata, do zanshin, the last movement because you have killed your enemy and don't want your enemy's soul to attack you. You must be alert by breathing in and out slowly and forming a psychic wall.

Question: What can you tell us about the relationship of meditation to Satori and its practise?

Answer: If you practice meditation, because people say that through it you achieve enlightenment – satori – don't expect to see a blinding flash of light or to experience ecstasy or the heavens opening up, etc. Through meditation your body undergoes chemical changes, building up chemicals similar to LSD in molecular structure, but in a way that your body can take it (no bad trips). When you achieve satori, people will think you are still the same person, you won't notice a line of demarcation — I have come this far

- but all of a sudden you will have come to grips with yourself and will have true happiness. You may have a blinding insight – all of a sudden you may realize who you are, but the heavens won't rip apart and no lights will flash.

The basic purpose of medication is to find happiness. If you master a kata, the satisfaction of that mastery will come to you someday as you are practising by yourself. If you meditate right, the physical manifestation will be a warm feeling starting at the base of the spine and going up it to the top of your head.

The martial arts should be practised in this way:

1) Rei. (Bow to your opponent.) Philosophically you are bowing to yourself although you have an opponent in your mind and bow to him.

2) Alertness. You must be very alert all the time.

3) Sound. You have to use the kiai. Use the kiai as a weapon that pushes (put your ki into it?). The kiai is important because it will make your intellect become aware of your body. The body and mind are inseparable, there is no demarcation. There is no such thing as a mind complete or a body complete by itself. Your mind is contained in every muscle cell in your body. Memory cells do exist in your body that go back to the first of your kind.

The Japanese also solved being overcrowded. Scientists discovered through experimentation that when rats were placed in overcrowded conditions, they developed cannibalism, they were fighting for space. They also developed homosexuality and apathy. The Japanese, however, as they became more and more overcrowded formed a rigid code of etiquette – everything became codified. Every person has his place in the sun in their culture and their language developed so that they didn't hurt their fellow man.

In pre war Japan, (before W.W.II) as it became more and more crowded, the language gradually changed. As each person's space became smaller and smaller, being extremely polite was the only thing that kept people sane. Language was the control that the rats didn't have, thus they turned to cannibalism. Human beings have the ability to adjust.

This is one reason why the martial arts was developed – it held them together under pressure. The American occupation at the end of WWII changed that – they banned the martial arts (except judo which they thought was a dance) and changed the etiquette. Now the Japanese are killing each other because the English language is not designed for their condition – it is not based on courtesy.

Question: Can you tell us more about Paqua?

Answer: Pa Kua is the simplest martial art in which to fight imaginary enemies since there are no set techniques. Whenever you practice, just place yourself in the centre of the T'ai Chi circle and imagine eight enemies surrounding you. No matter how you spin, the eight are around you – one in each position. No matter what movement you make, there is no set meaning for it, just circling and although the eight are always around you, you only concentrate on one at a time.

Concentrating on, let's say your forefinger, that's just one object, so that no matter where you are at, that one object is always in the same position. The one can be any of the eight enemies, it doesn't matter which one, it depends on where you are. That is why Pa Kua is so difficult and tiring, you are always spinning in the same place. It is not as interesting as some of the advanced karate katas that feature the linear principle. But there is no difference between the linear and the circular schools in the long run - they both achieve the same thing.

Once you see the first opponent, he stays with you although he may get help from the sides or rear.

Question: Can you tell us more about formal Za Zen?

Answer: There are two types of meditation, formal (za-zen) and informal (when you eat, you eat, you do not talk or read, etc. Do everything totally). One of the best ways to meditate is za-zen, sitting in the lotus position. Doing that lowers your body temperature 3-6 degrees, slows down your metabolism (so you don't age much for the period you are meditating). It is like finding the fountain of youth. If you have high blood pressure, that's the best posture to sit in as it lowers it. It also develops your awareness of your surroundings by sound. Certain sounds may distract you and others may not.

You may use all kinds of aids to help your concentration so you won't be easily distracted, chanting, counting breaths, staring at a candle, etc. If you are distracted it is no use sitting as you won't accomplish anything. After a period of time you won't be disturbed or distracted no matter what happens around you.

Meditating on the colour spectrum is not the road to enlightenment. It's only purpose is energizing. For instance if you are sexually satiated, then meditating on the colour red/orange will cause you to recover your energy and you will be able to go again. It is energizing but it won't bring you to satori. It is more of a process of developing energy than of meditation.

All is Energy

Courtesy of Martial Virtue Magazine

If you radiate energy out, it comes back. You receive what you give. Whatever you do will come back, evil deeds will come back. It all balances out with mathematical precision.

Love is the most valuable commodity in the universe.

We are three sided:

1 Knowledge

2 Attitude (between mediocrity and greatness is only one degree) get excited and you will be alive. The quicksand of mediocrity is your lack of love, money, and joy. Joy is the first universal law of increase, it is the building block of life. You cannot feel sorry for yourself if you feel joy. Guilt and fear will melt away at joy. Tell a joke you will experience joy.

3 Truth. Your body is the truth of life. You cannot activate yourself beyond your body, your body limits life's activity.

History of the Bo

In Japan, the stick is known as the bo and in China it is known as the kon. The bo originated in China during the Ming dynasty (1368-1644) but unfortunately none of the techniques were written down.

The techniques were instead handed down from teacher to student verbally. The same is true of Okinawan bo techniques. In Japan however all the techniques of a school (or ryu) were recorded on paper scrolls and handed down to each new successor. Okinawan bo techniques are based on the Chinese styles as the idea for their bo came from there. The 12th emperor of Japan, Keiko (71-130 AD), encouraged the use of the bo. The bo originally was used exclusively by the samurai class, but later it was handed down to the farmers and taken up by them.

Japan's society was feudal in nature and comprised five main classes listed below in order of social standing:

Emperor: Royalty
Shi: samurai
No: farmer
Ko: artisan
Sho: businessman

The farmers developed their bo techniques about 800 years ago during the Gempei era. In the Tokugawa period (1603-1867) the bo techniques were handed down and became the farmer's art permanently and the nomenclature of the bo became well defined. Before this there wasn't any nomenclature. From the Gempei era until the Tokugawa period all fighting styles and techniques were put to the test in actual combat due to the almost constant warfare that existed between the various clans.

The bo is a weapon capable of standing up against the sword and being made of a readily available material, namely wood, could be used by the poorer class, the farmers, in their numerous rebellions against samurai rule and taxation. The samurai eventually became disgusted at the farmers and their bos and started killing all the bo men. The farmers were able to preserve their bo even though suppressed because every time they had a festival they performed a dance (kata) with the bo, and this dance was always handed down to somebody to carry on the tradition.

The bo developed in Aichi-ken (prefecture) into two styles: Togun-ryu and Genji-te ryu. These two styles that the farmers developed have been preserved by them until this very day.

The bo never was developed into a complete way of life until it was handed down to the farmers. Before that the samurai would study many different weapons, although mainly the sword, and didn't concentrate only on one. The first bo developed was called the kanasai-bo (it was eight feet long) and it was made famous by Shinozuka-Iga-no-kami.

He developed his techniques and fighting style while dreaming that he was being attacked by many devils from all different directions. The bo was then used later in a six foot length depending on the school.

All Muso could think about after the fight was how could he defeat Musashi and his sword. He went to the mountains and train himself for five or six years. During this time he studied the sword, considering the blade and it's length, and tried to devise a bo style that could beat it. If the bo was too long, it would enable the swordsman to get inside. On the other hand if it was too short, it wouldn't be able to face the sword. In his efforts Muso had a moment of enlightenment and devised the bo length of four feet two inches. Now called a "jo".

This was eight to ten inches longer than regular sword and, considering his style, it equalized the cutting edge of the sword. This stick could use every sword technique and more. Muso developed seventeen techniques to be used with his new bo. While still in the mountains, he reach satori and found that Mongolian white oak had the strength to break any kind of metal blade made. This is why stick fighting became such a high art in Japan but not Korea. Mongolian white oak is found only in China and Japan.

Eventually Muso and Musashi fought again. This time Muso broke the blade of Musashi's sword and won the fight. He spared Musashi's life as Musashi spared his.

The most refined bo is a canoe paddle or an oar. A four foot two inch bo is also deadly, especially Shindo-Muso ryu, which has never been beaten except by Daito-ryu. (They are the only ones who study just the stick and no other weapons.)

There are three types of techniques with the stick:

1) Tsuki - thrust;

2) Harai - block; and

3) Ochi - hit.

The techniques are done to both sides of course.

The origin of the thrust is as follows, a Daito-ryu man of the Minamoto family was fighting his cousin with a spear, then suddenly the end of his spear was cut off. This left just the stick itself. Thus the only vulnerable areas to strike were the eyes, throat and groin and these could only be struck by poking them, thus the bo thrust was born.

You can perfect the sword in three years, but a stick man, with one year's training, is your equal. The stick can beat any weapon accept a gun.

Wood, being a natural substance, (was alive), is the best material for transmitting ki. You should practice with the same stick every time and constantly handle it until you know it well. The stick then develops spiritual qualities because your ki gets into it.

Your ki, if developed, will keep your body and other physical processes young. Your heart has the capability to live two hundred years, so should you.

Communication

There are four types of communication: Verbal, Non verbal, Intra-verbal, and Extra-verbal.

Verbal: This is a simple literal translation of a word. Let us use the word yes. If a person says yes they simply mean, "Yes".

Non-Verbal: This is where you read the persons body language and again let us use the word yes. If a person nods his head up and down it simply means yes.

Intra-Verbal: In this case when a person says the word yes he kind of has to have the word pulled out of him and his answer will be, "yyyyyesssss". In this case he really means yes but with with stipulations or reservations.

Extra-Verbal: This is where he says, "YES!" This time what he really means is yes emphatically and with out a doubt. Yes, yes, yes, yes, in other words.

Another point on the non-verbal is that there is a time lag between when the mind gives an order and the body reacts. The more stubborn the person is the greater this time lag is.

Exercise

Get up and exercise, even after serous illness. Bedrest is counter-corrective and you should get out of bed and get moving as soon as virtually possible. A Germany study was done and the results were that activity increased ones ability to heal.

In John Hopkins University, a six month study showed that putting someone on a tread mill increased their healing process ten fold. Two days after a heart transplant, the Mayo clinic puts people on the treadmill. Every week of bed rest results in a two to three percent loss of muscle mass. This starts a cycle of weakness and going back to bed. Loss of muscle mass may cause you to limit your nourishment and decrease your intake of nutrients that are important to the healing process.

Exercise makes you feel better about your self and increases your life span by as much as twenty years, it is estimated.

Six rules of working out:

1. Commit your self to training.
2. Be creative in your work out.
3. Cross train.
4. Train with a friend.
5. Mix it up, change the time of day to keep your interest up.
6. Just do it and enjoy.

The Great Life Force

This is the esoteric secret of the martial arts for bringing the miracle healing of the great life force to your loved ones.

You will find the following techniques easy to follow and 100% effective in its results. Do not let the simplicity fool you. Read the technique carefully and then follow the fail-proof instructions.

1. Form in your mind a clear idea of the injury or disease you wish cured through the power of the great life force.

2. Choose a place in which you are not likely to be disturbed and lie down or sit comfortably – preferably if your head can be supported.

3. Close your eyes and take a deep breath, following the passage of that breath through your entire body and back up into your brain – with your mind's eye. Relax your stomach muscles completely. Do it three times.

4. In your mind's eye form your own motion picture of your loved one's recovery. Through the power of your mind and the miracle healing of the great life force you can actually see the healing take place and the recovery become complete.

5. Add sound to your mental motion picture. Hear your loved one – with the picture firmly in your mind – tell you, "I am glad that I am cured, I am absolutely healthy and the sickness does not bother me.'

6. Allow yourself to feel the gladness and relief that comes with this recovery.

7. DO NOT ALLOW yourself to dwell on any negative thoughts or any doubt concerning the power of the great life force to bring on this miracle.

8. Relax for a few minutes and give thanks to God in appreciation of letting the great life force work through you to cure your loved ones.

9. Give your full undivided attention to this procedure and no more than 15 minutes to any one session.

10. Open your eyes and go about your daily life.

NB. Do not let the simplicity of this technique fool you!

Tradition and Standards

Early historic tradition has it that the martial arts go back 4,000 years into Chinese history. Traditional martial arts encompass all forms of external and internal, hard and soft, weapon and weaponless systems of fighting.

Legend has it that the origins of the martial arts can be traced back to the yellow emperor, Huang Ti, who wrote his classic treatise on internal medicine, the Nei Ching.

He also developed military practices involving the use of weapons and weaponless fighting.

The spiritual path with the advent of Confucianism and Taoism, developed from a physical to a spiritual path of existence,and a philosophical code underlying the arts took form. The core from which the modern martial arts developed emerged with Dharma (Bodhidharma) when he went to China from India.

He, introduced Zen Buddhism with the philosophical principle of the "empty mind" and satori At this point, the martial arts moved into the realm of religion as only monks practiced them. The arts reached their most perfected form of expression within Buddhism. It was within Buddhist eras that the most important forms of training were either innovated or notated for posterity.

In the 16th Century A.D, Shaolin martial arts rose to prominence with Master Pai Yu-Feng, who introduced the "five fists," each associated with a different animal.

Pai called it the five essences of man, namely:

1. Dragon Fist. Emphasized the training and development of the spirit. Lightness, stillness, and change were instilled.

2. Tiger Fist. Strengthening the bones, emphasizing jumping up and down with firmness of the shoulder and waist.

3. Leopard Fist. To develop strength and application of force, jumping and fighting.

4. Snake Fist. Practice of inner breathing to become sensitive and active with a pliable body.

5. Crane Fist. To train in concentration,stability, accuracy, and determination to defeat an enemy.

The five fists emphasized breathing correctly. These five fist combined the hard and soft elements that existed in various systems of movement and became the basis of the different styles throughout China and the Orient. From this traditional background, imbedded with the teachings of Confucianism, Taoism,and Zen Buddhism, the mastery of the martial arts is not only a physical endeavor, but also a philosophical accomplishment.

The Roots of Karate

Once, when a prominent sensei was lecturing, he said, “We cannot talk about karate as a martial art without understanding the history of karate in Japan and the impact of the man known as the father of karate, Master Gichin Funakoshi.”

We can safely say that modern karate dates from 1922, the year Gichin Funakoshi first demonstrated Okinawan Tode at a physical education exhibition sponsored by the Japanese Ministry of Education. The Tode that Funakoshi demonstrated has origins that went back into Chinese history, although it developed and matured in Okinawa.

“To” means China and “de” is translated as meaning technique, therefore,Tode means, “China hand technique”. In Japanese, the “to” can also be pronounced as “kara,” as “de” can be pronounced “te”; therefore, karate. the Japanese used a different character to write “kara,” so it no longer means “China”. The modern definition means “empty,” or “nothing.” Some have been confused and defined karate as “empty hand,”or “without weapons.” In reality, the emptiness is an emptiness of self, a freedom from the psychological obstructions of fear and self consciousness which hinder the free-and-total use of physical techniques. This definition of “emptiness,” coming from Zen, is the basic philosophy of the Japanese martial arts.

Long before the arrival of Funakoshi, the martial arts of Japan were known as Budo, Budo existed as a unified philosophy: kendo, judo, kyudo, etc., are only different in the method of techniques they employ.

Gichin Funakoshi, before he was chosen to go to Japan, had become the president of the Okinawan Martial Arts Society. Before he went, he consulted the great Tode masters on Okinawa and selected from them what he considered to be the best and most representative examples of Okinawan Tode. This was in the form of16 kata; 10 of the 15 being traditional forms, the other five the pinan kata devised by Itosu Yasutsune in the period from 1905-10. The exhibition lasted only a week, but it left an impact on the martial arts world of the Japanese and thus began the emergence of an art that was to overshadow the other budo arts, especially in the Western world.

The old techniques long held so mysterious were examined thoroughly and logically in the light of modern science,and gradually grew into karate as we know it today. Today when one enters the martial arts,one strives to become a "black belt". In a legitimate school, as the training of a student progresses he will become aware of the molding of himself into a better person, that the perfection of character is the goal set by the sensei.

Traditionally this has been the goal. The black belt is an award or honor given to a student who has sacrificed years in disciplining and honing his body and mind to achieve quintessence of physical, mental, and spiritual attainment.

Originally, the ranking system was established to provide a series of levels or steps by which the student could measure his progress. The first black belt awarded is a shodan. Further progress with result in dan ranks or degrees being conferred. This ranking system, from World War II, worked very well in motivating the student, but it also has resulted in some problems.

The disparity of standards has developed a problem that can be summed upas, The higher the number of grades the lesser the truth. Also, the awarding of 10th dans given by self-created organization to the "new" masters of the martial arts has become commonplace.

A proper ranking system should remain universally constant just as a man six feet tall is always equal in height to another six feet tall, if the measurement is done by the same standard. Judo and kendo, for example, have one international standard of testing which prevails throughout the world, This is due, in part, to both of them having their origins in Japan where the value, the rules of "rank" grew with the respective art. It is also due to the Dai Nippon Bu Toku Kai which, as a section of the Ministry of Education, since 1895, established standards and awarded all ranks, up to the end of World War II when it was disbanded by the occupation forces leader General Douglas MacArthur.

In 1954,the Bu Toku Kai was reactivated under the auspices of a member of the Japanese Diet named MaChino and the legendary Ohno Kumao.

The Bu Toku Kai is a martial art, organization which traces its origin to the Emperor Kanmu, the 50th emperor of Japan, 781-806 A.D. He opened up the Imperial grounds the Bu Toku Den in March, 797 (Eriryaku Jugonen).

In Emperor Kanmu's time, or May 5the Bu Toku Den tied in with the beginning of the Heian Shrine. This was the beginning of true samurai spirit and training.

When the Dai Nippon Bu Toku Kai opened as a section of the Ministry of Education in 1895, the prime movers were Prince Fushimi and Baron Oura.

Established in conjunction with the Shrine, Emperor Kanmu was revered as a deity in the shrine. The modern Bu TokuDen was opened in Kyoto, Japan in I 1899. Only kendo and judo were practiced at first.

Therefore, both of these arts developed one international standard for ranks which prevails until today.

The kendo section was headed by Naito Takahara, a swordsman of the Hokushi Itto Ryu, and the judo section was headed by one of Kano sensei's top students of the Kodokan, Isogai Hajime.

When the Dai Nippon Bu Toku Kai was established in 1895, the Sosai, or president was a member of the royal family Komatsu-Rio-Miya, Akihito Shinno Denka- the kaichoor chairman, was Watanabe. The Governor of Kyoto ' the Fuku-Kaicho or vice chairman, was Minobu, the Bishop of the Heian Shrine and other vice-chair man, was Toriumi, the head of the Kyoto Chamber of Commerce.

The first Bu Toku Matsuri (martial art festival) was held on October 25, 1896 ina makeshift tent and temporary hall, Kata and shiai were held in kendo and judo.

A few years after the opening of the permanent Bu Toku Den, the samurai titles of Hanshi and Kyoshi were conferred. The first recipients of the title of Hanshi were given in kendo, and the titles conferred on Watanabe Noboru, Ishiyama Magoroku, Takao Tesso, Eno Kanshiro, Sakabe Daisaku, Dobashi and Murasaki. On April1 st, 1906, the title of Kyoshi was conferred. The practice is continued up to the present time. A training apprentice title Renshi was also designated later.

In 1911, the Dai Nippon Bu Toku Kai opened a martial arts specialty school,the Bujutsu Semmon Gakko. Later on, it was changed to the Budo Semmon Gakko,popularly known as the Busen. Its aim and purpose was to promote and cultivate Budo in a true samurai spirit, to produce teachers to go out and propagate the real Japanese Martial Arts. The dan system was introduced by Kano Sensei,the founder of the Kodokan, and basically involved six steps known as kyu, three white belt steps and three brown belt steps, followed by the dans or grades, of which the shodan was the first grade. This was the first black bell degree or step. There were and are until today ten steps in the black belt ranks.

Modern Rank Abuses

Karate, from 1922, when it was introduced into Japan proper, up to the end of the Pacific war followed the judo ranking system. However, after 1950, many different schools sprung up, each having its own set of standards when it came to testing and conferring of dans. The Japanese martial arts were forbidden by the occupation, with the exception of judo,which was considered a sport. The central authority of the Bu Toku Kai was gone,hence the proliferation of many schools with many "new" masters. Thus, when karate was propagated internationally, the various countries embraced each style and each set of standards. A situation arose outside of Japan in which individuals set up their own organizations and handed out black belts without standards,but only for the money they could make. The end result today is there are as many black belts as there are students, who, frankly, are a disgrace to not only themselves but to the art of karate.

Since the Western public is not well aware of the differences in ranking and the ability of a real black belt, they are the losers. They may attend classes where the lure is an easy black belt which is not only dangerous to the student, but also denigrates the art of karate.

It is for these reasons that the Bu Toku Kai issued articles of standards and in1964, for the first time in the history of Japanese karate, an organization which unified all existing styles of karate came into being under the name of the Federation of All Japan Karate-Do Organization(FAJKO). While it proceeded with the task of bringing all karate groups under one administrative structure, it also worked to resolve the following two technical problems:

1) To standardize dan and kyu ranking systems worldwide which, until then, were left up the judgment of each organization.

2) To establish standardized uniform tournament rules.

The ranking standard, as set forth by the Bu Toku Kai, FAJKO, and the AAKF, is in accord with the international standard set forth by the ITKF (International Traditional Karate Federation), and granted recognition worldwide. They are as follows:

Definition

Ranking is the evaluation of an individual's progress toward the attainment of human perfection through the practice of karate. This evaluation is not based solely upon the physical techniques of karate. It encompasses the human being's entire physical, moral, and spiritual development. Promotions in rank are awarded in proportion to an individual's degree of development toward the karate goals of perfection. The established standards of progress and criteria for advancement are explained as follows:

Types of Ranking

There are three types of ranking and they are as follows:

Regular rank: The stage of progress of the human character as reached through physical and spiritual practice of karate.

Recommended rank: The stage of progress of the human character as reached through both an individual's continued practice, as well as one's total contribution and service to the development of karate.

Honorary rank: An award of rank as a result either directly or indirectly of one's service and support of the development of karate.

Regular Ranking Standards

The ranking standard for each development level is defined as follows: (We will forego the lower levels of kyu and start from the 1st kyu which is the level just before shodan, the first black belt level.)

ICHI-KYU

(1st Kyu) At this point, the individual must be capable of executing all fundamental body movements and techniques with proper application. This includes all hand and leg techniques.

SHO-DAN

(1st Dan) This level necessitates a further maturation of abilities. All basic body movements and techniques, including hand and leg techniques, can be applied with extended force and proper application in basic combinations.

Contents of Sho-Dan examination standards: KATA – intermediate kata.

KIHON – performs single techniques and basic combinations. KUMITE – from freestyle position is able to use basic techniques for defense and attack.

NI-DAN

(2nd Dan) This state requires the personal assimilation and performance of all basic body movements and techniques to such a degree that their application is in accord with the individual's own unique body demands. Examination standard: KATA – Advanced kata. KIHON – Combination of all basic techniques. KUMITE – Free sparring or self-defence from multiple positions, with or without weapons.

SAN-DAN

(3rd Dan) At this position, the individual has acquired the understanding of the underlying principles in all basic body movements and techniques. Moreover, this understanding can be demonstrated in the application of techniques under varied circumstances and conditions.

Examination standard: KATA – Advanced kata. KUMITE OR SELF-DEFENSE – Free.

YONDAN

(4th Dan) The individual attaining this standing has exemplified knowledge of the principle body movements and techniques and their application under varied conditions to such a degree that the ability to instruct others has been gained.

Examination standard: KATA – Advanced kata. INSTRUCTION – Must provide instruction with self demonstration.

GODAN

(5th Dan) This is the level wherein research has been completed in some limited area. This research includes its application in a mariner that is both relevant and applicable to the individual's particular physique.

Examination standard: KATA – Advanced kata with all required factors combining both physical and spiritual. RESEARCH – Presentation of favorite technique along with explanations and self-demonstration.

ROKUDAN

(6th Dan) The attainment of this position necessitates the performance of karate research in an area that by its nature has a universal benefit to be derived by its application.

Examination standard. Presentation of written report of karate research.

SHICHIDAN

(7th Dan) To achieve this level, the individual must have tinder-taken advanced research through actual application and extensive testing of the general research technique

Examination standard: Presentation of written report on karate research and the application and experience of such research.

HACHIDAN

(8th Dan) At this point, research must have been completed in anew and previously unknown area. Examination standard: Presentation of written research report on a new and yet untouched area.

KYUDAN

(9th Dan) The requirements for this standard call for an uncommon dedication for an extended period of time to the areas of individual achievement,research and technique, This dedication must have culminated in karate achievement and development of the highest and most extraordinary order. Moreover, this accumulated knowledge and expertise must have been utilized in the general service of karate development.

Examination standard: Review by central ranking committee.

JYUDAN

(10th Dan) This is the stage where the individual has finally neared the highest image of karate development. This has been brought about by the continuous practice and pursuit of the truth that is to be found in

1) Basic Techniques: Includes all stances, punching, striking, blocking, and kicking; 2) Each level of ranking requires that the individual has accomplished preceding ranking requirements.

Recommended Ranking Standards

1) Has applied oneself by hard work, through continuous practice to achieve a high spiritual development. However, there is a physical limitation or handicap.

2) Has provided distinguished service through instruction and continued practice but is limited or lacking in technique for respective rank.

3) Has fulfilled necessary regular ranking requirement but through unforeseen circumstances has been unable to be evaluated under required ranking procedures.

4) Any other circumstances other than described above and has contributed to the advancement of karate, such as research, development, etc.

Honorary Ranking Standards

In general must have the respect of the community by virtue of one's good character. The following is a detailed order of such ranking conditions:

1st Dan - Has provided indirect support of karate at the local community level within a country or territory.

2nd Dan - Has provided direct support of karate at the local community level within a country or territory

3rd Dan - Has provided indirect support of karate at the national level,

4th Dan - Has provided direct support of karate at a national level or may be a local dignitary or leader who has provided indirect support..

5th Dan - Has provided indirect support of karate as a national dignitary or leader in such areas as social, educational and financial, or may be a local dignitary or leader who has provided direct support.

6th Dan - Direct support of karate by a national leader.

7th Dan - Indirect support of karate by a national sovereign or top leader or highest official.

8th Dan - Direct support of karate by a national sovereign, top leader or highest official.

9th Dan - Indirect support of karate by an international leader or internationally-respected figure.

10th Dan - Direct support of karate by an international leader or internationally-respected figure.

Karate Ni Sente Nashi

Karate Ni Sente nashi literally means: "in karate one does not make the first move." It is a precept not much understood by karate ka the world over, Americans in particular.

Fortunately for karate today, Gichin Funakoshi was selected by the Okinawa pre-fectual government to demonstrate the art of karate in Japan and the impact that he made on the martial arts community in Japan was earth shaking because not only was he an expert's expert, he was also a philosopher. The greatness of Funakoshi can be attested to the fact that he created the philosophical concept of "karate ni sente nashi" to a level not thought of during his time.

The moral precepts of karate were slowly giving way to a pedantic attention to technical detail and the art of karate was in danger of going the way of jujitsu into eclipse.

Funakoshi knew from experience that civilization was a thin veneer and the whole fabric of karate without the warp and woof of moral philosophy could degenerate into mere street fighting and hippodrome. He was fully aware of the violence in man's nature therefore he emphasized and wove back into the fabric of karate the concept of " karate ni sente nashi" which was neglected because of emotional rigidity by some of his contemporaries.

Funakoshi taught not only the how of karate but also the way. The following story exemplifies one of the fundamental tenets of the martial arts. The sword of the true samurai is drawn under one condition – absolute necessity and dire peril. By the same token, the hands and feet of a karate ka are never used. The true karate ka never strikes first and never strikes in anger. You will notice that all katas, whether weapon or otherwise, start and end with a defensive movement.

The saying among karate men is: *"If your hand goes forth, hold back your anger, if your anger goes forth, hold back your hand."*

During the Satsuma Clan occupation of Okinawa, a Japanese samurai, who supplemented his income as an administrator by lending money, made a trip to Itoman Province where a certain fisherman to whom he had lent money lived. He had to travel a long way.

Unfortunately the fisherman had a bad year so in desperation he turned to flight and tried to hide from the samurai who had a reputation for a short temper. The samurai went to the fisherman's home and not locating him there, he made a round of the town looking for him. As the passage of time grew and the search proved of no avail, the samurai became furious. It was obvious that the fisherman was hiding from him so the samurai really searched hard.

Finally at twilight, as he was searching below what the Okinawans call the silver rocks cliffs – Shirogon – the samurai found the fisherman hiding in a crevice between two big rocks. He dragged him out into the open shouting: "You're avoiding me, you were hiding! What have you to say?"

"Well, said the fisherman who started to explain, but he was cut off by the samurai, "Don't talk. I know you haven't got the money to pay me. You're an ingrate. Do you realize how you came to borrow money from me? I'm not a cold-blooded money-lender trying to suck out your life's blood. You came to me to borrow money saying that your wife, children and everybody else in your family were in dire straits because of your poor catch that last year. You said that you needed money to tide yourself over and repair your nets but that it would take a long time to pay me back. It was you, not me, who said that it would take a year but you guaranteed to pay at the end of it. Now I'm here, at your word, after a year and you can't pay me?"

The fisherman replied, "No I can't".

The samurai drew his sword in anger and was going to drive it through the fisherman when the fisherman shouted out, "Wait. You have every reason to be angry but before you kill me, let me make a statement. I've studied a little martial arts and there is something that I have learned. Can you grant me this humble request?"

The samurai said, "You ingrate. I lent you money when you needed it and also gave you a year to pay, and now you give me this run around. Out with it before I change my mind. What martial art have you learned?"

In his mind the samurai was thinking, 'The hell with this guy! If he's been studying a martial art, I'll let him pick a weapon, then I won't be killing a helpless individual. In that way he could maintain his morality.'

"I'm not a samurai like you," stated the fisherman, "but I've started in the martial arts, although not with a sword, but in Okinawa karate. I have learned the meaning of the katas to philosophy that it entails. I questioned the reason for katas to start and end with a defensive movement. Now I know it's because of this Karate ni sente nashi. 'If your hand goes forth, withhold your temper; if your temper goes forth, withhold your hand.'"

The samurai was astounded to hear this from the lips of a simple fisherman and the effects of the words restained him. He put back his sword and told him, "Well, your teacher taught you right. After all, all samurai should know that it's a bushi saying. Thank your teacher for your life. Next year, one week from today, I'll be back. This time you must pay."

The fisherman agreed.

The samurai left for home. He had been gone for a week and it was very late at night when he arrived. As was the custom among Japanese, he shouted out, "Tadiima!" (I'm home), but there was no response. He went into the kitchen but the maid wasn't around. Being of violent temper, anxiety arose in him and he got mad, he reverted back to his normal self. Going around to his bedroom, he noticed a shaft of light streaming from his bedroom, as the door was slightly ajar. He peered intently from where he was standing and could see the faint outline of someone sleeping next to his wife. On the floor were his wife's clothes and those he recognized as belonging to a samurai.

He was startled and exploded in anger at the thought of his wife sleeping with another man. Although he couldn't see the man's face, there was no doubt about it for he could see a man's clothes. He drew his sword and stealthily crept towards the room. He lifted his sword and was just about to bust down the door and charge into the room when he saw the fisherman's face in front of him and heard the words, 'If your anger goes forth, hold back your hand; if your hand goes forth, hold back your anger."

At this the samurai thought to himself, 'if a simple fisherman like that can control himself, I, as a samurai, must also be able to control myself.'

He put his sword back and went around to the front of his house and shouted as loud as he could, "Tadiima!"

This time his wife heard him and got up and opened the door to greet him. She followed shortly by the samurai's mother. It seems that his mother, realizing that he would be gone a long time, had the idea of sleeping with his wife and leaving out his clothes to discourage any passing bandits who might look in. No one wanted to attack a samurai, especially in Okinawa where they were consider very formable opponents.

The year passed quickly and the samurai made the long trip again, come collection day. The fisherman was waiting for him. As the samurai approached his house, he ran out and said: "I had a good year. I've had nothing but good luck since you spared me. Here is your money, double as interest."

But the samurai refused it. He put his hand on the fisherman's shoulder and said, "Keep the money. You don't owe me anything. I do owe you. You taught me a lesson that I should have remembered from the days when I was learning to be a samurai."

He told him what had happened.

When the story spread, everyone got together and pooled their surplus money, the villagers and fishermen. With it they built what is known today as the white gold temple (Shirogon) in Itoman, Okinawa.

The Unlimited Universe and More

The universe has unlimited supply of all things – only in your mind do you create poverty. Somehow, this all ties into tithing 10%. It is more blessed to give then receive.

A poor man took care of pigs, and he was going to the library studying about how to become rich. He met a rich man and he asked him how he became rich. The rich man said how much do you make, about 100 dollars a month and he spent all his 100 dollars on rent and other goods. The rich man told him to take 10% and save it to invest. The philosophy is this the poor man always thinks he does not have enough. He is not kind to himself.

The strongest energy is 10 cycles per minute and this is the cycle one should tune into in order to charge the battery. Just before you get up in the morning is a good time to charge the battery. Start by rubbing your stomach in circles thirty six and twenty four times for women.

When you calm someone else this makes the wheel spin evenly. When you are upset the cycles are over 13 and the wheel wobbles, calming the person down centers the wheel.

Innocence by reason of insanity. Normal people are operating with an balanced wheel, insane people operate with a wobbly wheel. This is due to operating with different vibrations or cycles of brain activity.

The prisons in China were so bad that a year sentence was like a death penalty. No one lasted over a year.

O'sensei was describing Chinese prisons and jails during the late 1930s until the Japanese changed the system by taking the system over. O'sensei investigated the jail in Shanghai by staying in one over the weekend. He said it was so bad that he could only take it for one weekend.

Gay argument: if we allow women in the army then the idea of homosexuals in army should be able to be accommodated.

Faith is the evidence of things to come and not seen.

According to O'Sensei, only every second is reality, you can never say that this is it, because time is lineal and the universe is circular.

 God makes mistakes – he created the devil – so don't feel bad if you make a mistake.

Don't worry about life span, think about health span,and the secret to health is flexibility. ROM - range of motion.

When you see with the spiritual eye you see three hundred sixty degrees. With the physical eye you are limited to a narrow vision, in front of you and only peripheral vision. The way to develop the spiritual eye would be to do the katas in the dark. You develop the spiritual eye by seeing with your body, you see but you do not see, you hear but you do not hear.

We operate through three filters: 1) Language, 2) The society you live in, and 3) Personal experiences.

It is hard not to get angry when one is insulted; it's hard to not to look down on a beginner; and it's hard to keep oneself humble at all times. It's hard to find good friends; it's hard to endure the hardships of martial arts training, it's hard to endure the pain of regret and the pain of discipline, it's hard for a poor man to be generous, it's hard to teach others by knowing their abilities, it's hard not to argue about right and wrong, it's hard to find and learn a good method. When you think negative a gap opens and something jumps in that gap, and goes down into the subconscience mind and bubbles up the negativity so that it effects your behavior. Satan is the deity that does this. Because Satan will agree with you, this is why it is hard to be a Saint.

You have an unlimited source of energy in your body, the subconscious mind. This mind never rests or sleeps, it is inexhaustible, and controls your entire life. The left part of your brain needs rest, but not the right side... that controls the subconscious mind; the left side is the intellectual part. But the right side deals with orders, you must order it and give it goals, and this can only happen in the alphastate. The subconscious's mind has no morality. Morality is the property of the left mind.

When you hit the alpha level you have total retrieval of all information you have stored. This occurs at the state of 7 cycles. A hypnotist could also put you in this state and you must trust this person because the hypnotist can make one do what ever he wants because the sub-conscience mind has no morality. This is not by will power, this is only functional when one tunes in with the proper cycle. You can make anyone do anything.

The greatest thing that karate has is the kata, because of the use of imagination. The realm of the right brain, the subconscious mind can not tell what is real and what is imaginary, you can become the best in the world by training with the imagination. Seek and you shall find, ask and it shall be given. This is the whole secret of life. Mirror imaging – use the mirror to reinforce the subconscious mind.

Kogi Arioshi is the one person who beat Sensei Kim seven times. Until he was seven years old and Arikaki Sensei told him about strategy. Find out when Kogi Arioshi eats, wait until Kogi eats his biggest meal and attack him in the house.

Taking away guilt and fear, overcomes the fear of death. Do not be afraid of the man who kills your body, fear the man who can steal your soul. If you are not afraid to die, then you are free. Because all things will fall into place.

 Anything that is unpleasant develops energy, example kata.

Short Stories Teaching Philosophy and Psychology

In virtually every single class I ever attended with Sensei Kim, he would end it with a short story, usually teaching a principle of the samurai way of life or their philosophy.

He would, at the drop of a hat, go into a story with all the hand mannerisms for cutting with a sword or walking down the row of students as Musashi would have done. You would think you were right there when the story was actually happening, he was so convincing. He was a master storyteller and his facial and hand gestures were all a part of the finale of each and every class.

Five Causes of Poverty

At a seminar held in August 1986 in Vancouver, one of Sensei Kim's lectures involved poverty and its five causes.

1. Having the wrong friends. If you hang around people who are not interested in gaining wealth, you more then likely will not be as well, as all their conversation will be about non-wealth building ideas.

2. Having the wrong job. If you have a dead end job that pays you minimum wage and there is no opportunity for either learning or advancement, you will always be poor, as we always spend more then we make.

3. Having the wrong spouse. If your spouse is not interested in personal gain, then you will also not likely be interested in personal gain. You will

more then likely will be interested in what they are, whether it be being out doors or watching TV or whatever.

4. Having the wrong behavior or attitude. If your behavior is wrong and your attitude is wrong there is no way to the top. If you are a negative thinker and if you're a pessimist then there is only one way, and that way is not up.

5. Living in the wrong place. If you want to be financially successful and want to make it in the movie business, then you need to live where movies are made as this is where the opportunities are. They are not in some little urban community in the sticks somewhere.

We should also always remember that man has three constant urges that will never go away: 1. Sexual desire, 2. Self preservation, and 3. Pursuit of wealth.

The main difference between the rich and the poor is the difference in the attitude of the mind. The rich also realize that money cannot solve problems but it sure can calm the nerves.

Sensei talked at length about a person named Kenji Doihara, and that he had several ideas on wealth, as well. Doihara believed that men who surround themselves with beautiful women have a much better chance of making it then those who don't. He also believed that if you want to ever exploit a man look for his weaknesses in food, women and or money.

(Kenji Doihara was the one who approved the attack on Pearl Harbor and was hung for his war crimes in 1948 in Tokyo, Japan.)

Finally, Sensei Kim said that the proof about attaining money is that you must first give to get. It is that way in nature as it shows all the time. Before a plant or tree can have beautiful fruit it must first have beautiful flowers and before the beautiful flowers come beautiful leaves.

What is a Taker?

Some people can only take energy and not give it. They can't contain the energy you give and they overflow and the energy goes through them

 Types of ignorance: don't tell me; double ignorance over and over; refusing to learn.

like a sieve. Only if they can contain it will they give some back. These people (who can't give) are takers, these are the one's who that will kill you.

Jump

When Sensei was very young, he got into a fight at school and was beaten up by the school yard bully.

When he came home his mother said, "Go see your uncle, he will help you."

His uncle said, "Go see Jump... he will teach you to fight. He lives down this road and turn right, his house is the red one.

So off Sensei went looking for Jump. He finally got to the red house where Jump was supposed to live and there was a man with a big beer gut sitting on the porch. Sensei asked if Jump was home. The man asked who wanted to see him and Sensei said, "I would like to talk to him. My uncle said to come and see him as he would teach me how to fight because I was beaten up today at school.

The beer guzzling man jumped up and said, "I'm Jump and just get in there kid and kill him. Kid, kill him and don't stop. That is how you fight and win. Just get in there and give it to him and don't stop."

Never Mention Death to the Emperor of Japan

A long time ago in feudal Japan, the shogun and the Emperor were going to have a meeting and as was the norm in those days the person visiting would be given a gift upon his arrival.

In this case the Emperor was visiting the shogun. The shogun had a terrific idea a couple of days before the emperor arrived as to what he would give the emperor as a gift. His son had been studying with the best calligraphers in Japan and he would have his son create a calligraphy for the Emperor with a thoughtful and yet profound message.

So the morning arrived when the Emperor was to arrive and the son had locked himself in a room so that he could come up with the exact right calligraphy. Two hours before he arrived he was still locked in his room and no calligraphy. Finally the shogun saw the Emperor coming up the roadway with his retainers and entourage.

The shogun finally went to the room where his son had locked himself in and the father said, "Son, the emperor is coming up the roadway."

"I am almost finished," the son said from inside the locked room. "I will have it in a few seconds."

Finally, the son emerged from the room with the calligraphy. The father took one look at it and nearly fainted. "Son I can not give this to the Emperor of Japan – he will have my head!"

"But why father?" asked the son. "Why?

"The one thing you never mention to the Emperor is the word 'death'. This is the biggest insult you can give him."

"But father please read it again it is not insulting it is perfect."

He read it again:

Grandfather dies,
Father dies,
Son dies,
Grandson dies.

"This is the natural order, father. It is when this gets out of whack that life is not fair."

The father thought for a second, and thought, 'It is true. If my grandfather died I would be upset, but no where near as upset as if my son died."

He bowed and said, "You are right my son. Thank you. It is perfect."

Five Levels of Fighting

In the world of fighting, there are five levels of fighting that we must go through according to Sensei Kim.

 Law of dominant effect is when strong emotion takes over and the greatest emotion is fear.

The first level is the most basic, that every one can do. It is, simply, when someone attacks, you block and run away from the person.

The second level takes training and depending on the person this can come in a short or long time. It is when a person attacks, you block and counter the person.

The next level takes a great deal of training and many who study the martial arts experience this occasionally. It is when an opponent attacks, you block and counter the attack simultaneously.

The next step is one of the highest levels of fighting and rarely is it learned. It is when you attack the person the moment he is thinking about attacking you. You pick this up from your opponent because of the keen development of your senses and learning to perceive those things which can not be seen.

But there is one level even higher when it comes to martial arts and this is the level that only a true master reaches and that is when an attack comes you are just not be there at all. In other words, you have perceived the attack before it was even conceived and are just not there at all.

As an example of this, if you know that one particular bar is a rough bar, well, you just don't go to this place. The chances of a fight breaking out are much greater then if you go to a bar that that is known for its peaceful atmosphere.

Controlling Your Emotions

Somebody asked Chuang Tzu the question about controlling your emotions when giving vent to your anger. This person only wished another dead – if he had actually done it, he would have been beheaded. (Is it worthwhile to pay the price?)

Chuang Tzu said that it's simple and he gave a seemingly simple story that really wasn't:

A man was afraid of his shadow and he was afraid of it every day and since he wanted to get away from it, this particular day he ran as fast as he could. The shadow kept up with him. He went faster but the more he increased his speed, the faster the shadow went, keeping up with him. When he stopped, the shadow was there. It stayed right by his side. Finally, he came to the conclusion that he hadn't been running fast enough so he went all out this time but, unfortunately for him, it was too much for his body and he dropped dead of a heart attack.

He did not realize that if he had stood in one spot long enough, the shadow would have disappeared because of the sun – it would be underneath him when the sun was directly overhead.

In other words if you meet an emotion that seems to get away from you – that you cannot control – if you "sit" long enough, that emotion will disappear by itself because of your position (the pyramid position of the lotus posture). That's where meditation comes in; that's the reason that it's so important.

The lotus posture makes your body similar to that of a pyramid so that the vibrations come down in a certain way, from all over. If you concentrate below the belly button (the tanden), all the energy converges at that one spot, when you get the tanden in harmony. It brings a delightful feeling – a fantastic feeling of energy. When you send it back out, you harmonize with the universe and you can aid and abet, controlling this energy by a function that you have sounded. That's the reason why doing a mantra or sutra is effective. If you hit the right sound and get that vibration, you're in tune with the universe and you charge up your energy levels.

Bokuden and the Horse

Bokuden's students planted a horse on the path that Bokuden took for his daily walk. The horse was a notorious kicker, but Bokuden saw the horse and he simply walked around it.

That evening, his students were eating with Bokuden and one of them was not eating. Bokuden asked what was wrong. The student told Bokuden that he had put the horse on the path to see how he would defend against the horse.

Bokuden asked his students if they thought him to be a coward because he didn't fight the horse. They did not know what to say.

Bokuden simply said, "Only a fool would walk into a horse that kicks."

That day, he taught his students the art of fighting without fighting.

Behavior vs. Attitude

Which is most important, your behavior or your attitude?

According to Sensei Kim, your behavior is a result of your attitude and therefore it is your behavior that is most important.

A person's behavior is the answer to his success. A person can fake his attitude but he can not fake his behavior. A person can act as if they are a nice guy but eventually his true colors will come through when his behavior is shown.

You should also note that you are the last one to see your own behavior.

Samurai Ways

There were seven principles of the Samurai:

Gi – means making the right decision. If you must die, you must die. You must accept this fact emotionally.

Yu – means Bravery

Gin – means Universal Love

Rei – means Right Action

Makoto – means Sincerity

Meiyo – means Honor

Chugi – means Loyalty

There were four principles of the Samurai, which were absolute:

1. Pacification of the emotions.

2. Self control in the face of any event, composure.

3. They studied the phenomenon of death more than that of life. Otherwise, they would never get rid of fear.

4. They understood worldly desire for what it is.

The Samurai's seven principles of self healing:

1. Health is inner peace. Peace of mind should be good – guilt and fear must be let go of.

2. Quintessence of our existence is love. Therefore, our mind has no limits, for love has no limits. Do not fear death.

3. Giving is receiving. When your attention is on giving you have no fear.

4. All minds are joined, we are all part of the same energy.

5. All healing is self healing, science can help.

6. Learn to listen to nature. It has all the answers.

7. Forgiveness. Every time you meet someone, you must look at the meeting as an opportunity for growth.

Samurai Philosophy:

If someone pokes you with a needle, you poke him with a spike. If he pokes you with a spike, you poke him with a sword. If he pokes you with a sword, you poke him with a spear, and so on.

Zen Master on Choosing The Right City to Live

A Zen master was sitting at the top of a hill between two cities and was meditating on top of a rock when a samurai came walking by.

"Master," he said I am coming from that city as he pointed to the direction in which he had just come from and said, "I am going to that city." He pointed to as the direction in which he was traveling to. "I am wondering what the new city is like. Can you help me?"

The Zen Master said, "Yes, of course, but first I must know what was the city like that you just came from?"

"Well," said the samurai, "it was a terrible city as it was filled with liars cheats and thieves."

Pondering for a moment the Zen Master said, "I am very sorry to tell you but the city ahead is exactly the same."

The samurai said he would try any way and continued on his way.

A few minutes later another samurai came walking by and asked the exact same question as he had come from the exact same city and was going to the exact same city as the first samurai.

The zen master said "Yes, but first I must know what the city was like that you are coming from."

"Well," said the second samurai, "It was wonderful – the people were kind, loving and caring."

"Funny thing," said the zen master, "the city you are going to is exactly the same, the people are loving, kind and caring."

The second samurai said thank you and was on his way.

Yang and the Peking Duck

Yang Mu Ti was a martial artist so skilled that he never lost a battle. His reputation spread far and wide, but he never lost his humility.

One day, a rich man invited him to dinner because he was curious about this fearsome warrior who had never been defeated. Now Yang was a small man, only five-feet seven-inches, weighing about 140 pounds. It was the custom in China to put on a big fancy spread when you invited a guest to dinner. The highest honor the host could pay was to serve Peking duck.

The rich man had such a feast all prepared and ready, but when he saw the unpretentious Yang, he thought, 'This fellow doesn't look like much to me,' and ordered a very simple meal served instead.

Yang knew exactly what was in the man's head, but he said nothing. He ate the plain food, and drank the beer – why not?

After dinner, the rich man said to him, "Is there anyone you cannot beat?"

Yang replied with a smile, "There are only three kinds of people I cannot beat: a man made of wood, a man made of iron, and a man made of bronze."

"Well, I think my chief bodyguard is also one you cannot beat," said the rich man. "When he walks, the wind rustles, the leaves jump, and the tiger roars."

"Bring him on," replied Yang.

A big, fierce-looking man came into the room. He towered over the imperturbable Yang, but before he could make his move, Yang struck. Faster than the eye could see, he delivered a blow so powerful that the bodyguard went flying across the room. Instantly, the rich man leaped to his feet and shouted "Bring on the Peking duck!"

Who Is My Best Student?

Miyamoto Musashi was the most famous of all the samurai and one of the unique things about him was that he became famous in his own time.

Musashi was wandering through Japan and as was the custom of those days he would visit various sword schools and ask for food.

So one day he visited one of the schools and they recognized that it was Musashi and instantly invited him in to watch their sword class.

The Sensei said to Musashi, "Of all my students here, which one is my best student?"

Musashi, being polite, said, "It is obvious that you have many very talented people and it would be near impossible to pick just one."

The sensei said, "Musashi if you would like dinner I ask you most respectfully once again to tell me which one is the best."

Musashi was starving and yet he did not want to offend anyone so he said, "Well, there are so many high ranking students, they all look very good."

The sensei said, "Musashi, until you tell me who is the best I cannot feed you."

By now Musashi was smelling the food and his stomach growling, he was so hungry. He went to the lowest and newest white belt and looked deep inside their eyes and progressed up through the kyu belts and then the 1st dans and all the way up to the senior most student. He looked at the Sensei and said, “There is only one who is your best and it is the white belt beginner the one who just started.”

The Sensei was surprised and said, “Come on, don’t fool with me. Look at these 4th and 5th dans.”

“Yes,” said Musashi. “They are fine but you asked me and I told you who was your best.”

The sensei just could not understand so Musashi said, “I will prove it.” He said to the white belt, “Come over here.” He dismissed everyone else.

He asked the student and the Sensei to follow him into another small room. He then asked the student to kneel down on the floor in front of him and his teacher and as he handed him his tanto (short sword). He demanded the student to commit hara kiri in front of them.

The student looked at them in disbelief but then thought about it.

‘Here I am in front of the greatest swordsman in the world and my teacher. There is no way out.’

Musashi just stood there looking and finally the student decided that he may as well die with honor so he ripped open his gi top and grabbed the knife and raised it in the correct manner as to plunge it deep in his stomach and just before he started down with the knife Musashi yelled, “STOP.”

The student stopped and the teacher looked at Musashi with amazement and Musashi just looked at the teacher and asked “Which one of your senior students would have done that? This is why he is your best student – he will do exactly what you tell him and without question.”

The sensei understood. He, like many other senseis, have experienced the students who think they know more then their teachers.

Then they had the greatest meal Musashi had had in a long time.

Becoming a Buddha

Zazen (seated meditation) is necessary for spiritual awareness (satori).

A monk was seen by his master to be sitting down and meditating all day. He went up and asked him what he was doing. The monk replied that he wanted to become a Buddha. At this the master picked up a rock and began polishing it. The monk's curiosity got the better of him and he asked his master what he was doing. When his master told him that he was trying to make a mirror, the monk told him that no amount of polishing could turn a rock into a mirror. His master replied that no amount of sitting could make him a Buddha.

(Moral: If you seek Buddha-hood by thus sitting cross legged. You must free yourself from sitting or you will never come to the truth.)

We See Through Our Senses

We see the world through senses: sight, sound, smell, taste, touch, and intellect. The following story shows how your intellect is your enemy and holds you back.

A rich man who had three sons was dying so he called his sons together and told them that whoever passed the test specified in his will would inherit his estate.

The test involved picking up a vase filled to the brim with tea and carrying it over to another table without spilling a drop. Several days later the man died and the sons were notified that the test would be the next day. The first son was scared that his other brothers would have him assassinated and so he stayed up all night and had his room surrounded with guards. The following morning he instructed his guards to be especially on the alert for any strangers they met the way to the father's house.

This son expected an ambush around every turn and at every pass. When one didn't come and they were quite near their destination with only a small forest to pass through, the son ordered his guards to search behind every tree before he would cross. His fear was mounting with each step closer the house. Finally as he mounted the steps to his father's house, he couldn't take the suspense any longer and fainted, and couldn't take the test at the appointed time.

The second son was no coward but just to be on the safe side, he decided not to engaged in sex that night to be as sharp as possible on the morrow. Also he didn't eat that night. He went to bed early after thinking about how he would perform the test. The next day as he picked up the vase, he was trembling and dropped it, spilling all the water.

The third son did nothing unusual and nothing disturbed him. He ate a big dinner, had sex with his wife (who nagged him to take care of himself and get a good night's sleep), and returned home late after drinking with his friends. The day of the test he went right up, picked up the vase, and carried it over to the other table easily all without spilling a drop of tea. The other brothers suffered because their intellect made them worry.

(Moral: Do nothing and do!)

Two Monks and a Student

Two students who were friends were studying at a monastery to become monks and reach enlightenment. The abbot felt that one of them had reached the point at which he would benefit from studying with another master and so he told him to take a trip.

As he was packing, his friend asked if he could go along with him and when he asked why, his friend said so that he could learn from him. So he told his friend, "When I piss, it won't relieve you; when I eat, it won't satisfy you; and when I sleep, it won't do you any good."

His friend got the point.

(Moral: A teacher can show you the way but he can neither give it to you or do it for you.)

Tsukaru Bokuden

One of the greatest samurais of all times was Tsukaru Bokuden, along with Miyamoto Musashi. Sensei Kim loved to recount stories of these two legends.

One story of Bokuden goes like this:

Bokuden had three adopted sons and he was trying to decide which one he would have as his inheritor so he rigged up a wooden pillow above the door so that as soon as it was opened it would fall on each of the three sons. He would then be able to judge who should be the inheritor to his art.

Once it was rigged Bokuden called his youngest son in first. As he came through the door, he pulled his sword and cut the wooden pillow in half in mid air. The father complimented him on his speed.

The second son was then called in and, as the pillow fell on him, he side stepped it and cut it in half.

Finally, the eldest son came in the room and as the pillow fell he caught the pillow in mid air and asked his father where he should put it.

Bokuden then decided that his eldest son would be the inheritor as he resolved the problem with out drawing his sword.

True Dan Ranks

In today's day and age, dan ranks have come full circle and nowadays they mean very little, but the attitude is still there of those receiving their ranks.

Sensei told this story to his group years ago at a breakfast in Paris, France. The only thing that differs now is that you can probably differentiate this by saying the traditional martial artist and the non-traditional. Here we are talking about the traditional martial artist:

When someone receives a shodan, the common attitude is that the person who receives it can't wait to get home so he can show it off. He comes to class now more then ever so he can show everyone he is now a shodan.

The nidan is the person who drives home fast, honking his horn and showing all his friends his new ranking with stripes on his belt and can not wait to show off his old belt with the two stripes of white tape on them.

The person who gets to third dan is the one that climbs to the tallest mountain around and yells and shows off that he is now a third dan and a force to be reckoned with. He is the most egotistical of the bunch.

But when someone is given a fourth dan in a good traditional dojo he realizes that he really isn't that good and that he is actually humbled and a little embarrassed by the rank. He walks home with his belt hidden inside his gym bag and walks up against the walls so that he is inconspicuous as possible. He wants no one to see him nor does he want to be recognized for his new rank. This is when he is considered a real martial artist by his teachers and he is then in a traditional dojo allowed to teach the art.

When he enters the dojo everyone will notice him, even if he does not want to be noticed, as his charisma or his ki will be obvious to all in attendance.

Trees

Many people do not realize the power of the trees. They are extremely powerful as without them we would all die. It is the tree that gives off the oxygen that we breath.

One of the ways of harvesting the tree is to learn to embrace the trees for power.

You do this by lightly touching the tree and in your mind talking to it kindly like saying things like, "You are such a beautiful tree", "so strong and big and powerful", etc. The tree will turn the energy back to you.

The Jews have known this for years, as they plant trees all the time in Israel. They believe in the power of the tree, as well.

Learn to harvest the power from the tree and turn it inwards so you can use this energy for yourself.

The Zen Priest and the Baby

There was a knock at the door of the Zen priest. It was a woman crying and yelling at him hysterically.

"You evil man, you are simply evil. You took my daughter out and got her pregnant and now she or I will have to raise the child."

The Zen priest just looked at her and said "is that so." He said nothing else.

A few months went by and the mother came back, but this time yelling even more and she had with her the baby from her daughter. "This is all your fault. You take the child and you raise the child. It will ruin your life since it is your fault."

Again the Zen Priest just said, "Is that so."

Then about 2 years went by and the Zen priest had raised the child with all the nurturing needed to raise a perfectly healthy child. Then one day the mother came by and knocked quietly on the door and when the priest answered the door she fell on her knees begging his forgiveness.

"Master please forgive me. My daughter has just told us that it was not you that got her pregnant... it was the boy next door. I am so sorry. We would like to have the baby back now and raise him like our son and grandson. Is this possible?"

The master just looked at her and as he handed the baby over to her, said, "Is that so, is that so."

She never thought to consider all the problems her accusations had caused him and neither did he.

The Ultimate Decision

We are often faced with the question, should I do something or not?

I once asked Sensei Kim how does one know if you should do something or not? For example, is it right to make money in the martial arts as a teacher or is it wrong?

He answered two ways.

The way you will know the answer to this question is quite simple. If your service is small your payments should be small if your service is big then your payment should be big.

He went on to say that the samurai used another method to decide the answer to any question. They would ask themselves three questions. If the answer to any of them was no, they would not do it.

The three questions were:
Is it ethical?
Is it fair?
Can you look yourself in the mirror if you do it?

The Secret of the Zen Monks

Everything starts with thought. Lets say that you are angry with someone you must think of something funny and the anger goes away.

What is the seven minute mediation? The first three minutes you breathe in and out. The last three or four minutes you pray. It will calm you down. This is the secret of the Zen monks.

The mind has a terrific ability to heal and the Mozart effect. The sound is an important eliminate – light and sounds are very positive but the mind has to activate it first. The mind's ability to heal is not a psychic event. It is a physical phenomenon.

In America, scientists are reaching an understanding of the power of prayer. Faith and imagination are the pillars to successful communication and prayer.

Faith belongs to the sub-conscious. When you give an order to the sub-conscious it will follow it blindly and it will follow the order until it is completed. If you change the order, you must make the command in the same way that you gave it in the first place.

The Scorpion and the Turtle

One of Sensei's favorite stories was of the "Scorpion and the Turtle".

Apparently, one day a turtle was sitting at the edge of the pond and he saw a scorpion approaching him. He started to move fast to the pond but the scorpion said, ""Mr. Turtle, please wait – don't worry, I promise you I won't sting you.

The turtle hesitatingly stopped but stayed far enough away to see what the scorpion would say.

"Mr. Turtle, I need a small favor. I am going to the other side of the pond and I was wondering if you would give me a ride on the back of your shell?"

Mr. Turtle said, "Why would I do that? You are a scorpion and you will sting me."

"Mr. Turtle, I can't swim and if I sting you when we are crossing the pond we will both go under."

Mr. Turtle thought about it a second and said, "OK, you're right. Hop on and I will give you a ride."

Half way out, the scorpion says, "See Mr. Turtle? You have nothing to worry about."

"Well I guess you are right Mr. Scorpion. I apologize."

But, as they reached the other side and just before the scorpion jumped off the back of the turtle, he stung the turtle.

Mr. Turtle, in his dying breath, said, "Why did you do that? I was kind and nice to you?"

Mr. Scorpion said, "What did you expect? I am a scorpion and that is what I do. I sting."

 Body language: If you touch your nose you are usually lying.

The Rabbit and the Frogs

The rabbits called a meeting and they all went together to discuss what to do about their problems. They had many. Hunters were shooting them and predators were killing them. Farmers were poisoning them and they starved in the winter. They felt their problems were unsolvable so they took a vote on what to do and all agreed on suicide.

They marched down towards the river to drown themselves when they were spotted by the frogs. The frogs got scared at seeing all the rabbits marching towards them and jumped in the river. The rabbits were shocked by the actions of the frogs, and thinking that there was someone worse off than them, they didn't commit suicide after all.

(Moral: There is always someone worst off then you.)

Ai Uchi

In the Bu Toku Kai school of fighting strategy, we start with Ai Uchi or mutual death, but in most schools of fighting the basic philosophy is to win. Then, when winning is impossible, they go to Ai Uchi. This principal was discovered by Harigaya Sekiun, a samurai of exceptional ability.

The Ai Uchi is superior because when you go in, you will go in with all your heart and soul – nothing is held back. Then, you are prepared to die at all costs and if you win and are still alive this is a bonus.

He also talked about the fact that there are always three types of opponents we may face. The first is one who, no matter what, is inferior to us; the second is the one who is equal to us; and the third is the one who is superior to us.

When we fight we must always assume that the person we are fighting is superior to us, so we must always go full blast and full out. If we do this then we know that we have always given it our all, lessening that one chance of the inferior or equal opponent getting the lucky technique in on us.

The Old Lady and the Zen Master

There was an old woman whose husband was fooling around on her. She went to a Zen priest and told him her problem. He said, "I can solve this problem for you."

She was ecstatic. He told her to go home and bring the chicken into the house for one week and then come back and see him and see if her problem is still there.

One week later she returned saying that she still had the problem and now there was chicken droppings everywhere as well.

The Zen master said hers was an extreme case, and that he had only used this method once before – but it worked. He told her to go home, leave the chicken in the house and bring a sheep in as well. He said that this would resolve the problem and she should come back and see him in a week.

A week went by and she came back to see the priest and she said what are you crazy now I have this damn rooster crowing at 5:00 a.m. every morning and the damn sheep is eating our furniture. Yes but what about your husband. Yes yes he is still fooling around as well.

The priest said, "Well this is the worst case I have ever heard of. I only know one thing to do and my master told me it would work 100%. This is what you do... Go home leave the rooster in the house and the sheep and bring the cow into the house as well."

She said, "Are you crazy?"

He said, "I guarantee you this will work, 100%."

She went home, left the rooster and the sheep in the house and brought the cow into the tiny little Japanese house for one week and then went back to the zen priest.

He said, "So how are things?"

She said, "Now I know you are a crazy man because now I have a rooster the crows at 5:00 a.m., waking everyone up, a sheep that is still eating all our furniture and a cow that lays a plop down so big it almost fills our tiny living room. Life is a nightmare."

The zen priest said, "Yes but what about your other problem?"

She said, "What problem? I don't have anytime to solve these problems, little alone the other one."

The Miser and His Gold

There was a miser who loved money. He used it to buy gold. He always fondled the gold. To insure its safety he buried the gold in his garden every day after fondling it, digging it up the next day.

One day as he was burying it, a thief happened to see him. The first chance the thief had, he stole the gold. When the miser went to dig it up, it was gone. The miser sat at down in a heap, weeping, yelling, and cursing. A neighbor heard him and asked what was the matter.

When the miser told him about the gold the neighbor advised him to bury a rock and when he dug it up every day, treat it as if it were gold.

The Master and the Student

In feudal Japan it was customary for a student to sit outside a master's house for sometimes days on end before the student would be accepted.

In this case, a young boy wanted to devote his life to the sword and so he sat outside the master's home until one day the master accepted him.

When he came in, the master put him to work right away cleaning and shining the furniture and raking the yard. Finally after a few months the student asked the master when he would be able to start learning the sword. The master just said, "Soon".

The next day, the student was in the yard and the master took the broom and beat the heck out of him as he ran and tried to get away. The master just laughed. The next day the exact same thing finally when ever the master came around the student would just run away and again the master just laughed.

The next day the student was in the house with his back to the door washing the dishes and the master came in and began hitting him again but this time it was a stick. The student was sure by now that the master had gone insane but he stayed and just learned how to deflect the attacks as they came at him.

Then after he had learned to deflect the master's attacks with the stick, the master decided it was time to take it to the next level. So in the middle of the night while the student was sleeping he would wake him up and attack him with the stick. Of course, this really had the student going crazy as he didn't know when or where he was going to be attacked. It could be with the broom in the garden, while doing chores, or even in the middle of the night. He never knew when or where the attacks might come.

Finally the master couldn't get him and he decided to test the student one more time to see if he had really learned the art.

So he waited behind a door and when the student came through the door he would simply attack him across the chest with his jo.

The student approached the door and as he approached the door he simply ducked down and avoided the cut across the chest of the master.

It was then and only then that the master began his teaching of how to use the sword.

The Job of A Sensei

The job of the sensei is to supply good training and justice.

As an example. Let us say two students are fighting in the dojo and the Sensei is judging the fight. They both throw a punch at the same time and hit the solar plexus. They both think they scored but if one of the student's had their back foot in the air, his point does not score and the other with the planted foot does score.

Well it is the same in an argument.

Two people who are arguing can only see their own side of the argument, otherwise they would not be arguing. The sensei's job is to see the truth, as he is impartial and can see both sides of the story.

It is his job to then tell the truth and tell the students what the truth is.

Furthermore, the sensei's job is to motivate and activate his students so that the student achieves his inherent potential (Buddha hood) and becomes a master. If the teacher is successful and motivates correctly the student may break out and become a greater master than his teacher. Whenever you meet a sensei who wants to make you a carbon copy of himself, to fit you into his mould, then you know that he is not motivating you properly, because it will be almost impossible to exceed him. Most martial arts teachers, especially in karate, develop students stamped in their mould. Only in the basics should and can you do that, since you have to show them properly in the beginning, like teaching a baby to walk.

Yoshida Kotaro told me: "You are you and I am I. When the day comes when you achieve enlightenment, then you can say that I am a good sensei. Prior to that, I have taught you technical skill, all public knowledge, which meant nothing because if I hadn't shown you, somebody else would have."

The Farmer and the Wife

The farmer went to town and found a wife. On his way back from town after finding his wife, the horse they were riding stumbled and the farmer said, "That's one." The horse stumbled again and he said, "That's two." The horse stumbled again and he said, "That's three." And the farmer shot the horse.

The wife, complaining that if she knew that was the kind of man he was, she would not have married him. He said, "That's one."

They lived happily ever after.

Martial Artists and Satori

Why do martial artists often achieve satori after meeting an enlightened zen monk?

Yagyu Tajima-no-kami Muneyoshi achieved satori after meeting Takuan. It's because these swordsman met the monks as they had reached the breaking point and the monks where able to see it and apply the right stimulus to push them over the "line".

What did the swordsman go through before reaching the breaking point?

Diligent application of correct training. If you learn kata and practice it by yourself enough your expression will go into it. Your teacher, which you must have in order to progress, will polish your kata (thus you). He doesn't need to correct the technical aspects of your kata. A good teacher is able to see your ki (aura) as you do your kata, therefore he corrects your kata in a way as to adjust your ki to flow properly.

Kyo (Opening)

Question: Do animals create kyo?

Answer: No. Animals fight by: instinct, they have no intellect to get in the way. They can only fight the way they instinctively know. A dog always fights like a dog; it can't suddenly give a back kick. Since they don't think, there can be no kyo. Only a man can create kyo because the moment you can get your opponent to think, you have him. In the process of thinking or changing thoughts, he can't fight because he's thinking of strategy. He may even move – that's the best time to attack him.

A Japanese samurai will wait for you to start thinking or to make a move. He may even use gimmicks to do it, for instance giving a big kiai. You only get rattled when you are thinking. If you're like an animal and don't think, you're trained so much that when your opponent moves, you go right into your move without thinking about it ahead of time, thus there's no kyo. Since there's kyo only when your opponent's thinking, the moment he does so, you must take advantage of it and attack.

So the best defence in the world if somebody attacks you is to not think of the consequences. Don't say to yourself, 'I'm not going to succeed at this, so what happens if I miss?'

Thus the best attack is to his eyes (or groin); it will make him be wide open as he will now not want to be hit there (he'll have kyo) so you might instead be able to kick him in the groin or what not and get away.

Esoteric and Exoteric

These two words are very important to the martial arts. Esoteric means what is going on inside your mind and exoteric is what is going on outside your mind.

Here are a bunch of terms with their Exoteric and Esoteric equivalents:

TERM	*EXOTERIC*	*ESOTERIC*
Japanese	Public knowledge	Private or inside knowledge
Kiai	Shout	A form of telepathy therapy.
Uke	To Block	Experiences
Sensei	Teacher	Memory of the past
Shin	Mind or heart	Wisdom
Dojo	Training Hall	Place of enlightenment
Kata	Form or Dance	A shadow of the 5 elements, fire, water, earth, wind, and void.
Kihon	Basics	The void of non self
Te	Hand	Magical act

Mental Gravity

Sensei used to lecture us about mental gravity and how it is the same as physical gravity and we can not escape this.

We are always fighting against ego, greed and anger. No matter how much we do and no matter how humble, giving or passive we become these three evils will always be there tempting us.

We always think we are better then we actually are (ego), we always want more then we have (greed), and we always get upset at things (anger).

The job of the martial arts is to overcome these three but we must always be aware that they will never go away completely so we must always be ready for them when they raise their ugly heads.

Koan: Moon and the Water

Your mind must be like the moon shining on still water. If you throw a pebble in the water it causes ripples which breaks up the image of the moon into many reflections, giving a distorted view of the moon. Your mind must be empty of thought making it like still water which reflects all images truly. A disturbing thought causes a distorted view of reality, narrowing your awareness.

An empty mind state is called mushin (no-mind).

On Raising Your Children

When my daughters were very young, I asked Sensei Kim if he had any suggestions on raising children. He said that the most important thing with raising children is to raise them in the best neighborhoods you possibly can. The more prestigious the better it is.

The reason why is because they will be associating with other children whose parents are well educated and the conversation will not be 'will I go to College or not' but rather 'which College or University will I be going to'. Also the chances of them hanging around with kids who do drugs is less and they have a better chance of meeting someone who has big dreams and goals for themselves and their wife or husband.

Also it is very important when the mother is still carrying the child inside her to think and act positive all the time, think only good things, eat and drink healthy as this is what the child will be made out of. The mental qualities are just as important as the physical so make sure that pregnant women are always happy and thinking positive.

Old Man and Father Death

There was an old, extremely poor man who managed to make a meager living by collecting sticks and selling them.

One day he was walking along and picking up sticks to sell. He was carrying them on his back and he had finally had enough of living like this so he called out to "Father Death" to come and take him away. A second later he was walking along and he felt a tap on his shoulder.

He turned around and sure enough it was Father Death looking straight at him. Father Death said, "You called me?"

"Yes," said the startled man. "I, ah, was wondering if you could help straighten my bundle of sticks."

Heaven and Hell

A samurai came to the master Hakuin and asked, "Master, tell me, is there really a heaven and a hell?"

"Who are you?" asked Hakuin.

"I am a samurai of the great Emperor's personal guard."

"Nonsense" said Hakuin. "What kind of an Emperor would have you around? To me you look like a beggar."

At this the samurai started to rattle his big sword in anger.

"Oh!" said Hakuin, "So you have a sword. I wager it's much too dull to cut off my head!"

At this the samurai could not hold himself back. He drew his sword and threatened the master, who said, "Now you know half the answer! You are opening the gates to hell."

The samurai drew back, sheathed his sword, and bowed.

"Now you know the other half," said Hakuin "You have opened the gates of heaven."

Dojo Kun

Every Dojo has what is called a Dojo Kun or a dojo philosophy and this is the Dojo Kun that was used in the Chinese YMCA:

Seek perfection of character
Refrain from violent behavior
Respect others
Endeavor
Be faithful

Millionaire Ho Tung

Ho Tung was a multi millionaire that Sensei met in China when he was traveling through the Orient as a merchant marine.

He asked Ho Tung his secret to life, and he was told Ho Tung's three rules:

Never steal money

Never steal time

The more money you spend the more money you will make.

When it comes to money everyone is of the same religion.

Five Levels of Combat

At one of Sensei Kim's seminars he explained about the five levels of combat.

These are the five levels:

1. Block.
2. Block and counter.
3. Block, counter, take down with a throw.
4. Block, counter, take down with a throw followed by a controlling technique like an arm bar or a choke.
5. Block, counter, take down with a throw followed by a controlling technique like a arm bar or a choke and then a finishing technique like a stomp kick to the head.

You decide on how far to take the fight depending on the seriousness of the fight. For example, if it is a simple street fight and the guy throws a punch at you in a bar, you would probably take it as far as #2.

Now if the person has a knife you may take it as far as #4.

But if there are three guys attacking you, you would not want to take any chances on your opponent getting up, so you would more then likely take it to the #5 level.

On Self Defense

"In self defense, this is how it really works," said Sensei Kim. "The winner is usually the person who gets in the first good shot (because there is no padding and no mouth pieces in the street) and one good shot in the nose will stop most people."

Eighty per cent of street fights are won by the person with the fighting spirit or the right attitude, 15% of street fights are won by the person who is in the best shape or is the biggest and strongest. Only 5% of street fights are won by the person who has the best technique.

We should also remember one of the most valuable lessons Odagiri discovered about self defense and although it may seem simple, it is very profound.

There are three types of opponents only. The ones who are inferior to us; the ones who are equal to us; and the ones who are superior to us.

It is this third type of opponent that we must all train to beat. The first two we can beat always it is the third person who we can lose to.

A Monk vs. A Master Swordsman – Who Wins?

What if a monk practiced zen and reached satori, could he then compete against a master swordsman?

The answer is no. If the monk only achieved satori without martial arts training, the master swordsman could kill him in a match, although the monk will know what move he is going to attack with.

Hachi Maka

In 1977, some of us were fortunate enough to receive a dan rank from the then president of the Dai Nippon Bu Toku Kai, Ohno Kumao. This, of course, was greatly appreciated but what was more appreciated by some of us was the Hachi Maka that was given to us at the same time.

It said the following:

If in battle your hand is cut off,
You must use your feet.
If in battle your feet are cut off ,
You must use your stumps.
If in battle your stumps are cut off,
You must use your teeth.
If in battle your teeth are kicked out,
You must use your eyes.
If in battle your eyes are plucked out,
You must use your mind.
Never ever give up.

Koan: Man and Two Tigers

What is the meaning of the koan about the man hanging on to a breaking vine with a tiger above and a tiger below while he eats a grape and says: "How delicious!"

A martial artist or zen monk makes full use of every second, as it is right now. Whatever you do, you must do completely – do not be thinking of anything else (ichinen).

When you eat, you eat, it's a total commitment. Every act may be your last, so do it fully. If you can do that, even the most mundane or dull thing won't be mundane or dull because it will then have so much meaning. To capture that you must have had some kind of breakthrough.

Practicing the sutra will take away your fear.

Hitting the Wall

Since I returned to the United States in 1959, I have seen Karate in the United States grow like a hydroheaded monster resorting to cannibalism within itself. Karate is supposed to instill the qualities of virtue, integrity and wisdom in its practitioners but it appears that ambition, cupidity and duplicity have taken hold on the American scene.

The crooks we can deal with, because sooner or later they will be found out, but the rash of Shodans and other low-ranking practitioners who are opening up their own dojos (in Japan a Yondan or 4th degree is required) and do not belong to any central organization are the ones who have created, are creating, and will continue to create the quagmire that karate is floundering in. They are the ones who are giving out belts like it's going out of style.

Kata and Character

There are many ways to learn a man's true character. One way, said Sensei, was to watch the his kata.

If the kata is strong and powerful the student is probably strong and powerful inside and mentally. If his kata is weak and sloppy he is probably the same in his business dealings and the other areas of his life. If his kata is fast, strong and technically excellent, again more then likely so is his character.

"You see," said Sensei, "the kata is a mirror of the mind and what is in your mind is what will come out in your kata."

Therefore, if this is so, if the student concentrates on perfecting his kata he will also be concentrating on perfecting his mind.

He also said that the value of the kata is that we learn to pay attention to details. We learn this as we are our own adversary in the kata.

Dojo Oath

We will train our hearts and bodies for a firm, unshaking spirit.

We will pursue the true meaning of the martial way so that in time our senses may be alert. With true vigor, we will seek to cultivate a spirit of self-denial.

We will observe the rules of courtesy, respect our superiors, and refrain from violence.

We will pay homage to our creator and never forget the true virtue of humility.

We will look upwards to wisdom and strength, not seeking other desires.

Add to our lives, through the disciplines of budo, we will seek to fulfill the true meaning of the way.

How To Do Zazen

First of all, you do not need absolute quiet in order to do zazen. You need not sit in a full or half lotus, although it would be desirable as having the spine in that position affects you and your mind in a good way (steadies your alpha rhythm and slows your metabolism).

Your body should be elevated above your legs so place a cushion under your buttocks. After you sit down, rock your body forward as far as you can and at the same time purse your lips and exhale out your mouth. At the bottom position touch your tongue to your palate and inhale as you raise up,all the while imagining that your head is being pulled up to the ceiling. Repeat the process through smaller and smaller arcs until you are finally sitting straight up, You will now be in the proper posture. Then three times breathe in and exhale. Then go on to natural breathing. Be looking through half-closed eyes seven feet ahead.

In the first stage of your meditation your breath should be as follows:Breathe in with Om as if the air were coming in through all your pores; breathe out with Ah as if the air were leaving through all of your pores. Eventually you will feel as if your whole body were breathing and in tune with the universe.

A master who has achieved satori will time his meditation period by placing an, incense stick behind him. When it burns out, it gives off a characteristic high-frequency noise that only he can hear since he is so ‘in tune’ and in a heightened state of awareness.

When your meditation period is over, press the palms of your hands together. This is necessary because of the large electric currents going through your body that were produced by the meditation.

The Art of Fighting Without Fighting

In feudal Japan, Bokuden was challenged by a samurai while on a boat going from one place to another.

Bokuden accepted the challenge and said, “Okay, let’s fight on that Island over there.”

His opponent accepted most willingly.

When they got to the island, Bokuden knew what the young samurai was planning in advance, so when they arrived the young samurai jumped off the boat so as to gain the advantage and take up the best position for the fight.

Bokuden took his time getting off the boat and once the samurai was off and on the shore he took the oar and pushed the boat away from the island and started laughing at the samurai who was now on the island by himself.

Bokuden said, "Bye bye!" and laughed even more as he once again won by using the art of fighting without fighting.

Power of Ichiren

The father of the great Chinese martial artist Hakugen was killed by a tiger. His son swore he would not rest until he had killed the tiger.

The son had Ichiren (single mindedness). The son was a famous archer and thus decided to kill the tiger with an arrow. He made three extra long arrows especially for this purpose.

One evening the son was in the mountains and he saw what he thought was the tiger that had killed his father.

As he aimed at the tiger, he put all his soul and purpose into the arrow and then shot. Later he found that what he had seen was actually a rock and not the tiger.

As he looked closely at the rock he found that the arrow had gone through it. He was never able to duplicate this feat. He had had Ichiren at the time he shot the arrow.

The Cherry Blossom and the Carp

The samurai's most valuable possession, without a doubt, was his sword, which he valued over all else.

In the spring he would change the tsuba (sword guard) to be that of cherry blossoms and in the summer he might change it to be that of carp swimming in a pond.

Why the cherry blossom and why the carp? What did these two images have that were so important to the samurai?

The carp is the only fish that when caught will lay still on the cutting board, as he is able to accept death when it comes.

The samurai used the cherry blossom as their symbol, the reason for this is as follows. An ordinary man clutches at life, holds onto the very end. After he gets old and weak he still clutches to life, not wanting to die.

In contrast, the cherry blossom falls from the tree at the very peak of its beauty, whereas normal flowers wither and die then fall off.

This represents the fact that the samurai has mushin and does not fear death or cling to life, but leaves life at the peak of his glory.

The Carp and the Salmon

The Japanese have always admired the carp because of the way it struggles upstream against rushing water of rapids and waterfalls. It gives fierce struggle when hooked. Americans, hearing this from the Japanese, would say, 'Oh! We have a fish like that. It's called a salmon. It swims upstream against rapids to lay it's eggs and when hooked, it gives a terrific struggle.'

But the Japanese would ask, 'What does it do when it is on the chopping block and sees the knife?'

The Americans would reply that it still struggles hard to escape. It is here that the difference between the carp and the salmon lies.

The carp on the chopping block doesn't flop around in a futile effort to escape, instead it just lays there looking at you, seemingly saying, " Go on! Take your best shot."

It faces death calmly and unafraid.

Conclusion

In the compiling of this book, I kept asking myself, 'Well, who was Richard Kim really?'

Was he a fighter, was he in the infamous Kempei Tei, was he a philosopher, was he a psychologist, was he in the Black Dragon Society, was he a writer, was he a great Karate Sensei? Who was he, truthfully, and with no hype?

My resolve is that he was actually all of the above and a lot more as well.

I have been fortunate to travel the world with Sensei Kim, and on my own as well, meeting political figures and martial arts masters in many countries. I have also trained with some of the best karate masters of all times – names like Yamaguchi, Nakayama, Kanazawa, Enoeda, Higaonna, Merriman, Demura, Lewis, Tsuroka, and many more, but none have come close to Sensei Kim in so many ways.

I received my Shodan from the Zen Bei Bu Toku Kai in 1968 through my then Sensei Benny Allen, who was associated with Sensei Kim. Then, in 1973, we were to go to San Francisco to meet Sensei Kim. Somehow, Benny Allen didn't go and he asked me to go and give a package to Sensei Kim and bring back the dan rank certificates from him.

That trip, little did I know, would change my life forever. When I first met Sensei Kim, it was as if he stepped off of the pages of Karate Illustrated's "Classical Man" column.

He was everything I had ever wanted to be associated with. He was classy, he was in control, he knew all about martial arts philosophy and psychology – something that I had always wondered about. He was the man for me to become associated with, and I did.

When my colleague, Dennis Farbatiuk, and I returned to Canada, I started to make instant plans to bring Sensei Kim to Canada so everyone could meet him and share what I had experienced.

I will never forget the first time I met him at the airport when he came to Canada the first time, he said to me in quiet tone, (and it shook me to my bones), "Never again meet me dressed like that. Wear a shirt and tie from now on or I won't come back."

I was wearing an old leather coat and blue jeans. I couldn't believe it, but he was right and I never again met him without a shirt and tie.

The last time I was with Sensei was in Santa Cruz at the dan grading of Frank Gaviola. Sensei again embarrassed me by inviting me to the front to sit with him. It was if we knew we would not see each other again. We said nothing. Not even small talk. Then, he leaned over to me and said, "Warrener, you don't need any more dan ranking do you?"

I looked at him and said, "No, Sensei, I am just fine. Thank you very much."

He just smiled, and said, "I didn't think so."

A couple of minutes later, I said, "Sensei, I must leave now to get back to LA."

He just looked at me and said, "Yeah, Don, you better go... it's a long drive. Take good care of yourself, Don, I'll see you".

Somehow, when I looked back at him from the door in Rod Sanford's dojo, overseeing the grading as he sat erect and with his plaid suit jacket and his 'forever' bow tie and brush cut, I knew that it would be the last time I would see the man who changed my life for the better in so many ways. I can not even begin to express how much in these few pages.

I cannot tell you how blessed I feel, and I really mean the word 'blessed', to have been the one to write *The 20th Century Samurai*. It was like a trip down memory lane of the best 33 years of my life.

Sensei Kim was, is, and always will be *The 20th Century Samurai* and there will never again be someone like him. I am sure all of his students will agree.

The most important lesson I learned from Sensei is, without a doubt, that "A Martial Artist is An Artist Of Life". This says it all and is but one of the many lessons I will never forget.

I think I can speak for all his students when I say that not a day goes by that I do not think about him or use one of his precepts or philosophies on life. My hope is that this book will capture some of Sensei Kim for those of the future to experience.

His detractors must admit that they also learned a great deal from him. After all, if you stayed training with Sensei Kim for 20 or 30 years there is no way he could not have impacted your life in a positive way. Otherwise, you were simply just not listening, or were more interested in talking than listening, is all I can say to those people.

Throughout the 33 years I was associated with Sensei Kim, many of his detractors would come up to me and say, 'Why do you stay with this guy?' I even had one well known karate master offer me a 7th dan in 1980 to go with him, but I said no thank you.

Then I had Gogen "The Cat" Yamaguchi offer me the Presidency and Chief Instructor position of the Canadian Goju Kai in 1977, after Sensei Kim had introduced me to him. I again said, 'thank you but no thank you'.

Why did I stay? I could have made a lot more money and had more fame if I had of turned coat and gone for the next best thing.

Here is why:

I knew that Sensei Kim's karate was much different then mine. He taught Shorinji Ryu and I taught Goju Ryu and, being very honest, I already knew how to fight well from Benny Allen (in his dojo you either learned to fight quick or you got hurt and quit).

It was the 1960s... the Golden age of karate in North America.

The reason was simple – no one ever was able to capture my attention like Sensei Kim could. Sitting in on just one of his breakfast lectures or his late night fancy restaurant lectures was something none of his senior students could ever explain to those of you who were not as fortunate.

Did he have a temper? Was he harsh on some while easy on some? He sure did have a temper, as many can attest. But I think Jim Larkin said it best when he said, "Sensei Kim treated you the way you allowed him to treat you".

He was intriguing, he was funny as heck. As Eileen Dennis said, "He had the best jokes." He was interesting, always, with the latest scientific and psychology information. He was totally, 100%, informative and he was, above all, a real Sensei – like none I had ever met before, during our association, or since his passing.

HE WAS SENSEI RICHARD KIM!

A master of the martial arts par excellence. This was the man "I" knew, *The 20th Century Samurai*.

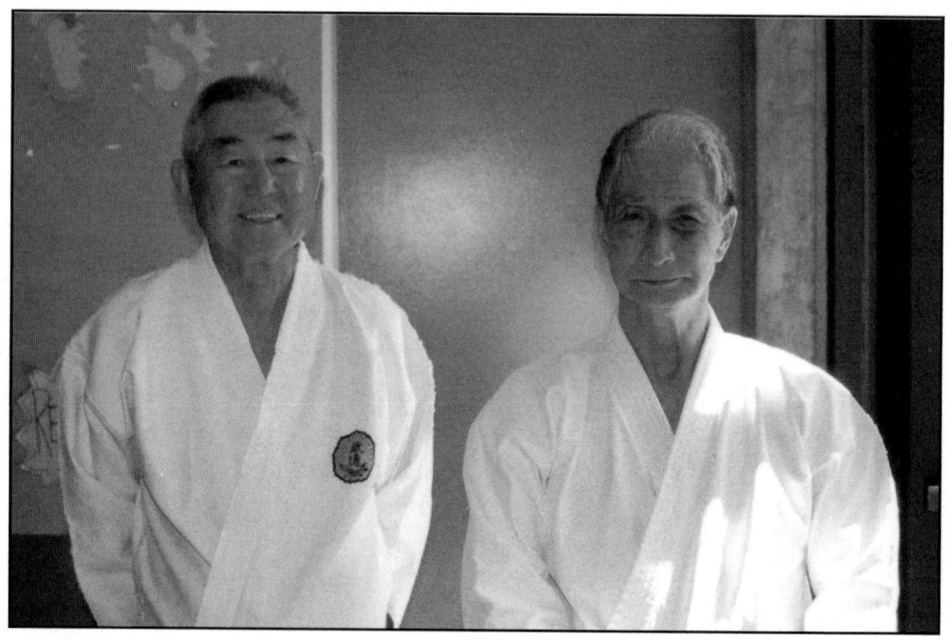

Sensei Richard Kim, with his dear friend and colleague, Hidetaka Nishiyama.

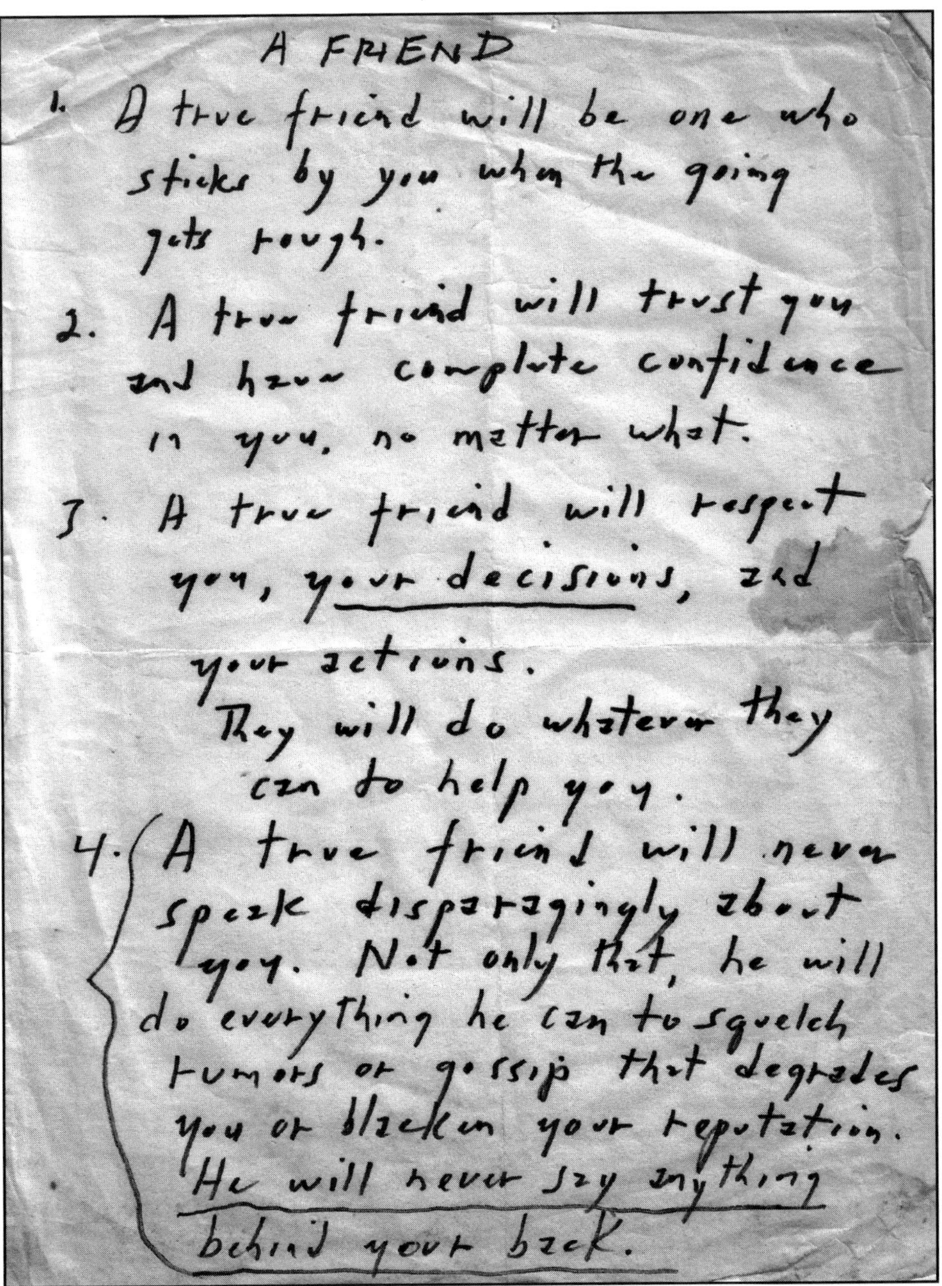

A FRIEND

1. A true friend will be one who sticks by you when the going gets rough.

2. A true friend will trust you and have complete confidence in you, no matter what.

3. A true friend will respect you, <u>your decisions</u>, and your actions. They will do whatever they can do help you.

4. A true friend will never speak disparagingly about you. Not only that, he will do everything he can to squelch rumors or gossip that degrades you or blacken your reputation. <u>He will never say anything behind your back.</u>

A note, written in Sensei Kim's own hand, detailing what a true friend is.

Ranking System in Modern Budo

Adopted by FAJKO on March 27, 1971

RANKS	AGE	TITLE
Ju-Dan (10th) over 10 yrs. after Ku-Dan	70 yrs. or over	*HANSHI – over 15 yrs. after Kyoshi; 55 yrs. old or over
Ku-Dan (9th) 10 yrs. after Hachi-Dan	60 yrs. or over	*HANSHI – over 15 yrs. after Kyoshi; 55 yrs. old or over
Hachi-Dan (8th) over 8 yrs. after Shichi-Dan	50 yrs. or over	*KYOSHI – over 10 yrs. after Renshi; 40 yrs. old or over
Shichi-Dan (7th) over 7 yrs. after Roku-Dan	42 yrs. or over	*KYOSHI – over 10 yrs. after Renshi; 40 yrs. old or over
Roku-Dan (6th) over 5 yrs. after Go-Dan	35 yrs. or over	*RENSHI – over 2 yrs. after 5th Dan; 35 yrs. old or over
Go-Dan (5th) over 3 yrs. after Yo-Dan	under 35 yrs.	*RENSHI – over 2 yrs. after 5th Dan; 35 yrs. old or over
Yo-Dan (4th) over 3 yrs. after San-Dan	under 35 yrs.	*RENSHI – over 2 yrs. after 5th Dan; 35 yrs. old or over
San-Dan (3rd) over two yrs. after Ni-Dan	under 35 yrs.	No formal title
Ni-Dan (2nd) over one year after Sho-Dan	under 35 yrs.	No formal title
Sho-Dan (1st) at least three yrs	under 35 yrs.	No formal title
Ikkyu (1st Brown) Nikyu (2nd Brown) Sankyu (3rd Brown) Yonkyu (4th class) Gokyu (5th class) Rokkyu (6th class)	No age specified	KYU (below brown identified by different colors) However, all kyus are considered white relative to the black belt.

**TITLES: May not be given irrespective of how high the rank; awarded for exceptional achievement and outstanding character.*

FAJKO: Federation of All Japan Karate-Do Organizations.

Sources

These are only some of the sources I used to compile this book.

WEB SITES

http://www.usmm.net/pownames.html
http://www.kyokushinmail.com/koya/letters/letter9.htm
http://www.theshipslist.com/ships/lines/americanpresident.htm
http://seinenkai.com/
http://www.blackbeltmag.com/
http://www.nationmaster.com/encyclopedia/Kenji-Doihara
http://en.wikipedia.org/wiki/Black_Dragon_Society
http://starbulletin.com/2001/07/09/news/obits.html
http://cnd.org/mirror/nanjing/NMTT.html
http://www.chinadaily.com.cn/english/doc/2005-06/08/content_449723.htm
http://hometown.aol.com/faessler98/ah17history.html
http://www.uscg.mil/hq/g-cj/appeals/cg0435.pdf
http://www.shsmu.edu.cn/english/university/index.jsp
http://www.aikidojournal.com/encyclopedia.php?entryID=783
http://personal.picusnet.com/butoku/
http://www.johsoveraa.com/Bilder/China/Shanghai/Shangh17.jpg
http://www.johsoveraa.com/Bilder/China/Shanghai/Shanghai.htm&h=1132&w=872&sz=96&tbnid=9JHUoAiCs0YJ:&tbnh=150&tbnw=115&hl=en&start=4&prev=/images%3Fq%3DSt%2BJohn%2527s%2BUniversity%2BShangHai%2BChina%26svnum%3D10%26hl%3Den%26lr%3D
http://hawaiikodanshakai.com/awardees.html

MAGAZINES

Countless magazines were researched – far too many to list – but thank you to all the publishers of these magazines that have analogued our history.

BOOKS

Beginning Ju Jitsu by Shortt and Hashimoto (Pg. #61) published by Paul Crompton
This Is Karate by Mas Oyama
What Is Karate?
Encyclopedia Of Martial Arts
Budo Jiten
A Comprehensive Dictionary of Japanese Martial Arts.
The Karate Sensei by Peter Urban
The Karate Dojo by Peter Urban
Captives of Shanghai by David H, Grover, Gretchen Grover, Western Maritime Press, 1999

PEOPLE

Hiroshi Kinjo, David H. Grover, Alex Bennett, Peter Urban, Jim Wilson, Charles Goodin, Pat McCarthy, Ken Shockey, Brian Ricci, Clarence Lee, Emil Farkas, Leroy Rodriguez, Robert Leong, Louis Jemison, Frank Gaviola and Neville Billemoria, to name but a few.

Glossary

Aikido: 1) Aikijutsu practiced as a way of life. 2) The aikijujutsu of Ueshiba Moreihei, a blend of basic techniques from Daito-ryu Jujutsu and the Omoto-kyo religion. The name was first registered by Hirai Minoru at the Butokukai in 1942. 3) Modern styles of aikijujutsu, as opposed to the older combat-oriented versions.

Bugei-juhappan: The 18 major forms of bujutsu: kyujutsu, bajutsu, kenjutsu, iai-jutsu, tantojutsu, sojutsu, naginata-jutsu, bojutsu, jojutsu, jutte-jutsu, hojojutsu, mittsu-dogu, shurikenjutsu, suieijutsu, kusarigama-jutsu, shinobijutsu, jujutsu, and hojutsu. *(Note: There are considerable differences of opinion as to exactly which bujutsu should be on this list.)*

bujin: 1) A warrior; a soldier. 2) A warrior not of the samurai class. 3) A warrior of any class.

Busen: Martial arts specialty school

Bu Toku Kai: Military Virtue Organization

Bu Toku Do: Hall of Military Virtues

Budo: Military Way

Bushi: Samurai Warrior

Budo Semmon Gaku: Martial arts specialty school

Chibana Chosin: (1887-1969) First president of the Okinawa Karate-do Renmei in 1956 and founder of the Okinawa Shorin-ryu Karate Kyokai in 1961. Awarded grade of hanshi in 1957. He was a student of Itosu Anko and called his style the Kobayashi Shorin-ryu in 1935.

Dai Nippon: All Japan

deshi: A disciple *(Note: A deshi has a sensei; a student has a teacher. There is a big difference.)*

dojo: 1) A training-hall for budo. 2) A Buddhist seminary.

Edo: The old name (until 1868) of Tokyo.

Fuko Kaicho: Vice Chairman

Funakoshi Tominakoshi Gichin: (1869-1957) Known as the father of modern karate. Funakoshi studied under Azato Anko and Itosu Yasutsune. He demonstrated his art to Ozawa Shintaro (an Okinawan school commissioner) in 1903, which resulted in karate becoming a part of the curriculum at the Men's Middle School in Shuri. In 1917 he gave a private demonstration of karate at the Butokuden, which was followed by a public demonstration in 1922. Kano Jigoro was so impressed that he invited Funakoshi to remain in Japan and teach at the Kodokan. Funakoshi accepted and shortly began teaching at the Keio University in Tokyo. He established the Shotokan (Shoto was his pen-name for calligraphy) in 1936, which led to the development of the JKA (Japan Karate Association).

gi: A martial art uniform; short for keiko-gi.

Hokushi Itto Ryu: A style of swordsmanship founded by Kawamura Michiyoshi

Hotei: A Chinese monk, c.800. He is the subject of many Zen paintings, usually being depicted carrying a sack over his shoulder.

Hozoin-ryu: A style of sojutsu founded at the Hozo-in monastery by Gakuzenbo Inei, c.1560. This style was long studied by the Takeda family. Takeda Shingen was an early supporter of the monastery.

Hanshi: Model Expert

Jitsu: en guard

Kaicho: Chairman

karate: 1) An art of empty-hand fighting, which was introduced to Japan by Funakoshi Gichin. 2) A symbolic motion of stretching one's arms outward and turning the palms toward heaven. *(Note: This term was first used by Hanagi Chomo in 1904 in his book Karate Soshu Hen. Funakoshi began using the term c.1925.)*

"Karate ni sente nashi": "There are no attacking techniques in karate!" (Funakoshi Gichin)

kata: 1) Any prearranged exercise. 2) A formal (prearranged) exercise.

Kodokan: The headquarters of Kodokan Judo in Tokyo.

Kyo: Unguarded

Kyoshi: Teaching Expert

makimono: A scroll.

Matsumura Sokon: (1809-1901) Okinawan karate pioneer known as Bushi, he was a master of Shuri-te and created the karate kata Chinto. He studied under Sukugawa Tode. His style is known as Matsumura-seito Shorin-ryu. This is the core-style from which many branches of Shorin-ryu have descended.

Motobu Choki: (1871-1944) An Okinawan karate instructor who is famous for defeating (with ease) a professional boxer in Kyoto in 1921.

mushin: 1) Heartlessly. 2) Without a thought. (All martial arts techniques should be done in this manner.)

ninja: A group of outcasts who served as spies and assassins in feudal Japan. They were considered sub-human, ranking with the eta, because they had no place in the Japanese caste system (samurai, farmer, artisan, merchant).

Ohno Kumao: He was responsible for the restructuring of the Dai Nippon Butoku Kai after WWII which was started in 1953

Ono Jiroemon Tenzen Tadaaki: (1565-1628) Student of Ito Ittosai, he inherited the Itto-ryu and called it the Ono-ha Itto-ryu. The kenjutsu instructor to the Tokugawa, he was one of the greatest swordsmen of his day.

Oyama Masutatsu: (b.1922) Founder of the Kyokushinkai in 1957. Oyama was born as Yong I-choi in Korea and moved to Japan in 1938. He studied karate under Funakoshi, Goju-ryu under Sou Neichu, and Daito-ryu under Yoshida Kotaru.

Renshi: apprentice teacher

ronin: A masterless samurai. (The name indicates someone who is washed about by the seas of fate.) Although romanticized by modern films, this was always considered to be a Very Bad Situation in feudal times.

Saigo Tanomo: (1830-1905) A minister of Aizu Han, he served as the 34th headmaster of the Daito-ryu. After the defeat of the Aizu Han during the Meiji restoration, he became an administrator at the Toshogu Shrine in Nikko, changed his name to Hoshina Genshin, and devoted the rest of his life to the study of shodo.

satori: Enlightenment; the realization of something's ultimate nature. Total satori creates a buddha.

sensei: 1) A title of respect for someone who is older (and wiser). 2) Your teacher. 3) Any teacher. (Note: There is nothing in the term sensei that suggests teaching; it only denotes wisdom. You should, therefore, never use the term to refer to yourself.)

Shinmen Musashi-no-kami Fujiwara Genshin: (1584-1645) Famous swordsman, known as Miyamoto Musashi, he was the author of Gorin-no-Sho and founder of the Niten Ichi-ryu.

So Doshin: The founder of Nippon-den Seito Shorinji Kempo, he studied Hakko-ryu and Chinese Kempo.

Takeda Sokaku Minamoto Masayoshi: (1860-1943) Second son of Takeda Sokichi and 35th headmaster (in 1898) of the Daito-ryu. By the age of 18 he had earned menkyo in the Ono-ha Itto-ryu, Jiki Shinkage-ryu, and Hozoin-ryu. Because of his abilities and small stature (4'11") he was known as the Aizu Kotengu (the little-demon of the Aizu). He never had his own dojo, but travelled throughout Japan teaching. With the exception of Ueshiba Moreihei and the members of the Sendai Army Regiment, he restricted his teaching to those people of power and influence.

Toyama Kanken: (1888-1966) Founder of the Zen Nippon Karate-do Renmei and Shudokan Karate.

Tsukahara Bokuden Takamoto: (1490-1571) A famous teacher of kenjutsu. He studied the Katori Shinto-ryu with his father and his uncle (Tsukahara Tosa-no-kami Yasumoto) and the Kage-ryu from Hidetsuna, and then founded the Kashima Shinto-ryu c.1530. Tsukahara Bokuden is widely considered to be the greatest swordsman in history.

uchideshi: 1) A live-in student. 2) A small group of students who receive special attention from the instructor.

Uechi Kanbun: (1877-1948) The founder of Uechi-ryu Karate, he studied under Chou Tsu Ho (a.k.a. Shu Shi Wa) in China from 1897 to 1907.

Ueshiba Moreihei: (1883-1969) A student of Takeda Sokaku, he merged the teachings of the Daito-ryu with the Omoto-kyo religion and founded modern aikido. Taking a lesson from Kodokan Judo, he began teaching it to the general public. *(Note: Ueshiba also used the personal names of Tsunemori and Moritaka.)*

yabusame: Archery on horseback. To make a smoother platform, Japanese war-horses were trained to run with a particular single-foot gait instead of the standard gallop. It became an annual event at the Hachiman Shrine in 1266. Originally, an archer was required to commit seppuku if he missed.

Yamaguchi Gogen: (b.1909) The founder of Japanese Goju-ryu. He was a student of Miyagi Chojun and started a karate club at the Ritsumeikan University in Kyoto in 1930. He also created a system of jiyu-kumite.

Yasutsune Itosu: (1830-1915) An Okinawan karate master, known as Anko, he was a student of Matsumura Sokon and Matsumora Kosaku. He created the Pinan Kata (1-5) while teaching karate in the Okinawa Dai-Ichi junior high school. He taught Funakoshi Gichin and Chibana Chosin.

Yoshida Kotaro: (c.1886-1964) A student of Takeda Sokaku, he introduced Ueshiba Moreihei to Sokaku at the Hisada Ryokan. Famous for his skill with a tessen (he once killed a bear with one), he also taught Oyama Masutatsu.

zanshin: Perfect finish, the instant of mugen after a perfect technique.

zazen: Seated Zen meditation.

Patience